THE LIBRARY
ST. MARY'S COLLEGE OF MARYLAND
ST. MARY'S CITY, MARYLAND 20686

THOMAS HARDY'S CORRESPONDENCE AT MAX GATE

A DESCRIPTIVE CHECK LIST

Compiled By
CARL J. WEBER and CLARA CARTER WEBER

WATERVILLE, MAINE
COLBY COLLEGE PRESS • 1968

Copyright 1968 by Colby College Press

CONTENTS

	Page
Preface	3
Introduction	5
A Summary of the Correspondence	12
Some Editorial Observations	16
Chronological List of Hardy's Correspondence	29
Alphabetical Index of Hardy's Correspondence	211
Index of References to Hardy's Works	236

PREFACE

THE SUBTITLE, *A Descriptive Check List*, makes clear that this is *not* a book of letters. It is a book *about* letters. Like a telephone directory, it is full of names and numerals; but, just as the directory does not provide a record of the telephone conversations which the use of the directory may lead to, so the present compilation makes no attempt to publish the text of Hardy's correspondence. It is merely a list of a part of that correspondence, a tool designed to facilitate for the scholarly-minded student an approach to and a use of the more than five thousand communications once retained in Hardy's files at Max Gate and now preserved in the Hardy Memorial Room in the Dorset County Museum at Dorchester.

When that room was opened on 10 May 1939 by the Poet Laureate, John Masefield, it was expected that it would shortly house all the books, papers, and other memorabilia which had been removed from Max Gate soon after the death of the second Mrs. Hardy. Unfortunately, the outbreak of World War II shortly thereafter delayed the transfer, and as a result the letters preserved by Hardy in his Max Gate files were not deposited in the Memorial Room until some years later, after the war had ended.

Students of Hardy's life and writings have since then been confronted by a lack of full and reliable information about these letters, for they have never been methodically catalogued, and they are not kept either in consistent chronological sequence or in strict alphabetical order. The letters of one correspondent may be found scattered among half a dozen different classifications. An informative list of these letters has therefore long been needed by the increasingly large number of persons interested in Hardy studies, especially by those who live in America. A grant-in-aid from the American Council of Learned Societies enabled the two undersigned workers to go to Dorchester, and there, with the kind permission of Curator R. N. R. Peers and the friendly cooperation of the Assistant Curator, Miss E. Maureen Samuel, they carried on the examination of the letters which has resulted in the present compilation. The pages that follow will tell other students what they can expect to find when they go to Dorchester to pursue their Hardy investigations "on the spot," and some of the pages that follow will offer suggestions as to what direction these investigations might profitably take.

PREFACE

We are glad to have this opportunity to acknowledge with thanks the helpful criticism given our manuscript by Mr. and Mrs. F. B. Pinion of Sheffield University, England, and the interest and assistance of Miss Irene Cooper Willis, Trustee (with Lloyds Bank, London) of the Hardy Estate. We also make grateful acknowledgment of the grant-in-aid of the American Council of Learned Societies and express our appreciation of the courtesies extended to us at the Dorset County Museum.

CARL J. WEBER
CLARA CARTER WEBER

Waterville, Maine

INTRODUCTION

SCHOLARS AND STUDENTS of the life and work of Thomas Hardy have long felt a need for reliable information about the letters he kept in his files at Max Gate—letters afterwards deposited in the Dorset County Museum under the terms of the will of the second Mrs. Hardy. In the absence of reliable information about these letters, much inaccurate reporting and not a little pure guesswork has been tossed about, both orally and in print. One scholar who visited the Museum reported his "estimate" that there were two thousand letters in the Max Gate file, while the 1964 *Year Book* of The American Philosophical Society stated (page 578) that there are "some 12,000" of Hardy's letters there. Neither statement is correct. One report has it that Hardy saved only his business letters; another, that he saved only his personal correspondence. Neither report is correct. And in the absence of any catalogue of the letters, inquiries addressed to the Curator at the Museum were certain to produce only vague and inconclusive replies. The present work is aimed at putting an end to the uncertainties and the contradictions.

The number of letters listed in the pages that follow would have been much larger if there had not been two great bonfires at Max Gate—one when Hardy himself fed letters to the flames, the other when the second Mrs. Hardy did the destroying. These two deliberate conflagrations reduced the number of Max Gate letters which survive to slightly more than five thousand.

On 7 May 1919 Thomas Hardy wrote to Sir George Douglas: "I have not been doing much—mainly destroying papers of the last thirty or forty years." Hardy was then seventy-eight years old; he had been living in Max Gate for thirty-four years, and the mass of papers that had accumulated in a span of years of that length was doubtless very great. There was hardly room for them all.

Hardy had an additional reason, however, for giving attention in 1919 to his "papers of the last thirty or forty years." He was preparing to write his autobiography (disguising it as the work of his wife, to be published after his death), and he often had to consult old letters or other papers to remind himself of what had happened earlier in the course of his long literary career. *The Later Years of Thomas Hardy* (published in 1930, two years after his death) contains frequent reminders of this reliance upon old letters. "Hardy's entries of his doings were always of a fitful and irregular kind" (page 37). "He had kept, at casual times, a record of his experiences in social life, though doing it had always been a drudgery to him" (page 66). "His memoranda get more and more meagre as the years go on, until we are almost entirely dependent on letter-references" (page 108).

Hardy's preservation of old letters had apparently been almost as "casual" and unmethodical as his keeping a record of his experiences, and in order to make the letters serviceable for the autobiography they had, first of all, to be put into chronological order. At a later date Mrs. Hardy informed an American bibliographer that, in the course of her assisting Hardy, the "letters were sorted and tied in bundles by years." On 6 February 1919 she wrote to Sydney Cockerell: "The letter sorting is still going on—nineteen years more to do." That is to say, the record had by 1919 been brought down to the year 1900. Mrs. Hardy added: "When they are all sorted, I am going to arrange them under initials, instead of dates." This attempt to substitute an alphabetical for a chronological arrangement led to difficulties and confusions about which we shall have more to say shortly.

The letters which Hardy decided to introduce into the biography, *The Early Life* and *The Later Years,* were put aside for preservation. Some others were likewise salvaged, but many more were destroyed. What Hardy allowed to survive is often useful in supplementing the information in the biography or in correcting its at times erroneous statements. An example may suffice. *The Later Years* states (page 133) that after Hardy had attended the Milton Tercentenary at Cambridge on 10 and 11 July 1908, "the remainder of the month was spent in Dorset." Surviving letters show that this was not so. In July 1908 Hardy sat twice to Hubert Herkomer in London, he attended a luncheon at the House of Commons, he made a trip out to Bushey, and he was present at the wedding of Edmund Gosse's son Philip in Kensington. The letters show how little was the time spent in Dorset. As Cardinal Newman once remarked: "Contemporary letters are facts." They help to keep the record straight. They protect us not only from the guesses and conjectures of biographers but from the hazy memories of ageing autobiographers as well.

The omissions or the errors in the autobiography are, however, not always the result of faulty memory or lack of information. Both *The Early Life* and *The Later Years* have significant silences. It is clear that in many instances Hardy chose to say nothing and that he decided to burn letters rather than to preserve them. There is nothing queer or unusual about this decision. Robert Browning once wrote to his "best and dearest friend" Isabella Blagden: "I read your letters, twice, and then burn them." According to an article in *Time* (28 August 1964, page 20), President Harry S. Truman once found his wife burning some of the letters he had written her. "Bess, you oughtn't to do that," he protested. "Why not?" replied his wife, "I've read them several times." "But think of history!" pleaded the President. "I have," murmured Mrs. Truman as she tossed the last bundle of letters into the fire.

Hardy, too, tossed many a letter into the fire; but, like Robert Browning, he was quite inconsistent in his treatment of old letters. Browning burnt all the letters Miss Blagden wrote to him, but when his letters to her were returned to him after her death, he preserved them all. Hardy acted in similar fashion. He destroyed all the letters written to him by Florence Henniker from 1893 to 1909; but when most of his letters to her were returned to Max Gate after her death, he preserved them all.

Fortunately for us, he preserved some letters that allow us to penetrate behind the veil of his silence. In the autobiography he said nothing about the offer of a knighthood which came to him from the Prime Minister eight or nine months after the publication of the third part of *The Dynasts*. Hardy's modesty in thus remaining silent need no longer deprive us of knowledge of the fact that on 2 November 1908 the Right Honorable H. H. Asquith wrote to ask "if I could persuade you to accept a Knighthood." Four days later Asquith wrote again to say that he understood Hardy's "desire to have fuller time to consider." The Prime Minister obviously informed his wife of the offer of a Knighthood, but he apparently failed to inform her that Hardy had declined the offer. The result was that Margot Asquith addressed him as "Dear Sir Thomas" and continued to write to "Dear Sir Thomas" long after she ought to have known that Hardy had decided that he would *not* become a "Sir."

As to the *full* extent and importance of what was tossed by Hardy into the fire, we have no way of knowing. Our ignorance is the greater because of the second destruction of old letters which was carried out shortly after Hardy's death on 11 January 1928. The Max Gate gardener has recently described what happened:

Within a week or so . . . , there was a grand clearance of . . . letters and other papers from his study. I was given the task of burning . . . bundles of newspapers on a bonfire in the garden. Mrs. Hardy stood by . . . to ensure that nothing escaped the flames . . . Mrs. Hardy herself burnt, on another bonfire, baskets full of the letters and private papers that I had carried down from the study to the garden under her supervision and watchful eye. She would not let me burn these, but insisted upon doing it herself, and after all the papers had been destroyed, she raked the ashes to be sure that not a single scrap or word remained . . . . My impression was she did not want any of the letters . . . to be seen by anyone . . . . Whether she was destroying them on her own initiative or carrying out the wishes of her late husband I never knew, and the world will never learn what went up in flames on that "bonfire day." (Bertie Norman Stephens, *Thomas Hardy in his Garden*, Beaminster, Dorset, The Toucan Press, 1963, pages 15-16.)

The letters, then, that are listed in this book are those that were allowed to survive the fires of 1919 and 1928. Mrs. Hardy in time began work on the plan she had announced to Sydney Cockerell in February 1919 of arranging the letters "under initials instead of dates," but she had not proceeded very far when difficulties began to show up. Should a letter from J.Comyns Carr about the dramatization of *Far from the Madding Crowd* really be filed under "Carr," or would it not be more logical to file it under "Dramatizations," or perhaps under *Far from the Madding Crowd?* Should a letter from Granville-Barker about the production of scenes from *The Dynasts* at the Kingsway Theatre be filed under *"Dynasts,"* or under "Barker," or under "Granville-Barker," or under "Theatre," or under "Kingsway?"

When ill-health forced Mrs. Hardy to suspend her work on the packets of letters, her secretary, Miss May O'Rourke (who had begun to work for Hardy in 1923), tried to carry on the sorting and re-arranging. Later still, the difficulties presented by the chaotic mass of letters were tackled at Florence Hardy's request by Miss Kitty Inglis, daughter of Colonel and Mrs. Inglis of Weymouth; but some of the puzzling questions had not been decided by the time of Mrs. Hardy's death in October 1937. The problem of dealing with the letters then passed into the hands of her executrix, Miss Irene Cooper Willis. The results of this combination of circumstances and this multiplicity of hands may still be seen in the Hardy Memorial Room of the Dorset County Museum. For when, some time after the close of World War II, the packets of letters finally reached the Museum, they were found to follow no consistent filing system. Some manila envelopes contain an alphabetical assortment, so that letters from, for example, Macmillan, Maitland, Meredith, Morley, Moule, and others, are all found together in an envelope marked "M." In other cases, letters from a single correspondent may be found scattered among half a dozen different envelopes. Others are largely chronological bundles, especially for the years after 1919, which seems to have been the last year for which Hardy himself dealt with the autobiographical writing. Thereafter the preservation and the later sorting of the letters became increasingly confused and inconsistent.

An attempt at indexing had been begun by Miss Inglis, and Miss Willis subsequently provided some useful cross-references in this index. But the marks of perplexity and confusion still remain.

Shortly before Hardy's death, Lady Pinney (of Racedown, Dorset) wrote Hardy about the true story of Mrs. Martha Brown, the Broadwindsor woman whose public execution at Dorchester Hardy had witnessed as a boy and whose story had held suggestions for him when he came to write *Tess of the D'Urbervilles*. Anyone who now reads Lady Pinney's letter is likely to conjecture that, in talking with Hardy, she had come to believe that he was not fully or accurately acquainted with the true story; she therefore wrote to set the facts straight, as she had come to know them. Where, now, should one file such a letter? Under "P" for Pinney, or under "T" for *Tess of the D'Urbervilles?* or under "1927," the year when Hardy received the letter? It finally landed in an envelope marked "B"—"B" for Martha Brown—where it is a close neighbor of an 1888 letter from Robert Browning.

What is attempted in the present compilation is, then, a systematic report on what the Max Gate file now contains. The pages that follow give, first, a chronological list showing all the letters in the order in which Hardy received them, together with brief identifications of the subject or nature of each; and second, an alphabetical index naming the writers of the letters with a consolidated listing of their letters. What this double compilation provides is information under both the arrangements Mrs. Hardy had in mind when she wrote Sydney Cockerell about sorting the letters "under initials instead of dates."

With very few exceptions, all the letters to Hardy are the originals received by him from the postman. (The letters from William Tinsley constitute a notable example of such exceptions.) As for the letters written by Hardy, some (notably 74 letters to the first Mrs. Hardy, 150 letters to Mrs. Florence Henniker, and two to her husband) are the originals sent through the mails; but the remaining 628 letters from Hardy are *not* the mailed communications but copies of one kind or another. Some detailed explanation of the nature of these copies is called for by reason of the fact that they testify to a wide variety of procedures on Hardy's part. There are at least six different kinds of copies, some made after the original letter had been penned and some made before the letter-to-be-mailed had been prepared for mailing.

(1) Probably the nearest to the posted originals are those copies which were made from wax impressions. The original letters were pressed into a jelly pan, and the ink deposited on the jelly or wax was then transferred to other sheets of paper—those that now survive among the Max Gate Letters. This mid-Victorian way of making copies of letters was a common one, in use for many years on both sides of the ocean, but very few of the surviving copies of letters in Hardy's files were made in this way.

(2) As soon as Florence Dugdale appeared upon the scene, bringing her typewriter with her, the use of carbon paper for making copies of the original letters put in its appearance; and these twentieth-century carbon copies are of course easily recognized.

(3) A third kind of copy is the handwritten one, sometimes in Hardy's hand, but more commonly in his wife's. Emma Hardy was often called upon to write a manuscript copy of one of Hardy's business letters, and in later years Florence Hardy sometimes (but not often) made similar handwritten copies.

(4) Most interesting of all, and most informative for giving us an insight into Hardy's habits as a correspondent, are those copies made by Hardy himself, some in ink, many in pencil. It is really not quite correct to call them copies: they are rather, strictly speaking, the originals. They are the preliminary rough drafts of Hardy's replies, and from these rough drafts the fair copies to be mailed were prepared. Some few of these "rough drafts" were intended, apparently, as letters-to-be-mailed; but before mailing them Hardy began revising the text; and after he had amended the phraseology, corrected the assertions, or otherwise tampered with his original thought to such an extent that the autograph letter had taken on a messy appearance, he then rewrote a fair copy and marked the word "Copy" on the original; and it is this original, in ink, which survives in the Dorset County Museum.

More numerous, however, are those rough drafts made with pencil, often written on the back of the letter Hardy was answering. These bear eloquent testimony to the care he took in composing such replies. The revisions, transpositions, deletions, all indicate the experienced and careful writer. They tell us one other thing, too: that letters received by various correspondents, letters signed by "M. O'Rourke, Sec." or by "F. E. [Hardy], Sec.," or signed in some such similar fashion, were really not by May O'Rourke and not by Florence Hardy at all. They were not dictations. They were not only composed by Hardy, but were also written (i.e., penned or penciled) by him. Very very few of the "copied" letters were dictated. Even when Hardy was complaining to his correspondents about the weakness of his eyes, he was penciling in very legible autograph the letters which Miss O'Rourke or Mrs. Hardy was then to type, sign, and mail as her own.

(5) Another kind of typed copy is that made by Mrs. Dorothy M. Meech at Florence Hardy's request. Such copies were made after Hardy's death, and in such cases both the original and the copy made from it survive.

(6) Another sort of typed copy is that made by (or supplied by) Howard Bliss: Hardy's letters to Clodd, for example, or to William Tinsley—copies made from the originals in Bliss's possession at the time the copies were made.

Mention should be made of the fact that surviving letters to Hardy provide abundant evidence that he wrote many replies without retaining copies of any kind. In other words, the 628 copies now extant in the Dorset County Museum fall far short of constituting a complete record of what Hardy wrote to his correspondents. One example of this may be cited. In the Hardy Collection of the late E. N. Sanders (of Parkstone, Dorset), presented by him to the Dorset County Museum, there are some sixty or more letters and postcards from Hardy to Hermann Lea (author of *Thomas Hardy's Wessex*, 1913). They contain abundant evidence that Lea often wrote to Hardy. (See "Hermann Lea's Recollections of Thomas Hardy" by Carl J. Weber, pages 39-48 in *The Dorset Year-Book for 1955-56*, Sidcup, Kent, England, 1955.) But among the Max Gate Letters there is not one from Hermann Lea, and not one copy of a reply from Hardy.

It is important, then, to keep in mind that the following pages tabulate only a part, perhaps only a very small part, of Thomas Hardy's correspondence. That fraction is, however, the part that he was willing to have survive, and the part that Mrs. Hardy also allowed to survive. Further comment on these letters will be found in the Summary and among the Editorial Observations.

Anyone who gives close attention to the pages that follow will note one aspect of the compilation which makes it unique. It demonstrates what the life of a professional author can become, when fame has crowned his labors. This compilation is unusual in that it is largely a record of incoming rather than of outgoing mail. Two volumes of Hardy's letters have already been published (one in 1954 and the other in 1963), and there will doubtless be, in time, a Collected Edition of his correspondence which will include the text of the 854 letters by Hardy listed in the present volume. But the bulk of the present compilation (more than eighty-three per cent) is made up of the 4185 letters written *to* him. They provide a unique demonstration of the lofty position he had come to hold in the public eye by the time he was eighty and of what that eminence involved. More than fifty per cent of the letters to him here recorded were written in the last eight years of his life, when he was not only acclaimed and applauded, but was also pushed, prodded, irked, and battered by a small army of actresses, animal lovers, anthologists, antiquarians, anti-vivisectionists, architects, artists, autograph hunters, biographers, book collectors, composers, critics, dramatists, editors, folklore addicts, geographers, hostesses, illustrators, journalists, lexicographers, literary agents, musicians, pacifists, painters, philologists, photographers, fellow poets, politicians, professors, publishers, reformers, reporters, reviewers, sculptors, society gossips, souvenir hunters, students, suffragists, topographers, tourists, and translators.

A SUMMARY OF THE CORRESPONDENCE

A close examination of the Chronological List reveals the fact that Hardy preserved

	18 letters	from	the 1860s
	119 "	"	the 1870s
	238 "	"	the 1880s
	293 "	"	the 1890s
	419 "	"	1900-1909
	994 "	"	1910-1919
	2104 "	"	the 1920s
Total	4185 letters		
	2 posthumous letters preserved by Mrs. Hardy		

4187 letters in all, more than half of them

written in the last seven or eight years of Hardy's life.

Add: 854 letters (or copies of letters) *from* Hardy

5041 grand total

Of the eighteen letters salvaged from the 1860s, 14 are from early friends in Dorchester (6 from Horace Moule, 7 from Henry Bastow, and 1 from Mrs. Martin), but none are from members of Hardy's family. He saved nothing from his mother, his father, his sister Mary, or his brother Harry. Two letters from his sister Kate are of very late vintage (17 July 1923 and 5 October 1924). Of his five years as a young architect in London (1862-67) there survives no contemporary trace among these letters. Four (1 from Alexander Macmillan and 3 from Frederick Chapman) deal with Hardy's first attempt at novel-writing, *The Poor Man and the Lady*, but there are no letters of the Sixties dealing with his first published work, "How I Built Myself a House" (published in March 1865).

The 119 letters from the 1870s tell a different story. More than a quarter of them have to do with Hardy's early novels. Leslie Stephen (who proved to be the best critic Hardy ever had) wrote 21 of them; George Smith wrote 4, and his firm (Smith, Elder & Co.) wrote 5 more. Most of these 30 letters from Stephen and Smith have to do with *Far from the Madding Crowd*. Three of the letters from Smith, Elder & Co. provide sardonic comment on the fluctuations in Hardy's reputation. After his modest success with *A Pair of Blue Eyes*, the firm offered him £400 for *Far from the Madding Crowd*. After the great success of this novel as a serial in the *Cornhill*, Smith, Elder offered £700 for *The Hand of Ethelberta*. After the comparative failure of this last-named novel, they offered only £200 for *The Return of the Native*, which (as Hardy once remarked to a member of his family) "some people say is my best." Thus, by one of "life's little ironies," he received for a great work like *The Return of the Native* only a little more than a quarter of what he had been paid for a failure like *Ethelberta*.

Of particular interest are the 6 letters from Henry Holt. Three were written before the serialization of *Far from the Madding Crowd* in the *Cornhill*. Holt's letter of 29 May 1873 and Lady Macmillan's letter of 18 April 1924—two letters written fifty-one years apart, and neither of them used by Hardy in his autobiography—testify to the efficiency of young Frederick Macmillan (*aetat.* 22) in promoting Hardy's Wessex wares in America. Holt's publication of Hardy in New York in the early 1870s brought the novelist many American readers but (at that date) no American correspondents.

The success of *Far from the Madding Crowd* in the *Cornhill* obviously led directly to the spread of Hardy's reputation on the European continent. The letter of 25 February 1876 regarding a German translation and the letter of 20 March 1876 regarding a Danish translation mark the beginning of what was destined to eventuate in world-wide fame for Hardy. The file of Max Gate Letters came to include communications from every corner of the globe:

Australia	France	Luxembourg	South Africa
Bohemia	Germany	New Zealand	Spain
Canada	Greece	Nigeria	Sweden
Ceylon	Holland	Norway	Switzerland
Chile	Hungary	Philippine Islands	Syria
China	India	Poland	Tasmania
Czechoslovakia	Ireland	Rumania	Turkey
Denmark	Italy	Russia	United States
Egypt	Japan	Scotland	Wales
Finland			Yugoslavia

In surveying the letters which Hardy salvaged from the 1870s one cannot fail to notice G. R. Crickmay's letter of 11 February 1870 asking "Can you go into Cornwall . . . ?"—the most important letter in Hardy's eyes that he ever received, for in Cornwall he met Emma Lavinia Gifford, whom he married on 17 September 1874. It is interesting to notice that, except for two letters from the Rev. E. H. Gifford, who officiated at Hardy's marriage, there are no letters about that event, other than Leslie Stephen's belated reference to it in his letter of 7 December 1874.

The 238 letters salvaged from the 1880s introduce a new aspect of Hardy's career. His election to membership in the Savile Club in London in 1878 led to his making the acquaintance of a number of able and distinguished men, and during the Eighties letters from J. M. Barrie, Walter Besant, Robert Browning, Edmund Gosse, and others began to make their appearance in his correspondence. Acquaintance with these men forced Hardy to recognize the inadequacy of his previously-held philosophical views—a shift recorded by him in *The Mayor of Casterbridge* where (in Chapter 17) he quotes Novalis's thesis that "Character is Fate."

The erection of Max Gate in 1883-85 and Hardy's establishment as a member of the "landed gentry" led to correspondence with and invitations from various "noble dames" who took pleasure in lionizing the author of *Far from the Madding Crowd* and *The Return of the Native*. Letters from Lord and Lady Carnarvon and one from Lady Winifred Herbert are found among the letters of the 1880s; and the absence from the Max Gate files of any letters from Lady Winifred's aunt, Lady Portsmouth, about whom Hardy wrote at length to his wife (in a letter of 13 March 1885), or from the Duchess of Abercorn, or Lady Hilda Broderick, or the Marchioness of Londonderry, about all of whom Hardy wrote in later letters to Emma, invites the conjecture that letters from these "noble dames" were among those destroyed by him in 1919 or by the second Mrs. Hardy in 1928.

The increase in the volume of Hardy's correspondence in the 1890s, from which he salvaged 293 letters, is largely the result of the public's interest in and response to *Tess of the D'Urbervilles*. On the first day of January 1892 Edmund Gosse wrote to Hardy: "In *Tess* . . . you have achieved the biggest success you have made since *The Return of the Native*. Your book is simply magnificent, and wherever I go I hear its praises . . . . Your success has been phenomenal." More than twenty years later, *Tess* was still ranked at the top. On 25 October 1913 Mrs. Florence Henniker wrote Hardy: "I can't help believing that *Tess* is your high-water mark." The letters listed in the present volume support the judgments expressed by Gosse and Mrs. Henniker. Prior to the publication of *Tess*, Hardy's entire correspondence resulted in no more than 250 letters which he regarded as worth salvaging; but in 1891-92 nearly 100 letters testify to the impact made by *Tess* upon those who wrote to the author. In 1895-96, when a dramatization of *Tess* attracted attention in both England and America, there was another marked expansion in the volume of Hardy's correspondence; and in 1924-25, when his own dramatic adaptation of the novel was produced both in Dorchester and in London, the volume of his correspondence was again swollen—more than 650 letters in 1924-25 alone. They make it quite clear that nothing Hardy ever wrote—neither *The Native* nor *The Dynasts*—ever succeeded as did *Tess of the D'Urbervilles* in making a powerful impression upon his friends and the public alike. The Index of References to Hardy's Works shows that there are only 22 letters in which *Jude the Obscure* is mentioned, in contrast with the much larger number in which *Tess* figures.

The fact that more than half of the surviving Max Gate Letters were written in the last decade of Hardy's life is probably to be explained, partly by his increased fame and by his attainment to the venerable age of eighty, but also partly by the fact that the bonfire of 1919 destroyed so many letters written in earlier years. Once the composition of the autobiography had been disposed of, Hardy was apparently content to take a more relaxed attitude toward his correspondence, and Miss May O'Rourke doubtless preserved for posterity many a letter which Hardy himself would have tossed into the fire. Such a letter is (we may conjecture) that of 26 October 1923 in which a frivolous girl in Yonkers, New York, asks Hardy "with your eyes shut" to draw a pig and send the drawing to her. An explanation of how such a trifling letter escaped Mrs. Hardy's bonfire in 1928 must be left to the reader's own conjecturing.

The extant correspondence contains little or no discussion of "novel-writing as an art" such as is found in Hardy's brief comment in *The Early Life* (page 232). Hardy was not a Henry James and not a Joseph Conrad, interested in lengthy discussions about the techniques of fiction. To Mrs. Henniker he once expressed surprise at George Meredith's perversity in infringing "the first rules of narrative art" (letter of 24 May 1909), but Hardy did not go into detail about what those "first rules" are. On the other hand, philosophical questions, such as those that appear in his argument with Alfred Noyes as to whether "the Power behind the Universe" is or is not "an imbecile jester" (see *Later Years*, pages 215-218), continued to interest him and to stimulate his correspondence throughout his life.

SOME EDITORIAL OBSERVATIONS

"If we were given fewer of a man's letters to his friends, and more of his friends' letters to him," so Lord Asquith once remarked, "we should get to know him better, because among other reasons we should be better able to realize how his personality affected and appealed to others."

In the light of this observation, Asquith would no doubt have praised the Max Gate Letters, for they certainly show how Hardy's personality affected and appealed to others. They thus serve to correct many erroneous views that have been expressed about him, and they contradict many of the false assertions that have been made and repeated. Hardy has, for example, been described as a prophet not without honor save in his own home town of Dorchester. These letters show, however, that he lived in friendly and cordial relations with many of his Dorchester neighbors: invitations and gifts and acknowledgments and inquiries and thanks went back and forth between him and other Dorchester people with a frequency and a cordiality that are unmistakable. Hardy has been described as an unsocial Dorset hermit, but these letters show him to be neither a hermit nor, in any exclusive sense, merely a Dorset countryman. He has sometimes been portrayed as a churlish, ill-mannered boor, "receptive but not responsive," but these letters often thank him for kind acts, generous gifts, sympathetic inquiries, and polite and prompt responses. He has been denounced for his refusal to autograph his books, but these letters supply the evidence that he often did autograph them, both his novels and his books of verse; and the list of people to whom he presented copies of his works is a long and impressive one. The interested reader can easily make his own list of recipients of presentation copies, but when made it will be found to include the names of Browning and Swinburne, of George Meredith and A. E. Housman, of Edmund Gosse and Sidney Colvin, of John Morley and Mrs. Humphry Ward, of Frederic Harrison and Sir Henry Newbolt, of John Galsworthy and A. C. Benson, of Leslie Stephen and John Masefield. Hardy has been criticized for being thin-skinned and over-sensitive when smarting under the unfavorable criticism of reviewers. But these letters show how frequently those same reviewers changed their tunes and admitted the unfairness of their remarks when Hardy struck back at them. John Hutton, for example, is (in Letter 49) "indeed shocked" that he had been so severe in condemning *Desperate Remedies* in his notoriously acidulous review in the *Spectator,* and Andrew Lang (in Letter 493) regrets the "tone of voice" he had used in his harsh review of *Tess*.

Attention has already been called to the fact that only a fraction of Hardy's replies to letters from his correspondents is represented by the "copies" he made and kept. Of all the letters he wrote to Leslie Stephen, for example, he retained a copy of only *one*. The observant reader will, however, have noted the fact that we can often infer the contents of Hardy's missing replies by studying some subsequent letter. A note asking permission to call at Max Gate may seem to have gone unanswered, but there is often another letter from the same inquirer or petitioner thanking Hardy for the call which he obviously had written to permit. Similarly there are letters announcing that a gift-book has been sent to Max Gate, or letters asking for an autograph in one of Hardy's own books, and the absence of any copy of his response to such letters might encourage the belief that he had churlishly made no response. A subsequent letter from his correspondent may, however, indicate that such an inference would be a mistake; for that later letter may thank Hardy for his "kind words" about the gift-book, or may thank him for autographing the book and posting it back to the reader.

The alert reader will also be able to make other useful observations. He will notice, for example, how much of Hardy's work, both in prose and in verse, was solicited—work written "by request." Editors began this solicitation as soon as *Far from the Madding Crowd* had made Hardy's name known, and in 1875 alone he received requests for his productions on at least five occasions (8 February, 24 May, 11 September, 12 October, and 2 November). In 1927, fifty-two years later, this editorial solicitation was still going on (see Romer's request in Letter 4980, written when Hardy was over 87), and Hardy's article on George Meredith was the result.

The reader will also notice how often one letter serves to correct another. In Letter 1395 Hardy remarks that the 1882 dramatization of *Far from the Madding Crowd* was "by J. Comyns Carr," and we read Hardy's unqualified assertion: "I had no hand in this beyond authorizing it." But the contemporary letters tell a different story. In Letter 211 to Hardy, William Black calls it "your play," and in Letter 214 Comyns Carr calls it "our piece."

Bertie Stephen's statement (quoted in the Introduction) that "the world will never learn what went up in flames on that 'bonfire day' " in 1928 when Florence Hardy raked the ashes, is doubtless in general true; but it is nevertheless possible to identify *some* of the letters the world has lost. The mere absence of some names in the preceding pages of this book is significant and informative. There are, for example, no letters from Emma Gifford, and none from Florence Dugdale—i.e., none written by her before her marriage. On the other hand, Hardy preserved four birthday greetings from Florence's parents—greetings sent him in 1922, '23, '25, and '26.

Hardy retained the letter of Stuart J. Reid (27 July 1892), asking whether he would like to receive a call from "a young lady —'charming and intellectual' " who was eager to meet him. This charming young lady was a Rebekah Owen of New York City. With her sister Catharine she came to Dorchester; with Hardy's permission she called at Max Gate on 5 August 1892 and so captivated the novelist that, in the preface to a new edition of *The Mayor of Casterbridge* (1895), he referred to her and her sister as "some good judges across the Atlantic." From that date on, Rebekah Owen continued to write to Hardy; she corresponded also with both of his wives. On 14 December 1915 Florence Hardy addressed her as "Best and Belovedest Betty" (Rebekah did not like to be called "Becky"), and in the year 1916 alone Florence wrote 33 letters to "Betty" Owen, who by this time had left New York and was living in England. But not one communication from Rebekah Owen survives among the Max Gate letters.

The destruction of Lena Milman's letters was almost as complete. Hardy met this young lady in June 1893 when her father, General George B. Milman, who was Major of Her Majesty's Tower of London, entertained Hardy at lunch there. On Friday, 9 June 1893, Hardy took Lena Milman to Toole's Theatre to see Barrie's play, *Walker, London*. Hardy wrote to her at least five times during the latter half of 1893. He sent her his photograph and asked for hers in return. When he failed to receive it, he wrote and asked again. After he had returned to Max Gate, he wrote yet again about her "portrait." She preserved all of Hardy's letters. He destroyed all of hers—all except one. On 17 August 1908 Lena Milman wrote Hardy: "I am engaged to be married."

The destruction of letters was not confined to personal correspondence. Business letters suffered the same fate. In 1877 H. S. King & Co. published a new edition of *A Pair of Blue Eyes*, but Hardy retained no letters from this publishing house. In 1889 he corresponded with Ward & Downey about the publication of a new edition of *Desperate Remedies*. His letters to this firm have survived, but there are no letters *from* Ward & Downey in the Max Gate files. In 1892 Heinemann published a third edition of *Desperate Remedies*, but there is nothing from Heinemann among the Max Gate letters. There is only one communication from the Tillotsons. In Letter 324, dated 16 March 1887, this Bolton firm solicited a novel for serialization—a request that led to Hardy's writing *Tess of the D'Urbervilles;* but all subsequent letters from the Tillotsons were destroyed. (The fact that only one communication from William Tinsley, dated 2 August 1872, survives among the Max Gate letters is *not* to be explained by either of the bonfires but by the transfer of the Tinsley letters from Max Gate to the Howard Bliss Collection of Hardiana.)

In some cases, instead of destroying the later communications of his correspondent, Hardy did just the opposite: he burned the earlier and retained the later letters. Before W. M. Parker wrote his letter of 30 March 1922, he had sent Hardy previous communications, but none of them survived the fire of 1919. The letters of William Lyon Phelps constitute another example. This Yale professor called on Hardy in September 1900 and began writing to him soon thereafter. Only one of Phelps's letters has survived, that of 9 December 1919. In December 1909 Paul Lemperly of Cleveland, Ohio, wrote to Hardy, and after this beginning he continued to correspond not only with the author but also with his wives—a correspondence that was continued up to the time of Hardy's death. But only two of Lemperly's letters have survived—birthday greetings to Hardy in 1925 and 1926.

In a few cases we can identify letters destroyed by Mrs. Hardy even after 1928—Sydney Cockerell's letters, for example. Having been appointed Hardy's literary executor, Cockerell continued to write to Mrs. Hardy for some time after her husband's death; but she retained none of his letters after 1927. The last one to Hardy himself is a birthday greeting dated 1 June 1927. (For an explanation of her destruction of Cockerell's letters, see Wilfrid Blunt's *Cockerell,* London: Hamish Hamilton, 1964, pp. 212-223.)

Hardy's old editor in the *Cornhill* office, Leslie Stephen, once declared that "no man is a real reading enthusiast until he is sensible of the pleasure of turning over [the pages of] some miscellaneous collection, lying like a trout in a stream, snapping up with the added charm of unsuspectedness any of the queer little morsels of oddity or pathos that may drift past him." Anyone who, "lying like a trout in a stream," turns over the pages of this book, will have abundant opportunity to snap up little morsels of one kind or another as they drift past. He will note that Hardy received his first "fan" letter at as early a date as 21 August 1874. Later on, such letters multiply. From Ellen Terry comes sincere appreciation of *Jude the Obscure* as "better than *Tess*: far finer than your finest," whereas Mrs. Humphry Ward feels moved to confess: "I am not going to pretend that I liked *Jude.*" Virginia Woolf tells Hardy that, in her opinion, his *Satires, Lyrics and Reveries* is " the most remarkable book to appear in my life time." Champ Clark, for more than a quarter of a century a Member of Congress and Speaker of the House of Representatives (1911-1919), considered (so we learn from a letter dated 20 June 1910) that *The Mayor of Casterbridge* is "the greatest novel in the English language," while Frederic Harrison believes (in Letter 895) that *Far from the Madding Crowd* "will last along with *Tom Jones* . . . and *Vanity Fair.*" A future Poet Laureate, John Masefield, declares (2 November 1911): "I should be very proud, if you, the greatest of living English poets, would accept from me this little English poem." And Edmund Gosse, calling Hardy his "most admired of friends," thanks him in 1919 "for the unbroken record of nearly forty-five years of precious intercourse. May we both live on to celebrate our Jubilee of Friendship!"

The reader who lies "like a trout in a stream, snapping up queer little morsels that may drift past him," will note with interest that the *Spectator's* review of *The Trumpet-Major* was written by Julian Hawthorne. He will learn with amazement that Sydney Cockerell, who had as yet read none of Hardy's novels—none!—could blithely propose, on 28 September 1911, to call on Hardy "tomorrow morning, to ask whether you have any manuscripts that you would be willing to give . . . ." He will note Vernon Rendell's query of 24 October 1919 as to whether George Eliot got the literary use of "Wessex" as a territorial designation from Hardy. She used the word (so we learn) three times in *Daniel Deronda* (1876); Hardy had used it in *Far from the Madding Crowd* in 1874. The reader will note Edgar Lee Masters's letter of 12 June 1919: "I admire your work and your spirit profoundly," and will prepare to re-examine more closely the influence of *Satires of Circumstance* upon the *Spoon River Anthology*. He will note (in the letter of 21 February 1918) the influence of "Wordsworth's first preface" upon Hardy, and will read Rockwell Kent's report (in the letter of 12 September 1919) of his "first discovery, years ago, of *Jude the Obscure*." He will note Philip Guedalla's confession of 9 August 1926 that *"The Dynasts*, almost more than anything else, made me try to write history."

And, among Hardy's own confessions, he will note that Chapter XVI in *Far from the Madding Crowd* was an afterthought, "written on the proof sheets," that in "The Burghers" (one of the poems in *Wessex Poems*) Hardy had Colliton House in Dorchester "in his mind as the scene of the enactment," and that in describing Napoleon's campaigns in *The Dynasts*, the Battle of Leipzig "bothered me much more than Jena or Ulm."

The Henniker part of the Max Gate Letters is unique in that it contains both sides—at least a *part* of both sides—of the correspondence: there are 150 letters *to* Florence Henniker and 38 letters *from* her. None of the letters from her is dated earlier than 1910 (i.e., her letters of 1893-1909 have not survived), and among Hardy's letters to her there are discernible at least six gaps of varying duration. The publication of the text of this correspondence may doubtless be expected at some future date; in the meantime it may be remarked that Hardy's letters to Mrs. Henniker are of special interest, if only because of the quantity of his comments about his own work. Of his fourteen novels, eleven are mentioned or discussed; half a dozen or so of the short stories are compared or named; *The Dynasts* and at least three of the books of poems are referred to, with special comment on the poems that are, as he puts it, "literally true." We learn that Hardy was more interested in writing *Jude the Obscure* "than in any [novel] I have written." In these letters, too, we learn of Hardy's wish that he "could be more in London" and of his regret that two marriages had left him with "no children." His brief remark on this last subject serves to enforce the equally brief but equally significant remark made by Gertrude Bugler in the talk on Hardy which she gave at the Corn Exchange in Dorchester on 7 April 1959: "I remember . . . my last visit to Max Gate during his lifetime . . . . He wondered how [if I went to London to play 'Tess' at the Haymarket Theatre] I should like playing with professional actors and how I could bear to leave my baby in other hands; he asked a number of questions about her, . . . looking a little sadly and wistfully beyond the object on which his eyes happened to be resting, and, instinctfully, I knew it was one of 'Life's Little Ironies' that he had no child of his own."

In 1928, when Mrs. Hardy was considering the publication of Hardy's correspondence with Mrs. Henniker, she asked James M. Barrie to read it. He did so, and we can imagine his surprise when he came upon her comments on him in two of the letters. On 5 March 1917 Florence Henniker wrote to Hardy: "How over-rated he [Barrie] is, don't you think? His great fame and huge fortune are probably neither of them deserved." And on 10 March 1922 she wrote again: "I think it is *absurd* to have given the 'O.M.' to Sir James Barrie . . . It might as well have been bestowed on Arthur Bouchier or Fay Compton!"

No editorial comment on the 74 letters to Mrs. Emma Gifford Hardy is needed here, for they have all been published with detailed annotation in *"Dearest Emmie"* (London: Macmillan, 1963; New York, St. Martin's Press, 1963).

Two of the largest groups of letters (next to those to Mrs. Henniker and to the first Mrs. Hardy) are those written to Sir Edmund Gosse and Sir Sydney Cockerell. In both these cases, both sides of the correspondence have survived, but in neither case is Hardy's part of it represented in Dorchester. His letters to Gosse are now privately owned in America, and the publication of this correspondence will have to await some future date. These letters are likely to prove most interesting and most rewarding, for Hardy wrote to Gosse with a freedom and an uninhibitedness that do not characterize his other letters. Even those to Florence Henniker often carry marks of his being ill at ease, especially after she had rebuked him for what he tried to pass off as "effusive" carelessness on his part. When "Dear Mrs. Henniker" seemed too formal a mode of address, he could not bring himself to writing (or dared not write) "Dear Florence" and so fell back upon an awkward absence of salutation of any kind, and eventually settled upon "My dear friend" as his habitual opening, exactly as he had done with Mary Jeune (Lady St. Helier). In writing to Mrs. Henniker he often signed himself "Tom," or "Tom H." There is none of this self-consciousness or awkwardness in Hardy's way of addressing Gosse. The two had become members of the Savile Club in 1878, when both were young men of 37 years of age, and both wrote with ease and naturalness to the other.

The letters from Sydney Cockerell outnumber those from Gosse. One difference between these two groups is seen in the fact that Cockerell's 68 letters were crowded into a period of sixteen years, whereas Gosse's 64 letters were spread over a period of forty-seven years. A similar contrast is presented by the letters written to and received from Lady St. Helier and Florence Henniker. The Max Gate files now contain only 10 letters to and 20 letters from Lady St. Helier, written over a period of 32 years; whereas the 150 letters to Mrs. Henniker were written over a period of thirty years. Of all these correspondents, Gosse was easily the most successful in "drawing Hardy out," and this is one of the reasons why, when the Gosse-Hardy correspondence is eventually published, it will reward public examination more than any other part of Hardy's letter-writing.

Two letters in the Max Gate files are apparently so insignificant as to call for no comment here; but for the reader interested in peering behind the scenes, there is more in these two letters than at first meets the eye. In Letter 2008 Hardy wrote (6 October 1915) to G. H. Thring:

As to your suggestion [made in a letter now missing] that I should draft . . . a letter [to Henry James, congratulating him on his admission to the Order of Merit], I feel that . . . I could not do it so appropriately . . . as some [other] members of the Society [of Authors] . . . . I therefore propose that they draw it up and send it down to me [at Max Gate] to sign.

The secretary of the Society moved with deliberation and it was three months before Hardy's proposal was acted upon. Then, in Letter 2036, Thring wrote (6 January 1916) to ask Hardy, as President of the Society, to sign the letter drafted by "our Chairman" Stanley Leathes. Hardy signed it and the letter was sent. It is now in the Houghton Library, Harvard University.

The two-page letter to James, typed on the official stationery of the Incorporated Society of Authors, is dated 10 January 1916, just seven weeks before James's death. It is addressed to "Dear Henry James" and is subscribed "with all good wishes" and signed "Thomas Hardy," but it is strewn throughout with phrases and expressions that are wholly foreign to Hardy's style: "my pleasure as well as my duty," "at one and the same time," "great and appropriate Honour," "member of a noble craft," "the Society over which I preside," etc. The state of James's health at the date when this letter was written gives us reason to think that he never saw it; but if he *had* seen the letter, he would doubtless have noticed the lack of cordiality in the trite phraseology and might have wondered whether Hardy had really phrased the letter himself. *We* know that he had not.

Hardy had known James for more than forty years. As fellow clubmen in London they saw each other frequently. At the annual dinner of the Rabelais Club on 6 June 1886 they sat amiably side by side. On 12 October 1892 they both attended Tennyson's funeral, and when Hardy wrote his wife to tell her about this occasion (see Letter 528), he mentioned Henry James's presence at the funeral. In 1898 Hardy told William Rothenstein that "certainly nobody" could write a brief comment on George Gissing "so well" as Henry James could write it. In 1903, when Mrs. Hardy was vacationing in Calais with her niece, Hardy wrote her on 29 November (Letter 997) and made a point of telling her that he had met Henry James at the Athenaeum Club in London. On 16 July 1908 Hardy wrote Emma again (Letter 1268) to tell her that he and James had sat side by side at the wedding of Edmund Gosse's son Philip. In 1909 Hardy and James both attended a memorial service to George Meredith in Westminster Abbey.

Despite all these intimations of friendship if not of cordiality, Hardy came later to remark that Henry James, "with his nebulous gaze" (*Early Life,* p. 217), had "a ponderously warm manner of saying nothing in infinite sentences" (*Early Life,* p. 237), and that his books showed him to be "a writer who has no grain of poetry, or humor, or spontaneity" (*Later Years*, p. 169). When Hardy died, he left a typescript, ready for Mrs. Hardy to publish, in which Henry James and Robert Louis Stevenson were referred to as "the Polonius and the Osric of novelists" (*Later Years*, pp. 7-8).

This coupling of the two younger writers perhaps enables us to conjecture what had gone wrong with Hardy's earlier friendship with James. Since the 1889 date when James had invited Hardy to dine with him on "a modest cutlet" (see Letter 388), something had obviously happened to produce the sour note found in Hardy's later remarks.

In 1920, when the *Letters of Henry James* were published, Hardy learned that James and Stevenson had discussed *Tess of the D'Urbervilles* back in 1892 and 1893 and had agreed that Tess was "vile." In 1920 these opinions were published for all the world to see. Hardy, along with other readers, learned that James had written to R.L.S. on 19 March 1892 to tell him that "the good little Thomas Hardy has scored a great success with *Tess of the D'Urbervilles,* which is chock-full of faults and falsity." Stevenson replied in a letter now lost but one obviously written in agreement with James's view; for, on 17 February 1893, James wrote again: "I grant you Hardy with all my heart . . . . Oh, yes, dear Louis, she is vile. The pretence of 'sexuality' is only equalled by the absence of it, and the abomination of the language by the author's reputation for style."

Hardy was not the man to let a posthumous attack like this go unavenged. James's caustic comment opened an old sore. On 1 May 1892 Andrew Lang had written to Edward Clodd: "I am sorry Hardy takes criticism so much to heart. My word, we should cultivate a little stoicism." But Hardy was no stoic—at least not in this respect. While he was preparing those pages which the second Mrs. Hardy was to issue in 1928 as *The Early Life,* Hardy devised his own brand of posthumous revenge. He wrote:

In December [1879] Hardy attended the inaugural dinner of the Rabelais Club, . . . instituted by Sir Walter Besant . . . as a declaration for virility in literature. Hardy was pressed to join as being the most virile writer . . . then in London; while . . . Henry James . . . was rejected for the lack of that quality, though he was afterwards invited as a guest (*Early Life,* pp. 172-73).

But when James attended the Rabelais Club dinners he was *not* there "as a guest" but as a regular member, and (what is more) as a charter member. When Robert Browning was invited to join, he was told (in a letter now in Waco, Texas) that Hardy and Henry James were both "already inscribed" as "original members." When, later on, the Club published its *Recreations,* Henry James was named as a member in each of the three volumes, and in Volume I his name was distinguished by an asterisk to mark him as a charter member of the Club. Hardy had a set of these *Recreations* in his own library; the set was in Lot No. 23 when the Hardy Library was sold at auction on 26 May 1938.

If there are readers who regard Hardy's conduct as an exhibition of petty malice if not of more blameworthy hostility, they can perhaps find some excuse for the wounded Master of Max Gate by remembering that Hardy was not the only one who found Henry James an uncongenial figure despite his impressive façade. After Ellen Glasgow had met James in London in 1914, she afterwards remarked that wherever she happened to see him, he invariably seemed "imposing, urbane, and delightful," but in "the involved sentences he was laboring to utter . . . there was a hollow ring somewhere. . . . When [in studying James's books] one industriously sifted his moral problems, there was little left but the smooth sands of decorum. . . . Placed beside Hardy . . . Henry James would have appeared, in spite of his size and his dignity, slightly foppish in manner" (*The Woman Within,* New York, 1954, p. 207).

Two other Americans have also given us their comments on the Polonius of English novelists. In "In Memory" T. S. Eliot remarked that Henry James "had a mind so fine that no idea could violate it" (*The Little Review,* August 1918). And in *The Thought and Character of William James* (Boston, 1934, Vol. II, p. 429), Ralph Barton Perry observed that in Henry James's letters "there is no philosophy at all." To a man with Hardy's well-known addiction to philosophizing, the lack of philosophy in Henry James would have made friendly intimacy impossible, even if James had not commented on the "faults and falsity" of *Tess of the D'Urbervilles* and had uttered no sneer at "the abomination of the language" of the novel by "the good little Thomas Hardy." It is therefore not surprising that the Max Gate files contain only four letters from Henry James, three of them dealing with Edith Wharton's request for a contribution to her war-time anthology.

On a previous page it has been remarked that the present volume bears some resemblance to a telephone directory: both are full of names and numerals. If this book, like a telephone directory, also contained classified "yellow pages," the reader's attention could thereby be directed to various aspects of Hardy's correspondence which must be left to the future labors of other interested students. Meanwhile, any reader can easily devise classifications of his own. For example, there are letters from

(1) Actors and actresses: Forbes-Robertson, Sir Henry Irving, Lillah McCarthy, Mrs. "Pat" Campbell, Olga Nethersole, Elizabeth Robins, Ellen Terry, Irene Vanbrugh, Sybil Thorndike, and Mrs. Fiske.

(2) Artists and Illustrators: Alma-Tadema, Augustus John, E. A. Abbey, Sir William Rothenstein, Helen Paterson, W. M. Barnes, John Collier, George Du Maurier, Parsons, Strang, Hopkins, and Blanche.

(3) Editors: Leslie Stephen, John Morley, T. P. O'Connor, C. K. Shorter, Arthur Locker, Mowbray Morris, and Henry M. Alden.

(4) Musicians: Elgar, Vaughan Williams, Gardiner, Gibbs, Holst, and Evelyn Suart.

(5) Fellow-novelists: Barrie, Arnold Bennett, Besant, Black, Blackmore, Galsworthy, Kipling, Meredith, H. G. Wells, and Virginia Woolf.

(6) Poets: Browning, Robert Bridges, Swinburne, De la Mare, A. E. Housman, John Masefield, Dobson, and Siegfried Sassoon.

(7) Publishers: Macmillan, Chapman, and Holt, William Tinsley, R. B. Marston, John Lane, C. Kegan Paul, George Smith, and Henry Harper.

Numerous other "yellow pages" classifications will occur to any interested reader, under topics like war, politics, dramatizations, etc. One topic, however, is conspicuous by its absence. The Max Gate letters make it abundantly clear that Hardy was not interested in lengthy discussions of the techniques of novel-writing and did not care to discuss the subtleties of unusual psychological situations. He was ready to write about minute observations of nature, or about farm-wagons, or about Roman excavations in Dorset, or about the preservation of ancient buildings, but *not* about how to plan, construct, and execute a novel. His correspondence reinforces the conclusions reached by those who have closely examined the MSS. of his novels, namely that he was largely an improviser who trusted to the impulse of the moment, to "instinct" and "intuition," for guidance through the mazes of novel construction.

Any close examination of Hardy's correspondence will, however, soon reveal the fact that there was one subject which was more certain than any other to arouse his interest and stimulate him into energetic and at times into indignant correspondence. In *The Return of the Native* he described Mrs. Yeobright as "a woman not disinclined to philosophize" and in possessing this trait she resembled her maker. Hardy, too, was not disinclined to philosophize; and the more he philosophized, the more convinced he became that life was just what he had called it in *The Return of the Native*, "a thing to be put up with." As early as 20 February 1888 his letters record this brooding, philosophizing tendency. In the letters of 3 April 1892, 20 April 1901, 15 January 1904, 28 May and 3 June 1907, 9 August 1909, 2 February 1915, 2 March 1918, and 17 December 1920, we can see how persistent was this habit of mind through the years. No comment on his correspondence would be a faithful report unless it emphasized this philosophizing aspect. Like the author of the Book of *Job,* Hardy even enjoyed imagining himself carrying on a philosophical discussion with God (see his poem "New Year's Eve"), and he could not understand why his readers regarded many of his brooding poems as gloomy and depressing. On 2 March 1918 Edmund Gosse wrote Hardy to ask: "Why does it make you so indignant to be called a 'pessimist'?" Hardy kept no copy of his reply to this question, but any reader of the "Apology" prefixed to *Late Lyrics* in 1922 will recognize how central and fundamental this subject was in the eyes of the man who (in that same "Apology") described his philosophy of life as "evolutionary meliorism."

When Hardy died, he left a book-length manuscript almost ready for the printer—it appeared in October 1928 as *Winter Words.* One of the poems in this volume is entitled "So Various." It describes a jury of twelve men: one, quite young; another, old and stiff; one is a man of sadness; another "a man so glad you never could conceive him sad"; one is a poor fellow who forgets everything said to him; another, a vindictive man who forgets nothing; etc., etc. The last stanza of this poem declares:

> All these specimens of men . . .
> Curious to say
> Were one man. Yea,
> *I* was all they.

The four thousand and more letters listed in the present volume were written to "all these specimens of men" even though they were addressed to "one man." Taken together, they provide convincing corroboration of the poetic judgment Hardy passed upon himself, that his personality was strikingly and impressively "various."

CHRONOLOGICAL LIST OF HARDY'S CORRESPONDENCE

[1860?]

1. No date: Horace M. Moule asks about going for a walk. Published in *Providence and Mr. Hardy* by Lois Deacon (London: Hutchinson, 1966), p. 87, See also *Early Life*, p. 43.

1861

2. January 22: Henry R. Bastow from Lancaster, Tasmania. See *Early Life*, p. 40.
3. February 17: Bastow from Hobart Town, Tasmania.
4. May 20: Bastow again from Hobart Town. Quoted in *Early Life*, p. 41.
5. July 26: Horace M. Moule is invited to come on Monday. Published in *Providence and Mr. Hardy*, p. 87.

1862

6. May 23: Bastow again from Hobart, Tasmania.

1863

7. March 2: Moule speaks of overwork. Published in *Providence and Mr. Hardy*, p. 88.
8. March 9: Mrs. Julia Augusta Martin (Hardy's first teacher) says to "Dear Tommy": "I suppose I ought hardly to address you in this way now." Published in *Thomas Hardy's Notebooks*, ed. Evelyn Hardy (London: Hogarth Press, 1955), p. 123.
9. July 2: Moule praises some analyses Hardy had sent him. Published in *Providence and Mr. Hardy*, pp. 88-89.
10. December 23: Bastow again from Hobart, Tasmania.

1864

11. February 21: Moule about good usage in English. Published in *Providence and Mr. Hardy*, pp. 90-91.
12. February 21: Bastow from "Hobarton."

1865

13. December 24: Bastow is now in Melbourne, Australia.

1867

14. June (30): Horace M. Moule about Hardy moving from London back to Dorchester. Quoted in *Providence and Mr. Hardy*, p. 92.
15. August 10: Alexander Macmillan has read through *The Poor Man and the Lady*. Quoted in part in *Early Life*, p. 77, and in full in *Letters of Alexander Macmillan*.

1869

16. February 8: Frederick Chapman says there is doubt about publication of *The Poor Man and the Lady*. Letters referred to in *Early Life*, p. 79.
17. February 26: Chapman asks Hardy to call on him to meet the gentleman who has read his manuscript. Referred to in *Early Life*, p. 80.
18. March 3: Chapman makes an appointment for Hardy to come to London to discuss his novel. See *Early Life*, p. 80.

1870

19. February 11: G. R. Crickmay asks if Hardy can go to Cornwall. Published in *Early Life*, pp. 85-86.
20. April 4: Alexander Macmillan expresses regret on returning the manuscript of *Desperate Remedies* because it is "too sensational."
21. April 7: William Tinsley about his receipt of the manuscript of *Desperate Remedies*.
22. n.d.: Horace M. Moule has two articles in the current number of *Echo*.
23. May 3: Tinsley reports on his reader's opinion of a manuscript of Hardy's.
24. May 5: Tinsley tells Hardy he must contribute to the expense of publishing *Desperate Remedies*.

25. May 9: Tinsley sends further details about publication costs of *Desperate Remedies*.
26. December 9: Tinsley reports arrival of corrected manuscript.
27. December 19: Tinsley approves the alterations Hardy has made.
28. December 21: Tinsley about terms for publication of *Desperate Remedies*. Copies of this and the six preceding letters from William Tinsley were supplied by Howard Bliss. Fifteen additional Tinsley letters (4 dated in 1871, 8 in 1872, one in 1873, and 2 in 1875) are listed and partly quoted in Purdy, pp. 330-335; but Purdy fails to list Tinsley's letter of 2 August 1872 (No. 38). Purdy (p. 329) says Tinsley's letters are now in the Bliss collection but he gives no explanation of how they got out of the Max Gate Collection into Bliss's, nor does he explain why Letter 38 did not go with the others.

1871

29. June 7: Hardy to William Tinsley: typed transcript, supplied by Howard Bliss, written from 3 Wooperton Street, Weymouth, about advertising *Desperate Remedies*.
30. August 11: M. K. Macmillan acknowledges receipt of a manuscript.
31. September 11: Macmillan forwards a criticism of a story by Hardy.
32. September (n.d.): John Morley criticizes *Under the Greenwood Tree*.
33. October 6: G. R. Crickmay about examining St. Juliot Church in Cornwall.
34. October 18: Alexander Macmillan has read Hardy's story but cannot publish it now because they are busy with Christmas books.
35. October 20: Hardy to Tinsley, from Cornwall: typed transcript; asks about returns on *Desperate Remedies* and refers to a new story (*Under the Greenwood Tree*) which Hardy had begun in the summer and which Macmillan had just declined.

1872

36. April 17: Horace M. Moule is in London.
37. July 27: Hardy to Tinsley, from London: typed transcript; about supplying *Tinsley's Magazine* with a serial entitled "A Winning Tongue Had He," later changed to *A Pair of Blue Eyes*.
38. August 2: Tinsley quotes terms for the publication of *A Pair of Blue Eyes*, both in *Tinsley's Magazine* and as a book. Not included in Purdy's list of Tinsley letters, p. 333. This is the only original Tinsley letter remaining in the Max Gate file. See Letter 28.
39. August 10: T. Roger Smith (London architect) would be glad to use part of Hardy's time.
40. August 30: Hardy to Tinsley, from St. Juliot Rectory, Cornwall: typed transcript; about the October installment of *A Pair of Blue Eyes*.
41. September 26: Mrs. Julia Augusta Martin thanks Hardy for a copy of *Under the Greenwood Tree*.

42. November 29: Rev. Caddell Holder, Rector of St. Juliot's says Miss Gifford, the young lady mentioned by Hardy, is still at St. Juliot's and sends her regards.
43. November 30: Leslie Stephen expresses pleasure in *Under the Greenwood Tree,* and asks Hardy about contributing a serial story to the *Cornhill.* Quoted in *Early Life,* p. 125.
44. December 4: Stephen regrets he cannot expect a story from Hardy as soon as he would like to have it. Paraphrased in *Early Life,* p. 125.

1873

45. March 12: Hardy to William Tinsley, from Bockhampton: typed transcript; asks about payment for *A Pair of Blue Eyes.*
46. March 31: Hardy to Tinsley: typed transcript; asks if it is desirable to change "Knight" to "Knighton" in *A Pair of Blue Eyes.*
47. April 7: Leslie Stephen asks about Hardy's progress on a new novel.
48. April 11: Stephen expects to have a vacancy in the *Cornhill* for a new story soon.
49. April 29: John Hutton about his review of *Desperate Remedies* in the *Spectator.*
50. May 11: Charles W. Moule (the original of Angel Clare in *Tess*) is going to Cambridge.
51. May 21: Horace M. Moule asks if Hardy would advise a man 24 years old to take up the profession of architect.
52. May 29: Henry Holt, New York publisher, is about to publish *Under the Greenwood Tree* on the recommendation of Frederick Macmillan. Letter published in Weber's *Hardy in America* (Waterville, Maine: Colby College Press, 1946), p. 15.
53. June 17: John Hutton asks if Hardy's publishers have sent *A Pair of Blue Eyes* to the *Spectator.*
54. June 26: Hutton expresses his delight in reading *A Pair of Blue Eyes* and *Under the Greenwood Tree.*
55. June 28: Emily Genevieve Smith thanks Hardy for the books lent by his mother, and says she has read *Under the Greenwood Tree.*
56. July 3: Hutton again about *A Pair of Blue Eyes.*
57. July 23: Henry Holt about publishing *A Pair of Blue Eyes* in New York. Letter published in *Hardy in America,* pp. 16-17.
58. September 6: Leslie Stephen asks to see the installment of Hardy's new novel that was promised him. Letter mentioned in *Early Life,* p. 126.
59. October 6: Stephen about his pleasure in reading the installment of *Far from the Madding Crowd.* Paraphrased in *Early Life,* p. 127.
60. October 20: Stephen hopes to begin publication of *Far from the Madding Crowd* in February.
61. November 18: Stephen reports publication of *Far from the Madding Crowd* should begin in January instead of February. See *Early Life,* p. 127; Hardy confuses Letters 60 and 61.
62. November 18: Smith, Elder & Co. ask Hardy's views about terms for the publication of *Far from the Madding Crowd.*
63. November 26: Smith, Elder & Co. offer £400 for *Madding Crowd.*

64. December 2: Smith, Elder & Co. acknowledge Hardy's acceptance of their offer.
65. December 8: Henry Holt is unable to make *A Pair of Blue Eyes* sell. Published in *Hardy in America*, pp. 20-21.

1874

66. January 8: Leslie Stephen sends congratulations. Quoted in *Early Life*, p. 129.
67. January 22: Henry Holt asks Hardy whether *Far from the Madding Crowd* is by him. Letter published in *Hardy in America*, p. 22.
68. February 17: Stephen has read the next installment of *Far from the Madding Crowd* with pleasure but finds portions "rather long."
69. March 12: Stephen thinks "the story improves as it goes on" but he wants the seduction of Fanny to be treated gingerly. Quoted in *Early Life*, p. 130.
70. April 13: Stephen speaks well of the story and comments on the Fanny Robin episodes further.
71. July 21: Stephen wants to talk to Hardy. (See *Early Life*, p. 139).
72. August 10: Henry Holt thanks Hardy for his photograph. Published in, *Hardy in America*, p. 23.
73. August 21: Mrs. Anne B. Procter praises Hardy's novel.
74. August 25: Leslie Stephen on Hardy's rustics, whose speech he finds out of character in *Far from the Madding Crowd*.
75. September 4: The Reverend Dr. E. Hamilton Gifford agrees to officiate at Hardy's marriage on 17 September 1874.
76. September 4: Mrs. Anne B. Procter again about Hardy's novel.
77. September 12: Dr. E. H. Gifford approves of Hardy's arrangements for his wedding.
78. November 12: Hardy to Henry Holt: about publication of *Far from the Madding Crowd* in New York. Transcript in the hand of Emma Lavinia Hardy, marked "Copy."
79. November 18: Katharine S. Macquoid about *Desperate Remedies* and about Bathsheba in *Far from the Madding Crowd*.
80. December 2: Leslie Stephen would like to begin a new story in the *Cornhill* and asks if Hardy has one to offer.
81. December 7: Stephen congratulates Hardy on his marriage to Emma Gifford.
82. December 23: John Hutton asks how Hardy liked a review in the *Spectator*.

1875

83. January 15: George Smith about publishing a second edition of *Far from the Madding Crowd*.
84. January 16: Mrs. Julia Augusta Martin tells Hardy of praise of his writings.

85. January 19: George Smith about corrections for the second edition of *Far from the Madding Crowd*.
86. January 20: Hardy to William Tinsley: typed transcript; about Tinsley's high price for the copyright of *Under the Greenwood Tree*; written from St. David's, Hook Road, Surbiton.
87. (c. January 30): George Du Maurier is glad Hardy is pleased with his illustrations for *The Hand of Ethelberta*.
88. February 8: J. H. Fyfe, from London, tells Hardy of a request for a story to be published in the *New York Times*.
89. February 15: Sir George B. Douglas, about his plan to write a romance.
90. March 5: L. J. Jennings accepts *The Hand of Ethelberta* for serialization in the *New York Times*.
91. March 9: George Smith expresses faith in *Ethelberta* and offers £700 for it.
92. March 22: Smith, Elder & Co. make a formal offer of £700 for *The Hand of Ethelberta*.
93. May 13: Leslie Stephen doubts the use of the word "amorous" by a lady in a story of Hardy's, and suggests "sentimental" as a substitute for it.
94. May 20: Stephen objects to the subtitle of *Ethelberta*, "A Comedy in Chapters." Quoted in *Early Life*, p. 136.
95. May 21: Hardy to Leslie Stephen (transcript), written from 18 Newton Road, Westbourne Grove; about the secondary title of *The Hand of Ethelberta*.
96. May 24. Charles F. Findlay solicits a story for *News of the Week*, Glasgow.
97. September 11: Richard Gowing wants a story for the January number of *The Gentleman's Magazine*. (Hardy sent a poem, "The Fire at Tranter Sweatley's.")
98. September 30: Gowing thanks Hardy for "the ballad."
99. October 12: William Isbister asks for a short story to run about six months in *Good Words*.
100. November 1: Mrs. Anne Procter again about Hardy's novel.
101. November 2: R. D. Blackmore sends thanks for the ballad Hardy sent him.
102. November 2: W. Minto asks for the next novel Hardy will write, to run weekly as a serial in *The Examiner*.
103. November 4: Hardy to Henry Holt (transcript marked "Copy," in the hand of Mrs. Emma Hardy), from West End Cottage, Swanage, Dorset; thanks Holt for getting "The Fire at Tranter Sweatley's" printed in *Appleton's Journal*, and states that he would like to continue connection with Holt.
104. November 10: R. D. Blackmore thanks Hardy for a letter.

1876

105. February 25: W. Lange about a German translation of *Far from the Madding Crowd*.
106. March 7: Smith, Elder and Co. about publishing cheap edition of *A Pair of Blue Eyes* and *Far from the Madding Crowd*.

107. March 20: A. Hansen about a Danish translation of *Far from the Madding Crowd*.
108. April 11: Freiherr von Tauchnitz about publishing Tauchnitz Editions of Hardy's novels.
109. May 16: Leslie Stephen about Hardy's kindness in accepting his criticisms. Quoted in *Early Life*, p. 143.
110. May 22: Tauchnitz about his editions of Hardy's works.
111. "Thursday Night": William Blake accepts an invitation to lunch.
112. August 21: J. H. Nodal about the Dorset dialect.
113. November 24: Léon Boncher, from Besançon, about *Far from the Madding Crowd* and his review of it.
114. (n. d.): Thomas Overy sends some verses dated "1876."
115. (n. d.): Mrs. Anne Procter again about Hardy's novels.

1877

116. April 4: Mrs. Procter again about Hardy's novels.
117. April 13: C. Kegan Paul, London publisher, about publishing a new edition of *A Pair of Blue Eyes*.
118. May 28: Stephen about *The Return of the Native*.
119. September 29: George Binghams about some research he has done relative to the "threatened invasion of 1803."
120. October 22: Tauchnitz about Tauchnitz Editions.
121. December 1: Tauchnitz again about publishing Hardy's works for sale on the continent.

1878

122. January 3: Arthur W. Blomfield (Hardy's first employer) invites him to attend some private theatricals.
123. January 8: Tauchnitz about another Tauchnitz edition.
124. January 14: Francis Hueffer solicits a story for publication in the *New Quarterly Magazine*.
125. February 5: Arthur Hopkins about the illustrations for *The Return of the Native* as serialized in *Belgravia*.
126. February 19: Hopkins again about the drawings for *The Return of the Native* and the illustrator's need for the author's help, especially "on Eustacia."
127. April 18: Edward Abbott, from Boston, Massachusetts, asks for a sketch about Hardy for use in *The Literary World*.
128. May 1: Chatto & Windus repeat Hueffer's request (Letter 124); also ask for a short story for the July number of the *New Quarterly Magazine*. (Hardy sent "An Indiscretion in the Life of an Heiress.")
129. June 8: Henry Holt, from New York, has succeeded in disposing of *Indiscretion in the Life of an Heiress*. Letter published in *Hardy in America*, p. 28.
130. September 19: George Smith will be happy to publish *The Return of the Native* in an edition of 1000 copies but offers only £200 for it.

131. September 23: Chatto & Windus about publishing *The Return of the Native* in a library edition uniform with *Far from the Madding Crowd*.
132. November 2: Tauchnitz again about a continental Tauchnitz Edition.

1879

133. February 17: Leslie Stephen asks to see *The Trumpet-Major* when it is further advanced.
134. March 7: Walter Besant about forming a Rabelais Club, and enclosing a "List of Original Members" in which, after Hardy's name, comes that of W. H. Pollock and then Henry James.
135. March 24: Annie S. Franklyn about a character in *The Return of the Native*.
136. May 20: George A. Macmillan acknowledges receipt of a manuscript. This letter provides what is perhaps the sole surviving evidence that Hardy submitted *The Trumpet-Major* to Macmillan, his fourth attempt and his fourth failure to win Macmillan acceptance. Within the next three months this novel was accepted for serialization in *Good Words*.
137. May 30: C. J. A. Rumbold about his grandfather, Sir Thomas Rumbold, who is mentioned in *The Return of the Native*.
138. June 2: John Blackwood will be glad to see the manuscript of another novel by Hardy.
139. June 25: Donald Macleod is glad to learn Hardy is contributing a story to *Good Words* in 1880, and then outlines what he, as editor of the magazine, desires to find in its stories.
140. August 22: Macleod has received the proofs of Hardy's opening chapter and asks about illustrations.
141. August 29: John Collier wishes to illustrate a story of Hardy's.
142. September 6: Hardy to William Isbister, publisher of *Good Words*: typed transcript; from 1 Arundel Terrace about the artist John Collier and proofs of *The Trumpet-Major*.
143. September 29: C. Kegan Paul about the "sketch map" in *The Native*.
144. October 19: Paul about a review by Mrs. Sutherland Orr, a sister of Sir Frederick Leighton.
145. October 26: Alexandra Leighton Orr about her article that Kegan Paul had written about.
146. November 20: John Collier, the artist, is pleased with the sketches for use in illustrating *The Trumpet-Major*.
147. November 25: Walter Besant about the inaugural dinner of the Rabelais Club.
148. December 30: Besant congratulates Hardy on the opening chapters of *The Trumpet-Major*.

1880

149. January 14: H. E. Tullidge comments on finding a character named Tullidge in *The Trumpet-Major*.

CHRONOLOGICAL LIST

150. January 17: Tauchnitz about another Tauchnitz Edition.
151. February 1: Frederick Locker tells of his pleasure in reading *Far from the Madding Crowd* and invites Hardy to call on him. Hardy's reply published in *Early Life*, pp. 174-175.
152. March 6: Hallam Tennyson tells Mrs. Anne Procter he and his mother will be glad to have a call from her and Mr. Hardy.
153. March 7: Mrs. Procter passes Tennyson's letter on to Hardy.
154. March 21: Mrs. Procter again.
155. April 1: Henry M. Alden informs Hardy Harper & Brothers of New York plan to issue an English Edition of their magazine. Letter published in *Hardy in America*, p. 44.
156. April 16: Hardy to Harper & Brothers (a copy signed "Thomas Hardy"): answers Alden's letter, agreeing to supply a serial for publication in *Harper's Magazine*, both the New York and the London editions, for £100 for each monthly installment.
157. April 20: George Smith says this would be a good time to send a MS. for the *Cornhill* to Mr. Stephen.
158. May 2: Mrs. Anne Procter friendly letter.
159. May 24: Harper & Brothers accept Hardy's offer of a new story, *A Laodicean*. Letter published in *Hardy in America*, pp. 44-45.
160. June 5: Helen Paterson (Mrs. William Allingham) cannot illustrate another novel for Hardy because she has given up book illustration.
161. June 7: Frank Dicksen declines Hardy's request that he illustrate a novel for him.
162. June 9: George Du Maurier will illustrate Hardy's tale and his price will be "twenty guineas for each drawing."
163. June 11: Hardy to Harpers, New York: about the engravings for *A Laodicean* of the illustrations to be made by Du Maurier, in a letter written from No. 1, Arundel Terrace, Upper Tooting. A transcript in Emma Hardy's hand, marked "Copy" in his hand.
164. June 14: William Lowell belatedly says he would be glad to illustrate Hardy's story.
165. June 23: Du Maurier is pleased at the prospect of illustrating Hardy's novel.
166. July 12: Du Maurier invites Hardy to dine with him, in order to consult about the drawings for *A Laodicean*.
167. July 14: W. P. Frith (artist) will be at the Grosvenor Restaurant at 7:30 on the 20th.
168. July 28: George Du Maurier sets date for meeting Hardy at lunch.
169. August 17: Du Maurier asks about *Part III*.
170. August 31: George Manville Fenn asks permission to quote.
171. September 3: Fenn thanks Hardy for his permission.
172. (n. d., c. September): Du Maurier about the illustrations for *A Laodicean*.
173. September 16: James Russell Lowell about a proposed Copyright Treaty between the U.S.A. and England.
174. November 8: Walter Besant about a letter from R. D. Blackmore.
175. November 19: Leslie Stephen regrets a lapse of relations with Hardy.
176. December 8: George Du Maurier is glad Hardy likes a recent sketch.

177. December 9: Sir Henry F. Ponsonby (secretary to Queen Victoria) thanks Hardy for the three volumes of *The Trumpet-Major*, which the Queen hopes to read.
178. December 10: Besant on *The Trumpet-Major*.
179. December 11: Lady Agatha Russell thanks Hardy for *The Trumpet-Major*.
180. (n. d.): Edmund Gosse praises *The Trumpet-Major*.
181. (December ?): J. Comyns Carr says work is progressing on the dramatization of *Far from the Madding Crowd*.
182. December 10: Paul Jüngling about a German translation of *The Trumpet-Major*.

1881

183. January 17: John Hutton asks if Hardy was pleased with the review of *The Trumpet-Major* in the *Spectator*, written by Julian Hawthorne.
184. February 7: C. Kegan Paul about *Part III* of *A Laodicean*.
185. February 24: Paul suggests a doctor for Hardy's illness and says he is writing "rather a good review" of him.
186. April 20: Hardy to G. Thyen: wax impression copy of Hardy's letter signifying his intention to vacate the house at Upper Tooting.
187. April 21: Bernard Derosne asks permission to translate *The Trumpet-Major*. into French.
188. April 23: Hardy gives Bernard Derosne permission to translate *The Trumpet-Major* into French. A copy in ink, signed "Thomas Hardy."
189. April 26: Derosne asks about the possibility of his making other translations of Hardy's books into French.
190. May 16: Hardy to G. Thyen: since Hardy has not yet found a house, he would be glad to remain at Upper Tooting through August.
191. June 25: Derosne has finished translating *The Trumpet-Major*.
192. July 5: Lord Carnarvon will be very glad to propose Hardy's name at the Athenaeum Club.
193. July 8: Besant sends an invitation.
194. July 9: Besant notifies Hardy about the annual dinner of the Rabelais Club.
195. July 26: Henry J. Moule (Curator of the Dorset County Museum) accepts Hardy's invitation to call on him at Wimborne.
196. August 24: Moule would like to visit again "the Avenue" at Wimborne where Hardy and his wife are living.
197. September 28: Thomas Bailey Aldrich solicits "a serial story" to run through six or more numbers of the *Atlantic Monthly*.
198. October 3: Moule replies to a letter from Hardy.
199. October 9: Mrs. Anne Procter writes a friendly letter.
200. October 13: Henry Stevens informs Hardy that Houghton Mifflin & Co. desire a serial story for the *Atlantic Monthly* in 1882.
201. October 18: W. R. A. Ralston writes about "Tourgueneff, the Russian Novelist."
202. October 18: Reginald Smith thanks Hardy for the William Barnes obituary in the *Athenaeum*.

CHRONOLOGICAL LIST

203. October 20: Hardy to W. R. A. Ralston; typed transcript from The Avenue, Wimborne, about Tourgueneff's visit.
204. November 26: Harper & Brothers make final payment for *A Laodicean*. Letter published in *Hardy in America*, p. 46.
205. December 8: Thomas Woolner about getting a book of Hardy's to read.
206. December 12: Alexandra (Mrs. Sutherland) Orr about Paula's quest of Somerset in *A Laodicean*.
207. December 12: W. C. Unwin answers inquiries from Hardy as he prepares to write *Two on a Tower*.
208. December (30?): J. Comyns Carr tells Hardy a play founded on a novel of his has been produced in London with no acknowledgment to Hardy.
209. December 31: Judge H. Tindal Atkinson sends an invitation.

1882

210. January 1: John Thomas about Pinero's plagiarism in *The Squire*.
211. January 2: William Black on the way a play of Hardy's is being treated.
212. January 6: Dolores Drummond (actress) solicits a chance to play Bathsheba in Hardy's play based on *Far from the Madding Crowd*.
213. January 7: Frederick Greenwood will be glad to write a favorable statement about Hardy and his works.
214. January 20: J. Comyns Carr discusses Hardy's adaptation of his novel, *Far from the Madding Crowd*.
215. January (30?): Carr about the controversy over Pinero's play, and about plans for the production of the Hardy-Carr play, which opens at Liverpool 27 February 1882.
216. February 28: Carr, from Liverpool, dealing with changes and revisions in the Hardy-Carr play and answering Hardy's complaints that his suggestions had been ignored.
217. March 7: Thomas Bailey Aldrich about Hardy's appearance in *Atlantic Monthly*. This letter published in part in "Thomas Hardy and his New England Editors" by Carl J. Weber, *New England Quarterly*, XV (December 1942), 685-686, and in full in *Hardy in America*, p. 73.
218. March 8: Henry Stevens invites Hardy to dinner at the Freemason's Tavern.
219. March 9: Henry J. Moule, of Dorchester, friendly letter.
220. (c. April 1): Carr has made arrangements for the production of *Far from the Madding Crowd* in London in the Globe Theatre. It opened on April 29, 1882.
221. April 3: Aldrich reports the arrival in Boston of the second installment of *Two on a Tower*. This letter published in part in "Thomas Hardy and his New England Editors" by Carl J. Weber, *New England Quarterly*, XV (December 1942), 686, 692; and in full in *Hardy in America*, p. 74.
222. May 18: Henry Stevens accepts Hardy's invitation to dine with the Rabelais Club.

223. July 18: Richard H. Hutton criticizes Hardy's "Withered Arm" and calls it disagreeable.
224. July 20: Mrs. M. O. W. Oliphant asks Hardy to write a paper for *Longman's Magazine* on the Dorset "labouring poor."
225. August 4: Hardy to James Hogg: copy from "The Avenue, Wimborne," asks about a contribution to the periodical, *London Society;* signed "Thomas Hardy" but "not written by me."
226. August 9: James Hogg informs Hardy the contribution to his periodical was by "another Thomas Hardy."
227. August 15: Hardy to James Hogg: copy, thanking Hogg for his reply of 9 August.
228. November 12: C. Kegan Paul about *A Laodicean* and *Two on a Tower*.
229. December 15: Tauchnitz about another Tauchnitz Edition.
230. (n. d.): William Blake about meeting Hardy at Phillippi.
231. "Sunday": Mrs. Anne Procter sends a friendly letter.
232. (n. d.): Leslie Stephen regrets his inability to accept an invitation from Hardy.

1883

233. January 8: R. B. Marston (London publisher) is pleased with *Two on a Tower*.
234. January 13: Harper & Brothers make grateful acknowledgment of Hardy's letter in the London *Athenaeum*. Published in *Hardy in America*, p. 48.
235. January 19: Frederick Greenwood sends a note.
236. January 28: J. B. Daly about reviews of *Two on a Tower*.
237. February 5: A. G. McFadden questions Hardy about his heroines.
238. February 20: Wilfred Meynell wants an article on the English rustic.
239. February 22: Edwin A. Abbey is glad Hardy can come on Monday (26 February 1883). This letter is almost the sole surviving relic of an early friendship that faded.
240. March 14: W. Davenport Adams about a collection of "Songs from the Novelists."
241. April 19: Mrs. Anne Procter friendly letter.
242. April 20: Walter Besant writes as a fellow novelist.
243. April 22: Havelock Ellis acknowledges Hardy's letter (of 19 April 1883) about Ellis's article on Hardy's novels in the *Westminster Review*.
244. May 2: Havelock Ellis again about his article.
245. May 27: Arthur Rouht asks permission to translate *Two on a Tower* into German.
246. June 11: Edmund Gosse invites Hardy to dinner at the Savile Club to meet W. D. Howells from America.
247. June 26: John Morley promises something on an article by Hardy in the *Pall Mall Gazette*.
248. August 29: William H. Peet about errors in *Far from the Madding Crowd*.
249. October 12: Bernard Derosne, after translating *The Trumpet-Major* into French, asks about making other French translations.

250. October 15: Edward W. Bok invites Hardy to write to him.
251. October 29: Walter Besant about the publishers of *Good Words*.
252. October 29: Horace Seymour, from 10 Downing Street, expresses W. E. Gladstone's thanks for Hardy's article in *Longman's Magazine*.
253. November 6: Besant reports his efforts with the publishers of *Good Words*.
254. November 11: Judge H. Tindal Atkinson, from Wimborne.
255. December 29: Judge Atkinson sends holiday greetings.
256. December 31: Henry J. Moule sends Good Wishes for 1884.

1884

257. January 28: Mary Muchall asks permission to translate four of Hardy's novels into German.
258. March 4: Mrs. Anne Procter, after nearly a year's silence, another friendly letter.
259. March 4: William H. York sends a rough plan of the site for Max Gate which has been granted to Hardy by the Duchy of Cornwall.
260. March 14: Mary Muchall repeats her request of 28 January 1884.
261. March 27: Mary Muchall thanks Hardy for the permission granted by him.
262. May 2: Mrs. Procter another friendly letter.
263. May 18: Bernard Derosne about further French translations.
264. June 2: Mrs. Anne Procter birthday letter. Published in *Early Life*, p. 216.
265. June 9: Laura (Mrs. Lawrence) Alma-Tadema about "Interlopers at the Knap"; mentions her husband.
266. July 3: Judge H. T. Atkinson, from Wimborne.
267. October 8: Mrs. Procter, last of her 15 friendly letters to Hardy.
268. October 15: John Morley solicits a novel for serialization in *Macmillan's Magazine*.
269. "Thursday" (n. d.): William Black about a dinner engagement.

1885

270. January 16: William Black about salmon-fishing with E. A. Abbey.
271. March 6: B. Fossett Lock, of Dorchester, asks Hardy to preside when Lock lectures on the poetry of William Barnes.
272. March 13: Hardy to his wife: about his visit to Devon. Published in *Dearest Emmie* (London, 1963), pp. 1-2.
273. March 15: Lock regrets Hardy could not be present when Lock lectured on the poetry of William Barnes.
274. March 17: Alexander Macmillan pleased that Hardy is to give the firm a novel for *Macmillan's Magazine*.
275. April 27: Lady Winifred Herbert informs Hardy that Lady Carnarvon wants to make his acquaintance.

276. May 12: Lady Carnarvon invites Hardy and Mrs. Hardy to a small party.
277. May 16: Hardy to his wife: tells her about the Carnarvon party in London. Published in *Dearest Emmie*, pp. 2-4.
278. June 12: Frederic Harrison invites Hardy to lunch.
279. June 15: Harrison sends another invitation.
280. July 17: William H. York sends a receipt for Hardy's cheque in payment for the site of Max Gate.
281. August 14: John Hutton grieves for Hardy in the loss of a friend, and is interested in Hardy's comment on Lord Houghton.
282. August 24: Robert Louis Stevenson proposes to call at Max Gate.
283. September 1: Hardy to George Wilmshurst: copy, signed "T. H." in ink, about paying £450 for the ground on which his house stands.
284. September 4: G. Herriot about the purchase of the site of Max Gate.
285. September 16: Judge J. S. Udal about a meeting of the Field Club and of his wish to meet Hardy.
286. October 20: Arthur Locker (editor of *The Graphic*) about arrangements made with Harper & Brothers for the publication of *The Mayor of Casterbridge* in *Harper's Weekly* after its serial appearance in *The Graphic*. Partly quoted in Purdy, p. 53.
287. October 23: G. Herriot about "Tithe Rent Charge" on the Max Gate site.
288. November 20: Hardy to John Morley: copy made by Howard Bliss of letter about "disestablishment."
289. November 23: John Morley acknowledges Hardy's letter of the 20th.
290. November 25: Leslie Stephen is pleased Hardy wrote to him.
291. December 3: Alexander Macmillan about beginning the serialization of *The Woodlanders* in *Macmillan's Magazine*.
292. December 14: Thomas Bailey Aldrich about the final chapters of *Two on a Tower* and his dislike of the situation there depicted. Part of this letter was published in "Thomas Hardy and his New England Editors" by Carl J. Weber, *New England Quarterly*, XV (December 1942), 688-89, 696; and also in *Hardy in America*, pp. 75, 85.
293. December 14: Christine (Mrs. Henry) Reeve about her father's reading *The Trumpet-Major*.
294. December 19: William Black sends Christmas greetings.

1886

295. January 3: Judge H. T. Atkinson thanks Hardy for *The Mayor of Casterbridge*.
296. January 9: Lady Winifred Herbert thanks Hardy for remembering a promise to immortalize her name. (However, Saxelby's *Hardy Dictionary* lists no "Winifred" and no "Herbert.")
297. March 29: Alexander Macmillan is delighted with the first installment of *The Woodlanders*.
298. May 29: C. Kegan Paul about a reviewer of a book by Hardy.

299. May 31: Alexander Macmillan sends proofs of Part III of *The Woodlanders*.
300. June 7: Macmillan about adding *The Mayor of Casterbridge* to Macmillan's "Colonial Library."
301. June 28: Hardy to Christine (Mrs. Henry) Reeve: copy, not in Hardy's hand, about *The Trumpet-Major*.
302. July 1: George Meredith will be glad to welcome Hardy any day he can call.
303. (n. d.): Robert Louis Stevenson praises *The Mayor of Casterbridge* and Henchard. Published in *Early Life*, page 235.
304. (n. d.): Stevenson invites Hardy to call at the British Museum for a talk in Sidney Colvin's office.
305. September 3: Edmund Gosse thanks Hardy for a visit.
306. September 19: Mowbray Morris has had to shorten *The Woodlanders*, and gives Hardy a suggestion about handling one of his characters.
307. September 29: M. Holzmann says the Duchy of Cornwall asks payment of £450 for the property at Max Gate.
308. October 9: N. MacColl invites Hardy to write an obituary article on William Barnes for the *Athenaeum*.
309. October 11: MacColl thanks Hardy for being willing to write the requested article on Barnes.
310. October (21?): MacColl thanks Hardy for his article.
311. November 1: Edward A. Arnold solicits a short story for *Murray's Magazine* and mentions 'Vernon Lee.'
312. November 13: Coventry Patmore invites Hardy to visit him at Hastings.
313. November 19: Edmund McClure solicits a story with a "moral backbone."
314. December (6?): L. L. Barnes about Hardy's obituary notice of William Barnes.
315. December 7: Mrs. Lucy E. Baxter (daughter of William Barnes) solicits help in her attempt to write a biography of her father.
316. December 16: M. Holzmann sends Hardy the deed conveying Max Gate and land to him from the Duchy of Cornwall.
317. December 17: Mrs. Lucy Baxter thanks Hardy for his letter in response to her appeal of 7 December 1886.
318. December 22: Henry J. Moule regrets Hardy's unwillingness to write "a memoirette" of William Barnes, and refers to Hardy's article about Barnes in the *Athenaeum*.
319. December 28: Caroline Tolbort, a cousin of Hardy's friend, Hooper Tolbort who died in India three years earlier, writes to Hardy. See *Early Life*, p. 211.

1887

320. January 5: J. J. Foster invites Hardy to become a member of The Folk-Lore Society.
321. (n. d.): James Payne sends some thanks.
322. February 1: Payne repeats his gratitude.
323. February 21: Alexander Macmillan about the publication date set for *The Woodlanders*, 15 March 1887.

324. March 16: Tillotson & Son suggest Hardy write another novel as long as *The Woodlanders* and offer a thousand guineas for serial rights. (This offer led to Hardy's writing *Tess*.)
325. March 22: Edmund Gosse thanks Hardy for *The Woodlanders*.
326. April 21: Mrs. Julia Augusta Martin to "Dear Tom," who was her pupil. Published in *Thomas Hardy's Notebooks*, p. 127.
327. May 2: Arthur W. Blomfield proposes to call on Hardy in Dorchester.
328. May 5: Alexander Macmillan, concerning royalty on *The Woodlanders*.
329. May 12: A. C. Swinburne is grateful to receive a copy of a new book of Hardy's from the author himself.
330. (n. d.): Sir Frederick Leighton is pleased Hardy sent him a copy of *The Woodlanders*.
331. (May 25?): James Payne invites Hardy to dine.
332. June 3: E. Roscoe Mullins, about to sculpture a statue of the late William Barnes, solicits Hardy's help.
333. "Tuesday" (n. d.): J. R. Robinson invites Hardy to dinner.
334. July 8: A. Herbert thanks Hardy for an invitation to dinner.
335. July 22: Justin McCarthy regrets his inability to accept an invitation.
336. July 23: Lord Lytton, Vice-Roy of India, thanks Hardy for his letter of 12 July 1887.
337. August 8: John H. Lock thinks the bells of St. Peter's Church, Dorchester, are inaccurately described in *The Mayor of Casterbridge*.
338. August 18: L. G. Metcalf solicits an article on "The Profitable Reading of Fiction" for publication in *The Forum*, New York City, and offers forty guineas for it.
339. August 28: Edmund Gosse reports Robert Louis Stevenson is off to Colorado and is taking with him a copy of *The Woodlanders*.
340. September 26: George Bainton inquires about Hardy's training for the formation of style.
341. September 27: C. J. Longman, while glad to get Hardy's story, "The Withered Arm," is disappointed in it. (The story appeared later in *Blackwood's Magazine*.)
342. September 30: Hardy to Metcalf: about his request of 18 August 1887; sent the article later and it was published in *The Forum*, March 1888.
343. October 21: Walter Besant about French translations.
344. October 26: William Blackwood accepts "The Withered Arm."
345. November 30: G. M. Fenn praises *The Woodlanders*.
346. December 2: Henry J. Moule sends a letter of Dorset gossip.
347. December 5: Moule sends more Dorset news.
348. December 9: Blackwood sends proofs of "The Withered Arm."
349. December 16: Harper & Brothers about "The Waiting Supper" and about the paperback edition of *The Woodlanders*. Letter published in *Hardy in America*, p. 51.
350. December 30: Blackwood sends £24 in payment for "The Withered Arm."
351. (n. d.): Arthur M. Hind about a drawing of an old barn at Minterne Parva and in praise of *The Woodlanders*.
352. (n. d.) John W. Ogle about *Far from the Madding Crowd*.

1888

353. January 1: Edmund Gosse about Cotter Morison (obit. 1888).
354. January 1: A. Herbert thanks Hardy for *Wessex Tales*.
355. February 3: L. G. Metcalf sends £40 for an article on "The Profitable Reading of Fiction."
356. February 20: A. B. Grosart about the difficulty of reconciling the existence of evil with the idea of omnipotent goodness.
357. (c. February 21): Hardy to A. B. Grosart: pencil draft of reply to Grosart's inquiry of 20 February 1888. Published in *Early Life*, p. 269.
358. February 23: John Sarum about the migration of Dorset peasantry.
359. March 6: Alexander Macmillan about royalty on *Wessex Tales*.
360. March 20: Sarum again about the migration of Dorset peasantry.
361. April 24: William Miles Barnes about *The Life of William Barnes* by W. M. B.'s sister, Lucy Baxter, and about "the illustrations."
362. (c. May 7): Lady Catherine Milnes Gaskell thanks Hardy for a copy of *Wessex Tales*.
363. May 8: Robert Browning thanks Hardy for the copy of *Wessex Tales* Hardy had sent him on 7 May 1888 (Browning's birthday).
364. Thursday (May 10?): Justice Sir Charles Darling thanks Hardy for a copy of *Wessex Tales*.
365. May 11: Hall Caine about theatre seats for Hardy.
366. June 1: Frederic Harrison about *Wessex Tales*.
367. July 13: Harry Quilter is glad Hardy will write a story for publication in *The Universal Review*.
368. August 7: Quilter asks questions about the story Hardy had promised to write.
369. August 27: Quilter again about the story.
370. September 13: Bernard Derosne (French translator) about *Desperate Remedies*.
371. October 24: Edmund Gosse about an article in *Longman's*.
372. October 26: Gosse again about a magazine article.
373. (? October): Quilter again about a story for *The Universal Review*.
374. November 19: Leslie Stephen about the *Dictionary of National Biography*. Quoted in *Early Life*, p. 290.
375. December 18: Laura (Mrs. Laurence) Alma-Tadema thanks Hardy for a story.
376. December 21: Mrs. Lynn Linton thanks Hardy for a story.

1889

377. January 1: Edmund Gosse praises Hardy's story, "A Tragedy of Two Ambitions."
378. January 4: E. R. Pearce Edgcumbe invites Hardy and his wife to lunch.
379. March 27: James M. Barrie about "A Tragedy of Two Ambitions."
380. April 9: John Addington Symonds praises *The Return of the Native*.

381. May 11: Mrs. Julia Augusta Martin thanks Hardy for some books. Published in *Thomas Hardy's Notebooks*, p. 129.
382. May 26: Walter Besant invites Hardy to dinner.
383. May 28: Arthur W. Blomfield, just knighted, thanks Hardy for his letter of congratulation.
384. June 7: Rosamund (Mrs. Arthur) Tomson sends a book.
385. June (15?): Mrs. Tomson acknowledges a letter from Hardy.
386. June 28: George Gissing, from Wakefield.
387. July 3: Mrs. Lynn Linton hopes to meet Hardy and Mrs. Hardy.
388. July 13: Henry James invites Hardy to dinner.
389. July 15: William M. Thomas solicits permission for J. T. Grein and C. W. Jarvis to dramatize *The Woodlanders*.
390. July 16: Jarvis asks permission to adapt *The Woodlanders* for the stage. (The letter is signed also by Jack T. Grein).
391. July 19: Hardy to Charles W. Jarvis: autograph letter from the Savile Club, London, signed by Hardy but marked "Copy," granting permission to adapt *The Woodlanders* to the stage.
392. July 20: James M. Barrie thanks Hardy for his letter.
393. September 6: Barrie hopes to meet Hardy.
394. September 16: Charles W. Jarvis reports he and Grein have finished a first sketch of their dramatization of *The Woodlanders*.
395. October 7: Edward A. Arnold (editor of *Murray's Magazine*), to whom Hardy had offered *Tess*, about payment for serial installments.
396. October 23: Bernard Derosne about French publication.
397. November 15: Edward A. Arnold declines to publish *Tess*.
398. November 15: Walter Besant note.
399. November 25: Mowbray Morris, having read the MS. of *Tess*, thinks it unwise to publish it in *Macmillan's Magazine*.
400. (n. d.): Lady Catherine Gaskell invites Hardy and Mrs. Hardy to lunch.
401. (n. d.): Besant about future short stories.

1890

402. (n. d.): Andrew Lang about Howells and Trollope. See Letter 246.
403. (n. d.): Lang about Howells and Thackeray.
404. May 13: J. M. Barrie invites Hardy to dine at the Garrick Club.
405. May 17: Lord Lytton thanks Hardy for a recent letter.
406. May 28: Edmund Gosse invites Hardy to lunch to meet Kipling.
407. June 25: Arthur Locker gives reasons why *The Graphic* cannot publish *A Group of Noble Dames* as the text of these tales now stands.
408. July 2: Heron B. Verity asks for a copy of Hardy's most recent "work" so that it may receive notice in the *Journal* of the Royal Institute of British Architects.
409. July 7: Havelock Ellis asks for information to use in connection with Ellis's "investigations" of recent writers.
410. (July 8?): Hardy to Havelock Ellis: pencil draft of a page of information to be sent in response to Letter 409; e.g., "*Desperate Remedies* . . . owed its existence to [George] Meredith."

411. July 24: Hardy to his wife: about Locker's objections to *A Group of Noble Dames* (see Letter 407), and other matters. Letter published in *Dearest Emmie*, pp. 6-7.
412. August 12: Alfred Parsons wishes to come to Dorchester and let Hardy show him a certain place, so that he may draw an illustration for *Harper's Magazine*. Parson's headpiece appeared in the March 1891 issue.
413. September 14: Edmund Gosse about his pleasant visit to Max Gate.
414. October 1: Gosse has received bad news from R. L. Stevenson.
415. October 4: Charles J. Robinson about Hardy's pedigree.
416. October 18: Christopher Childs about Hardy's pedigree.
417. October 20: Rosamund Tomson about old shepherd's crooks.
418. October 22: Sir Henry Thompson invites Hardy to 35 Wimpole Street.
419. October 26: Childs again about Hardy's pedigree.
420. October 27: Borlase Childs about Hardy's pedigree.
421. October 27: J. A. Steuart about a book of *Letters to Living Authors*.
422. October 29: Gosse asks if Kipling's brother-in-law, Balestier, may call on Hardy at Max Gate.
423. October 29: Rosamund Tomson again about shepherd's crooks.
424. November 25: Thackeray Turner about the preservation of the old Stratton Parish Church.
425. December 3: Hardy to his wife: reports safe arrival in London despite a fog. Published in *Dearest Emmie*, pp. 7-8.
426. December 4: James R. Osgood (American publisher) reports the passage of the new Copyright Bill in Congress. Published in Weber, *The Rise and Fall of James Ripley Osgood*, 1959, p. 248.
427. December 5: Hardy to his wife: the copyright of *Tess* in America may be saved. Letter published in *Dearest Emmie*, pp. 8-9.
428. December 9: Hardy to his wife: Kipling has published an attack, "The Rhyme of the Three Captains," on him in the *Athenaeum* for 6 December 1890. Letter published in *Dearest Emmie*, pp. 10-11.
429. December 10: Hardy to his wife: he is staying with Mrs. Jeune at 37 Wimpole Street, London. Letter published in *Dearest Emmie*, pp. 11-12.
430. December 14: Thackeray Turner again about the preservation of the Stratton Parish Church.

1891

431. January 24: Hardy to his wife: about dining *chez* Mrs. Jeune with Sir Henry Irving and Ellen Terry. Letter published in *Dearest Emmie*, pp. 12-14.
432. February 3: T. Wemyss Reid invites Hardy to dinner at the Reform Club.
433. March 6: Hardy to H. Blanchamp: typed transcript, acknowledging receipt of £17 for his story, "For Conscience' Sake," published in the *Fortnightly*.
434. March 22: Alfred Parsons is glad his drawing of High Street, Dorchester, pleased Hardy.

435. April 1: Charles W. Jarvis says the dramatization of *The Woodlanders* has been read by various actors and others, but nobody has yet been found to produce it.
436. April 11: Hardy to his wife: about the publication of *A Group of Noble Dames* and other matters. Published in *Dearest Emmie,* pp. 14-15.
437. April 13: Hardy to his wife: about rewriting "The Midnight Baptism" (lifted from the MS. of *Tess*) for the May issue of the *Fortnightly,* and about other matters. Published in *Dearest Emmie,* pp. 15-16.
438. April 14: The *Fortnightly Review* writes about the title for the Baptism Scene lifted from the MS. of *Tess.*
439. April 16: Hardy to his wife: more about "The Midnight Baptism," and other matters. Published in *Dearest Emmie,* p. 17.
440. April 18: Hardy to his wife: about talking with H. Rider Haggard who has just returned from Mexico. Published in *Dearest Emmie,* pp. 17-18.
441. April 21: Ernest A. Vizetelly asks Hardy to sign an Appeal, on behalf of Vizetelly's father who is in prison for having published some of Zola's novels.
442. April 28: Sir Henry Irving returns a dramatization of *The Woodlanders.* Hardy's pencil note on this letter states that Hardy did not submit, or send, the play. (It was by C. W. Jarvis.)
443. May 4: Walter Besant about publishing arrangements with Tillotson and Tauchnitz.
444. May 6: Charles W. Jarvis reports Irving's decision about the dramatization of *The Woodlanders.*
445. (May ?): Lady Dorothy Nevill invites Hardy to luncheon.
446. June 8: Clement K. Shorter solicits a short story for the Christmas number of the *Illustrated London News* and asks for a portrait of the author for publication.
447. June 27: John Lane proposes a Bibliography of Hardy's works.
448. "Friday": W. Robertson Nicoll hopes for a contribution from Hardy.
449. July 4: Lady Dorothy Nevill invites Hardy to luncheon.
450. July 8: Henry Bradley about Dorset words in the *Oxford Dictionary.*
451. July 8: Lord Lytton thanks Hardy for *A Group of Noble Dames.*
452. July 13: J. V. Foster about "a Dorset Mummers' play."
453. July 18: Foster about "the Dorset Play of St. George."
454. July 28: Lord Lytton writes a long letter about *A Group of Noble Dames.*
455. August 6: Sir William Watson sends a copy of *Wordsworth's Grave.*
456. August 14: W. Robertson Nicoll about a notice of *A Group of Noble Dames* in the New York *Nation.*
457. August 17: W. R. Nicoll thanks Hardy for his kindness.
458. August 27: Clarence W. McIlvaine about publication of *Tess.*
459. October 22: W. E. G. (?) to W. E. Henley about *Noble Dames.*
460. November 5: W. Robertson Nicoll asks if honors should be conferred by the state on literary men.
461. (November 6?): Hardy to Nicoll: rough draft of reply to Nicoll's letter of 5 November 1891.

462. December 12: Rosamund (Mrs. Arthur) Tomson sends a book of verses.
463. December 14: Hardy to Mrs. Graham Tomson: typed transcript (supplied by Howard Bliss?) of letter to accompany a copy of the Tauchnitz Edition of *A Group of Noble Dames*.
464. December 19: William Morris has read *Far from the Madding Crowd* and *The Return of the Native* and liked *Madding Crowd* better.
465. December 25: C. Kegan Paul long letter about *Tess*.
466. December 29: Frederic Harrison praises a book by Hardy.
467. December 29: S. H. Spencer Smith is grateful for the loan of a copy of *Tess*.

1892

468. January 6: John Addington Symonds comments on Hardy's command of the tragic aspects of life.
469. January 7: T. P. O'Connor about *Tess* and other matters.
470. January 15: Frederick Wetmore thinks highly of *Tess*.
471. January 17: Symonds about living among Swiss peasants; adds a postscript on 19 January 1892.
472. January 18: Alfred Austin critical comment about *Tess*.
473. February 4: Hardy to Edward Clodd: about Andrew Lang's adverse criticism of *Tess*: typed transcript (Supplied by Howard Bliss?).
474. February 22: Mary St. Leger Kingsley (pen-name "Lucas Malet") thanks Hardy for *Tess*.
475. (n. d.): Lady Dorothy Nevill thanks Hardy for *Tess*.
476. March 6: Earl of Pembroke about a passage in *Tess* on the effect of "depopulation" in villages.
477. March 13: Pembroke says he loves *Tess*.
478. March 16: Mary St. Leger Kingsley has enjoyed *Tess*.
479. March 30: Marie von Wendheim is grateful for permission to translate *The Mayor of Casterbridge* into German.
480. April 1: Hardy to Edward Clodd: assures him the superstitions and customs described in the novels are based on true records. Typed transcript.
481. April 2: Mary St. Leger Kingsley wants Hardy to call on her.
482. April 3: Hardy to Roden Noel about pessimism and other matters.
483. April 4: Mary St. Leger Kingsley will be delighted to see Hardy.
484. April 5: Hardy to his wife: another dinner party at Lady Jeune's. Published in *Dearest Emmie*, pp. 18-19.
485. April 5: Millicent Fawcett asks Hardy to write a short story for working boys and girls about treating love lightly.
486. April 11: Marya Aberconway is glad to know the creator of *Tess*.
487. April 11: Mary A. Ward (Mrs. Humphry Ward) asks permission to call and solicit a contribution to the "Columbus Album."
488. April 12: Earl of Pembroke thanks Hardy for a magazine.
489. April 22: Marquis of Crewe, second Lord Houghton, invites Hardy to visit him in Dublin.
490. April 24: Millicent Fawcett again about a short story for working boys and girls.

491. April 27: William Dean Howells wants one or more short stories for the *Cosmopolitan Magazine* in New York.
492. May 2: Andrew Lang states he did not mean to be unfair in writing his short notice of *Tess*.
493. May 5: Lang regrets his harsh review of *Tess*.
494. May 18: Walter Besant about an unnamed book.
495. May 23: Hardy to his wife: about the funeral of his publisher, James R. Osgood, which Hardy had attended that afternoon. Published in *Dearest Emmie*, pp. 19-20.
496. May 26: Hardy to his wife, from London: about Max Gate matters. Published in *Dearest Emmie*, pp. 20-21.
497. (n. d.): William Strang about his etched portrait of Hardy.
498. June 1: Margaret Deland, after reading *Tess* in America, asks if she could find the Vale of Blackmoor if she came to England.
499. June 7: Joseph Eldridge solicits support of Pearce Edgcumbe as a political candidate.
500. June 8: Hardy to Eldridge: rough draft of reply to Letter 499; Hardy regrets being unable to participate in politics.
501. June 13: George, Lord Curzon, would like to persuade Hardy to dine with him some evening.
502. June 17: Roden Noel (son of Lord Barham) invites Hardy to supper.
503. June 30: Mathilda Blind invites Hardy to a little party.
504. (n. d.): Madame Mary Darmesteter (later Mme Duclaux), whom Hardy had met at Gosse's on 12 April 1891, about *The Three Strangers*.
505. (n. d. July ?): Lady Dorothy Nevill has now read *Tess*.
506. July 6: Lord Crewe invites Hardy to Fryston; says his sister, Mrs. Henniker, will be staying with him.
507. July 9: Lord Crewe does not want an answer very soon because he is aware Hardy's father is ill.
508. July 18: John W. Hales asks about the expression "Good now" in *Under the Greenwood Tree*.
509. July 19: Hardy to Hales: pencil draft, signed "T. H.," of reply to letter 508. Says the expression is still in use in the county.
510. July 21: Henry J. Moule answers a note from Hardy.
511. July 23: Hales thanks Hardy for his letter of 19 July.
512. July 25: Lord Crewe sends condolences upon the death of Hardy's father.
513. July 27: Stuart J. Reid asks if Hardy would care to receive a call from a young lady who wishes to meet him. (She was Rebekah Owen of New York City; with Hardy's permission she called at Max Gate on 5 August 1892.)
514. July 31: Vera Spassky asks permission to translate *Tess* into Russian.
515. (n. d.): Lady Dorothy Nevill friendly note.
516. August 30: Clement K. Shorter asks permission to call on 3 September.
517. September 1: Robert Buchanan (author of *Come Live with Me and Be My Love*, dedicated to Thomas Hardy) says he dedicated the story to Hardy out of admiration for his works.
518. September 3: John Morley thanks Hardy for a letter.

519. September 6: Sir George Alexander about a conversation at Lady Jeune's.
520. September 12: Sir Frederick Pollock praises *Tess*.
521. September 13: Alexander thanks Hardy for his reply, and asks him to write a play for him.
522. September 14: Vera Spassky again about translating *Tess* into Russian.
523. September 17: Vera Spassky thanks Hardy for a letter.
524. September 19: Mary St. Leger Kingsley about the literary agent, Mr. [A. P.] Watt.
525. October 1: Tauchnitz about a Tauchnitz Edition of *Tess*.
526. October 6: J. M. Barrie about *Tess*.
527. October 10: Sir George Douglas about the death of Tennyson.
528. October 12: Hardy to his wife: about Tennyson's funeral in Westminster Abbey. Published in *Dearest Emmie*, p. 21.
529. October 26: Vera Spassky has completed translating the first two phases of *Tess* into Russian.
530. October 31: J. Alexander Smith about the baptism of infants in *Tess*.
531. (c. November 1): Hardy to J. A. Smith: pencil draft, unsigned, of reply to Smith's letter of 31 October 1892.
532. November 16: Sir James Crichton Browne admires *Tess*.
533. November 23: W. Morrison proposes some changes on the last page of *Tess*.
534. (n. d.): Lady Dorothy Nevill friendly note.
535. December 11: Miss Anna Williams praises *Tess*.
536. December 19: W. Robertson Nicoll solicits a line about Hardy's health for publication in *The Bookman*.
537. December 28: Sir Henry Irving thanks Hardy for the trouble he took with the pedigree of Irving's family.

1893

538. March 21: Frederick Wedmore asks about William Barnes's *Poems*.
539. April 19: James M. Barrie suggests Hardy make a one-act play out of "The Three Strangers."
540. April 24: Barrie is delighted with Hardy's acceptance of the idea of the one-act play.
541. June 3: Hardy to The Hon. Mrs. Arthur Henniker, from 70 Hamilton Terrace, London; acknowledges receipt of her note about arriving in London. (Hardy's letters to Florence Henniker were returned to Max Gate upon her death in 1923.)
542. June 4: Lady St. Helier (Mary, Lady Jeune) was delighted with Hardy's play she has just seen.
543. June 5: Barrie expresses delight over the success of *The Three Wayfarers*.
544. June 8: Sir Squire Bancroft note.
545. June 10: Hardy to Florence Henniker: about Barrie's play, *Walker, London*. He promises to send her a sermon about *Tess*. Letter partly published in *Later Years*, 1930, pp. 21-22.

546. (June 15): Hardy to Florence Henniker: about her novel, *Foiled.*
547. (June 19): Hardy to Florence Henniker: sends the sermon he promised, and says he went to Oxford recently.
548. (June 21): Hardy to Florence Henniker, from the Athenaeum Club, London: he is to receive tickets for the 27th when Ada Rehan will play the Shrew at Daly's Theatre.
549. June 30: Hardy to Florence Henniker: has mailed her a copy of the Summer Number of the *Illustrated.*
550. (July 2): Hardy to Florence Henniker: she must see Miss Rehan, and Miss Milman is going with Mrs. Hardy to a party at Alma-Tadema's Tuesday night.
551. (c. July 4): Hardy to Florence Henniker: about the opening pages of *A Laodicean,* and Mrs. Henniker's being unfaithful to "the Shelley cult."
552. July 13: Hardy to F. Henniker, from Max Gate: sends *A Laodicean* and other books.
553. July 16: Hardy to F. Henniker: thanks her for a book of ballads and comments on a friendship that came to an end promptly.
554. July 16: John Morley thanks Hardy for the gift of a book.
555. July 17: Hardy to "Miss Milman": transcript (supplied by Howard Bliss) of letter, from Max Gate, to General Milman's daughter about Browne's *Urn Burial,* etc.
556. July 21: Lady Catherine Gaskell enjoyed her talk with Hardy.
557. July 24: Hardy to his wife, written from the London home of Sir Francis and Lady Jeune: about his having attended the Irving farewell performance Saturday. Published in *Dearest Emmie,* pp. 22-23.
558. July 27: Hardy to Florence Henniker, from the home of the Jeunes in London: possibility of Hardy's collaborating with her in writing a story.
559. August 17: Hardy to Florence Henniker, from Max Gate: reminds her of his letter of an earlier date (now missing).
560. (August ?) 18: Vera Spassky has to give up translating *Tess* into Russian because of ill health.
561. September 4: Hardy to Lena Milman: sends his photograph and asks for hers.
562. September 6: Hardy to Florence Henniker: discusses a collection of her stories and proposes some "amendments" in them.
563. September 6: Lady Catherine Gaskell thanks Hardy for a copy of *The Trumpet-Major.*
564. September 10: Hardy to Florence Henniker from Max Gate: about his walks to scenes of *The Trumpet-Major* with "a young American lady" [Rebekah Owen] who is staying in Dorchester with her elder sister.
565. September 10: Hardy to Henry Arthur Jones: transcript (probably supplied by Howard Bliss) of letter written from Max Gate: was present at the reading of a play by Jones.
566. September 13: Hardy to Florence Henniker, from Max Gate: has refused to go with Miss Owen to visit the tomb of the Turbervilles at Bere Regis because he hopes to take her there some day.
567. September 16: Hardy to Florence Henniker, from Max Gate: is sending her *The Woodlanders* and *Desperate Remedies,* and her

chilling letters from Dublin made him regret having sent the letters he wrote in reply.
568. September 18: Hardy to Lena Milman: transcript, about her photograph requested two weeks previously.
569. September 22: Hardy to Mrs. Henniker: thanks her for the poems of Lord Houghton (her brother).
570. October 6: Hardy to Florence Henniker: about a story of theirs.
571. October 22: Hardy to Florence Henniker: about seeing her again, and about "The Spectre of the Real" in which they were collaborating.
572. October 25: Hardy to Florence Henniker: advice about the terms offered by Hutchinson for publishing her stories.
573. October 28: Hardy to Florence Henniker: discusses the story they have been collaborating on and proposes various titles.
574. October 30: Hardy to Florence Henniker: advises her to accept the Hutchinsons' offer.
575. November 9: Hardy to Lena Milman: transcript, from Max Gate, about footnotes in a Russian translation of *Tess*.
576. (November 22?): Thomas Boggs solicits a story at once.
577. December 1: Hardy to Florence Henniker: about an article of his in the December *English Illustrated Magazine*.
578. December 18: Hardy to Florence Henniker: he has sent the story to Mr. Shorter.
579. December 23: Hardy to Lena Milman: transcript from Max Gate, about her portrait.
580. (n. d.): Mary, Lady Jeune about Princess Mary.
581. (n. d.): Lady Dorothy Nevill invites Hardy to luncheon.

1894

582. January 1: Justin McCarthy introduces his friend Mrs. Forbes.
583. January 15: Hardy to Florence Henniker: *Life's Little Ironies* will be published at the end of the month; tells her not to order it.
584. February 14: Lord DeTabley about his work.
585. February 23: Hardy to Lady Jeune: typed transcript, inviting her to reply to remarks on *Life's Little Ironies* that appeared in the *Daily Chronicle*.
586. March 3: Lord Curzon invites Hardy to lunch.
587. March 8: Lord Randolph Churchill thanks Hardy for an autographed copy of *Life's Little Ironies*.
588. March 8: Lord Curzon again invites Hardy to lunch.
589. March 12: Henry Arthur Jones invites Hardy to dinner and tells him he is reading *Life's Little Ironies*.
590. March 31: Hardy to his wife, from the Jeunes' home in London: he is to take Lady Jeune's daughters to the theatre that evening. Published in *Dearest Emmie*, p. 25.
591. April 1: Hardy to his wife: Lady Jeune thinks she ought to wear spectacles; he reports on last night's visit to the theatre and on dinner and luncheon engagements. Published in *Dearest Emmie*, pp. 26-27.

592. April 3: Hardy to his wife, from the Savile Club, London: about lunching with Lady Pembroke on the 2nd and with Lord Curzon on the 5th. Published in *Dearest Emmie*, pp. 27-28.
593. May 5: Edward Clodd sends a copy of a letter in the *Daily Chronicle* defending Hardy's position regarding morals in his novels.
594. May 5: Hardy to Clodd: transcript, thanking him for the letter in the *Chronicle*.
595. May 21: Hardy to Henry Arthur Jones: transcript (supplied by Howard Bliss?), from 16 Pelham Crescent, South Kensington, about *The Masqueraders*.
596. May 27: Marie von Wendheim about her translation of *The Mayor of Casterbridge* into German.
597. June 5: Lord DeTabley invites Hardy to dinner.
598. (n. d.): Winifred Thomson to Lady Jeune: about her desire to paint a portrait of Hardy.
599. (n. d.): Lady Jeune introduces Miss Thomson and forwards her letter to Hardy.
600. (n. d.): Winifred Thomson to Lady Jeune: about the Hardy portrait.
601. August 23: A. Berger about making a German translation of "A Tragedy of Two Ambitions" and of "On the Western Circuit."
602. September 7: Henry J. Moule about Dorset problems.
603. October 4: Ellen Terry praises *The Return of the Native* and *Tess*.
604. November 19: Olga Nethersole (actress) begs Hardy to dramatize *Tess* and to let her have the play.
605. November 27: C. Sothern Lewis about the suicide in "The Spectre of the Real."
606. December 9: Clara (Mrs. Theodore?) Watts-Dunton about a promised MS. of Swinburne.
607. December 21: Henry J. Moule about a sketch of his.

1895

608. January 2: Grant Allen thanks Hardy for a copy of *Far from the Madding Crowd*.
609. January 9: G. Herriot about a false report of the purchase of the Max Gate site.
610. January 10: Hardy to Herriot: copy, signed "T. H.," of reply to Letter 609.
611. January 17: Hardy to Herriot: further reply to Letter 609.
612. January 19: Herriot thanks Hardy for his letters.
613. January 20: G. Henschel asks about a German translation of *Tess*.
614. February 12: T. P. O'Connor solicits an essay of 1500 to 2000 words.
615. February 23: George Saintsbury about the situation after Waterloo.
616. March 3: Saintsbury thanks Hardy for his reply to Saintsbury's letter.
617. April 3: Hardy to his wife: has looked at houses and flats in London, and mentions the South Kensington Museum. Published in *Dearest Emmie*, pp. 28-29.

618. April 3: Sir Johnston Forbes-Robertson about putting *Tess* on the stage.
619. April 3: Mrs. Eliza Lynn Linton letter, at the age of 73.
620. April 8: Hardy to his wife: he has heard that Mrs. Linton wants to let her flat and asks if he should communicate with her about it. Published in *Dearest Emmie*, pp. 29-31.
621. April 17: Mrs. Lynn Linton would be glad to have Hardy and Mrs. Hardy as tenants of her flat.
622. April 24: Hardy to his wife: he has taken a place at 90 Ashley Gardens in Westminster, and is very busy with proofs of the 16-vol. Collected Uniform Edition of his works. Published in *Dearest Emmie*, pp. 31-32.
623. April 26: Hardy to his wife: about her move from Max Gate to the London flat he has taken for the season. Published in *Dearest Emmie*, pp. 32-33.
624. April 27: Hardy to his wife: more about Emma's move from Dorchester to London. Published in *Dearest Emmie*, pp. 33-34.
625. May 17: Winifred Thomson about beginning to paint Hardy's portrait.
626. May 24: Mrs. Pearl Craigie invites Hardy and his wife to lunch at the Bath Club.
627. (c. June 1): Winifred Thomson's illness prevents for the moment her continuing to work on his portrait.
628. June 3: Lord DeTabley invites Hardy to dinner.
629. June 3: Sir Johnston Forbes-Robertson has read *Tess* with extreme interest.
630. (c. June 4): Beatrice (Mrs. "Pat") Campbell about her deep interest in *Tess*.
631. (c. June 30): Mrs. Campbell wants to know what Hardy has done with regard to the first act of *Tess*.
632. July 8: Sir William Watson intends to call on Hardy.
633. July 10: Mrs. Pat Campbell wants to hear from Hardy soon.
634. (c. July 11): Frank R. Benson asks permission to produce his dramatic version of *Far from the Madding Crowd*.
635. July 15: Benson is disappointed that Hardy does not sanction a dramatic version of *Far from the Madding Crowd*.
636. July 24: Hardy to his wife: he is to meet Forbes-Robertson to talk further about the *Tess* dramatization. Published in *Dearest Emmie*, pp. 34-35.
637. July 27: Mrs. Lynn Linton asks permission to introduce a friend of hers, Maud Welman.
638. July 30: J. M. Barrie solicits support of W. E. Henley as a candidate for the chair of English Literature at Edinburgh University.
639. August 4: Hardy to Florence Henniker: has been too ill to write her.
640. August 12: Hardy to Florence Henniker: about *Jude the Obscure*.
641. August 26: Olga Nethersole about the dramatization of *Tess*.
642. (c. August 31): Mrs. Pat Campbell would be free for *Tess* in the autumn if it were ready for production.
643. September 3: Hardy from Max Gate to Florence Henniker in Marienbad: he has just returned from a visit, about which he wrote in "The Dame of Athelhall."
644. September 3: George Gissing has just visited George Meredith.

645. September 11: Hardy to Florence Henniker: describes a week's pleasant visit to General Pitt-Rivers at Rushmore. See *Later Years*, p. 38.
646. October 27: Hardy to his wife, from the Reigate home of Lady Henry Somerset. Published in *Dearest Emmie*, pp. 35-36.
647. November 5: A. G. Swinburne thanks Hardy for his gift of a copy of *Jude*. Partly published in *Later Years*, pp. 39-40.
648. November 8: Augustine Birrell sends thanks for Hardy's newest book.
649. November 8: Sir Johnston Forbes-Robertson asks about Hardy finishing *Tess*.
650. November 10: Hardy to Edward Clodd: transcript, about *Jude* and the marriage question.
651. November 10: Hardy to Florence Henniker: he hesitated to send a copy of *Jude* because he thought it might have bored her.
652. November 15: Hardy to the Editor of *The Animal's Friend*: autograph letter marked "Copy" about the slaughtering of animals, giving the editor permission to republish the scene in *Jude*, gratuitously.
653. November 15: Arthur Stirling (of Osgood, McIlvaine & Co.) acknowledges Hardy's letter of the 14th about *Jude*. Published in *Hardy in America*, p. 169.
654. November 19: Mrs. Pearl Craigie admiration of *Jude*.
655. November 22: George Egerton, author of *Keynotes*, thanks Hardy for *Jude*, which he has just read.
656. November 28: Ellen Terry comment on *Jude*.
657. November 30: Hardy to Florence Henniker: accepts an invitation to lunch; comments on incoming letters about *Jude*.
658. December 4: Sir Johnston Forbes-Robertson thanks Hardy for his note about *Tess*.
659. December 12: W. T. Stead invites Hardy to name hymns that have helped him, for use in an article in the *Review of Reviews*.
660. (c. December 16): Hardy to W. T. Stead: unsigned reply, in pencil, to Stead's inquiry of the 12th, naming three hymns. Published in *Later Years*, p. 45.
661. (n. d.): Lady Jeune illegible letter.
662. December 26: Sir Johnston Forbes-Robertson, who is reading *Jude*, asks to have the [*Tess*] play as soon as possible.

1896

663. January 1: Sir George Douglas, who has just written on "Some Critics of *Jude The Obscure*" (London *Bookman*, January 1896), sends New Year's greetings.
664. January 3: Sir Johnston Forbes-Robertson tells Hardy Mrs. Patrick Campbell is in Dorchester and will call on him about *Tess*. Quoted in Marguerite Roberts's *Tess in the Theatre* (1950), where the date is given as January 5.
665. (c. January 4): Mrs. Campbell, from the King's Arms Hotel at Dorchester, says she and her daughter will be happy to have lunch with Hardy.

666. January 5: Grant Allen praises *Jude*.
667. (January 7): Mrs. Campbell thanks Hardy for a gift.
668. January (14?): Forbes-Robertson asks to be allowed to read *Tess* through.
669. (c. January 21): Mrs. Campbell is brokenhearted over the hesitatation about producing *Tess*.
670. February 2: Hardy to his wife: about lunching with Winifred Thomson, calling on Mrs. Crackanthorpe, walking with Elizabeth Robins (the actress), and calling on Florence Henniker. Published in *Dearest Emmie*, pp. 36-37.
671. February 3: Hardy to his wife: about calling on Lady Jeune, and attending the funeral of Frederick Leighton. Published in *Dearest Emmie*, pp. 37-38.
672. February 5: Hardy to his wife, from the Savile Club: about attending a masked ball, and a possible *Tess* production. Published in *Dearest Emmie*, pp. 38-39.
673. February 9: Hardy to Harper & Brothers: autograph copy; says he has finished the dramatization of *Tess* and can now write about arrangements to be made.
674. February 11: Hardy to Florence Henniker: sends copy of the *Saturday Review* with a comment on *Jude*; refers to *Tess* and plans its production in New York.
675. February 14: Hardy to Harper & Brothers: autograph copy; about Lorimer Stoddard's *Tess*.
676. February 14: Sir Johnston Forbes-Robertson about royalties and fees if *Tess* is produced.
677. February 22: William Clibborn about the original of the physician Vilbert in *Jude*.
678. February 25: Leon Kellner asks about a German translation of one of the stories in *Life's Little Ironies*.
679. February 26: Mrs. Pearl Craigie note.
680. February 28: Daniel Frohman, to Harper & Brothers: an offer of terms for an American production of *Tess*.
681. March 3: Harper & Brothers acknowledge the receipt of letters from Hardy about the dramatization of *Tess*.
682. March 4: Frederic Harrison about a London production of *Tess*.
683. March 9: Elizabeth Robins (actress) asks if she may read *Tess*, with a view to showing it to a manager.
684. March 15: Hardy, from Max Gate, to Henry Arthur Jones: transcript (supplied by Howard Bliss?); what are good or bad terms for a play.
685. March 18: Elizabeth Robins again about *Tess*. She is perplexed to learn Hardy has entered into negotiations with Mrs. Campbell to play the part of Tess since he had assured her that he expected her to play Tess and it was so announced in the papers.
686. March 25: Sir Laurence Alma-Tadema suggests Hardy have the *Tess* play translated into Italian or French for Madame Duse.
687. April 28: Harper & Brothers about terms for the American production of *Tess* by Mrs. Fiske.
688. May 9: Madeleine Rolland about translating *Tess* into French.
689. May 13: James V. Nimmo invites Hardy to stand as a candidate for the Lord Rectorship at Glasgow University.

690. May 16: Hardy to Nimmo: copy in ink, from Brighton; expresses regrets and thanks.
691. June 1: Hardy to Florence Henniker: sends some books for a bazaar, and is sorry to learn of Major Henniker's illness. Also comments on "free love" and says he has no theory at all on the subject.
692. June 1: Herman Raulbach about a German translation of *Tess*.
693. June 9: Mlle Madeleine Rolland about translating *Tess* into French.
694. June 12: Sir Henry Lucy invites Hardy to dinner.
695. June 20: Blanche (Mrs. Montague) Crackanthorpe has told John Hare about *The Three Wayfarers* and the impression it made on her.
696. June 25: John Hare thanks Mrs. Crackanthorpe for her interest in his behalf.
697. July 6: Mrs. Patrick Campbell tells what her terms will be for the production of *Tess*.
698. July 13: Jeannette L. Gilder notorious letter to Hardy. Letter referred to in *Later Years*, p. 50.
699. July 16: Hardy to Jeannette L. Gilder: typed copy, from the Savile Club, in answer to hers of the 13th. Published in *Later Years*, p. 51.
700. July 17: Jeannette L. Gilder very appreciative letter to Hardy. Published in *Later Years*, p. 52.
701. July 17: John Hare asks about fee for permission to produce *The Three Wayfarers*.
702. July 18: Hare suggests two guineas as a fee for each performance of *The Three Wayfarers*.
703. July 28: Hare has received *The Three Wayfarers*.
704. August 4: Mrs. Campbell regrets Hardy is not going to have *Tess* produced.
705. August 7. Hardy to Mrs. Campbell: he has decided not to consider a production of *Tess* in England soon, if ever.
706. September 24: Hardy to Florence Henniker, from Liege, Belgium; about bicycling, and other Belgian matters.
707. (n. d.): Sir Bertram C. A. Windle about the topography of Dorset.
708. September 29: Windle again about Dorset topography.
709. October 12: Hardy to Florence Henniker: he is now back at Max Gate; about his travels in Belgium and his visits to art galleries.
710. November 2: Robert Young about his uncle, Sergeant Young, who will appear shortly in *The Dynasts*.
711. November 8: Hardy to Florence Henniker: expresses pleasure that her stories are selling.
712. November 29: Hardy to Florence Henniker: his story, "The Duke's Reappearance," is scheduled for publication in the Christmas Supplement of *The Saturday Review*.
713. December 6: Hardy to Florence Henniker: expresses regret at not having seen her in London.
714. December 24: Henry J. Moule thanks Hardy for a copy of *Under the Greenwood Tree*.
715. December 30: Hardy to Florence Henniker: thanks her for Christmas card and kind letters.

1897

716. January 24: Hardy to Florence Henniker: about the status of an author with Dorset landowners, and other comments.
717. January 28: Madeleine Rolland again, in French, about translating *Tess* into French.
718. February 2: Sir George Alexander says the role of Tess is perfect for Miss Neilson.
719. February 16: Hardy to Henry Arthur Jones: transcript of a letter about the dramatization of *Tess*.
720. February 17: Sir George Alexander about a copyright for the *Tess* play.
721. February 19: Hardy to Florence Henniker: about his getting up a copyright performance of *Tess*, to come out in America.
722. February 26: William Rothenstein, a young artist, asks Hardy to sit for one of a series of lithograph portraits which R. proposes doing.
723. (n. d.): Mrs. Minnie Maddern Fiske thanks Hardy for his suggestions about the role of Tess.
724. March 2: Hardy to his wife: about the copyright performance of *Tess* at the St. James's Theatre, etc. Published in *Dearest Emmie*, pp. 39-40.
725. (c. March 3): Mrs. Patrick Campbell about the success of *Tess* in New York.
726. (same date as Letter 725): Mrs. Campbell about *Tess* again.
727. March 4: Hardy to Florence Henniker: he is sorry she has a cold.
728. March 5: Harper & Brothers report on Mrs. Fiske's production of the *Tess* play, which opened 2 March 1897 at the Fifth Avenue Theatre in New York.
729. March 8: Olga Nethersole about the *Tess* play.
730. March 9: Mrs. Campbell about the *Tess* play.
731. March 16: Edmund Gosse consoles Hardy after a bitter attack has been made on *The Well-Beloved*.
732. March 20: Mrs. Pearl Craigie says the review of *The Well-Beloved* in *The Academy* was written by a pupil of W. P. Ker.
733. (c. March 25): Clement K. Shorter solicits a contribution to the Jubilee Number of the *Illustrated London News*.
734. March 26: C. Lewis Hind about an article on *The Well-Beloved* in *The World*.
735. March 28: A. C. Swinburne thanks Hardy for a book.
736. March 29: Hardy to the Editor of *The Academy*: transcript of a letter about his review of *The Well-Beloved*.
737. March 31: Hardy to Florence Henniker: about criticism of *The Well-Beloved* by *The World*.
738. April 1: Edmund Gosse says he was most unhappy about the review of *Tess* in *The World*.
739. (c. April 2): Clement Shorter about Hardy appearing in the Jubilee Number of the *Illustrated London News*.
740. April 9: Mrs. Campbell expresses regret at not having seen Hardy.
741. April 10: G. E. Buckle, editor of *The Times*, about *The Well-Beloved*.

742. April 27: Hardy to Florence Henniker: in spite of adverse reviews *The Well-Beloved* is selling remarkably well, and the *Tess* play is a success in America.
743. April 30: Olga Nethersole regrets Hardy is unable to make arrangements with her for the production of *Tess*.
744. June 7: William Terriss offers to make arrangements for the dramatization of *Tess* for the English stage.
745. June 12: Terriss thanks Hardy for a letter.
746. (June 14?): Sir George Douglas mentions the Jubilee.
747. June 30: H. B. Irving says his wife wants to play the title role in *Tess*.
748. July 3: Hardy to Florence Henniker, from Geneva: reports his travels in Switzerland, and mentions *The Well-Beloved*.
749. July 9: H. B. Irving thanks Hardy for a letter and mentions Mrs. Fiske's American company in *Tess*.
750. July 16: Rudyard Kipling solicits Hardy's help in finding a house near him.
751. September 29: Kipling still seeking a house in Dorset.
752. (c. October 2): Kipling again about finding a house.
753. October 4: Kipling about his house-hunting.
754. October 31: Hardy to Winifred H. Thomson: transcript of letter in which Hardy reports he has bought a bicycle.
755. November 6: E. H. Coombs offers Hardy the presidency of The Wessex Society of Manchester.
756. November 10: Hardy to Coombs: accepts his offer; pencil draft, unsigned.
757. November 20: Rudyard Kipling about a memorial on behalf of W. E. Henley.
758. November 26: W. J. Locke invites Hardy to respond on behalf of Literature at the Dinner of the Royal Institute of British Architects.
759. November 27: Hardy to Locke; pencil draft of reply to the invitation of the 26th; declines for reasons of health.
760. (n. d.): Kipling about meeting at the railway station for a house-hunting expedition.
761. (n. d.): Mme Blaze de Bury has lectured in France on *Tess* and *Far from the Madding Crowd*; asks him to give her some notes on his career.
762 December (15?): Sir George Douglas thanks Hardy for pointing out various misprints, some of them in *Jude*.

1898

763. January 3: Edmund Gosse sends New Year's greetings and refers to George Meredith's approaching 70th birthday.
764. January 13: Hippisley Smith about the pedigree of the Hardy family.
765. February 12: Mrs. Pearl Craigie, 31-year-old author of *School For Saints* (1897), published under her pen-name of John Oliver Hobbes, values his kind words about her romance.
766. May 5. Hippisley Smith again about the Hardy family pedigree.

767. June 21: Henry J. Moule about an article on Hardy.
768. July 22: Hardy to Florence Henniker: about a hot bicycle journey to Bristol, Gloucester, and Cheltenham.
769. August 6: H. B. Irving asks about the provincial rights of *Tess*.
770. August 9: A. G. Greenhill wants Hardy to collaborate with some musician on a book of old English dances.
771. August 12: Hardy to Florence Henniker: about the publication of her short stories.
772. August 30: Hardy to Florence Henniker: about various matters, including his making sketches to illustrate the projected *Wessex Poems*.
773. September 22: Hardy to Florence Henniker: about bicycling to Exeter, and making sketches for *Wessex Poems*.
774. September 29: George Moore to Bram Stoker (journalist), sending him proofs of *Evelyn Innes*: a typed transcript, the presence of which in Hardy's files has not been explained. Stoker called on Hardy at his London flat in April 1907.
775. October 7: Hardy to Edward Clodd: transcript; praises Clodd's *Tom Tit Tot*.
776. October 17: Hardy to Florence Henniker: more about the illustrations for *Wessex Poems*.
777. November 13: Hardy to Florence Henniker: about a story of hers.
778. December 6: Frederick Harrison wants an article on Wessex traditions.
779. December 14: Mrs. Minnie Maddern Fiske thanks Hardy for the consideration he has shown her in regard to *Tess*.
780. December 15: Sir Johnston Forbes-Robertson wants to know who has the rights of *Tess*.
781. December 26: A. C. Swinburne thanks Hardy for a copy of *Wessex Poems*.

1899

782. January 1: Hardy to Florence Henniker: wishes her a happy New Year and expresses pleasure at hearing she was pleased with "some poems" [sent by him to her?].
783. January 3: Leslie Stephen thanks Hardy for *Wessex Poems*.
784. January 4: W. T. Stead about the Crusade of Peace.
785. January 9: Hardy to W. T. Stead: reply to inquiry of 4 January.
786. January 30: Hardy to Florence Henniker: more about *Wessex Poems*.
787. February 9: W. R. Paton about the use of horses in war.
788. February 14: Edmund Gosse about *Wessex Poems*.
789. February 15: Hardy to Florence Henniker: about her story, "The Three Corporals."
790. February 18: Lionel Johnson is glad that Hardy was pleased with Johnson's review of *Wessex Poems* in *The Outlook*, 28 January 1899.
791. February 23: Theodore Watts-Dunton praises *Wessex Poems*.
792. March 14: Mrs. Pearl Craigie about a play she has written.

793. March 14: Mrs. Coventry Patmore about her husband having *A Pair of Blue Eyes* read aloud to him.
794. March 29: Hardy to Edward Clodd: transcript; about the illustrations in *Wessex Poems*.
795. (n. d.): Theodore Watts-Dunton is reading *Tess* again.
796. (April 8): Walter Besant about society.
797. April 13: Hardy to Florence Henniker: expresses delight at the prospect of her getting one of her stories onto the stage; mentions *Wessex Poems*.
798. April 16: William Dean Howells introduces Hamlin Garland. Letter mentioned in *Hardy in America*, p. 154.
799. May 10: James Sully solicits Hardy's signature on a petition to be sent to the Czar about the Finns.
800. May 13: Hardy to his wife: he is sorry to learn she has sprained her ankle, and reports he has toothache. Published in *Dearest Emmie*, p. 41.
801. May 16: T. P. O'Connor solicits a short story for *T. P.'s Weekly*.
802. May 24: Hamlin Garland presents Howells' letter of 16 April 1899 and asks to see Hardy.
803. May 30: Madeleine Rolland about coming to see Hardy in Dorchester.
804. June 13: George Meredith invites Hardy to dinner.
805. July 19: Madeleine Rolland again about coming to Dorchester to call.
806. July 25: Hardy to Florence Henniker: he is about to start on a 2 or 3 day's bicycle tour in the New Forest.
807. August 9: H. D. Traill solicits a prose essay for publication in *Literature*.
808. August 13: Hardy to Florence Henniker from Max Gate: about his fatigue after the bicycle tour.
809. August 23: Hardy to Florence Henniker: thanks her for a book and reports on a recent caller from the *Daily Chronicle*.
810. (c. 26 August): Hardy to Florence Henniker: acknowledges receipt of a note from her.
811. September 17: Hardy to Florence Henniker: about meeting Sir Francis and Lady Jeune at Stonehenge.
812: (n. d.): Lady Dorothy Nevill invites Hardy to luncheon.
813. October 11: Hardy to Florence Henniker: he is disappointed in Swinburne's sonnet in today's *Times*.
814. October 19: Hardy to Major Arthur Henniker: best wishes as he sets out for South Africa and hopes he will return soon.
815. October 25: Edmund Gosse sends congratulations and praises Hardy's verses.
816. November 8: George Gissing, from Paris, about books, scenery, etc.
817. November 9: Hardy to Florence Henniker: about the illness of her brother, and Hardy's sonnet on the departure of the ship in which Major Henniker sailed for South Africa.
818. November 24: Hardy to Florence Henniker: refers to his poem "The Dead Drummer" in *Literature* this week.
819. (n. d.): Lady Dorothy Nevill about being at home the next day.
820. December 2: Laurence Pike about the condition of horses wounded on the battlefield.
821. December 19: Hardy to Florence Henniker: war news.

822. (n. d.): Lady Dorothy Nevill friendly note.
823. December 23: J. A. Spender thanks Hardy for his poem, "A Christmas Ghost-Story," for publication in the *Westminster Gazette*.
824. December 26: Hardy to Miss Winifred H. Thomson: transcript of letter about her sending the portrait she had painted of him to an Exhibition.

1900

825. January 23: Charles J. Blomfield thanks Hardy for returning the St. Cross drawings.
826. January 24: Hardy to Blomfield: pencil draft of reply to Blomfield's letter of 23 January 1900; refers to Gordon Gifford, Hardy's nephew.
827. January 26: Hardy to Florence Henniker: praises her *Lady Gilian*, especially the opening scene.
828. February 20: Lord Crewe (Mrs. Henniker's brother) belated reply to Hardy's letter of last November.
829. February 25: Hardy to Florence Henniker: he was glad to get her letter.
830. March 8: Alfred Sutro solicits Hardy's help at the Savile Club.
831. March 12: Hardy to his wife: has had a good report of her nephew Gordon Gifford, now employed at Blomfield's office in London. Published in *Dearest Emmie*, pp. 41-42.
832. March 15: Hardy to his wife: more about her nephew Gordon Gifford, and her niece Lilian Gifford. Published in *Dearest Emmie*, pp. 42-43.
833. March 29: A. E. Housman accepts an invitation to come to Dorchester.
834. April 1: Edmund H. New asks Hardy to look at the maps he has drawn for a book on *Wessex* by Professor Windle.
835. April 2: Lord Wolseley praises Hardy's poem, "Souls of the Slain," in the April *Cornhill Magazine*.
836. April 3: Hardy to Florence Henniker: about her story in the *Universal Magazine*.
837. April 18: Sir T. Clifford Allbutt about Hardy's poem in the *Cornhill*.
838. May 1: Sir Frederick Treves about his remarks at the Reform Club.
839. May 9: Lord Curzon invites Hardy to lunch.
840. May 23: Thomas Seccombe about Hardy's vignette of William Barnes in *The Athenaeum*.
841. May 30: Seccombe thanks Hardy for his letter about Barnes.
842. June 1: Hardy to Florence Henniker: about his visit to Stoke Court, and two or three weeks spent in London.
843. June 9: William Rothenstein would like to do another drawing of Hardy. See Letter 722.
844. June 14: William Dean Howells asks for a story like "The Distracted Young Preacher." ("Enter a Dragoon" appeared in *Harper's Monthly*, December 1900.)

845. June 18: Sir Frederick Pollock praises *The Well-Beloved*.
846. June 21: Pollock about marriage customs and property deeds.
847. June 24: Charlotte Pendleton asks approval of her libretto for an operatic version of *Tess* to be composed by Elliott Schenck.
848. June 26: Hardy to Charlotte Pendleton: copy; he will not object to her adapting the words of *Tess* for an operatic version.
849. July 11: A. E. Housman fixes 4 August as date for his visit to Max Gate.
850. July 21: An American friend of J. C. Young asks Hardy to inscribe some volumes of his works for Mr. Young's library.
851. July 29: Hardy to Florence Henniker: about her story in the *Pall Mall Magazine*.
852. July 30. A. E. Housman about the train from Waterloo Station to Dorchester.
853. August 14: Richard Nichol Howard will be glad to see Hardy and his friend, Sir Frederick Pollock.
854. August 15: Pollock about visiting the "isle of Portland" with Hardy.
855. August 26: Pollock about early forms of conveying land.
856. August 29: Edmund H. New about making a sketch from a watercolor Hardy showed him, to be included in B. C. A. Windle's *The Wessex of Thomas Hardy* (London, 1902).
857. September 17: Henry J. Moule asks about Hardy's paper published in an earlier issue of the *Proceedings* of the Dorset Field Club.
858. September 20: Moule thanks Hardy for his letter.
859. September 26: Arthur Symons wants facts and dates about Hardy for use in an article for the new Supplement to the *Encyclopaedia Britannica*.
860. October 22: Hardy to Florence Henniker: asks about Colonel Henniker and refers to *The Three Wayfarers*.
861. (c. October 31): Hardy to Mrs. Frank D. Higbee: about the American Red Cross Society. Published in *Later Years*, p. 86.
862. November 2: Henry D. Davray about French translations.
863. November 29: J. Nicol Dunn is pleased to have the "Song [of the Soldiers' Wives"] for publication in the *Morning Post* (30 November 1900).
864. November 30: Mary A. (Mrs. Humphry) Ward comments on *Jude*.
865. December 11: Hardy to his wife: expresses concern lest she has broken down while nursing her sister Helen Catherine (Mrs. Holder) in her last illness. Published in *Dearest Emmie*, pp. 43-44.
866. December 24: Hardy to Florence Henniker: is sending her his Christmas card, and expresses disappointment in Quiller-Couch's *Oxford Book of Verse*.
867. (n. d.): J. Evelyn Ball solicits help in getting her poetry published.
868. (n. d.): Mrs. Patrick Campbell returns his one-act play and asks if she may have *Tess*, the original version. (This was Mrs. Campbell's final appeal.)
869. (n. d.): Stephen Phillips says Hardy was very kind to speak to Mrs. Campbell.
870. (n. d.): F. H. Heidbrink inquires about Clym's song in *The Return of the Native*. (Hardy had quoted the first and third stanzas of a poem by C. G. Etienne.)

871. (n. d.): Marchioness of Queensberry regrets she cannot come; she thinks *Under the Greenwood Tree* delightful.

1901

872. January 7: Clive Holland asks if members of the Whitefriars Club may call at Max Gate next June. See Letter 893.
873. January 28: Lady Dorothy Nevill friendly note.
874. February 15: Hardy to Florence Henniker: William Archer came to interview him about a week ago.
875. March 16: Sir Arthur Spurgeon invites Hardy to become an Honorary Member of the Whitefriars Club.
876. March 22: Reginald Lund thanks Hardy for his contribution, "The Superseded," to *The May Book*, published in aid of the Charing Cross Hospital.
877. April 4: Hardy to Florence Henniker: the death of his favorite cat and the cat's interest in music.
878. April 19: Hardy to his wife, from London: about seeing Sir Henry Irving in *Coriolanus*, and looking for lodgings. Published in *Dearest Emmie*, pp. 46-47.
879. April 20: Arnaldo Cervesato, from Rome, asks Hardy's opinion as to a revival of Idealism.
880. April 24: Hardy to his wife: about her coming to London and their looking for lodgings. Published in *Dearest Emmie*, pp. 47-48.
881. April 27: Hardy to his wife: about looking for lodgings in London, and about the Harrisons, the Gosses, the Abbeys, Mrs. Henniker, and what one should wear on one's head now that Queen Victoria has died. Published in *Dearest Emmie*, pp. 48-49.
882. May 16: Hardy to Florence Henniker, from 27 Oxford Terrace, London: a cold prevents his acceptance of her invitation to her farm.
883. June 2: Hardy to Florence Henniker: is pleased she has remembered his birthday, and about his recent visit to Edward Clodd at Aldeburgh.
884. June 4: Cyril R. Everett about the Hardy family pedigree.
885. June 8: Maurice H. Hewlett invites Hardy to come on the 13th to meet Sarah Bernhardt.
886. June 18: Henry S. Salt about stag hunting, and asks support of a protest against cruel sports.
887. June 20: Hardy to Arnaldo Cervesato: pencil draft of a reply to Letter 879. Published in *Later Years*, p. 90.
888. June 24: Richard Garnett plans to call at Max Gate.
889. June 27: Garnett sends details about his proposed visit.
890. June 27: Hardy to Henry S. Salt: transcript of reply to Letter 886; expresses disapproval of killing animals "by cunning."
891. July ?: William Savage Johnson asks permission to call.
892. July 3: Salt thanks Hardy for his letter of 27 June; it was read at the meeting of the Humanitarian League.
893. July 5: Sir Arthur Spurgeon thanks Hardy for the visit of the Whitefriars Club to Max Gate.

894. July 25: Hardy to Florence Henniker: refers to an afternoon he spent with her and asked her to let him know when she will depart for Germany.
895. July 27: Frederick Harrison has just read *Far from the Madding Crowd;* believes it will last along with *Tom Jones* and *Vanity Fair.*
896. July 31: Harrison regrets his inability to accept an invitation from Hardy.
897. July ?: Richard Garnett about the Dorset dialectal word "inkledog" as a queer name for the earthworm.
898. August 10: Frederic Harrison thanks Hardy for a copy of *A Pair of Blue Eyes.*
899. August 20: Harrison says *A Pair of Blue Eyes* has been consoling.
900. August 28: Canon H. D. Rawnsley, Vicar at Keswick, solicits help in raising money.
901. September 2: J. Nicol Dunn gives permission to reprint the "Song of the Soldiers' Wives." See Letter 863.
902. September 5: Richard Garnett about books, etc.
903. October 18: Frederic Harrison asks help in blasting the murderers and anarchists who are dragging England to infamy.
904. October 29: Henry J. Moule sends some local gossip.
905. November 6: Edmund H. New sends a copy of Windle's book on *Wessex,* illustrated by New.
906. November 24: Lord Roseberry thanks Hardy for *Poems of the Past and the Present,* published the week before.
907. November 24: Mary A. (Mrs. Humphry) Ward thanks Hardy for his poems.
908. December 3: Theodore Watts-Dunton acknowledges Hardy's generous comment on Watts-Dunton's poem, "Christmas at the Mermaid."

1902

909. January 10: A. Weber appreciation, from Bradford.
910. January 11: John Morley acknowledges gift of *Poems of the Past and the Present.*
911. January 21: Watts-Dunton about a grudging review of Hardy's *Poems.*
912. January 24: Vicomte J. de Porthays, from Paris, solicits comment on the Boer War for publication in the *Revue Bleue.*
913. January 25: Hardy to his wife: about attending the wedding of the daughter of the Marquis and Marchioness of Londonderry. Published in *Dearest Emmie,* pp. 49-50.
914. February 1: Hardy to Vicomte J. de Porthays: pencil draft of reply to Letter 912.
915. February 14: Mario Borsa invites Hardy to join in commemorating the centenary of the birth of Victor Hugo.
916. (c. February 16): Hardy to Mario Borsa: pencil draft, signed "T. H.," of reply to Letter 915. Published with slight changes in *Later Years,* p. 92.
917. February 17: Sir Bertram C. A. Windle invites Hardy to address the Birmingham Literary Club.

918. February 27: Hardy to Edward Clodd: transcript of letter praising Clodd's *Life of Huxley.*
919. February 27: Clarence W. McIlvaine discusses a renewal of Hardy's contract with Osgood, McIlvaine & Co., about to expire at the end of its seven-year term.
920. February 28: Hardy to Clarence W. McIlvaine: Hardy's copy; his reasons for not wishing to renew his contract with Osgood, McIlvaine & Co. when it expires on 4 April 1902.
921. March 3: Hardy to McIlvaine: Hardy's copy; feels he must let the contract lapse.
922. March 4: Hardy to G. Herbert Thring, Solicitor to the Society of Authors: a transcript by Hardy, marked "Copy"; asks Thring's opinion about Hardy's plan to let his contract with Osgood, McIlvaine & Co. lapse.
923. March 5: Thring says Hardy would be justified in letting his contract lapse.
924. March 6: H. Rider Haggard asks about Hardy's views on agricultural conditions in Dorset.
925. March 7: Anthony Hope Hawkins tells Hardy it is all right for him to change publishers.
926. (c. March 7): Hardy to Haggard: rough draft; lengthy reply to his letter.
927. March 10: Hawkins tells Hardy the Macmillans are very reliable.
928. March 11: Haggard thanks Hardy for Letter 926.
929. March 13: Richard Garnett about a plan to set up a library of modern English authors.
930. March 16: Mario Borsa about the Italian version of *Tess.*
931. March 18: Hardy to Frederick Macmillan: rough draft; offers his works to the House of Macmillan.
932. March 25: Arthur C. Benson offers Hardy a copy of his poem "Ode to Japan."
933. March 26: Arthur Waugh solicits a MS. from Hardy for publication.
934. April 9: A. C. Benson thanks Hardy for his letter of 1 April 1902, about Benson's "Ode to Japan." Hardy's letter published in *Letters of Thomas Hardy* (Colby, 1954) p. 60.
935. April 28: Hardy to the Town Clerk, Dorchester: rough draft in ink, unsigned but all in Hardy's hand, of "Suggestions" for the *Guide to Dorchester.*
936. May 17: Henry Newbolt thanks Hardy for his contribution, "The Dear," to *The Monthly Review.*
937. May 19: Frederick Macmillan expresses the delight of the firm about having Hardy's books on their list.
938. May 26: Hardy to the Editor of the *Dorset County Chronicle*: rough draft in pencil, in Hardy's hand, of an anonymous letter regarding Edmund Kean in Dorchester. Published in the *Dorset County Chronicle,* 12 June 1902, p. 10.
939. July 21: Baron Frederic d'Erlanger asks for an interview in order to discuss an operatic *Tess.*
940. September 25: Hardy to Florence Henniker: pleased he will soon be able to see her and Colonel Henniker again, and about the new edition of his books soon to be brought out by Macmillan.

941. October 7: Benjamin De Casseres sends a copy of *The Bookman* containing his essay on Hardy's work.
942. October 8: Charles Whibley thanks Hardy for a copy of *Tess*.
943. November 13: T. P. O'Connor about an "attempt" in *T. P.'s Weekly*.
944. November 28: Hardy to Florence Henniker: death of the daughter of Barnes, the poet; says he wrote an obituary notice of her that appeared in the *Times*.
945. December 7: Hardy to Florence Henniker: more about the obituary of Barnes's daughter [Mrs. Baxter], and about Madeleine Stanley's marriage to a Mr. Brodrick.
946. December 7: Alfred de la Fontaine thanks Hardy for the kind offer of a tree.
947. December 14: Maarten Martens, from Holland, says *Jude* is gripping.
948. December 22: Hardy to Edward Clodd: transcript; "his friend" is welcome to call at Max Gate.

1903

949. January 3: Charles W. Moule friendly letter.
950. January 4: Hardy to Florence Henniker: thanks for an edition of *A Shropshire Lad*, and best wishes for the New Year.
951. January 5: Frederic Harrison is pleased with a letter from Hardy.
952. February 10: Sir Arthur Quiller-Couch about a war poem by Hardy.
953. February 21: Edmund Gosse asks Hardy to identify a passage about birds.
954. February 23: Harrison asks advice about submitting a manuscript to Harper & Brothers.
955. February 23: William Rothenstein asks permission to make a third drawing of Hardy.
956. March 6: John Royce invites Hardy to attend the Jubilee of the Manchester Public Free Libraries.
957. (c. March 9): Hardy to Royce: pencil draft; reply to Royce's invitation, with regrets.
958. March 11: Maynard Shipley asks for Hardy's views on capital punishment.
959. (c. March 12): Hardy to Shipley: rough draft of reply to Shipley's inquiry.
960. March 17: Hardy to Florence Henniker: has been reading Henry James's *The Wings of the Dove* with his wife.
961. March 29: Hardy to Florence Henniker: thanks her for a letter.
962. April 7: Henry J. Moule is grateful for the loan of Max Gate.
963. May 21: Moule again grateful for Hardy's kindness.
964. May 29: Moule writes from Max Gate.
965. May 30: Moule again thanks Hardy for the loan of Max Gate.
966 June 16: Moule, still at Max Gate, sends his last letter to Hardy.
967. June 25: Hardy to his wife: asks her to lock the drawers in his study at Max Gate. Published in *Dearest Emmie*, pp. 50-51.

968. June 27: Hardy to his wife: Mrs. Moulton has arrived [from America], and she wants them to attend her afternoon teas. Published in *Dearest Emmie*, pp. 51-52.
969. June 28: Hardy to his wife: asks her to hunt up the illustration to the "Leipzig" poem in *Wessex Poems*. Published in *Dearest Emmie*, pp. 52-53.
970. July 2: Hardy to his wife: about Americans being at his lodgings now, so he is ready to leave. Published in *Dearest Emmie*, pp. 53-54.
971. July 7: Frederic Harrison invites Hardy to visit him.
972. July 9: Sir Hugh Clifford solicits autograph in a copy of *The Well-Beloved*.
973. July 13: Henry Woodd Nevinson is grateful for Hardy's note about his article in the June *English Illustrated Magazine*.
974. July 18: Laurence Housman solicits a poem for publication in *The Venture*.
975. July 21: Hardy to Housman: pencil draft of a reply to Letter 974; he may send something.
976. July 22: Charles Hughes about Dorsetshire allusions in the Elizabethan poem *Willobies Avisa*.
977. July 28: G. E. Peters about the strength of the beer in *The Mayor of Casterbridge*.
978. August 3: Millicent, Duchess of Sutherland (later Lady Millicent Hawes) solicits a poem for a book to be sold for the benefit of the Newcastle Cripples' Guild.
979. August 13: Duchess of Sutherland thanks Hardy for his verses, "Life's Opportunity," published by her in *Wayfarer's Love* (October 1904), p. 16.
980. August 19: W. Bromley about a memorial brass to be placed in the Stinsford Church.
981. August 29: Arthur E. Moule (brother of Curator Moule) friendly letter from China.
982. September 1: Housman repeats his request in Letter 974.
983. September 2: Hardy to Housman: rough draft of reply, enclosing "The Market Girl" for publication in *The Venture*.
984. September 10: Edward B. Caulfeild [sic] writes about Browning's "The Statue and the Bust."
985. September 13: Hardy to Florence Henniker: about refusing to see summer tourists in the morning and their resentment at being told to come back later.
986. September 18: Thomas White sends two copies of the musical setting of "The Sergeant's Song" from *The Trumpet-Major*.
987. September 20: George Gissing, from the Pyrenees, about the scenery, books, etc.
988. October 24: Caulfeild again about Browning's "The Statue and the Bust."
989. November 13: Hardy to his wife, who is in Dover: he is finishing reading the proofs of *Part I* of *The Dynasts*. Published in *Dearest Emmie*, pp. 54-55.
990. November 13: Edmund Gosse praises "The Tramp-Woman's Tragedy," published in the *North American Review* after being rejected by the *Cornhill*.

991. November 16: Hardy to his wife, who is in France: about her cats and other news from Dorchester. Published in *Dearest Emmie*, pp. 55-57.
992. November 19: Hardy to his wife: has received her card from Calais, and nothing has happened at Max Gate. Published in *Dearest Emmie*, p. 57.
993. November 19: Louis Dumur (the unidentified "editor" of *L'Européen* of *Later Years*, p. 101) solicits Hardy's opinion as to France's alleged decadence.
994. November 21: Hardy to his wife: reports on her four cats. Published in *Dearest Emmie*, pp. 57-59.
995. November 24: Hardy, in London, to his wife, in France. Published in *Dearest Emmie*, p. 59.
996. November 26: Hardy to his wife, about a visit to St. Paul's Cathedral and other London matters. Published in *Dearest Emmie*, pp. 60-61.
997. November 29: Hardy to his wife: reports his return to Max Gate after two days in London in the rain, which gave him influenza. Has met Henry James at the Athenaeum Club. Published in *Dearest Emmie*, pp. 61-62.
998. November 30: Arthur E. Moule replies to a letter from Hardy.
999. December 3: Hardy to Charles Hannan, who wishes to dramatize *Two on a Tower*: Hardy does not wish to have it done.
1000. December 4: Hardy to Louis Dumur: copy in ink of Hardy's reply to Letter 993. Published in *Later Years*, p. 101.
1001. December 23: Hardy to Florence Henniker: wishes her a happy Christmas and New Year; had hoped to send her a copy of *The Dynasts, Part I*, but it will not be out until January.
1002. December 26: H. Balfour Gardiner sends a copy of "The Stranger's Song."
1003. "Monday" (n. d.): Alfred Pretor about theology and Platonism.
1004. (n. d.): Pretor again, about Sophocles, etc.

1904

1005. January 4: William Sharp about William Dean Howell's high opinion of Hardy's works.
1006. January 12: Frederick Macmillan about granting permission for the use of the word "Wessex."
1007. January 15: Henry Jackson to Alfred Pretor about metaphysics.
1008. January 20: Frederic Harrison has read *The Dynasts* and does not know what to think of its audacity.
1009. January 21: Edmund Gosse praises *The Dynasts, Part I*.
1010. January 23: A. C. Swinburne thanks Hardy for *The Dynasts, Part I*.
1011. January 29: Frederic Harrison about the dramatic form of *The Dynasts*.
1012. January 31: Lord Roseberry thanks Hardy for *The Dynasts*.
1013. February 6: Leslie Cope Cornford asks permission to dramatize *The Trumpet-Major*.

1014. February 8: Sir Henry Newbolt about the Omar Khayyam Club dinner.
1015. February 9: Aline Lady Sassoon asks permission to translate and adapt Hardy's *Tess* for the (French) stage.
1016. February 10: George A. Macmillan about the desire of Charles Hannan to dramatize *Two on a Tower*.
1017. February 11: Hardy to George A. Macmillan: rough draft of reply to Letter 1016; conditions under which Hardy would permit Hannan to dramatize *Two on a Tower*.
1018. February 15: J. Nicol Dunn invites support of a memorial to W. E. Henley.
1019. February 16: Hardy to J. Nicol Dunn: rough draft, signed "T. H.," of reply to Letter 1018. Asks Dunn to omit his name.
1020. February 27: G. Herbert Thring about infringement of copyright.
1021. March 2: W. Hugh Spottiswoode about reproducing two pages of *The Dynasts*.
1022. March 5: Hardy to Charles Hannan: rough draft in ink, signed "T. Hardy" and marked "Copy," of letter reversing Hardy's statement in Letter 999. Now states his willingness to let Hannan dramatize *Two on a Tower* and stipulates in detail the conditions which must govern any such dramatization.
1023. March 7: Charles Hannan regrets he must give up all thought of dramatizing *Two On a Tower*.
1024. March 9: Manuel Math is grateful to Hardy for granting him the rights to dramatize *Tess* in Spanish.
1025. March 11: Albert Pont asks permission to make a French translation.
1026. March 14: Hardy to Florence Henniker: says he has had much correspondence about *The Dynasts*, and praises her criticism of it.
1027. March 14: Henry W. Nevinson solicits a favor for the Balkan Committee.
1028. March 16: Sir Henry Newbolt about the Omar Khayyam Club dinner.
1029. March 29: James Knowles will look at a poem that Hardy offered him for publication in the *Nineteenth Century*. (It was apparently declined.)
1030. April 18: Hardy to Florence Henniker: thanks her for message at the time of his mother's death.
1031. April 29: E. Pasco thanks Hardy for his reply to a query about the Turberville coach.
1032. May 3: Joseph H. Choate, the American ambassador, solicits an essay for publication on the centenary of the birth of Nathaniel Hawthorne.
1033. May 5: Frederic Harrison invites Hardy to visit him.
1034. May 11: Eden Phillpotts asks about the "doleful-bell" flower in *Far from the Madding Crowd*.
1035. May 14: Phillpotts thanks Hardy for his prompt reply.
1036. May 27: Hardy to L. C. Cornford: grants permission to dramatize *The Trumpet-Major*. See Letter 1013.
1037. June 3: Joseph H. Choate about the contribution requested in Letter 1032.
1038. (c. June 24): Violet Hunt about the reviews of *The Dynasts*, Part I.

1039. June 27: Hardy to Violet Hunt: transcript, from 13 Abercorn Place, London, about *The Dynasts.*
1040. July 3: Elizabeth Robins invites Hardy to dinner.
1041. July 5: Elizabeth Robins hopes Hardy will call on her as he said he would.
1042. July 20: James Sully thanks Hardy for his letter in *The Times* of 28 June about Tolstoy's "sermon" on war. Letter reprinted in *Later Years,* p. 107.
1043. August 16: Mrs. B. A. Crackanthorpe answers Hardy's inquiry about the husband of 'Lawrence Hope.'
1044. August 23: G. L. Clothier to John Lane about the inn at Marshall's Elm in Hardy's "A Trampwoman's Tragedy."
1045. August 24: Israel Zangwill offers Hardy two seats to *Merely Mary Ann.*
1046. September 4: Arthur Symons about *Jude* and other matters.
1047. September 25: Hardy to Florence Henniker: about her being in Ireland and the memories this brings back to him. He is working on *The Dynasts, Part II.*
1048. October 1: Edward Hutton after reading *Jude*
1049. October 12: Frederick Macmillan about permitting a Mr. Heywood to translate *The Well-Beloved* into French.
1050. October 17: Edmund Gosse thanks Hardy for a visit to Max Gate.
1051. October 23: S. H. Butcher about *The Dynasts.*
1052. October 24: George A. B. Dewar sends a book.
1053. October 28: Sir George Douglas thanks Hardy for his note and for his invitation to Max Gate.
1054. November 7: R. Vaughan Williams asks permission to print the words of "In a Wood" on a music program.
1055. November 25: Edward Garnett replies to an inquiry about his "Amaryllis at the Fair," and refers to *The Country of The Pointed Firs* by Sarah Orne Jewett.
1056. November 29: Lady Dorothy Nevill asks when he will call on them.
1057. December 22: Hardy to Florence Henniker: thinks she is right in preferring *Fellow Townsmen* to *The Three Strangers.*
1058. December 30: S. H. Butcher is grateful for a message from Hardy.

1905

1059. January 2: Edmund Gosse invites Hardy to dine.
1060. January 10: Sir Henry Newbolt about the Trafalgar centenary.
1061. January 12: Newbolt thanks Hardy for permission to reprint "The Night of Trafalgar" from *The Dynasts, Part I.*
1062. January 26: Joseph Pennell invites Hardy to be a guest of the International Society of Sculptors, Painters and Gravers on 20 February at the Cafe Royal, for the opening of the Whistler Memorial Exhibition.
1063. January 26: John Pollock about his review of *The Dynasts* in the October 1904 *Independent Review.*
1064. January 31: William Rothenstein about recent events in Russia.
1065. February 1: Wallace Reid sends a book of his verses.

1066. February 12: Sir Frederick Treves invites Hardy to the inaugural dinner of the Society of Dorset Men in London.
1067. February 16: Treves disappointed that Hardy will be unable to attend the dinner of the Society.
1068. February 23: Sir Arthur W. Pinero about a protest to *The Times*.
1069. February 26: Hardy to Florence Henniker: sorry not to be able to see her at the Empress Club in London.
1070. February 28: Donaldson R. Thorn says the University of Aberdeen is going to confer the Honorary Degree of Doctor of Laws on Hardy on 7 April 1905.
1071. March 5: H. J. C. Grierson invites Hardy to be his guest while in Aberdeen in April.
1072. March 9: Sir James Frazer (author of *The Golden Bough*) would like to call.
1073. March 10: John Marshall Lang (Principal of Aberdeen University) thanks Hardy for a letter.
1074. March 14: Sir James Murray about arrangements for Hardy's going to Aberdeen in April.
1075. March 17: Lang about arrangements for Hardy's coming to Aberdeen in April.
1076. April 12: Frazer writes that he and his wife will call.
1077. April 25: R. B. Cunningham Graham has just read *The Trumpet-Major*.
1078. April 30: J. L. Garvin is glad to have a poem of Hardy's ["Geographical Knowledge"] in last week's *Outlook*.
1079. May 2: Mary MacCartie about a lady in *The Dynasts*.
1080. May 2: F. N. Maitland asks for Hardy's reminiscences of Leslie Stephen.
1081. May 4: Maitland thanks Hardy for his prompt reply.
1082. May 11: Frederic Harrison invites Hardy to visit him.
1083. May 23: Sir Sidney Lee invites Hardy to lunch.
1084. June 11: Maitland thanks Hardy again for his response.
1085. June 19: Walter Tyndall about an exhibition of his paintings of "The Thomas Hardy Country"—i.e., the paintings from which the illustrations for Clive Holland's *Wessex* (London; A. & C. Black, 1906) were to be made.
1086. June 20: Israel Gollancz invites Hardy to attend a meeting of the Shakespeare Memorial Committee.
1087. June 22: George Meredith tells Hardy (who had proposed calling) he is always welcome.
1088. June 26. Hardy to Gollancz: rough draft, signed "T. H.," of reply to Gollancz's invitation of 20 June.
1089. July 13: Clive Holland about a visit to Wessex by some journalists.
1090. July 17: Maitland thanks Hardy for his contribution to the *Life of Leslie Stephen*.
1091. August 22: Jacques-Emile Blanche to the Duchess of Sutherland: praises *Far from the Madding Crowd* and says he would like to paint a portrait of Hardy.
1092. August 27: Millicent, Duchess of Sutherland introduces Monsieur Blanche, a French artist.
1093. September 4: Blanche, presents the letter of introduction from the Duchess of Sutherland and expresses the desire to paint Hardy's portrait.

1094. September 8: J. Meade Falkner, from Durham, about a book on Dorchester antiquities on which Henry Moule was working.
1095. September 12: Hardy to Florence Henniker: he is going to Aldeburgh for the Crabbe celebration and would like to call on her while in that part of the country.
1096. September 18: Frank Adlam about old hymn tunes.
1097. October 9: Blanche praises *Jude*.
1098. October 9: J. L. Garvin wants for publication in *The Outlook* (London), a poem celebrating the Trafalgar anniversary next week.
1099. October 11: Madeleine Rolland first letter to Hardy in English.
1100. October 21: Hardy to Florence Henniker: he has finished the second part of *The Dynasts*.
1101. November 5: Edmund Gosse asks how *The Dynasts* is progressing.
1102. November 5: Hardy to Clive Holland: about Hardy's family history, etc. The presence of this letter in the Max Gate files, in ink, and signed "Yours very truly, Thomas Hardy," suggests that Hardy never sent it.
1103. November 22: Frederic Harrison has been writing a play.
1104. November 29: Bradford K. Daniels, from Balayan, Philippine Islands, says he has just finished reading *Tess* and does not find Hardy a pessimist.
1105. November (n. d.): G. Herbert Thring solicits support in recommending Swinburne for the Nobel Prize. (Hardy signed.)
1106. December 10: J. W. Frankland, from New Zealand, has received Hardy's card acknowledging Frankland's brochure.
1107. December 19: C. Lewis Hind asks permission to call at Max Gate.
1108. December 19: William Rothenstein about the need for a better understanding with Germany.
1109. (December 20): Hardy to Rothenstein: rough draft, in pencil, unsigned, of reply (14 lines) to Rothenstein's letter of 19 December 1905. This is the only one of Hardy's many letters to Rothenstein (the originals of which are now in the Houghton Library, Harvard University) of which Hardy retained a copy.
1110. December 21: Hardy to Florence Henniker: wants to proceed with *The Dynasts* but feels slowed down.
1111. (n. d.): R. Bosworth Smith about a meeting of the Field Club.

1906

1112. January 1: Edmund Gosse wants to know what has delayed *The Dynasts, Part II*.
1113. January 5: C. Lewis Hind returns a borrowed copy of the *North American Review*.
1114. January 24: Hardy to an unknown correspondent: typed transcript (presumably supplied by Howard Bliss from the original in his possession), from Max Gate, about a photograph of 8 Adelphi Terrace in London, where Hardy once worked.
1115. January 30: Sir James Murray inquires about a Dorset word in *Two on a Tower*.

1116. February 8: Frederic d'Erlanger tells Hardy his operatic version of *Tess* has been accepted for performance at Naples.
1117. February 10: Frederic Harrison thanks Hardy for *The Dynasts, Part II*.
1118. February 11: Hardy to Florence Henniker: he wants to send *Part II* of *The Dynasts*.
1119. February 12: Hardy to Edward Clodd: typescript copy, acknowledging receipt of Clodd's *Animism*, and a copy of *The Dynasts, Part II*, is on its way.
1120. February 12: Sir Henry Newbolt thanks Hardy for his book.
1121. February 14: Sir Sidney Lee thanks Hardy for *The Dynasts, Part II*.
1122. February 25: Edward Clodd acknowledges receipt of *The Dynasts, Part II*.
1123. February 25: Arthur Symons about *The Dynasts*.
1124. February 26: Edmund Gosse congratulates Hardy on *The Dynasts, Part II*.
1125. March 30: *Cornhill* Magazine welcomes "The Spring Call" poem.
1126. April 15: Frederic d'Erlanger thanks Hardy for his letter.
1127. April 21: d'Erlanger says an eruption of Mt. Vesuvius spoiled the performance of the *Tess* opera at Naples.
1128. (c. April 28): Jacques-Emile Blanche about Hardy's sitting for his portrait.
1129. May 2: Henry W. Nevinson gratitude for Hardy's kindness.
1130. May 4: Blanche about seeing Hardy again.
1131. May 4: Thackeray Turner thanks Hardy for his letter of 30 April 1906. Colonel Balfour has agreed to read it at a meeting of the Society for the Protection of Ancient Buildings.
1132. May 11: Blanche to Mrs. Emma Hardy: about calling on her.
1133. May 16: Hardy to Florence Henniker: thanks her for appreciation of *The Dynasts, Part II*.
1134. May 21: Hardy to General Arthur Henniker: thanks for letting him know about Mrs. Henniker's operation.
1135. May 21: Blanche to Mrs. Emma Hardy: about calling on her.
1136. June 1: F. W. Maitland asks for all of a letter of which Hardy had sent only a part.
1137. June 3: Henry Arthur Jones invites Hardy to lunch and to see *Othello*.
1138. June 4: Hardy to Jones: transcript; accepts Jones's invitation.
1139. June 5: Hardy to H. Stephens Richardson: transcript, from the Athenaeum Club, London, about joining the Field Club for a visit to Wool, Dorset.
1140. June 5: Maitland about a sonnet of Hardy's.
1141. June 9: Max Beerbohm regrets he cannot come to tea.
1142. June 12: Hardy to Florence Henniker: about her recovery from second operation.
1143. June 21: Irene Vanbrugh to Mrs. Emma Hardy: regrets having failed to see her recently and sends regards to Hardy.
1144. June 29: Hardy to Florence Henniker, from 1 Hyde Park Mansions, London: his portrait has been painted by Monsieur Blanche.
1145. July 1: George A. Macmillan asks about permitting the publication of Alexander Macmillan's letter to Hardy about *The Poor Man*.

1146. July 4: Reginald J. Smith about printing Hardy's papers on Church Restorations in the *Cornhill*.
1147. July 5: Edmund Gosse calls attention to a monograph on Hardy's writings (by Firmin Roz) in the *Revue des Deux Mondes* for 1 July 1906, pp. 176-207.
1148. July 17: Desmond McCarthy solicits a poem for *The Speaker*.
1149. July 18: Maitland reminder about the letter he had asked for on 1 June 1906.
1150. July 20: Maitland sends proofs of Hardy's contribution to *The Life of Leslie Stephen*.
1151. July 21: Blanche sends thanks for some books.
1152. July 22: Maitland writes further about the proofs sent to Hardy.
1153. July 23: Gosse about the illustrations in the first edition of *Far from the Madding Crowd*.
1154. July 25: Maitland again about *The Life of Leslie Stephen*.
1155. July 29: Edward Clodd thanks Hardy for the *Cornhill*.
1156. August 1: Maitland asks to see the original of a Leslie Stephen letter.
1157. August 1: John Slater thanks Hardy for his paper on Church Restorations.
1158. August 3: Maitland expresses gratitude.
1159. August 8: Firmin Roz asks permission to make a French translation of *Jude*. (He translated *The Woodlanders* into French.)
1160. August 13: Sir Arthur Quiller-Couch on *The Dynasts;* asks permission to quote a passage by Hardy in an anthology.
1161. August 20: J. Meade Falkner about F. Roz's article on Hardy in the July *Revue des Deux Mondes*.
1162. August 23: The Rev. T. Perkins about Dorset archaeology.
1163. August (n. d.): Lady Betty Balfour (daughter of Lord Lytton) requests letters her father had written to Hardy be sent to her.
1164. September 3: Lady Balfour thanks Hardy for letters from her father and asks for permission to publish the one dated 10 July 1887 about *The Woodlanders*.
1165. September 5: Edward Thomas asks permission to reprint "The Darkling Thrush" in an anthology.
1166. September 7: Madeleine Rolland about the translation of *The Mayor of Casterbridge* into French by Louis Barron.
1167. (c. September 8): Arthur Symons about Hardy's sonnet in the *Saturday Review*. ("A Church Romance" appeared in *S. R.* for 8 September 1906.)
1168. September 12: Hardy to Florence Henniker: about his paper on Ancient Churches, and that the author of *A Man of Property* sent him the book which he began to read but found uninteresting and too materialistic and sordid.
1169. September 27: Henry W. Nevinson sends proofs of an article he has written about Hardy.
1170. September 28: Charles Roden Buxton thanks Hardy for letting him hope for a contribution to the first number of the *Nation*.
1171. October 7: H. Brown about the Turberville family in *Tess*.
1172. October 21: Frederic Harrison on pessimism.
1173. October 29: Edmund Gosse about the Literary Supplement of the *Daily Mail*.
1174. October 29: James Rose asks about the Hardy family pedigree.

1175. October 30: Arthur G. Ferard about the Keats-Shelley Memorial.
1176. (n. d.): Doris Davidsohn asks permission to translate *The Well-Beloved* into German.
1177. November 21: Sir Sidney Lee about the formation of an English Association.
1178. November 22: Mrs. M. G. Fawcett asks Hardy's opinion about women's suffrage.
1179. November 29: Maitland thanks Hardy for his kind words.
1180. November 30: W. L. Courtney accepts the poem "New Year's Eve" for publication in the January issue of the *Fortnightly Review*.
1181. November 30: Hardy to Mrs. M. G. Fawcett: rough draft, signed "Thomas Hardy," of reply to her request of 22 November 1906 for his opinion.
1182. December 4: Mrs. Fawcett thanks Hardy for his letter.
1183. December 21: Hardy to Florence Henniker: some verses of his are coming out in the January *Fortnightly Review*.
1184. December (n. d.): Sir Harold Boulton invites Hardy to be a member of the Keats-Shelley Memorial committee.
1185. (n. d.): E. Topham Forrest to Lady St. Helier; returns a letter of Hardy's she had left with him.
1186. (n. d.): Mr. John Morgan Richards thanks Hardy for sending him letters to Hardy from his daughter to be copied (Mrs. Pearl Craigie, née Pearl Richards, pen-name John Oliver Hobbs, died in 1906.)
1187. "Monday": R. Bosworth Smith illegible letter of congratulations on *The Dynasts, Part II;* Hardy added, in pencil, his decipherings of Smith's scrawl.

1907

1188. (c. January 1): Hardy to Edward Clodd: thanks him for Munro's *Lucretius* and wishing him a Happy New Year; typed transcript of the original letter presumably in the possession of Howard Bliss.
1189. January 14: Sir Walter Raleigh asks help in the preparation of a volume of poems by William Barnes for publication by the Oxford University Press.
1190. January 20: J. M. Barrie thanks Hardy for a volume of his poems.
1191. January 20: Sir Walter Raleigh thanks Hardy for being willing to make a selection of Barnes's Dorset poems for publication.
1192. February 6: M. Beer asks permission to translate *Jude* into German.
1193. February 14: Hardy to M. Beer: pencil draft, unsigned but in Hardy's hand, of a reply to Beer's request of 6 February. Points out that *Jude* had already been translated into German and published in 1897, so Beer is free to translate it without payment of any fee.
1194. April 25: George A. B. Dewar sends a book.
1195. May 13: Hardy to the Committee of the Humanitarian League: typed transcript, from 1 Hyde Park Mansions, London, about cruelty to animals.
1196. May 28: Henry R. Bastow, after a silence of 41 years, writes that his son Arthur is returning from India.

78 MAX GATE CORRESPONDENCE

1197. May 28: Edward Wright inquires about "the Unconscious Will" in *The Dynasts*.
1198. June 2: Hardy to Wright: reply to Letter 1197, the philosophy of *The Dynasts;* rough draft, signed "T. H." Published in *Later Years*, pp. 124-125.
1199. June 3: Wright thanks Hardy for his letter of 2 June.
1200. June 8: K. Minoura, from Tokio, Japan.
1201. June 18: Edmund Gosse thanks Hardy for some poems [by Barnes?]
1202. June 20: Austin Dobson about a poem by Hardy.
1203. August 8: Hardy to Florence Henniker: about his work on *The Dynasts, Part III*.
1204. August 12: Frank A. Hedgcock, from the University of Paris, asks many questions, for use in preparing a thesis on the Wessex Novels.
1205. August 13: Hardy to K. Minoura; pencil draft of reply to Letter 1200; unable to express well-defined opinion on Japan.
1206. September 7: Thomas Seccombe sends a book.
1207. September 17: Henry Jackson to Alfred Pretor: on metaphysical matters.
1208. September 19: Jackson again to Pretor on metaphysics.
1209. September 23: Reginald J. Smith accepts for publication in the *Cornhill Magazine* "The Apotheosis of the Mind" by Florence Dugdale.
1210. September 27: Mrs. Dorothy Allhusen (née Dorothy Stanley, daughter of Lady St. Helier) to "My dear Uncle Tom," using her mother's way of addressing Hardy. Thanks for his letter.
1211. September 29: Hardy to Florence Henniker: thanks for *Our Fatal Shadows*, which he thinks an improvement over her previous novels. He is still working on *The Dynasts*.
1212. October 3: W. L. Courtney declines Hardy's offer of "A Sunday Morning Tragedy," which the *Fortnightly Review* could not publish because of its subject.
1213. October 7: J. M. Barrie asks support in opposing censorship in the theater.
1214. October 11: Major W. R. Arnold, from Madras, India, asks about Dorset songs that could be used by a military band.
1215. October 15: Madeleine Rolland refers to the day she spent with Hardy and Mrs. Hardy at Max Gate, and returns some proofs.
1216. October 25: John Marshall Lang glad to receive a letter from Hardy introducing the Rev. Herbert Pentin who wished to become Chaplain at Aberdeen University.
1217. October 31: Edmund Gosse is sending a copy of an anonymous book which has just been published, *Father and Son*. Gosse's authorship was disclosed later.
1218. November 10: Barrie again about opposition to censorship in the theatre.
1219. November 11: Arthur Cochrane about *The Dynasts*.
1220. November 23: Hardy to Major Arnold: pencil draft of reply to Letter 1214 about Dorset songs.
1221. December 2: Frank A. Hedgcock outlines plan he has in mind for writing his thesis on Hardy's novels at the University of Paris.
1222. December 16: Arnold thanks Hardy for his letter of 23 November.

1223. December 28: A. M. Broadley asks if *Part III* of *The Dynasts* will be available in the spring.
1224. December 31: Hardy to Florence Henniker: thanks for her Christmas card and wishes for a happy new year. He has almost finished the proofs of *The Dynasts, Part III*.
1225. (n. d.): Charles Roden Buxton solicits a contribution to the *Independent Review*, which he edits.
1226. (n. d.): Yrjo Hion inquires about a Finnish translation of *A Group of Noble Dames* and *Life's Little Ironies*.
1227. (n. d.): Lady St. Helier invites Hardy to pay her a visit.

1908

1228. January 5: Jacques-Emile Blanche asks if Hardy would accept Membership in the International Society.
1229. January 10: Captain John E. Acland about the site of the old Dorchester theatre, erected in 1828.
1230. January 26: Sir Walter A. Raleigh solicits further help in preparing a volume of Barnes's poetry.
1231. January 30. Raleigh thanks Hardy for his help about the poems of Barnes.
1232. February 8: H. W. Smith solicits an article on George Meredith for publication in the *Daily News*.
1233. (c. February 9): Hardy to Smith: rough draft, signed "T. H.," of reply to Letter 1232; cannot write a detached critical estimate.
1234. February 12: Charles Cartwright asks for permission to adapt *The Mayor of Casterbridge* for the stage; he had played in *Far from the Madding Crowd*.
1235. February 12: Edmund Gosse thanks Hardy for *The Dynasts, Part III*.
1236. February 17: Sir Frederick Pollock about the greatness of *The Dynasts*.
1237. February 20: Hardy to Cartwright: rough draft of reply to Letter 1234: remembers Cartwright in the role of Sergeant Troy, and refers to the possibility of *The Mayor of Casterbridge* as a play.
1238. February 20: Hardy to Edward Clodd: typed transcript; says *The Dynasts, Part III*, like *Paradise Lost*, proves nothing.
1239. March 4: Gosse praises *The Dynasts, Part III*.
1240. March 4: Arthur Symons says *The Dynasts* is magnificent.
1241. March 5: C. Hagberg asks Hardy to serve on a committee to arrange for the celebration of Tolstoi's 80th birthday.
1242. March 7: Frederic Harrison congratulates Hardy on completing *The Dynasts* and gives it high praise.
1243. March 10: Sir Hubert von Herkomer praises *The Dynasts* and asks Hardy if he will revise a book on The House of Herkomer.
1244. March 22: A. G. Gardiner thanks Hardy for explaining his views of life.
1245. March 30: Sir William Watson thanks Hardy for *The Dynasts*.
1246. April 5: Judge B. Fossett Lock on *The Dynasts*.

1247. April 6: Nelson W. Richardson invites Hardy to become an Honorary Member of the Dorset Field Club.
1248. April 24: George A. Macmillan about publicizing *The Dynasts*.
1249. May 7: Robert Donald about a Shakespeare Memorial Theatre.
1250. May 9: William Watkins about the Society of Dorset Men in London.
1251. May 9: C. Hagberg Wright again about the celebration of Tolstoi's 80th birthday.
1252. May 10: Hardy to Robert Donald: rough draft in pencil of reply to Letter 1249: Letter published in *Later Years*, pp. 131-132.
1253. May 12: Lord Curzon invites Hardy to visit him.
1254. May 15: Curzon urges Hardy to visit him.
1255. May 18: Alfred G. Gardiner distressed about Hardy's misunderstanding of his article.
1256. May 21: Hardy to Florence Henniker, from the Athenaeum Club, London: expresses pleasure about her comment on *The Dynasts*, and also the pleasure of the publisher of the book.
1257. May 25: Hardy to his wife: looking for lodgings in or near London. Published in *Dearest Emmie*, pp. 66-67.
1258. May 26: Ian MacAlister invites Hardy to be present on June 23 at the meeting of the Royal Institute of British Architects.
1259. June 2: Lord Curzon postpones the date set for Hardy's visit.
1260. June 9: Austin Dobson thanks Hardy for a song in *The Dynasts*.
1261. June 27: Sir Walter Raleigh solicits a few words as a Preface for the volume of *Poems* by William Barnes.
1262. June 28: Hardy to his wife: about dining at the home of his publisher, Frederick Macmillan. Published in *Dearest Emmie*, p. 67.
1263. (c. July 1): Violet Hunt is sending her books.
1264. July 2: Hardy to his wife: about her coming to town, leaving Florence Dugdale in charge at Max Gate. Published in *Dearest Emmie*, pp. 67-69.
1265. July 3: Hardy to his wife: about sitting to Hubert Herkomer for a portrait. Published in *Dearest Emmie*, p. 69.
1266. July 6: Hardy, in London, to his wife at Max Gate: he is going to Cambridge for the Milton Tercentenary. Published in *Dearest Emmie*, pp. 70-71.
1267. July 13: Hardy to his wife: he had a good time for two days in Cambridge. Published in *Dearest Emmie*, p. 71.
1268. July 16: Hardy to his wife: he sat next to Henry James at the wedding of Gosse's son Philip and Gertrude Hay. Published in *Dearest Emmie*, pp. 71-72.
1269. July 16: Laurence Binyon about *The Dynasts*.
1270. August 17: Lena Milman on her engagement to be married. (Hardy sent her his photograph in 1893.)
1271. September 15: Hardy, from Max Gate, to his wife in Calais; dull at home. Published in *Dearest Emmie*, pp. 72-74.
1272. September 15: Harold Child thanks Hardy for information about the projected performance of a dramatization of *The Trumpet-Major*; is glad to accept Hardy's invitation.
1273. September 16: May Sinclair would like to call, bringing a friend, Miss Amy Moss, who some years ago wrote a fine article on the Wessex Novels in the *Atlantic Monthly*.

1274. September 19: Hardy to his wife: about the digging in the Amphitheatre. Published in *Dearest Emmie*, pp. 74-75.
1275. September 24: Hardy to his wife in Calais: plans for a November performance of A. H. Evans's dramatization of *The Trumpet-Major*. Letter published in *Dearest Emmie*, pp. 75-76.
1276. September 30: Hardy to his wife in Calais: about her cats, the heat, and an expected call from May Sinclair. Published in *Dearest Emmie*, pp. 76-78.
1277. September 30: Moberly Bell solicits an article on "Maumbury Ring" for publication in *The Times*. (It appeared on 9 October 1908.)
1278. (c. September 30): May Sinclair thanks Hardy (see Letter 1273); she and her friend will come at 3.
1279. October 3: Madeleine Rolland sends a translation she has made. (She had previously translated *Tess* into French.)
1280. October 5: Hardy to his wife: she had better stay in Calais because of confusion at Max Gate where a new room is being constructed in the attic. Published in *Dearest Emmie*, p. 78.
1281. October 9: Hardy to his wife in Calais: the cats are well, and Rebekah Owen has become a Roman Catholic. Published in *Dearest Emmie*, pp. 78-80.
1282. October 9: Sir Squire Bancroft about Hardy's article on "Maumbury Ring."
1283. October 9: G. E. Buckle about the "Maumbury Ring" article. (It was published as a little book by the Colby College Library in August 1942.)
1284. October 9: William Watkins about the Society of Dorset Men in London.
1285. October 12: Hardy to his wife: the cats are well. Published in *Dearest Emmie*, pp. 81-82.
1286. October 12: Watkins again about the Society of Dorset Men in London.
1287. October 16: L. P. Jacks solicits an article for the *Hibbert Journal*.
1288. October 18: Laurence Binyon sends a book of his.
1289. October 18: Harold Child has been commissioned by *The Times* to go to Dorchester and write about the play, *The Trumpet-Major*, in November.
1290. October 25: Valery Larbaud, from Vichy, France, has just published, through *La Phalange*, an essay on *The Dynasts*.
1291. November 2: The Right Honorable H. H. Asquith (Prime Minister) asks if he could persuade Hardy to accept a Knighthood.
(This unpublished letter provides the evidence long sought and until now not found for contradicting such statements as that of Rupert Hart-Davis in his biography of Hugh Walpole (New York, Macmillan, 1952). After quoting from Walpole's journal of May 1937: "I must confess that . . . I can't think of a good novelist who accepted a knighthood . . . . Hardy . . . refused" [page 381], Hart-Davis remarks: "I know of no evidence that Hardy was ever offered a knighthood." Letter 1291 supplies that evidence; and Letter 1293 shows that Hardy promptly declined the offer.)
1292. November 5: Desmond McCarthy solicits a poem for the *New Quarterly*.

1293. November 6: Prime Minister Asquith understands Hardy's need for time to consider the offer of a knighthood.
1294. (c. November 10): R. Vaughan Williams thanks Hardy for permission to set to music the Soldier's Song in *The Dynasts*.
1295. November 11: H. Balfour Gardiner wants to make a one-act opera out of "The Three Strangers."
1296. (c. November 12): Hardy to Gardiner: pencil draft of reply to Letter 1295: asks why not choose scenes from *The Dynasts* as more worthy of music.
1297. November 26: Frederic d'Erlanger reports Hardy's *Tess* opera has been successfully produced at Milan.
1298. December 1: Gardiner asks for a copy of the dramatic version of "The Three Strangers" (i.e., *The Three Wayfarers*).
1299. December 3: Sir Frederick Treves thanks Hardy for a copy of his edition of the *Poems* of William Barnes.
1300. December 8: Hardy to his wife, from London, asks her to send him some clothes. Published in *Dearest Emmie*, pp. 82-83.
1301. December 12: Charles W. Kent invites Hardy to attend a celebration of the 100th anniversary of the birth of Edgar Allan Poe at the University of Virginia.
1302. December 21: A. Helen Ward asks support of Women's Suffrage.
1303. December 22: Hardy to Helen Ward: rough draft in ink; is unable to let his name appear, but is not opposed to Women's Suffrage.
1304. December 22: Hubert J. Elliott about seeing, in his father's autograph book, Hardy's "How fares the Truth?" written just above George Meredith's autograph.
1305. December 23: Hardy to Florence Henniker: the performance of *The Trumpet-Major* (as dramatized by A. H. Evans) and performed on 18 and 19 November 1908 was received with great interest. (In the typescript of this letter, made by Mrs. Meech, the year, not mentioned in Hardy's dating, was erroneously taken to be 1909 and the letter was accordingly assigned a place in the transcript that was a year too late.)

1909

1306. (c. January 4): Hardy to Charles W. Kent: rough draft of reply to Letter 1301, thanking him for the invitation. The rest of Hardy's reply was published in *Later Years*, p. 134.
1307. January 5: H. Balfour Gardiner again about his desire to make an opera out of *The Three Wayfarers*.
1308. January 14: Sir Henry Newbolt about his article on *The Dynasts* in the *Quarterly Review* of January 1909, pp. 193-209.
1309. January 18: A. G. Symonds about the Dorchester Grammar School.
1310. February 6: L. J. Zivny about a Bohemian translation of *Tess*.
1311. February 15: W. H. Helm thanks Hardy for replying to his question.
1312. February 16: Helen Garwood six-page letter from Philadelphia about Schopenhauer. Her University of Pennsylvania doctoral dissertation, *Thomas Hardy, An Illustration of the Philosophy of*

Schopenhauer, was published two years later (Philadelphia, Winston, 1911), at which time Miss Garwood sent Hardy a copy. He acknowledged receipt of it; his letter quoted in *Hardy of Wessex* (New York, 1940), p. 203.

1313. March 2: George Meredith thanks Hardy for *The Dynasts.*
1314. April 16: Walter Armstrong about the portrait of Quin, "a man of varied parts," in *The Dynasts, Part I,* Act VI, Scene VI.
1315. May 6: P. G. Mitchell appreciation from Philadelphia.
1316. May 7: R. B. Cunningham Graham is reading the poems of Barnes.
1317. May 7: Bertha Johnston appreciation from Brooklyn, New York.
1318. May 22: Maurice Hewlett, from Salisbury, invites Hardy to spend a weekend with him.
1319. May 24: Hardy to Florence Henniker: about the death of George Meredith, and *The Egoist.*
1320. May 26: G. M. Trevelyan thanks Hardy for the poem on Meredith, published in *The Times,* 22 May 1909.
1321. June 7: Maurice Hewlett asks Hardy to accept the Presidency of the Society of Authors, vacated by the death of Meredith.
1322. June 8: F. M. Bland about a case almost parallel with Tess Durbeyfield's.
1323. June 9: Hardy to Hewlett: copy of reply to Letter 1321, declining the Presidency of the Society of Authors.
1324. June 10. Hewlett urges Hardy to reconsider.
1325. June 11: Hardy to Hewlett: rough draft of reply to Letter 1324; he cannot alter his decision to decline.
1326. June 13: Hewlett again on the same subject.
1327. June 14: Hardy to Hewlett: rough draft; is considering what Hewlett has said.
1328. June 14: Laurence Binyon about Sir John Moore in *The Dynasts.*
1329. July 5: Lady Augusta Gregory praises *The Dynasts.*
1330. July 5: Hewlett repeats his hope that Hardy will accept the Presidency of the Society of Authors. [He did.]
1331. July 8: Frederic d'Erlanger about plans for the London performance of the *Tess* opera.
1332. July 9: Hardy, from London, to his wife at Max Gate: about the London performance of d'Erlanger's *Tess* opera. Asks her if she will come. Published in *Dearest Emmie,* pp. 83-84.
1333. July 9: May Sinclair invites Hardy to lunch.
1334. July 16: Neil Fosyth thanks Hardy for his letter about the *Tess* opera at Covent Garden.
1335. July 17: d'Erlanger thanks Hardy for his letter to the management of Covent Garden.
1336. July 19: Hardy to Florence Henniker, from Max Gate: he seems to be in a state of depression.
1337. July 21: May Sinclair on the psychology of *Tess.*
1338. July 22: d'Erlanger on the second performance of the *Tess* opera, which went very well.
1339. July 30: John Galsworthy thanks Hardy for his letter.
1340. August 9: Fred Harsley asks for a statement for use by Dr. Max Dessoir at the University of Berlin.
1341. August (12?): Hardy to Harsley: copy, signed "Thomas Hardy," of reply to Letter 1340. Two sentences published in *Later Years,* p. 139.

1342. August 19: William M. Meredith returns George Meredith's letters of 1886 and 1909 which Hardy had lent to Meredith's son.
1343. August 20: Inez S. Maskeleyne sends a musical setting for Hardy's "New Year poem."
1344. August 25: Israel Zangwill congratulates Hardy on *The Dynasts*.
1345. August 29: Lady Augusta Gregory asks if Hardy will sign a Memorial aimed at getting W. B. Yeats onto the Civil List.
1346. September 6: Wilfrid Meynell about the Portsmouth address of George Meredith's grandfather.
1347. September 6: Henry W. Nevinson last of his five letters to Hardy. [His "The Son of Earth" about Hardy was published in *Essays in Freedom* (London: Duckworth, 1909).]
1348. September 15: Sir Sidney Lee solicits a contribution.
1349. September 21: George A. B. Dewar gives permission to reprint a sonnet which had appeared in *Nineteenth Century*.
1350. September 21: Madame Eve (Paul) Margueritte about a French translation of *The Well-Beloved* and *A Pair of Blue Eyes*.
1351. September 24: Maurice Lanoire sends a copy of his article published in the *Journal des Debats* on *The Dynasts*.
1352. September 28: Evelyn Stuart (concert pianist) about three settings by Gustav Holst for poems by Hardy.
1353. October 1: Mary C. Sturgeon asks permission to quote from Hardy's work.
1354. (c. October 4): Hardy to Messrs. Macmillan: asks them to notify Mary Sturgeon she may have permission to quote for one guinea.
1355. October 13: Sir T. Herbert Warren about his use of a poem of Hardy's [about the comet].
1356. October 14: Frederic Harrison congratulates Hardy on succeeding Meredith as President of the Society of Authors.
1357. October 20: Hardy to Henry Arthur Jones: typed transcript of letter from Max Gate, about protesting against censorship in the theatre.
1358. October 27: Warren again about the comet and Hardy's poem.
1359. November 6: Pat à Beckett solicits a contribution for printing in the Souvenir Programme at a game, for a charitable purpose.
1360. November 11: à Beckett sends thanks for his gift of "Budmouth Dears," from *The Dynasts, Part III*, in response to her appeal of 6 November.
1361. November 16: Warren sends a volume.
1362. November 22: E. Jean North thanks Hardy for one of his books.
1363. November 25: Hardy to A. M. Broadley: transcript (supplied by Howard Bliss?), about Samuel Johnson and Mrs. Thrale, published in *Hardy Letters*, pp. 79-80.
1364. November 28: Hardy to Florence Henniker: *Time's Laughingstocks* is to be published soon; comments on a performance in London by a company of amateur actors, of *Far from the Madding Crowd*. He indicates that his spirits are low—at 69.
1365. November 30: W. H. Williams invites Hardy to be the guest of the Town of Liverpool at a dinner.
1366. December 3: Hardy to Williams: rough draft of reply to Letter 1365: he is compelled to decline.
1367. December 5: Clodd on Hardy's poems in *Time's Laughingstocks*, published 3 December 1909.

1368. December 7: Gosse thanks Hardy for *Time's Laughingstocks.*
1369. December 9: Drinkwater sends two sonnets addressed to Hardy.
1370. December 11: Gilbert Murray thanks Hardy for *Time's Laughingstocks.*
1371. December 19: Lord Crewe (brother of Florence Henniker) thanks Hardy for *Time's Laughingstocks.*
1372. December 26: Drinkwater asks permission to print the two sonnets, he had sent on 9 December 1909.
1373. (n. d.): William Bayard Hale asks permission to call.
1374. (n. d.): Austin Harrison (son of Frederic Harrison) about *Time's Laughingstocks.*
1375. (n. d.): Ralph Vaughan Williams sends two songs, setting Barnes to music.

1910

1376. January 1: Madeleine Rolland expresses pleasure in reading Hardy's most recent poems.
1377. January 3: John Drinkwater praises Hardy's poems.
1378. January 17: John Ayscough praises *Tess, The Mayor, The Return of the Native,* and *The Woodlanders.*
1379. January 25: William Adams Brown has been reading *The Dynasts* in New York City with admiration.
1380. (c. January 26): Frances (Mrs. F. M.) Cornford asks if she and her husband may call.
1381. January 30: Sir Francis Darwin thanks Hardy for letting his daughter and her husband (F. M. Cornford) call at Max Gate.
1382. February 13: Edmund Gosse about founding an English Academy of Letters.
1383. February 15: Hubert von Herkomer about painting Hardy's portrait.
1384. February 25: Algernon Rose about the Author's Club.
1385. March 8: Harold Child asks if he may call and bring a friend.
1386. April 2: Edward Whymper about the tombstone of his grandfather in Ipswich Cemetery.
1387. April 10: Hardy to the Secretary of the Humanitarian League: rough draft; expresses pleasure about its age of twenty years.
1388. April 13: Ernest George about Hardy's nomination for election as an Honorary Associate of the Royal Institute of British Architects.
1389. April 15: Newman Flower, a native of Dorset, would like to do an anthology of Hardy's work.
1390. April 21: Thomas B. Wells inquires about a possible autobiography for Harper & Brothers to publish. Letter published in *Hardy in America,* p. 103.
1391. April 22: Hardy, from London, to his wife: has been looking for flats and lodgings for three days. Published in *Dearest Emmie,* pp. 85-86.
1392. April 24: Hardy to Wells: rough draft of reply to Letter 1390; he could not appear in a better place than *Harper's Magazine* but it is unlikely he will ever produce his reminiscences. Letter partly published in *Hardy in America,* p. 103.

MAX GATE CORRESPONDENCE

1393. April 27: Hardy to his wife: he has found an acceptable flat at Blomfield Court, Maida Vale, London. Published in *Dearest Emmie*, pp. 86-87.
1394. April (?): G. Herbert Thring asks for a list of Hardy's plays.
1395. April (?): Hardy to Thring: lists only two plays, *The Three Wayfarers* and *Tess*; adds that a dramatization by J. Comyns Carr of *Far from the Madding Crowd* was produced in 1882, but he had no hand in it beyond authorizing it. See Letters 208, 214, 215, 216.
1396. April 30: Hardy to his wife: about the flat at Blomfield Court. Published in *Dearest Emmie*, pp. 87-88.
1397. May 2: Hardy to his wife: he has made an offer for the flat at 4 Blomfield Court. Published in *Dearest Emmie*, p. 88-89.
1398. May 3: Hardy to his wife: discusses her move from Max Gate to London. Published in *Dearest Emmie*, pp. 89-90.
1399. May 30: Florence Henniker invites Hardy to luncheon; she is sorry Mrs. Hardy has been ill. (This is the first letter from Mrs. Henniker preserved in the Max Gate files. All those written from 1893 to 1909 were destroyed.)
1400. June 1: Mrs. B. A. Crackenthorpe about Mrs. Granville-Barker who wants to play the part of Tess.
1401. June 2: Alfred East sends birthday greetings.
1402. June 3: Lord Curzon sends birthday greetings.
1403. June 3: Edmund Gosse greets Hardy on his 70th birthday.
1404. June 3: Frederic Harrison sends birthday greetings.
1405. June 6: Frederic d'Erlanger sends thanks for an invitation from Mrs. Hardy.
1406. June 9: Mrs. Dorothy Allhusen invites Hardy to Stoke Poges.
1407. June 10: Maurice Hewlett invites Hardy to dinner.
1408. June 13: Henry C. Duffin offers to submit to Hardy's scrutiny the manuscript of his book on Hardy (published in 1916 by Manchester University Press).
1409. June 14: Sir Henry Newbolt sends a book.
1410. June 15: Lillah McCarthy (Mrs. Granville-Barker) thanks Hardy for letting her read *Tess* and indicates her personal interest in it.
1411. June 16: Hardy to Henry Arthur Jones: typed transcript of a letter from Blomfield Court, Maida Vale, about *Rebellious Susan*.
1412. June 17: Hardy to Lillah McCarthy: autograph letter, signed "Thomas Hardy," with stipulations about the text of the *Tess* play and other matters related to the play.
1413. June 20: J. M. Barrie invites Hardy to lunch.
1414. June 20: Genevieve Bennett (Mrs. Champ) Clark wishes to see him; she has read *Tess* many times, and her husband thinks *The Mayor of Casterbridge* is a great novel.
1415. June 21: J. M. Barrie is pleased that Hardy will come to lunch.
1416. June 21: Josephine Preston Peabody (Mrs. Lionel Marks) asks permission to call. (She had written Hardy on 16 July 1907 on a previous visit from America to London and had obtained his consent to autograph three of his books for her. Hardy did not retain her letter of 16 July 1907. His reply is in the Houghton Library, Harvard University.)
1417. June (?): Commander W. W. Fisher invites Hardy to visit H.M.S. *Dreadnought* and afterwards the American flagship U.S.S. *Louisiana*.

1418. July 2: Prime Minister H. H. Asquith on the King's proposal to confer the Order of Merit upon Hardy.
1419: July 2: Hubert von Herkomer about painting Hardy's portrait.
1420. July 4: Asquith requests his letter of 2 July 1910 be kept private.
1421. July 4: Lord Knollys informs Hardy officially of the King's pleasure to confer the Order of Merit upon him.
1422. July 4: William Dean Howells invites Hardy to call at 18 Half Moon Street where Howells and his daughter are staying while in London.

Congratulations on the award of the ORDER OF MERIT, various dates, received from 49 persons:

1423. Sir Clifford Allbutt (10 July)
1424. C. Moberly Bell (17 July)
1425. F. Mackenzie Bell
1426. Lucy (Mrs. W. K.) Clifford
1427. Stephen Collins (13 July)
1428. Montague Crackenthorpe
1429. Betty de la Pasture ("June 6")
1430. Austin Dobson (11 July)
1431. Sir George Douglas (12 July)
1432. A. Conan Doyle
1433. Alfred and Annie East
1434. Sir Robert Edgcumbe (13 August)
1435. Capt. Fisher, R.N.
1436. George Frampton
1437. Charles E. Gifford
1438. Edmund Gosse
1439. Lady Agnes Grove (23 July)
1440. Rider Haggard
1441. Austin Harrison
1442. Sir Robert Hart
1443. Anthony Hope Hawkins
1444. Florence Henniker
1445. Hubert von Herkomer (11 July)
1446. Maurice Hewlett
1447. Sir Robert Hudson (11 July)
1448. Sir Sidney Lee (11 July 1910)
1449. F. S. A. Lowndes (11 July)
1450. Seymour Lucas
1451. Vernon Lushington (12 July)
1452. Sir Frederick Macmillan
1453. J. Ellis McTaggart (12 July)
1454. Julia Maguire (19 July)
1455. Colonel MountBatten (11 July)
1456. Lady Dorothy Nevill
1457. Lord Northcliffe
1458. Alfred Parsons
1459. Sir Frederick Pollock
1460. Lady St. Helier
1461. T. Bailey Saunders (10 July)
1462. Thomas Seccombe
1463. Clement K. Shorter
1464. Evangeline F. Smith (21 July)
1465. William Strang
1466. Henry R. Tedder
1467. Sir Frederick Treves (11 July)
1468. G. Herbert Thring
1469. John Tussaud
1470. Theodore Watts-Dunton (20 July)
1471. Charles Whibley

1472. July 11: Col. Douglas Dawson informs Hardy the King will receive him on the 19th to invest him with the insignia of the Order of Merit.
1473. July 11: D. Lewis Poole invites Hardy to accept Honorary Life Membership in the Royal Societies Club.
1474. July 5: Hardy to his wife: is glad to hear she got home safely; tells her to put "O. M." *only* on the envelope after his name. Published in *Dearest Emmie*, pp. 91-92.
1475. July 18: Hardy to his wife: how he is managing without her at the London flat. Published in *Dearest Emmie*, pp. 92-93.
1476. July 19: Frank A. Hedgcock about calling at Max Gate.

1477. July 21: J. W. Fortescue, librarian at Windsor Castle, about having a portrait as "O. M." made for the King.
1478. July 22: William Strang wishes to arrange a sitting for a portrait of members of the Order of Merit.
1479. July 25: L. P. Jacks is opposed to the practice of sending out presentation copies of one's book.
1480. July 25: Strang thanks Hardy for being willing to sit for a portrait.
1481. July 27: Colonel Henry S. Legge about the Order of Merit.
1482. July 28: Sir William Crookes is sorry Hardy is not able to give a talk at the Royal Institution.
1483. August 5: Hardy to Clodd: typed transcript; a proposed visit to Aldeburgh.
1484. August 27: Florence Henniker about her recent reading; she recommends *A Man of Property* and asks who Mr. Galsworthy is.
1485. August 28: Judge J. S. Udal about his work on Dorset folklore.
1486. August 29: Jean-Marie Carré asks if Hardy has ever been attracted by Goethe, "and if not, why?"
1487. September 15: A. C. Bradley asks Hardy to be President of The English Association.
1488. September 20: Strang will be happy to come to Dorchester to paint the portrait of Hardy for the King.
1489. September 22: Maarten Martens sends his new book from Doorn, Holland.
1490. October 6: Nelson Gardner letter from New Jersey.
1491. October 6: Gustav Holst sends a musical setting of a poem. ("The Homecoming" was published in London by Stainer & Bell in 1913.)
1492. October 6: E. L. Ling, Mayor of Dorchester, about presenting Hardy with the Freedom of Dorchester.
1493. October 17: Blanche A. (Mrs. Montague) Crackanthorpe about the Hardy play, *The Mellstock Quire*, to be given by the Dorchester players, and about the fortunes of the *English Review*.
1494. October 24: Montague Crackanthorpe sends a copy of his article in the *Nineteenth Century*.
1495. October 24: Sir James Murray inquires about various Dorset words in Hardy's books.
1496. October 29: John Burrows about the survival of the custom of putting a man in the stocks.
1497. November 3: Valery Larbaud writes, in French, about *Tess*, *Jude* and *Time's Laughingstocks*. See Letter 1290.
1498. November 17: Sir James Crichton Browne invites Hardy to give a lecture at the Royal Institution.
1499. November 18: Charles E. Gifford congratulates Hardy on his being granted the Freedom of Dorchester.
1500. November 25: Alfred Noyes says his essay on Hardy's poetry is to appear in the *North American Review* soon. (It appeared in the July 1911 issue, pp. 96-105.)
1501. November 25: F. O. Saxelby asks consent to his preparing a Dictionary of Hardy's Characters and Places.
1502. November 29: Genevieve (Mrs. Champ) Clark, from Washington, D. C., where her husband is a Member of Congress, has been proclaiming she saw Hardy last summer. See Letter 1414.
1503. November 31: (*sic!*): Gosse about the *Mellstock Quire* play.

1504. December 5: Capt. Albert Gleaves regrets not having had Hardy visit the U.S.S. *North Dakota* when it was in Portland harbor.
1505. December 7: Angus Machlachlen about a musical setting for a poem by Hardy.
1506. December 8: Lyman A. Cotten thanks Hardy for an autographed copy of *The Dynasts* presented to the Ward Room Mess of the U.S.S. *Connecticut*.
1507. December 9: J. Cuthbert Hadden about church music.
1508. December 13: F. M. Cornford asks permission to call again at Max Gate. (He and Mrs. Cornford had called c. 28 January 1910.)
1509. December 19: Hardy to Florence Henniker: is glad she likes Miss Dugdale, who has recently been with her; praises Miss Dugdale's literary judgment, and closes with a happy Christmas.
1510. December 21: Angus Machlachlen about setting Hardy's poems to music.
1511. December 22: John E. Acland tells where the Bow stood in Dorchester. See Letter 1229.
1512. December 24: Hardy to Florence Henniker: recalls her luncheon in London (see Letter 1399). The publishers are going to reprint *Time's Laughingstocks*. (Hardy dated this letter merely "Christmas Eve," without naming the year. In making the typed transcript, now in the Museum at Dorchester, the year was assumed to be 1921, an error caused by ignoring the 1910 date in the text of the letter.)
1513. December 24: Madeleine Rolland thanks Hardy for his kindness to a pupil of hers.
1514. December 26: Hardy to Saxelby: rough draft, in pencil, of reply to Letter 1501.
1515. December 28: Saxelby gives details of his plan for a Hardy Dictionary.
1516. December 30: Saxelby gives further details of his plan.
1517. (n. d.): Lady Dorothy Nevill friendly note.
1518. (n. d.): May Sinclair tells Hardy book is coming to him [presumably a copy of her novel *The Creators*].

1911

1519. January 1: Sir Frederick Treves thanks Hardy for the gift of *The Dynasts* (published in one volume in November 1910).
1520. January 3: Saxelby about the possibility of including the *Poems* in the projected Hardy Dictionary.
1521. January 4: Hardy to Saxelby: rough draft, in pencil, warning him Hardy will accept no responsibility for the Hardy Dictionary.
1522. January 4: Prime Minister H. H. Asquith thanks Hardy for *The Dynasts*.
1523. January 6: Gustav Holst sends thanks for a gift from Hardy.
1524. January 14: A. R. Andrews about the Wessex Society of Manchester.
1525. January 18: Isaac Levine asks permission to set "To Life" to music.

MAX GATE CORRESPONDENCE

1526. January 28: Sir Harold Boulton about the Keats-Shelley Memorial Association.
1527. February 2: John Oliver asks about Sir John Moore's fiancée in *The Dynasts*. (Hardy's reply, dated 6 February 1911, published in *Hardy Letters At Colby*, pp. 85-86.)
1528. February 7: Hardy to Isaac Levine. rough draft, in pencil, signed "T. H.," of reply to Letter 1525; gives permission and asks for a copy of the musical setting.
1529. February 13: Prince Alexander George of Teck asks support of the Middlesex Hospital.
1530. February 22: Lady Ritchie (Thackeray's daughter) about the Jubilee of the *Cornhill*, of which her father was the first editor.
1531. March 13: Georges Bazile asks permission to make a French translation of one of Hardy's short stories.
1532. March 17: Hardy to Florence Henniker: refers to her brother's accident. Wishes he could be in London more but he gets influenza if he goes there.
1533. March 26. Emile Bergerat invites a testimonial on the centenary of Théophile Gautier.
1534. March 27: Alfred East, after an illness, thanks Hardy for his kind wishes.
1535. March 30: Hardy to Emile Bergerat: rough draft; reply to Letter 1533. Very glad to accept the invitation.
1536. April 3: Sir James Murray inquires about various Dorset words in Hardy's works.
1537. April 9: A. Herbert Evans about the possibility of his dramatizing *The Mayor of Casterbridge*, not for the Dorchester Dramatic Society but for professional presentation.
1538. April 13: Lord Curzon about an inaugural dinner.
1539. April 15: Darnkhanavola appreciation from Bombay.
1540. April 23: Hardy to A. H. Evans: rough draft, in pencil, unsigned but in Hardy's hand, of reply to Letter 1537. Would prefer not to have the dramatizing done unless he does it himself.
1541. April 23: Isaac Levine sends a copy of his musical setting for "To Life."
1542. May 3: Hardy to Florence Henniker: about his plans to be in London soon. He is pleased she liked "A Darkling Thrush" and "Rain on the Windows." He likes them, too.
1543. May 19: Lady Elizabeth Lewis invites Hardy to lunch.
1544. May 26: Hardy to Florence Henniker: has read her short story with interest. Could not call on her because he was getting a cold.
1545. May 30: J. B. Bury about superstitions in *The Woodlanders*.
1546. June 2: John Richmond sends birthday greetings.
1547. (n. d.): Alfred East says he has been away.
1548. June 5: Lady Elizabeth Lewis appreciates the gift of a book.
1549. June 10: Hardy, again in London, writes his last letter to his wife, "Dear E": he is going to the theatre with Mrs. Crackanthorpe, and he thinks Lady Lewis a very pleasant woman. Published in *Dearest Emmie*, p. 96.
1550. June 11. Hardy to Hamilton Fyfe: rough draft, unsigned but in Hardy's hand, of reply to a letter of 6 June 1911 (not preserved by Hardy) about Tolstoy's "proposed League of Thinkers."

CHRONOLOGICAL LIST

1551. June 13: John Galsworthy invites support of an appeal about the use of airplanes in war.
1552. June 13: Sir James Murray inquires about Dorset words in *Wessex Poems*.
1553. June 22: Isaac Levine sends a MS. copy of the musical setting for "To Life."
1554. June 28: Galsworthy thanks Hardy for a letter.
1555. July 9: Galsworthy sends a revised version of the "Memorial" protesting against the use of airplanes in war.
1556. July 11: Bruce L. Richmond would like to bicycle over from Shillingstone to lunch with Hardy.
1557. July 21: Yone Noguchi sends a book from Kamakura, Japan.
1558. August 1: W. Stebbing sends thanks from an early and constant admirer.
1559. August 2: Austin Harrison reports on another attack.
1560. August 4: Isaac Levine thanks Hardy for a letter.
1561. August 22: Hardy to Florence Henniker: reply to her letter about seeing the Coronation. He tells her the Macmillans are proposing an *edition de luxe*.
1562. September 9: Hardy to Saxelby, rough draft, in pencil, of letter returning the proofs of *A Thomas Hardy Dictionary* (London: Routledge, 1911).
1563. September 11: S. Valaskaki about Hardy's books from Cairo, Egypt.
1564. September 15: Gustav Holst thanks Hardy for permission to use the words (of "The Sergeant's Song"?) in another musical setting.
1565. September 20: George E. Moule is glad to have met Hardy once more. (They had been boys in Dorchester together.)
1566. September 28: Sydney C. Cockerell (who has not yet read any of Hardy's books) proposes to call on Hardy to ask if he has any manuscript that he would be willing to give the Fitzwilliam Museum at Cambridge.
1567. October 3: Hardy to Florence Henniker: about her reading, his views on marriage and divorce, and other matters.
1568. October 3: Cockerell about the gift of Hardy MSS. to the British Museum.
1569. October 6: Cockerell about the gift of other Hardy MSS. to other libraries.
1570. October 8: Cockerell about giving MSS. to Birmingham and Manchester.
1571. October 11: Hardy to Cockerell: rough draft; about the MSS. of the Wessex Novels; sends the remaining MSS. to Cockerell.
1572. October 12: Cockerell about giving the MS. of *The Trumpet-Major* to the Royal Library at Windsor Castle.
1573. October 13: Cockerell thanks Hardy for giving MSS. of *Jude* and *Time's Laughingstocks* to the Fitzwilliam Museum at Cambridge.
1574. October 13: Cockerell about giving various Hardy MSS. to various libraries.
1575. October 14: Gustav Holst has no hopes of having his songs published and Hardy may keep them as long as he likes.
1576. October 16: John W. Fortescue says the MS. of *The Trumpet-Major* will be a welcome accession to the Royal Library.

1577. October 18: F. G. Kenyon thanks Hardy for giving the British Museum the original MSS. of *Tess* and *The Dynasts*.
1578. October 19: John W. Fortescue writes that His Majesty accepts with much pleasure the gift of the MS. of *The Trumpet-Major*.
1579. October 19: F. Madan thanks Hardy for giving the original MS. of *Poems of the Past and the Present* to the Bodleian Library at Oxford.
1580. October 20: Cockerell reports on the gift to libraries of all the manuscripts Hardy sent him.
1581. October 20: Sir George Douglas thanks Hardy for his letter.
1582. October 24: Whitworth Wallis sends personal thanks for the gift of the MS. of *Wessex Poems* to the Birmingham Museum.
1583. October 27: Cockerell again about the gift of the MSS. to various libraries.
1584. November 2: John Masefield presents a poem to Hardy.
1585. November 11: Gordon Craig appreciation of Hardy's statement regarding his work.
1586. November 14: John E. Acland thanks Hardy for the gift of the MS. of *The Mayor of Casterbridge* to the Dorset County Museum.
1587. November 15: M. Anderson thanks Hardy for giving the original MS. of "An Imaginative Woman" to the Aberdeen University Library.
1588. November 16: Herbert Putnam to Sydney Cockerell acknowledging Hardy's gift of the original MS. of *A Group of Noble Dames* to the Library of Congress, Washington, D. C.
1589. November 17: Helen, Lady Ilchester enjoyed seeing Hardy's plays, *The Three Wayfarers* and *The Distracted Preacher*, in Dorchester the day before.
1590. November 23: H. Rider Haggard is glad Hardy likes the Mahatma.
1591. December 4: J. M. Barrie "was away" at a certain time.
1592. December 8: J. Meade Falkner praises *Time's Laughingstocks*.
1593. December 14: Henry Guppy sends thanks for the gift of the autograph MS. of "A Tragedy of Two Ambitions" to the John Rylands Library at Manchester.
1594. December 18: Edith (Mrs. Alfred) Lyttleton asks permission for several performances of *The Three Wayfarers*.
1595. December 25: Lady Elizabeth Lewis thanks Hardy for his sympathy on the death of her husband.
1596. December 31: Mrs. Dorothy Allhusen thanks Hardy for his Christmas thought of her.
1597. (n. d.): Sir Henry Newbolt has just read *Under the Greenwood Tree* again.
1598. (n. d.): John S. Sargent about pictures and birds.

1912

1599. (c. January 1): Lascelles Abercrombie has been commissioned to write a critical study of Hardy's work.
1600. January 6: Perriton Maxwell asks support of a move to change the law regarding marriage and divorce.

1601. January 8: Hardy to Maxwell: rough draft, in pencil, of reply to Letter 1600; he blames the present marriage laws for much of the misery of the community, and thinks "we live in a barbarous age."
1602. January 19: Josephine Preston Peabody wishes Hardy a Happy New Year and sends a copy of her book of poems, *The Singing Man*. (His letter of 7 February 1912 in reply is in the Houghton Library, Harvard University.)
1603. February 1: J. M. Barrie asks help in regard to censorship.
1604. February 7: Barrie again about censorship in the theatre.
1605. February 12: Barrie thanks Hardy for his letter.
1606. February 22: William Rothenstein sends a copy of Hammond's book on the last Peasant Revolt.
1607. **February 23:** Whitworth Wallis sends official thanks for the MS. of *Wessex Poems* given to the Birmingham Museum.
1608. March 2: Helen, Lady Ilchester invites Hardy to come and spend a day.
1609. March 18: Angus Machlachlen about setting Hardy's poems to music.
1610. March 25: William Dean Howells thanks Hardy for his letter about Howells' birthday. (Howells' letter quoted in *Hardy in America*, pp. 60-61.)
1611. March 26: Clarence W. McIlvaine acknowledges receipt of two MSS. ("The Abbey Mason" and *The Romantic Adventures of a Milkmaid*) bought by J. Pierpont Morgan, to be held for Mr. Morgan's arrival in London.
1612. April 3: Lady Ilchester has been ill but will shortly suggest a day for the proposed visit by Hardy.
1613. April 4: Lady St. Helier will be glad to have him call.
1614. April 21: Hardy to Florence Henniker: thanks for her gift of her new novel; is busy correcting proofs of a new edition of his books.
1615. April 30: Percy W. Ames informs Hardy the Royal Society of Literature has awarded him its Gold Medal.
1616. May 2: Hardy to Ames: rough draft; acknowledgment of Letter 1615.
1617. May 2: Thomas W. Hand solicits a MS. for the Leeds Public Library.
1618. May 3: Sydney C. Cockerell is disappointed that the usual honorary degrees are not to be given this year at Cambridge.
1619. May 6: Ames again about the Gold Medal Hardy is to receive.
1620. May 22: Hardy to Florence Henniker: is busy correcting proofs of twenty volumes.
1621. May 22: Lady Ilchester asks if the 28th or 29th would be convenient for a visit by Hardy.
1622. May 26: Lady Ilchester will see him on Tuesday (28th).
1623. May 29: Sir Henry Newbolt accepts an invitation to call at Max Gate and bring William Butler Yeats with him.
1624. May 29: W. B. Yeats informs Hardy he and Newbolt will arrive together.
1625. May 31: Newbolt appreciative letter.
1626. June 2: Frederic Harrison sends birthday greetings on Hardy's **72nd.**

1627. June 2: William Rothenstein sends birthday greetings.
1628. June 3: Theodore Watts-Dunton sends birthday greetings.
1629. June 4: E. S. Beesly about Hardy's 72nd birthday.
1630. June 4: John Morley about Hardy's "Plea for Pure English" as reported in *The Times*, 4 June 1912.
1031. June 12: James Gow presents a petition.
1632. June 21: Cockerell is going on a trip into Devonshire and will call on Hardy on Monday the 24th.
1633. June 21: Edmund Gosse says their friendship has lasted nearly forty years and it is very precious to him.
1634. June 21: Lillah McCarthy (Mrs. Granville-Barker) has been looking for [the MS. of] the play *Tess* and will send it back as soon as she finds it; regrets being unable to produce it.
1635. June 27: Arthur Compton-Rickett solicits an interview with a view to writing a book on Hardy's literary methods.
1636. (c. June 28): Hardy to Arthur Compton-Rickett: copy of reply to Letter 1635; he can lend no assistance and is unable to consent to interviews.
1637. July 1: Alice Balfour thanks Hardy for *The Dynasts*.
1638. July 4: Lady Ilchester invites Hardy to luncheon.
1639. July 8: Lady Ilchester fixes the time for Hardy's coming to luncheon.
1640. August 25: Walter Parrott about King George I.
1641. August 27: Sir Arthur Quiller-Couch is preparing an *Oxford Book Of Victorian Verse* and asks permission to include four poems by Hardy.
1642. August 31: B. F. Stevens & Brown ask information about the publication of *The Three Wayfarers*.
1643. September 1: Herbert C. Gorst, from Liverpool, in praise of the poem "God's Funeral."
1644. September 5: Sir Francis Darwin invites Hardy to spend a few days at Cambridge.
1645. September 7: A. C. Benson sends Mrs. Hardy a "thank you" note after a visit.
1646. September 15: Charles E. A. L. Rumbold about Sir T. Rumbold in *The Return of the Native*, III, VI.
1647. October 8: Frederic d'Erlanger tells Hardy the *Tess* opera has not proved a financial success.
1648. October 28: Miss Leonie Gifford sends thanks for a book.
1649. November 5: A. Symons about pumping from Sewage Tanks by the Town of Dorchester.
1650. November 6: Hardy to Symons: rough draft, in ink, signed "T. H.," of reply to Letter 1649.
1651. November 6: James Douglas solicits support in protesting against a "grave abuse." See *Later Years*, p. 152.
1652. November 10: Hardy to James Douglas: rough draft, in pencil, signed "T. H.," of reply to Letter 1651. Partly published in *Later Years*, p. 153.
1653. November 19: James Sully on Hardy's letter in *The Times* about "the biographical novel" (see Letter 1652).

Letters of sympathy and condolence, upon the death of Mrs. Emma Hardy, were received from at least 29 persons (letters from others are missing, for example, Mrs. Henniker's).

1654. Sir Clifford Allbutt
1655. Percy Ames (14 Dec.)
1656. Author's Club
1657. Squire Bancroft (30 Nov.)
1658. J. M. Barrie (9 Dec.)
1659. Mrs. Blanche Crackanthorpe
1660. Frederic d'Erlanger (2 Dec.)
1661. Sir George Douglas (29 Nov.)
1662. George Frampton (1 Dec.)
1663. Charles E. Gifford
1664. Florence Golland (30 Nov.)
1665. Ellen (Mrs. Edmund) Gosse (30 Nov.)
1666. Frederic Harrison (30 Nov.)
1667. Maurice Hewlett
1668. A. E. Housman
1669. "Betty" Lady Lewis
1670. Susan Lushington (1 Dec.)
1671. Sir Frederick Macmillan
1672. George Macmillan (29 Nov.)
1673. Helen (Mrs. Maurice) Macmillan
1674. Alfred Parsons
1675. Mary Lady St. Helier
1676. P. Schwartz (22 Dec.)
1677. William Serjeant
1678. Mary Sheridan
1679. Sir Frederick Treves (29 Nov.)
1680. William Watkins
1681. Sir William Watson (29 Nov.)
1682. Theodore Watts-Dunton (7 Dec.)

1683. November 30: James Sully about the new philosophy.
1684. (c. December 4): Lady St. Helier 3-page letter in supplement to her expression of sympathy on 29 November.
1685. December 17: Hardy to Florence Henniker: appreciates her writing to him, tells her about the death, and the dramatization of *The Trumpet-Major*.
1686. December 21: Hardy to Sir George Douglas: transcript (made by Florence E. Dugdale?) of letter about the death of Mrs. Hardy.
1687. December 22: Charles Whibley thanks Hardy for the afternoon he spent at Max Gate.
1688. December 28: Hardy to A. G. Symonds: rough draft, in pencil, of letter about the Dorchester Grammar School.
1689. December 30: Symonds acknowledges Hardy's letter of the 28th.

1913

1690. January 3: Hardy to A. G. Symonds: rough draft, in pencil, in Florence Dugdale's hand, of letter about the Dorchester Grammar School.
1691. January 13: Lady Ilchester sends sympathy upon Emma's death.
1692. January 14: Sir Frederick Pollock asks Hardy to second his son's nomination at the Athenaeum Club.
1693. January 19: George A. B. Dewar sends the *Saturday Review* with an article on "the Land Question."
1694. January 25: Madeleine Rolland recalls Mrs. Hardy's welcome when Mlle Rolland visited Max Gate.
1695. (c. January 26): F. Mabel Robinson about Hardy's bereavement.
1696. January 27: James Curle about excavations on the site of the Roman fort at Newstead, near Melrose, in Scotland.

MAX GATE CORRESPONDENCE

1697. January 27: Max Goschen asks permission to reprint four poems from *Time's Laughingstocks*.
1698. February 7: Symonds about the Dorchester Grammar School.
1699. February 11: F. Maddison invites a testimonial to Andrew Carnegie.
1700: February 13: Hardy to Maddison; rough draft, in pencil, signed "T. H.," of reply to Letter 1699; he approves and his name may be used.
1701. February 13: Violet Churchill, from the British Consulate in Amsterdam, says she and her husband want to see Hardy and shake his hand.
1702. March 11: K. Shinohara asks permission to include some of Hardy's stories in a Japanese schoolbook.
1703. March 31: John H. Dickinson about the restorations at St. Juliot Church in Cornwall.
1704. April 1: Joseph Geach quotes a price for making a wall tablet and hanging it in St. Juliot Church.
1705. April 1: Alfred Parsons about sketching Dorset scenes.
1706. April 7: Geach acknowledges receipt of Hardy's order for a wall tablet for the St. Juliot Church.
1707. April 15: The Rev. H. G. B. Cowley about Emma's tombstone in the Stinsford churchyard.
1708. April 16: J. Ellis McTaggart congratulates Hardy on being awarded a Litt.D. degree by Cambridge University.
1709. April 18: George, Lord Curzon invites support of a certain Fund.
1710. April 23: May Morris about a little barn at Little Oxwell.
1711. April 25: S. A. Donaldson invites Hardy to become an honorary Fellow of Magdalene College, Cambridge.
1712. May 14: Lady St. Helier invites Hardy to come to London and stay.
1713. May 17: W. Stebbing thanks Hardy for a birthday letter.
1714. May 19: Frank William George (Hardy's cousin) about applying for a call to the Bar.
1715. May 23. G. E. O'Dell asks permission to reprint the Stonehenge scene from *Tess*.
1716. May 30: Geach says the work of hanging the wall tablet at St. Juliot is completed.
1717. June 2: A. W. Ward invites Hardy to dinner at Cambridge.
1718. June 3: Dickinson again about the restoration at St. Juliot Church in Cornwall.
1719. June 4: Sir James Barrie responds to Hardy's letter of 3 June 1913 expressing pleasure at Barrie's being made a Baronet. (Hardy's letter, now in the Colby College Library, published in *Hardy Letters*, p. 96.)
1720. June 4: Edmund Gosse greets Hardy on his 73rd birthday.
1721. June 5: J. Montague Butler invites Hardy to dinner after receiving his honorary degree at Cambridge.
1722. June 7: Wilfrid Meynell sends a book of poems.
1723. June 9: A. C. Bradley forwards a request.
1724. June 12: Sir Sidney Colvin invites Hardy to dinner.
1725. June 17. Gosse has had a call from Henry James, who was pleased to have news of Hardy.
1726. June 29: Sydney C. Cockerell praises *The Dynasts*.

CHRONOLOGICAL LIST

1727. July 1: Margot Asquith invites Hardy to tea.
1728. July 3: Margot Asquith invites Hardy to lunch.
1729. July 4: Charles E. Gifford thanks Hardy for a photograph of the grave of his aunt, Emma Hardy.
1730. July 6: Hardy to Henry Stainsby: rough draft, typed, unsigned; gives permission to put his books, prose or verse, into Braille.
1731. July 7: Gifford thanks Hardy for a suggestion.
1732. July 7: Stainsby thanks Hardy for permission to reproduce his works in Braille.
1733. July 8: Florence Golland (Emma Hardy's cousin) thanks Hardy for a photograph of Emma's grave.
1734. July 10: W. T. Bradley thanks Hardy for the gift of the MS. of his poem about Swinburne to the Newnes Public Library at Putney.
1735. July 11: Cockerell about the gift of the MS. of Hardy's poem on Swinburne.
1736. July 11: Sidney Colvin accepts an invitation to visit Hardy at Max Gate.
1737. July 17: Colvin will arrive at Max Gate on Sunday, 20 July 1913.
1738. July 20: George A. B. Dewar is assuming the editorship of the *Saturday Review*.
1739. July 22: Sir Edward Elgar has been told that Hardy would consider working with him.
1740. July 22: John Lane invites Hardy to be his guest at Blandford.
1741. July 23: S. A. Donaldson has been elected an Hon. Fellow of Magdalene College.
1742. (c. July 29): Elgar about his efforts to work with Hardy.
1743. July 30: Arthur C. Benson congratulates Hardy on his election as Hon. Fellow of Magdalene College.
1744. July 30: Gosse thanks Hardy for the gift of the MS. of "Wessex Folk."
1745. August 10: Lord Portman replies to an inquiry.
1746. August 17: Sir George Douglas suggests Hardy write "some Reminiscences of Wessex Life."
1747. August 18: H. Rider Haggard letter of sympathy.
1748. August 20: Frederic Harrison asks Hardy to visit him at Bath.
1749. August 27: John E. Acland about the Town Pump and Obelisk erected in Dorchester in 1784.
1750. August 28: Douglas acknowledges a letter from Hardy.
1751. August 29: Acland is glad Hardy approves of his suggestion.
1752. August 30: W. Townley Searle solicits support of a plea for permission to give dramatic performances in public parks.
1753. (c. August 31): Hardy to Searle: he is unable to take part in Searle's suggestion.
1754. September 2: Stephen, Lord Coleridge asks permission to call at Max Gate on the 5th.
1755. September 6: Lord Coleridge apologizes for his failure to call.
1756. September 15: Hardy to F. A. Duneka, of Harper & Brothers: typed transcript; about terms for the publication of *A Changed Man*.
1757. September 17: H. Nagaoka, from Japan, asks permission to call at Max Gate.
1758. September 20: Frederic Harrison hopes to reach Dorchester at 1:35 on Monday the 22nd.

1759. September 21: Roma Green asks permission to set "Autumn in the Park" to music. (Hardy endorsed this letter, in pencil: "Permission given. Oct 11, '13".)
1760. September 26: George A. B. Dewar about "Ah, are you digging at my grave?"
1761. October 2: Logan Pearsall Smith sends a pamphlet about forming a Society for Pure English.
1762. (c. October 4): Hardy to Smith: rough draft of reply to Letter 1761: he is willing to have his name added to the list of members.
1763. October 9: Donaldson invites Hardy to come to Cambridge on 1 November 1913 for his induction as Hon. Fellow of Magdalene.
1764. October 9: Kurt Urlan, a German student who wishes to study the Dorset dialect, asks permission to call at Max Gate.
1765. October 14: Sydney M. Baber invites Hardy to attend a film showing of *Tess* at the Cinematograph Theatre in London on 21 October 1913.
1766. October 14: Sir Frederick Pollock will see Hardy's cousin, Frank George, next week.
1767. October 15: R. E. F. Maitland about painting a portrait of Hardy for Magdalene College.
1768. October 20: Sir James Murray asks about "tranter" and other Dorset words.
1769. October 23: Donaldson about Hardy's coming to Cambridge.
1770. October 25: Florence Henniker about *Tess;* thinks it is his major work.
1771. October 26: Murray thanks Hardy for his reply to Letter 1768.
1772. October 27: Frank W. George tells Hardy Pollock gave him the introduction he needed. See Letters 1714 and 1766.
1773. November 2: Hardy to Florence Henniker: glad she likes to have *A Changed Man,* and informs her he is now an "honorary Fellow" of General Henniker's College at Cambridge.
1774. November 4: A. E. Housman sends some ghost stories.
1775. November 5: A. C. Benson sends a copy of the *Cambridge Review.*
1776. November 8: Benson is glad Hardy approves of Maitland's portrait of him.
1777. November 8: Mary (Mrs. Algernon) Sheridan asks permission to call.
1778. November 9: The Marchioness of Londonderry has just read Hardy's *A Changed Man and Other Tales.*
1779. November 10: Frederic Harrison congratulates Hardy on the honorary Fellowship at Cambridge.
1780. November 18: Lady Ilchester thanks Hardy for his book. She hopes to see *The Woodlanders* played tomorrow.
1781. November 20: Florence Henniker is pleased Hardy wrote her from Cambridge; Magdalene must be proud to have him as a Fellow.
1782. November 21: Handley C. G. Moule, Bishop of Durham, sends a book.
1783. November 25: Thomas Barclay about honoring Anatole France.
1784. November 27: Lillian Gifford sends a lamp.
1785. December 8: John Lane proposes a new edition of Lionel Johnson's book, *The Art of Thomas Hardy.*
1786. December 16: Margot Asquith thinks Hardy is "the best living writer of English."

1787. December 17: Leon Bradzky about the lines of verse in *Under the Greenwood Tree.*
1788. (n. d.) Commander W. W. Fisher invites Hardy to bring Miss Dugdale to tea on board H.M.S. *St. Vincent* (in Portland Harbour?).
1789. December 21: Hardy to Florence Henniker: about his niece and Miss Dugdale taking care of his wants; with a Christmas greeting.
1790. (n. d.): Commander Fisher asks Hardy and Miss Dugdale to go to see his mother in Weymouth.

1914

1791. January 4: Hardy to Mrs. Cecil Popham: copy made in ink by Florence Dugdale, telling Mrs. Popham her father saw the soldiers come just as "described in the first chapter of *The Trumpet-Major.*"
1792. January 7: E. A. Ffooks about the Dorchester Grammar School.
1793. January 17: Florence Henniker sends thanks for the poem ("To Meet, or Otherwise") in the *Sphere* [20 December 1913]. Says it is sad but "there are beautiful lines in it."
1794. January 18. W. O. Beament invites Hardy to become an Honorary Member of a philosophical society at Selwyn College, Cambridge, (Beament erroneously dated his invitation "1913.")
1795. January 21: Hardy to Beament: rough draft, in pencil, signed "T. H.," of reply to letter 1794. He is happy to accede. (Clearly dated by Hardy "Jan. 21, 1914.")
1796. January 24: S. A. Donaldson invites Hardy to Cambridge for the celebration of the birthday of Samuel Pepys.
1797. January 24: B. F. Stevens & Brown ask permission to reprint *The Three Wayfarers.*
1798. January 25: Hardy to Stevens & Brown: rough draft, in pencil, for "F. D." (Florence Dugdale) to sign, of reply to Letter 1797; he does not want to publish *The Three Wayfarers* at present.
1799. February 5: Alida Lady Hoare asks help in behalf of animals.
1800. February 11: Hardy to Florence Henniker: he was married to Florence Dugdale yesterday.

Congratulations and Best Wishes on his second marriage (10 February 1914) were written to Hardy on 11 February or the later date indicated by these 17 persons:

1801. Sir Clifford Allbutt (16 Feb.)
1802. Arthur C. Benson (25 Feb.)
1803. Stephen Lord Coleridge (12 Feb.)
1804. Sir George Douglas
1805. Kate Gifford
1806. Edmund Gosse
1807. Lady Agnes Grove
1808. Frederic Harrison (13 Feb.)
1809. Florence Henniker
1810. "Betty" Lady Lewis
1811. Sir Frederick Macmillan
1812. George Macmillan (12 Feb.)
1813. Helen (Mrs. Maurice) Macmillan (16 Feb.)
1814. F. Mabel Robinson
1815. Mary, Lady St. Helier
1816. William Strang
1817. Sir Frederick Treves (14 Feb.)

1818. February 19: Dowager Lady Ilchester about the journals of Lady Susan O'Brien.

1819. February 26: Dowager Lady Ilchester again about the O'Brien journals.
1820. March 9: Hardy to Florence Henniker: about his marriage to Florence Dugdale; he was "lonely and helpless" after his wife (Emma) died.
1821. March 13. Hardy to Mr. Hankey: transcript of letter written from the Athenaeum Club, London, about cruelty to animals.
1822. March 20: Florence Henniker is glad to have some verses Hardy sent her, and she praises Florence Dugdale.
1823. March 21: Frederic Harrison critical comment on Henry James.
1824. March 24: Dowager Lady Ilchester again about the O'Brien journals.
1825. March 24: Shudscanoff appreciation from Turkey.
1826. March 29: Sydney C. Cockerell is pleased with 'The Year's Awakening' in *The New Weekly.*
1827. April 21: Margaret ("Maggie"), Lady Herkomer thanks Hardy for letter of sympathy after her husband's death.
1828. April 26: J. Ellis McTaggart invites Hardy to lunch.
1829. May 5: Mary G. Creczowska asks permission to translate *Far from the Madding Crowd* and *Jude* into Polish.
1830. May 6: Phil Aronstein sends an article from Berlin, and asks permission to reprint certain poems.
1831. May 11: James Stanley Little about the Shelley Memorial.
1832. May 26: Frederic Harrison asks help in commemorating the seventh centenary of the birth of Roger Bacon.
1833. (c. May 31): Harrison again about the Bacon centenary.
1834. June 1: Lord Curzon sends birthday greetings.
1835. June 8: W. H. Grattan Flood sends a copy of the words and music of a ballad Hardy quotes partly in *Under The Greenwood Tree.*
1836. (c. June 10): Hardy to Flood: rough draft; he may set to music any of Hardy's lyrics.
1837. June 18: Harrison again about the Roger Bacon centenary.
1838. June 10: Florence Henniker sends late birthday wishes.
1839. June 11: Hardy to Florence Henniker: about his motoring to Plymouth with Mrs. Hardy.
1840. June 13. Sidney Colvin solicits help in determining what part of the southern coast of England Keats visited on his voyage to Italy.
1841. June 16: Colvin thanks Hardy for suggesting Lulworth as the place Keats went ashore.
1842. June 16: Dowager Lady Ilchester again about the O'Brien journals.
1843. June 23: Hall Caine thanks Hardy for his contribution and is glad Hardy wrote it in his own hand.
1844. June 24: Israel Gollancz about celebrating the Shakespeare Tercentenary in 1916.
1845. June 25: Lord Bryce invites Hardy to attend a meeting on the Shakespeare Tercentenary.
1846. July 6: Clouderley Brereton says Hardy is kind to have written on her verses.
1847. July 11: Florence Henniker hopes Hardy had a nice time with Lady St. Helier.
1848. July 17: Hardy to Florence Henniker: refers to the poems he wrote just after Emma died; expresses concern for fear he had

not treated her as well as he might have in her later life, and says he will publish these poems as amends.

1849. July 28: Colvin about Keats's landing on the coast of Devonshire.
1850. August 2: Wilkinson Sherren replies to Hardy's question about where the old theatre at Weymouth used to stand.
1851. August 21: Cockerell feels honored at being asked to be one of Hardy's literary executors—a function he exercised until 1962.
1852. August 27: Frederic Harrison about his visit to Paris and Switzerland.
1853. August 28: Hardy to Edward Clodd: transcript of letter referring to the War atmosphere, etc.
1854. August 29: Robert Lynd solicits an article on the war for the *Daily News*, on "England and the Last Great War" in case Hardy prefers not to write on the present one.
1855. August 30: Cockerell description of Paris and France at the end of the first month of the World War.
1856. August 31: Sir Claud Schuster about organizing a campaign to combat Germany's attempts to influence public opinion in neutral countries.
1857. September 9: Schuster again about the campaign to influence public opinion.
1858. September 10: Hardy to Schuster: rough draft of reply to Letter 1857.
1859. September 11: Edmund Gosse tells Hardy his poem ["Song of the Soldiers," in *The Times*, 9 September 1914] touched him deeply.
1860. September 15: F. A. Duneka, of Harper & Brothers, praises the "Song of the Soldiers," and expresses "the sympathy and good will of all the American people."
1861. September 22: Schuster again about his campaign to influence public opinion in neutral countries.
1862. September 25: Harley Granville-Barker asks if Hardy would like a production of *The Dynasts*.
1863. September 27: Hardy to Granville-Barker: would be much interested in a production of *The Dynasts* at Barker's theatre; rough draft, and also a typed transcript (either made by Florence Hardy, or, more likely, supplied by Howard Bliss) of the original letter.
1864. September 28: Hardy to Duneka: typed transcript of reply to Letter 1860. He has not heard from Harpers about *The Dynasts*.
1865. September 28: Granville-Barker thanks Hardy for consenting to a production of Scenes from *The Dynasts*.
1866. (c. October 1): Charles F. A. Masterman thanks Hardy for his letter.
1867. October 5: Masterman about *The Dynasts*, and thanks Hardy again.
1868. October 8: D. R. Landesberger is amazed Hardy has little esteem for Nietzsche.
1869. October 10: F. R. Yerbury invites Hardy to read a paper on Rheims Cathedral at a meeting of the Architectural Association.
1870. (n. d.): Hardy to Yerbury: rough draft, in pencil, in the hand of Florence E. Hardy, of reply to Letter 1869: Hardy is unable to give an address at the meeting.
1871. October 13: Granville-Barker about the matter of copyright involved in producing *The Dynasts*.

1872. October 14: Hall Caine about literary matters and the war.
1873. October 15: Hardy to Granville-Barker: typed transcript of letter sending Barker some lines to be used in *The Dynasts*.
1874. October 18: Amy Lowell autograph letter about the day (1 August 1914) she and a friend arrived at Hardy's door.
1875. October 21: Hardy to Granville-Barker: about the program for the production of *The Dynasts*. (Two copies; a rough draft in pencil and a typed transcript.)
1876. October 28: Hardy to Barker: again about the program for *The Dynasts* production.
1877. October 28: Caine asks permission to reproduce Hardy's photograph in *King Albert's Book*.
1878. (c. October 31): J. F. Symons-Jeune supplies some information.
1879. November 1: Florence Henniker about Hardy's poem, "Song of the Soldiers."
1880. November 2: A. C. Benson thanks Hardy for his letter about Benson's brother.
1881. November 10: Ester Sutro (Mrs. Alfred Sutro) invites Hardy to tea and asks about a musical setting composed by her nephew.
1882. (c. November 11): Hardy to Mrs. Sutro: rough draft; her nephew may publish without charge.
1883. November 11: Prime Minister Asquith thanks Hardy for his suggestions about recruiting.
1884. November 12: Sir C. P. Ibert inquires about a historical point connected with the Militia.
1885. November 18: A. E. Drinkwater asks about filming a performance of *The Dynasts* for cinema use later on.
1886. (c. November 19): Hardy to Drinkwater: rough draft of reply to Letter 1885: thinks the idea is a good one.
1887. November 19: John Masefield thanks Hardy for the gift of *Satires of Circumstance* and praises his poetry.
1888. November 21: Lord Crewe thanks Hardy for *Satires of Circumstance*.
1889. November 21: Alfred Sutro thanks Hardy for his letter.
1890. November 22: Cockerell praises Hardy's new book of poems.
1891. November 24: Margot Asquith thanks Hardy for his note.
1892. November 25: Kate Gifford thanks Hardy for *Satires of Circumstance*.
1893. November 25: Edmund Gosse praises Hardy's recent poems.
1894. November 25: Lady St. Helier invites Hardy to visit.
1895. November 26: Masefield is grateful for the pleasure of seeing *The Dynasts* at the theatre.
1896. November 27: A. C. Benson thanks Hardy for a copy of his new poems.
1897. November 27: A. E. Housman thanks Hardy for the gift of his poems.
1898. November 27: "Rosalind Travers" (Mrs. H. M. Hyndman) invites Hardy to call.
1899. November 28: Florence Henniker is grateful for a volume of Hardy's poems.
1900. November 29: Henry Ainley asks Hardy to autograph a copy of *The Dynasts*.

CHRONOLOGICAL LIST 103

1901. November 29: Sir Frederick Macmillan has seen *The Dynasts* and enjoyed it.
1902. November 30: Hardy to Clodd: transcript; about Granville-Barker's production of *The Dynasts*.
1903. December 4: Sir Frederick Pollock saw *The Dynasts* recently and thought it brilliant.
1904. December 5: Elizabeth Asquith asks for a contribution to an album in aid of the Arts Fund.
1905. December 5: Ethel Clifford Dilke after seeing *The Dynasts*.
1906. December 9: W. A. M. Goode solicits a contribution. (Hardy sent two stanzas called "An Appeal to America on Behalf of the Belgian Destitute.")
1907. December 10: George A. B. Dewar about Hardy's new volume of poems.
1908. December 11: Lascelles Abercrombie writes again.
1909. December 16: Ellinor Lady Grogan praises the performance of *The Dynasts*.
1910. December 16: Dr. C. W. Saleeby about *The Dynasts*.
1911. December 17: Mrs. Dorothy Allhusen went to see *The Dynasts*.
1912. December 18: Charles Whibley thanks Hardy for *Satires of Circumstance*.
1913. December 20: Edward Clodd, like Hardy, has recently married.
1914. December 21: Elizabeth Asquith thanks Hardy for sending her (in answer to Letter 1904) "A Jingle on the Times."
1915. December 23: Hardy to Florence Henniker: he and his wife went to London to see *The Dynasts* and found it more impressive than he had expected.
1916. December 28: C. W. Saleeby about *The Dynasts* and militarism.
1917. December 29: Saleeby about *The Dynasts* and Bergson's *élan vital*.

1915

1918. January 2: A. C. Benson thanks Hardy for his letter.
1919. January 5: Sir Hama Thornycroft about *The Dynasts*.
1920. January 11: Valentina Capocci inquires about an Italian translation of *Tess*.
1921. January 13: Edith Holman-Hunt about her interest in *The Dynasts*.
1922. January 17: Virginia (Mrs. Leonard) Woolf tells Hardy his poem to her father, Leslie Stephen, touched her deeply. She also calls *Satires of Circumstance* "remarkable."
1923. (c. January 18?): Hardy to Lady St. Helier: typed transcript (supplied by Howard Bliss?); about his illnesses.
1924. January 19: Mrs. Dorothy Allhusen expresses sympathy in Hardy's illness.
1925. January 19: Esmé Beringer about the effect of *The Dynasts* on her.
1926. January 21: Vere E. Cotton sends a print of Magdalene College, Cambridge.
1927. February 2: Hardy to Dr. C. W. Saleeby: rough draft, in pencil, unsigned, of reply to letter of 29 December 1914 about Bergson,

Herbert Spencer, etc. (This reply later revised by Hardy and both versions of the letter published in *Later Years*, pp. 167-168, 270-272.)
1928. February 6: Mrs. Blanche Crackanthorpe about having seen *The Dynasts* before it closed on 30 January 1915.
1929. February 8: Amy Lowell has *Satires of Circumstance* at last.
1930. February 12: Commander W. W. Fisher, from on board H.M.S. *St. Vincent*, gives an account of a naval engagement.
1931. February 19: Frank Theodore has recently read *Tess*.
1932. February 21: Bruce L. Richmond about calling at Max Gate.
1933. February 22: J. S. Furley invites Hardy to give an address at the College at Winchester.
1934. February 22: Harper & Brothers about the MS. of "A Hundred Years Since."
1935. February 23: Thornycroft wants to model a head of Hardy.
1936. February 25: Furley regrets Hardy's inability to come to Winchester.
1937. February 26: John H. Dickinson about restorations at St. Juliot Church in Cornwall.
1938. February 26: Thornycroft proposes various dates for modeling a head of T. H. (Hardy selected 20 April 1915).
1939. (n. d.): Mrs. Winnie Fairweather, from South Australia, of her reading about Scenes from *The Dynasts* in Adelaide.
1940. March 2: Dowager Lady Ilchester, from London, about the O'Brien journals.
1941. March 10: The Marchioness of Londonderry thanks Hardy for writing on the death of her husband.
1942. March 15: Helen, Lady Ilchester thanks Hardy for his letter of sympathy on the death of her father.
1943. March 15: Charles Whibley agrees with Hardy about the war.
1944. March 17: Saleeby accepts an invitation to Dorchester.
1945. March 17: Sir William Watson comments on Hardy's praise.
1946. March 18: Edward Thomas asks permission to quote a poem.
1947. March 20: W. H. Davies praises *Time's Laughingstocks*.
1948. March 20: Sir Evelyn Wood asks Hardy to forward a letter to Major Hannay.
1949. March 21: Edward Thomas thanks Hardy for permission to quote.
1950. March 23: Hardy to Florence Henniker: comments on the war; and Mrs. Hardy has been ill with sciatica.
1951. March 25: Thomas thanks Hardy again for permission to quote.
1952. March 27: Editor Brougham asks for revised texts of Hardy's war writings that he is willing to see appear again. (Hardy responded on 29 April 1915.)
1953. March 31: Florence Henniker about the war.
1954. April 4: Hardy to Lady St. Helier: copy of a letter about calling on her in London (presumably supplied by Howard Bliss).
1955. April 4: Frank W. George has been attached to the 5th Dorset regiment.
1956. April 7: Sir George Douglas is pleased to receive news of Hardy.
1957. April 9: Sidney Colvin sends some reminiscences of old Mrs. Procter about Keats, Hazlitt, and others.
1958. (c. April 12): Thornycroft proposes coming to Max Gate on 20 April 1915 to model Hardy's head.
1959. April 14: William Rothenstein would like to call.

1960. (c. April 21): Rothenstein is going to call the next day.
1961. April 24: Dowager Lady Ilchester, from Dorset, about the O'Brien journals.
1962. April 30: Hardy to Lady St. Helier: typescript copy (supplied by Howard Bliss?); regrets inability to accept her invitation.
1963. April 30: John Cowper Powys sends a book of essays, one of which is about Hardy.
1964. (c. May 1?): Lady St. Helier invites Florence Hardy to stay at her house.
1965. May 2: Harold Child asks permission to come to Max Gate to listen to Hardy talk about his life and work, in preparation for a book about Hardy in the series "Writers of the Day."
1966. May 5: Grant Watson appreciation.
1967. (c. May 8): Hardy to Florence Henniker: invites her to meet him at Lady St. Helier's in London.
1968. May 8: Child again about the book on Hardy.
1969. May 8: John Drinkwater sends his new book of poems and also a short play of his, and says he has seen a performance of *The Dynasts*.
1970. (c. May 20): Hardy to Florence Henniker: he is living near a large Cavalry Camp and hears reveille at 5 in the morning.
1971. May 23. Florence Henniker asks for a testimonial about a German maid of hers who may be interned or deported.
1972. May 23: J. F. Symons-Jeune thanks Hardy for a letter of sympathy.
1973. May 25: Hardy to Florence Henniker: sends the testimonial she requested and says he dislikes being in London.
1974. May 31: Hardy to Lady St. Helier: typed transcript (supplied by Howard Bliss?); is sending a scarce reprint for her Red Cross Sale.
1975. June 1: Dowager Lady Ilchester about the O'Brien journals.
1976. June 1: John Cowper Powys about Hardy's poetry.
1977. June 2: Mary (Mrs. Algernon) Sheridan sends birthday greetings on Hardy's 75th.
1978. June 5: H. C. MacIlvaine asks permission to arrange *The Dynasts* for cinema filming.
1979. June 12: Percy Withers thanks Hardy for his signature to an appeal on behalf of Abercrombie.
1980. June 17: Maurice Macmillan about calling at Max Gate.
1981. June 19: Paul Lamboth invites Hardy to be a patron for a lecture by Maurice Maeterlinck, for benevolent purposes, in London.
1982. June 21: Lamboth thanks Hardy for accepting his invitation of the 19th.
1983. June 28: Gertrude L. E. G. Cecil invites Mrs. Hardy for a weekend visit.
1984. July 4: Sir James Wilson about *Notes* on the New Forest Dialect.
1985. July 16: Thornycroft about modeling Hardy's head.
1986. July 21: Henry James solicits the contribution of a poem to Edith Wharton's book.
1987. July 27: W. M. Flinders Petrie asks permission to call at Max Gate.
1988. July 28: James repeats his request for a poem for Mrs. Wharton's book. (On 8 August 1915 Hardy sent the "Cry of the Homeless.")

1989. August 9: Mrs. Wharton thanks Hardy for his contribution to *The Book of the Homeless.*
1990. August 10: James thanks Hardy for the "Cry of the Homeless."
1991. August 12: Captain Stair A. Gillon is off to the Dardanelles.
1992. August 12: Mrs. Wharton again thanks Hardy for his contribution to *The Book of the Homeless.*
1993. August 13: Lieut. Frank George, from Gallipoli.
1994. August 18: Lt. George to his mother: his last letter from Gallipoli, where he was killed in action four days later.
1995. August 24: Brigadier-General Cathcart Hannay about the death of his cousin, Lt. George.
1996. August 26: John Galsworthy thanks Hardy for his letter and refers to ghastly business of the war.
1997. September 1: Charles E. A. L. Rumbold solicits another Wessex novel on the lines of *The Trumpet-Major.*
1998. September 2: Hardy to Florence Henniker: about the death of Lt. George.
1999. September 2: Shudscanoff appreciation, from Turkey.
2000. September 3: James P. Grieves asks for particulars about the death of Lt. George.
2001. September 6: W. L. Courtney solicits a poem for publication in the *Fortnightly Review.*
2002. September 14: Dorothy (Mrs. Cecil) Hanbury thanks Hardy for a copy of *Under the Greenwood Tree.*
2003. September 14: Sir Evelyn Wood thanks Hardy for telling him about the death of Lt. George.
2004. September 21: Sir Ray Lankester would like to call.
2005. September 25: Captain Gillon war-time letter from the Dardenelles.
2006. September 29: Dorothy (Mrs. Cecil) Hanbury thanks Hardy for his signed photo.
2007. September (?): Sir Frederick Pollock thanks Hardy for his support.
2008. October 6: Hardy to G. Herbert Thring: rough draft, in pencil, unsigned, of letter in response to Thring's inquiry (now missing) regarding a congratulatory letter to Henry James. Hardy proposes the letter be drawn up and sent to him to sign. (This proposal was carried out; Hardy's signature, as President of the Society of Authors, was added to the letter drawn up in London; it is now in the Houghton Library, Harvard University.)
2009. October 9: Dorothy Shapcote asks about the Giffords, the family of the first Mrs. Hardy.
2010. October 13: Mary (Mrs. Algernon) Sheridan thanks Hardy for his words of sympathy on the death of her son.
2011. (c. October 15): Hardy to Lady St. Helier: typed transcript (supplied by Howard Bliss?); he has a cold.
2012. October 22: Israel Gollancz solicits a contribution to the book planned for the Shakespeare Tercentenary in 1916.
2013. October 28. Robert P. Porter solicits a contribution to the Recruiting Supplement of the London *Times.*
2014. October 29: Hardy to Gollancz: rough draft, in pencil, signed "T. H.," of reply to Letter 2012; will bear in mind the request (that he considers an honor.)

2015. (c. October 29): Hardy to Porter: rough draft of reply to Letter 2013; suggests a certain passage in the eleventh book of the *Aeneid* is appropriate to the recruiting movement when a change of a few words is made.
2016. (n. d.): Thornycroft, having completed the modeling of Hardy's head, writes about books, art, and other subjects.
2017. November 2: F. H. Waters solicits a brief resumé of *Far from the Madding Crowd* for use on the program for a showing of the Turner Films version of the novel at the West End Cinema in London on 16 November.
2018. (c. November 3): Hardy to Waters: rough draft of a 450-word synopsis of *Far from the Madding Crowd*. It was printed in the program for the showing of the film at the West End Cinema on 16 November.
2019. November 3: A. C. Benson is glad to have a letter from Hardy.
2020. November 5: Hardy to MacIlvaine: rough draft of reply to Letter 1978; denied the permission asked for.
2021. November 5: Sir Oliver Lodge thanks Hardy for accepting his pamphlet.
2022. November 6: Dowager Lady Ilchester from London about the O'Brien journals.
2023. November 10: K. Amy Turner asks permission to quote from Hardy's works.
2024. November (?): Hardy to Lady St. Helier: rough draft; accepts invitation to stay at her house.
2025. November 21: Benson thanks Hardy for his letter.
2026. November 21: Captain Gillon war-time letter from the Mediterranean area.
2027. November 28: Sir George Douglas sympathy on the death of Hardy's sister Mary.
2028. December 7: Sydney C. Cockerell about the death of Hardy's sister Mary.
2029. December 17: Robert Nichols sends a book.
2030. December 22: Harold Bolce asks for help in war propaganda.
2031. December 26: Hardy to Bolce: rough draft of reply to Letter 2030; encloses two paragraphs (both from *The Dynasts*) that may serve the purpose.
2032. December 29: G. Levenson Gower writes about the Keats-Shelley Memorial.
2033. December 31: George A. B. Dewar about the poem on Beeny Cliff and other poems.
2034. December 31: Edmund Gosse is worried about Henry James's health.

1916

2035. January 5: Sir Claud Schuster about a manifesto aimed at influencing public opinion in Spain.
2036. January 6: G. Herbert Thring asks Hardy (as President of the Society of Authors) to sign a letter congratulating Henry James on his admission to the Order of Merit. (Hardy complied; the letter is now in the Houghton Library, Harvard University.)

2037. January 7: Schuster thanks Hardy for his reply to Letter 2035.
2038. January 18: Sir Hama Thornycroft about the bronze head of Hardy modeled in April 1915.
2039. January 26: W. M. Flinders Petrie solicits Hardy's signature on a letter to the London *Times*.
2040. January 29: Harold Child is sending a copy of his book, *Thomas Hardy* (London: Nisbet, 1916), with a Bibliography by Arundell Esdaile.
2041. January 30: Mrs. Blanche Crackanthorpe sends Hardy some war news.
2042. January 31: Edmund Gosse asks for a gift of books for a Red Cross sale.
2043. January 31: Siegfried Sassoon asks permission to dedicate a book of poems to Hardy.
2044. February 1: William Rothenstein asks permission to make a new drawing of Hardy for a set of portraits to be published by Harold Munro.
2045. February 4: Harriet Monroe cables from Chicago to ask permission to include some of Hardy's poems in an anthology of *New Poetry*.
2046. February 4: Hardy to Monroe: he has no objection.
2047. February 6: Hardy to Monroe: rough draft, in pencil, unsigned but in Hardy's hand, of further reply to Letter 2045; asks her to add "When I Set out for Lyonnesse" to the poems to be included in her anthology.
2048. February 7: Israel Gollancz solicits a contribution to a *Book of Homage to Shakespeare*.
2049. February 10: Rothenstein is going to call on the following day.
2050. February 15: Edith Wharton sends a copy of *The Book of the Homeless* containing Hardy's poem.
2051. February 18: Gollancz thanks Hardy for his poem written in response to Letter 2048.
2052. February 18: Rothenstein thanks Hardy for his help in the drawings; had found Hardy a difficult subject.
2053. February 19: The Marchioness of Londonderry sends a photograph of her picture by Sargent.
2054. February 23: Sydney C. Cockerell about a proposed Bibliography of Hardy's works by Henry Danielson.
2055. February 24: Sassoon tells Hardy the book of his poems will be sent soon.
2056. February 26: Cockerell about a committee of Hardy ?rary executors.
2057. March 2: Muriel Stuart sends a volume of her poems.
2058. (c. March 3): Hardy to Muriel Stuart: rough draft, in Hardy's hand; acknowledges her volume of verse and tells her some of the poems are "promising."
2059. March 3: Sir Frederick Macmillan has just returned from the funeral of Henry James.
2060. March 5: Lillian Gifford about seeing the film of *Far from the Madding Crowd* in a London cinema.
2061. March 14: Edmund Gosse asks for a book or a manuscript for a Red Cross sale.
2062. March 24: H. B. Middleton on his marriage in a church in Chilton Canfield in which Hardy "had a hand."

2063. March 27: Galsworthy about *The Dynasts*.
2064. (c. March 31): Galsworthy thanks Hardy for a letter.
2065. April 17: Thring acknowledges receipt of a letter from Hardy.
2066. April 21: Captain S. A. Gillon war-time letter from the Mediterranean area.
2067. April 28: Thornycroft about his bronze head of Hardy.
2068. May 10: Henry W. Tyler, from Boston, Mass., has been elected a Foreign Honorary Member of the American Academy of Arts and Sciences.
2069. May 15: W. Lock invites Hardy to visit him at Keble College, Oxford.
2070. May 27: Arthur Compton-Rickett asks permission to quote a letter from Hardy.
2071. May 28: Florence Henniker about the war.
2072. May 28: J. L. Reayner about a production of scenes from *The Dynasts* at Weymouth.
2073. (c. May 29): Hardy to Reayner: rough draft of reply to Letter 2072.
2074. May 29: E. H. Blakeney asks permission to quote from Hardy's Shakespeare poem.
2075. June 1: Arthur J. G. Russell has received help and pleasure and enlightenment from Hardy's works.
2076. June 2: Lord Curzon is pleased Hardy remembered him.
2077. June 5: J. F. Symons-Jeune sends belated good wishes for Hardy's 76th birthday.
2078. June 6: Constance, Countess of Shaftesbury asks permission for a performance of scenes from *The Dynasts* at Poole in the autumn.
2079. June 6: Thring on Hardy's proposal that the Society of Authors act as Literary Executors.
2080. June 7: Edward D. Brooks, of Minneapolis, Minnesota, sends a check for five pounds and requests a signed autograph copy of the poem "To Meet or Otherwise."
2081. June 11: The Countess of Shaftesbury sends thanks for the permission requested in Letter 2078.
2082. June 12: The Countess of Shaftesbury thanks Hardy for his letter.
2083. June 17: Frederic Harrison is grateful for Hardy's message after the death of Mrs. Harrison.
2084. June 21: B. Fossett Lock has received a letter from the American Ambassador which was very helpful.
2085. June 23: Alan Laurie reports Hardy's play was a success at Weymouth.
2086. June 24: Robert S. Comber, Mayor of Weymouth, thanks Hardy for his interest in the local effort for the Red Cross work.
2087. June 28: Hardy to Florence Henniker: the Wessex Scenes from *The Dynasts* were performed at Weymouth by the Dorchester players.
2088. July 2: Captain Gillon war-time letter.
2089. July 3: Mrs. Genevieve Bennett Clark from Washington, D. C., is grateful for Hardy's books.
2090. July 3: Clement K. Shorter solicits Hardy's signature on a petition Conan Doyle has drawn up.

2091. July 7: Hardy to Clement Shorter: rough draft of reply to Letter 2090; he cannot attempt to interfere with the government in its treatment of Irish rebels.
2092. July 9: Austin Philips is grateful to Hardy for allowing him to call last November.
2093. July 17: Thring tells Hardy his proposal that the Society of Authors act as Literary Executors would involve an expense of something under £100.
2094. (c. July 18): Hardy to Thring: rough draft, in Hardy's hand, of reply to Letter 2093: has requested his executors (Sydney Cockerell and Florence Hardy) to consult the Society of Authors in the event of any difficulty.
2095. July 18: C. W. Saleeby solicits support in a movement to suspend all Liquor Traffic during the war.
2096. July 25: George A. Macmillan thanks Hardy for a birthday gift.
2097. July 25: Captain Gillon another war-time letter from the Mediterranean area.
2098. July 28: Brigadier-General John H. Morgan asks permission to call.
2099. July 31: Thornycroft, who did the bronze head of Hardy in April 1915, again.
2100. August 4: Thornycroft discusses books, art, etc.
2101. August 10: J. W. Mackail sends a "little thing" of his own.
2102. August 11: Eneas MacKay asks Hardy to sign an etched portrait of him by William Strang for sale in support of the Red Cross Fund.
2103. August 13: Hardy to MacKay: rough draft of reply; agrees, for the two guineas offered in Letter 2102, to go to the Red Cross headquarters and sign the portrait.
2104. August 15: Captain Gillon another war-time letter.
2105. August 21: J. L. Garvin about his son's death in the war.
2106. August 26: Dorothy (Mrs. Cecil) Hanbury thanks Hardy for his generous cheque for the Supply Depot.
2107. August 28: F. W. Slater, of Harper & Brothers, inquires about the announcement of a Bibliography of his works prepared by Mrs. Hardy.
2108. August 29: J. W. Mackail about Hardy's comment on Iago.
2109. August 30: Hardy to Slater: rough draft; is puzzled by his trouble getting published in an American newspaper.
2110. September 4: John H. Dickinson about a sketch made by the first Mrs. Hardy at St. Juliot in Cornwall.
2111. September 4: Florence Henniker again about her German servant girl and the war. See Letter 1971.
2112. September 4: Hardy to Florence Henniker: he proposes to make a trip to Cornwall to see the tablet erected in St. Juliot Church to Emma; the Macmillans are going to include a selection from his poems in their Golden Treasury series.
2113. September 4: Jean Jullien, from Paris, offers Hardy honorary membership in the Société des Gens de Lettres.
2114. September 6: Josephine Preston Peabody about *The Dynasts*.
2115. September 16: Hardy to Jullien: rough draft, in pencil, unsigned but in Hardy's hand, of reply to Letter 2113: accepts the honor.

CHRONOLOGICAL LIST

2116. September 27: Brooks thanks Hardy for the MS. solicited in Letter 2080.
2117. October 5: Humphry Ward asks Hardy to contribute an article on William Barnes to Volume 5 of Ward's *English Poets*.
2118. October 6: A. C. Benson invites Hardy to Cambridge.
2119. October 6: Thornycroft about art, books, etc.
2120. October 13: Harriet Monroe acknowledges Hardy's help and names the poems to be included in the anthology about which she wrote in Letter 2045.
2121. October 14: Benson thanks Hardy for his book.
2122. October 14: Ward thanks Hardy for being willing to write about William Barnes.
2123. October 15: H. J. C. Grierson acknowledges from Edinburgh the gift of Hardy's *Selected Poems* (published 3 October 1916) and generously praises the volume.
2124. October 16: Sir Arthur Quiller-Couch about *Selected Poems*.
2125. October 20: Arthur E. Clayton about Hardy's suggestion that a memorial stone be placed on the Esplanade at Weymouth; asks Hardy to submit further suggestions about such a stone.
2126. October 21: C. K. Ogden about efforts to make known to the public the Foreign Press reaction to the war situation.
2127. October 22: Lady Alice Stuart of Wortley appreciation of Hardy's *Selected Poems*.
2128. October 24: Lady Ilchester about getting seats for the performance of "Wessex Scenes from *The Dynasts*" to be given in Dorchester on 6 and 7 December.
2129. October 25: Hardy to Arthur E. Clayton: rough draft, in pencil, unsigned; about erecting a stone to commemorate the visits to Weymouth by King George III, with a design for a tablet.
2130. October 25: H. Granville-Barker sends thanks for a book of poems.
2131. October 25: Lady C. Wimborne asks Hardy to write a couplet and sign it, for sale to raise funds for use by the Dorset Guild of Workers. (Hardy complied.)
2132. (c. October 27): Hardy to Lady Wimborne: rough draft of response to Letter 2131, with four lines copied from *Wessex Poems*.
2133. October 30: Ogden thanks Hardy for his response to Letter 2126.
2134. October 30: Thornycroft about art and other subjects.
2135. October 30: Lady Wimborne thanks Hardy for his autograph MS. of lines from *Wessex Poems*.
2136. November 1: Lady Ilchester cannot attend the matinee on the 9th, but her daughter will substitute for her.
2137. November 3: Captain Gillon again from the Mediterranean area of the war.
2138. November 3: Lady Ritchie (Thackeray's daughter) thanks Hardy for his kindness to her niece, Peggy Ritchie.
2139. (c. November 5): H. G. Wells refers to the Golden Treasury volume of Hardy's poetry, *The Dynasts*, *Under the Greenwood Tree*, and *The Trumpet-Major*.
2140. November 6: Evelyn Sharp asks support for Adult Suffrage.
2141. November 7: Hardy to Evelyn Sharp: rough draft of reply to Letter 2140: refuses her request.
2142. November 9: Lady Ritchie thanks Hardy for a book of his poems.

2143. November 12: Lady Ilchester about the date for the Dorchester performance of "Wessex Scenes from *The Dynasts*."
2144. November 16: H. C. Bulkeley thanks Hardy for books for German prisoners of war interned in Dorset.
2145. November 19: Sir George Douglas about the effect of the War on people's faith.
2146. November 21: Hardy to Captain John H. Morgan: transcript; thanks for a copy of *Land and Water* with his article in it.
2147. November 26: Humphrey Ward thanks Hardy for writing about Barnes for Ward's *English Poets* series.
2148. November 30: Evelyn Gifford thanks Hardy for his book and note.
2149. December 1: Mrs. Hanbury thanks Hardy for an invitation to attend a rehearsal of the "Wessex Scenes from *The Dynasts*."
2150. December 1: P. H. Lee Warner asks permission to quote "The Oxen" on a Christmas card.
2151. December 4: W. Reginald Wheeler asks permission to quote three poems in a Yale anthology.
2152. December 8: Blanche Crackanthorpe about the stage presentation of *The Dynasts*.
2153. December 8: Thring solicits support of a resolution by The Society of Authors.
2154. December 9: H. B. Elliott asks permission to quote six poems in an anthology.
2155. December 12: A. C. Benson tells of the pleasure Hardy's book has given him.
2156. December 13: Stanley Leathes about the Society of Authors.
2157. December 14: Elliott detailed information about the anthology referred to in Letter 2154.
2158. December 16: R. N. Dawes to Mrs. Hardy about the outfitting expenses for the Dorchester production of *The Dynasts*.
2159. December 19: Arthur Symons sends a copy of his new book of prose.
2160. December 22: Hardy to Florence Henniker: is glad she liked "the Golden Treasury Selection" of his poems.
2161. December 23: Benson thanks Hardy for his letter.
2162. December 29: Mackail sends good wishes for the New Year.
2163. December 29: Novello & Co. ask permission to publish a musical setting of the "Song of the Soldiers."
2164. December 30: Hardy to Lady St. Helier: typescript copy; sends New Year's greetings.
2165. December 30: Hardy to Novello & Co.: rough draft of letter granting permission to publish his "Song of the Soldiers" with a musical setting by F. Wilson Parish.
2166. (n. d.): Louisa Conyers about the Turberville coach in *Tess*.
2167. (n. d.): Bruce L. Richmond thanks Hardy for his letter.

1917

2168. January 6: Hardy to Novello & Co.: rough draft in pencil; about errors in their proposed publication of his poem (see Letter 2165); sends a correct copy.

CHRONOLOGICAL LIST 113

2169. January 6: Captain S. A. Gillon war-time letter from 3rd Army Corps headquarters.
2170. January 17: Bruce Glasier asks permission to quote a poem.
2171. January 18: Sydney C. Cockerell thanks Hardy for a letter.
2172. January 28: Madeleine Lady Middleton personal letter.
2173. February 6: James M. Barrie sends thanks for a letter.
2174. February (7?): Percy W. Ames about promoting an Intellectual Entente.
2175. February 8: Hardy to Ames: rough draft, in pencil, signed "T. H.," of reply to Letter 2174; regrets he cannot attend; has written in favor of these views for many years.
2176. February 16: A. C. Benson sends thanks for a letter.
2177. February 16: H. Stephens Richardson invites Hardy to be a Vice-President of the Strength of Britain Movement.
2178. February 16: Siegfried Sassoon thanks Hardy for his poem in the *Nineteenth Century*.
2179. (c. February 17): Hardy to Richardson: rough draft, in pencil, unsigned, of reply to Letter 2177; he is "much honored" but not able to take any real part in the movement.
2180. March 4: Hardy to Florence Henniker: about the German prisoners working in his garden, and Barrie came and stayed for the play of *The Dynasts*, and other matters.
2181. March 5: Florence Henniker suggests Barrie is overrated and probably does not deserve his fame and fortune. Her new story is honored by being dedicated to Hardy.
2182. March 6: Dr. L. Litwinski solicits aid in commemorating Verhaeren and Sienkiewich.
2183. March 7: Hardy to Dr. Litwinski: rough draft, in pencil, unsigned, of reply to Letter 2182; is sorry but he "must refrain."
2184. March 12: C. K. Ogden asks support of a protest "drafted by Professor [Gilbert] Murray" against a recent attack upon the *Cambridge Magazine*.
2185. March 13: John McClure asks permission to quote two poems.
2186. March 14: Hardy to Ogden: rough draft in pencil, responding to Letter 2184 in protest against the recent attack on the *Cambridge Magazine*.
2187. March 14: E. A. Ffooks about the Dorchester Grammar School.
2188. March 16: Israel Gollancz about forming a Shakespeare Association in France.
2189. March 22: Arthur Maquarie about promoting an Intellectual Entente.
2190. (c. March 23): Hardy to Maquarie: reply to Letter 2189: thinks the idea is a sound one, rough draft, in pencil, unsigned.
2191. March 30: H. S. Milford asks permission to quote.
2192. April 7: F. F. Foster about his book on *Dorset Worthies*.
2193. April 11: A. C. Benson thanks Hardy for the "Mellstock lyric."
2194. April 11: Arthur E. Morgan about the need for improved facilities for University education in southwest England.
2195. April 21: Miss M. E. Paul (daughter of publisher Kegan Paul) asks Hardy about translations of his works.
2196. April 25: Captain Gillon another war-time letter.
2197. May 2: John F. Childs about the Hardy family pedigree.

2198. May 6: Arthur E. Morgan asks for aid in trying to improve educational facilities in southwest England.
2199. May 8: Hardy to Morgan: rough draft of reply to Letter 2198; will be glad to add his name.
2200. May 11: Childs about the Hardy family pedigree.
2201. May 20: Hardy to Florence Henniker: about Stevenson, Galsworthy, Gosse, and Sassoon.
2202. May 20: Siegfried Sassoon says Hardy's letter pleased him.
2203. May 22: Childs again about the Hardy pedigree.
2204. May 25: Childs again about the Hardy pedigree.
2205. June 6: Richard Bagot about a Shakespeare Monument in Rome.
2206. June 9: Bagot again about a Shakespeare Monument in Rome.
2207. June 18: John Buchan sends Hardy an official invitation to accompany Barrie on a visit to the War front in France.
2208. June 24: John Galsworthy asks permission to dedicate his new novel, *Beyond*, to Hardy.
2209. June 29: Barrie accepts Hardy's decision about going to the War front in France. (Hardy's decision *not* to go was sent to Barrie on 23 June 1917. This letter, now in the Colby College Library, published in *Hardy Letters*, pp. 103-104.)
2210. June 29: Galsworthy thanks Hardy for the permission requested.
2211. July 11: George Herbert Clarke, a Canadian professor, asks permission to quote.
2212. July 20: Hardy to Lady St. Helier: typed transcript; invites her to call in London.
2213. July 23: Frederic Harrison about Hardy's "stories of Wessex." (In an immediate reply Hardy referred Harrison to *The Hand of Ethelberta*.)
2214. July 24: Harrison says he knows Hardy's *Ethelberta*.
2215. July 28: Raymond Abbott on various matters.
2216. August 3: Milford again asks permission to quote.
2217. August 14: Sir William Watson about an unfortunate literary worker.
2218. August 25: Daphne Bankes solicits Hardy's autograph.
2219. August 29: James Bernard asks permission for public readings of *The Dynasts*.
2220. September 17: Harrison asks why Hardy has neglected Lyme Regis.
2221. September 19: Hardy to John H. Morgan: transcript; thanks him for his humorous sketch of Wessex life.
2222. September 24: Lady Alice Stuart of Wortley sends greetings from Tintagel in Cornwall.
2223. October 20: James D. Barker asks permission to set the "Song of the Soldiers" to music.
2224. October 23: W. J. Roberts solicits a poem for the War Seal Foundation album of original contributions.
2225. (c. October 24): Hardy to Roberts: rough draft of reply to Letter 2224: encloses a holograph, signed, of a sonnet on the War generally which had not yet been published.
2226. October 24: Charlotte L. Baker, a 20-year-old girl in Newton, Massachusetts, loved *The Woodlanders*.
2227. October 25: Hardy to Barker: grants the permission requested in Letter 2223.

CHRONOLOGICAL LIST

2228. (n. d.): Hardy to A. G. Symonds: rough draft; about the Dorchester Grammar School.
2229. October 29: Roberts is grateful for Hardy's contribution to the War Seal Foundation's album.
2230. November 2: Sir Henry Newbolt is distressed about the *Times* report of what he said about Hardy's poetry.
2231. November 9: Grace E. (Mrs. T. H.) Marshall, from Canandaigua, New York, about the plot of *The Return of the Native*.
2232. November 9: Thornycroft on art and other subjects.
2233. November 22: W. Stebbing sends thanks from a *Times* "leader-writer" (who later left Hardy a legacy of £30).
2234. November 23: Childs about the Hardy family pedigree.
2235. November 23: R. B. Cunningham Graham praises *Jude*.
2236. November 25: Thornycroft about books, art, etc.
2237. November 30: Bertram Lloyd asks permission to quote.
2238. December 1: Dean W. R. Inge, from the Deanery of St. Paul's Cathedral, thanks Hardy for a copy of his *Moments of Vision* (published 30 November 1917).
2239. December 5: George Bazile asks permission to publish a French translation of "An Imaginative Woman."
2240. December 7: Raymond Abbott thanks Hardy for a copy of *Moments of Vision*.
2241. December 7: Cockerell thanks Hardy for *Moments of Vision*.
2242. December 9: Galsworthy thanks Hardy for *Moments of Vision*.
2243. December 15: Lord Coleridge thanks Hardy for his latest volume of poems.
2244. December 16: Edmund Gosse thanks Hardy for an inscription in a copy of *Moments of Vision*.
2245. December 17: Laurence Binyon sends a poem on Stonehenge.
2246. December 22: H. C. Bulkeley asks Hardy to autograph some books.
2247. December 26: David A. Robertson asks if Hardy plans to visit the United States after the war.
2248. December 31: Mrs. Allhusen sends best wishes for 1918.
2249. December 31: Barrie asks Hardy to serve on a committee to arrange for a Red Cross sale of books and manuscripts.

1918

2250. January 1: Sir George Douglas thinks the effect of the War on literature is depressing.
2251. January 1: John Galsworthy sends New Year's greetings.
2252. January 1: Brigadier-General John H. Morgan sends an article on "Literature and Politics."
2253. January 1: Lady St. Helier sends New Year's greetings from one who is "nearly 78." (She and Hardy were both born in 1840.)
2254. (c. January 2): Hardy to Barrie: rough draft of reply to Letter 2249; agrees to let his name appear on the Committee list.
2255. January 2: Sir Frederick Macmillan warns Hardy against granting "general permission" to anthologists to quote.

2256. January 12: Barrie asks for one or two poems for a War-relief sale.
2257. January 14: Walter Pouncy asks permission to issue Hardy's portrait on a postcard, to raise money for the Dorset Fund.
2258. January 15: Hardy to Pouncy: has no objection to Pouncy's request. Rough draft in Hardy's hand, to be signed by his secretary.
2259. January 21: Isabel M. Smith reports finding, at the office of Smith, Elder & Co., the MS. of *Far from the Madding Crowd;* asks permission to send it to the Red Cross for sale.
2260. January 23: Robert S. Comber invites Hardy to suggest an inscription for a commemorative tablet on or near the Gloucester Hotel, Weymouth.
2261. January 24: Samuel C. Chew, from Bryn Mawr, Pennsylvania, asks permission to quote Hardy in a book about Swinburne which Chew is writing.
2262. January 24: Isabel M. Smith thanks Hardy for permission to send the MS. of *Far from the Madding Crowd* to the Red Cross for sale.
2263. January 26: Edmund Gosse asks Hardy to date certain of his poems, to aid Gosse in writing a study of his work as a poet which he has been asked to write for the *Edinburgh Review.* (The article appeared in the April 1918 issue.)
2264. January 29. H. Tomabeclus asks permission to translate *The Mayor of Casterbridge* into Japanese.
2265. January 31: Hall Caine about the possible publication of a letter by Hardy as a contribution to "the controversy."
2266. February 1: Sir Francis Darwin sends a book.
2267. February 7: Hardy to Florence Henniker: expresses disappointment in the reviews his poems have been receiving; and indicates "At Lanivet," "At the Word 'Farewell,'" and "Why Did I Sketch" are literally true.
2268. February 7: Hardy to Robertson: rough draft of reply to Letter 2247; it is not probable he will visit the United States after the war. Partly published in *Later Years,* pp. 185-186.
2269. February 7: E. V. Lucas about the sale of the manuscript of *Far from the Madding Crowd* at the Red Cross auction, suggesting an article on it, and on "the author's second thoughts" as revealed by the MS.
2270. February 7: Winifred Thomson has given three of his letters to the Red Cross sale.
2271. February 9: Hardy to Chew: rough draft of reply to Letter 2261: grants permission and says Swinburne corresponded with him about many of his poems.
2272. February 9: Hardy to Lucas: rough draft of reply to Letter 2269: has no objection to an article.
2273. February 11: Wimborne asks about cinema rights in *Jude.*
2274. February 13: L. G. Harrison asks for information about old Burton Bradstock.
2275. (c. February 14): Hardy to Harrison: rough draft of reply to Letter 2274; has no special knowledge of old Burton Bradstock.
2276. February 18: Hardy to Wimborne: rough draft of reply to Letter 2273; refers Wimborne to his agents, the Messrs. Macmillan.
2277. February 20: C. Dampier Whetham about a herd of pedigree cattle near Cerne Abbas, Dorset.

2278. February 21: Edmund Gosse had spotted of his own accord the influence of Wordsworth's first preface on Hardy. [Gosse's article on Hardy's poetry was collected by him in *Some Diversions of a Man of Letters,* London: Heinemann, 1919.]
2279. February 22: Whetham invites Hardy to come to see the pedigree cattle at Cerne Abbas.
2280. February 23: H. W. Massingham asks permission to call.
2281. February 26: Arthur Machen asks Hardy to write his reminiscenses for the *Evening News.*
2282. (c. February 27): Hardy to Machen: rough draft of reply to Letter 2281; would not like to write any account of himself for publication.
2283. February 27: Massingham thanks Hardy for his call at Max Gate.
2284. February 28: Chew asks permission to quote from Hardy's writings.
2285. March 2: Gosse asks why it makes Hardy indignant to be called a pessimist.
2286. March 14: John Drinkwater hopes to call on the 24th.
2287. March 21: Hardy to Chew: rough draft of reply to Letter 2284; gives permission for quotations.
2288. April 2: Blanche Warre Cornish thanks Hardy for his letter of sympathy.
2289. April 22: J. F. Symons-Jeune is sending a book by Gosse.
2290. April 26: Winifred Thomson reports that Hardy's letter which she contributed to the Red Cross sale fetched four pounds.
2291. May 15: Rendel Harris about the establishment of an Anglo-American University at Plymouth.
2292. May 18: Hall Caine invites Hardy to co-operate in the preparation of a national cinema film to present "the ideals for which we are fighting" in this War.
2293. May 19: Caine again about a film to present England's War ideals.
2294. May 20: Hardy to Harris: rough draft of reply to Letter 2291; is interested in Harris' proposals and hopes the idea will mature.
2295. May 21: Hardy to Caine: rough draft of reply to Letter 2292; sends best wishes for the scheme, but he can do better independently.
2296. May 21: Caine about his scheme for a film on War ideals.
2297. (c. May 21): Harris thanks Hardy for his letter.
2298. May 22: Caine again, about a film on England's ideals.
2299. May 27: Caine about the correspondence in the *Sunday Observer,* 27 January 1918.
2300. May 30: A. C. Moule about his Uncle Horace, Hardy's boyhood friend.
2301. June 1: Sydney C. Cockerell sends best wishes for Hardy's 78th birthday.
2302. June 1: Mary Fox-Strangways sends birthday greetings.
2303. June 1: Lady Ilchester sends birthday greetings.
2304. June 1: Maurice Macmillan sends best wishes on Hardy's birthday.
2305. June 1: Henry Stone sends birthday greetings from one "of the little band who studied Architecture with Sir Arthur Blomfield . . . over fifty years ago."
2306. June 2: Charles Whibley sends birthday greetings.
2307. June 3: W. M. Stone asks permission to reproduce *The Woodlanders* and *The Return of the Native* in Braille.

2308. June 5: Hardy to Florence Henniker: thanks for her good wishes on his birthday. (He apparently did not preserve her letter.) While dining recently at the King's Arms he recalled that the last time he was in it was when she came to Dorchester to see one of the performances of the local players.
2309. June 10: A. C. Deane sends belated birthday greetings.
2310. June 12: Hardy to Deane: rough draft of reply to Letter 2309; sends sincere thanks.
2311. June 13: Stone thanks Hardy for the permission requested in Letter 2307.
2312. June 26: A. Edward Newton about the fate of the manuscript of *Far from the Madding Crowd*. Says he bought it recently from a bookseller in New York and it is now in Newton's library at Daylesford, Pennsylvania.
2313. June 30: H. M. Hyndman about politics, and his pleasure over a recent visit to Dorchester.
2314. July 3: Robert Edgcumbe solicits encouragement of Miss May O'Rourke who has the ambition to be a poet.
2315. July 4: Charles W. Moule about Sydney Cockerell at Cambridge.
2316. July 4: Bruce L. Richmond asks permission to call.
2317. July 4: Arthur Symons asks Hardy to write his name in a book of his.
2318. July 10: John C. Powys, says *Moments of Vision* is better than *Satires of Circumstance;* he lectured on Hardy in San Francisco, California, in May.
2319. July 14: Mrs. Genevieve Bennett Clark about politics and war news from Washington, D. C.
2320. July 23: Hardy to The Lord Mayor of London: rough draft; regrets inability to accept an invitation to luncheon at the Mansion House.
2321. July 25: Sir Arthur Quiller-Couch about a "French Chair" at Cambridge University.
2322. July 30: John Galsworthy solicits a poem for publication in *Reveillé*.
2323. July 31: Howard D. Widger asks permission to quote Hardy in an American high school volume of war verse.
2324. August 4: Ernest R. Debenham invites Hardy to lunch and to see his cottages at Moreton, Dorset.
2325. August 11: Cockerell about the war news.
2326. August 16: E. Malcolm Venables sends a sonnet.
2327. August 25: Lord Northcliffe has just finished his third reading of *Tess*.
2328. August 31: Clark again asks permission to quote.
2329. August 31: Sir Frederick Pollock is reading *The Woodlanders* again; calls it "one of the best."
2330. September 1: Henry Winslow asks permission to call.
2331 (n. d.): Mrs. Dorothy Allhusen friendly letter.
2332. September 3: Pollock about legal matters, Shakespearean chronology, etc.
2333. September 3: Siegfried Sassoon is glad to hear John Drinkwater has seen Hardy.
2334. September 8: Hardy to Arnold Bennett: rough draft of reply to Bennett's solicitation of 4 September 1918 (not preserved by

Hardy) of Hardy's signature to a War Manifesto. Has scruples against signing it, and makes further comment.
2335. September 9: Bennett sends thanks, but he is desolate.
2336. September 24: Winslow thanks Hardy for the pleasure of his call at Max Gate.
2337. September 25: Rabbi J. H. Hertz sends a *Book of Jewish Thoughts*.
2338. September 30: M. R. James thanks Hardy for his good wishes.
2339. October 12: Cecil Palmer asks permission to print something by Hardy in a publication in appreciation of the services of the Air Force.
2340. (c. October 13): Hardy to Palmer: rough draft of reply to Letter 2339; permission is given to print "Jezreel" in *Air Pie*.
2341. October 16: Lady Alice Stuart of Wortley has not been to St. Juliot.
2342. October 23: Clarke thanks Hardy for permission to quote.
2343. October 27: Hardy to Florence Henniker: is glad she liked "Jezreel"; was written very rapidly (24-25 September 1918) and published in the *Times*, 27 September.
2344. October (?). H. F. Bulkeley sends a sonnet.
2345. November 6: Walter de la Mare cannot tell how much Hardy's letter means to him.
2346. November 13: Mrs. Allhusen friendly letter two days after the Armistice.
2347. November 14: E. Marsh thanks Hardy for autographing a book.
2348. November 14: Sassoon enjoyed his visit at Max Gate.
2349. November 28: Barker sends Hardy a copy of his musical setting for the "Song of the Soldiers" and says he plans to consult a professional musician for an opinion as to its merits.
2350. November 28: Kostos Palamas, called the greatest living Greek poet, writes in French to send Hardy a poem in Greek entitled "Tess d'Urbervilles," together with a French translation of the poem.
2351. November 30: Hardy to Barker: rough draft of reply to Letter 2349; likes Barker's plan.
2352. November 30: Canon A. Nairne thanks Hardy for his letter.
2353. December 8: W. Courthope Forman asks about amber-colored butterflies which Egdon produced in *The Return of the Native*.
2354. December 19: Anna (Mrs. David) Johnson solicits a contribution to a book to be sold to raise money for "the Fatherless Children of France."
2355. December 20: George T. Keating wants Hardy's autograph in two books.
2356. December 21: Amy Lowell sends her new volume of short epics.
2357. December 21: C. A. Speyer about a musical setting he has composed for "When I set out for Lyonnesse."
2358. December 22: Raymond Abbott, from Ventnor, Isle of Wight.
2359. December 24: Augustine Birrell asks permission to quote a letter Hardy wrote to B.'s father-in-law Frederick Locker.
2360. December 28: Hardy to Florence Henniker: Birrell is going to print a little book about his father-in-law Frederick Locker.
2361. December 28: Hardy to Speyer: in reply to Letter 2357, rough draft in pencil; explains the meaning of "The rime was on the spray" and says "Lyonnesse" in the poem is a vague term denoting the north and west coast of Cornwall.

2362. December 29: Birrell thanks Hardy for the permission requested in Letter 2359.
2363. (n. d.): Paul Jordan Smith, from Claremont, California, in appreciation.

1919

2364. January 4: Robert Graves solicits a contribution to *The Owl*.
2365. January 7: Kineton Parkes asks permission to dedicate a poem to Hardy. (Hardy declined.)
2366. January 7: C. A. Speyer would like to come to Max Gate and play his musical setting for "When I set out for Lyonnesse."
2367. January 8: Harold Child about his review of *Moments of Vision* for *The Observer*.
2368. January 9: Graves is grateful for Hardy's promise to contribute to *The Owl*.
2369. January 14: George Morris Philips solicits an autograph.
2370. January 17: H. D. Strange asks if Hardy would be prepared to have a telephone installed at Max Gate.
2371. January 19: Hardy to Strange: rough draft of reply to inquiry about the telephone; would be interested, depending on the cost.
2372. January 19: Child thanks Hardy for offering to correct his copy of *Moments of Vision*.
2373. January 20: Frederic Harrison asks for Hardy's autograph for a Mrs. Will Gordon.
2374. January 25: Clara Watts-Dunton about Hardy's poem "A Singer Asleep."
2375. January 25: Marguerite Wilkinson asks permission to quote poems.
2376. (c. January 26): H. G. Wells, from Weymouth, asks if he may see Hardy one day.
2377. January 29: Harrison is glad to hear from Hardy.
2378. February 4: James Milne asks permission to call, in preparation for writing an article on Hardy.
2379. February 10: Guy N. Pocock thanks Hardy for permission to quote.
2380. February 13: Child is glad Hardy likes the review of *Moments of Vision* in *The Observer*.
2381. February 14: W. H. Morris inquires about Mr. Gordon Gifford.
2382. February 17: A. R. Powys about repairs to St. Sophia church in Constantinople.
2383. February 18: Hardy to Powys: rough draft of reply to Letter 2382; approves that a memorial be addressed to the Foreign Secretary.
2384. February 18: D. R. Cousin to the Rev. H. G. B. Cowley, asks about the grave of William Dewy in *Under the Greenwood Tree* (a copy made, in pencil, by Hardy).
2385. February 18: Sir Arthur Quiller-Couch answers a "jolly letter" about a Byron lecture; has difficulty replying in kind because he has just received news of his son's death in the War.
2386. February 20: J. Middleton Murry solicits a poem for the first number of the new *Athenaeum*.

CHRONOLOGICAL LIST

2387. February 21: Rev. Cowley forwards an inquiry from D. R. Cousin (Letter 2384).
2388. February 27: Stair A. Gillon thanks Hardy for his letter and his volume of poems.
2389. March 2: Hardy to Middleton Murry: rough draft of reply to Letter 2386: has been unable to find anything suitable.
2390. March 3: Murry again asks for a contribution to the new *Athenaeum*.
2391. March 8: Henry C. Lyon replies to Hardy's inquiry as to where the Order of Merit ranks among other Orders.
2392. March 10: G. Herbert Thring about an alleged American piracy of *The Mayor of Casterbridge*.
2393. March 12: Arnold H. Lewis thanks Hardy for permission to set "Budmouth Dears" to music.
2394. March 12: Murry thanks Hardy for a contribution to the new *Athenaeum*.
2395. March 12: Humphry Ward apologizes for his failure, more than two years ago, to send Hardy his fee for the article on Barnes in Vol. 5 of Ward's *English Poets*.
2396. March 15: Hardy to Thring: copy of a typed reply to inquiry of 10 March 1919; prefers to have nothing to do with reprints of his books published before 1891, they were not copyright in America.
2397. March 17: J. Paul Cooper solicits a poem for the quarterly news sheet of the Arts & Crafts Exhibition Society.
2398. (c. March 18): Hardy to Cooper: rough draft of reply to Letter 2397; he is unable to send poems or articles.
2399. March 24: Catherine D. Whetham about her volume of War Verses.
2400. April 5: Graves wants Hardy's contribution (to *The Owl*) Now.
2401. April 11: James Barrie is pleased with Hardy's letter.
2402. April 18: Milton Bronner, from Washington, asks for help.
2403. April 23: Siegfried Sassoon about Hardy's poem in the *Athenaeum*.
2404. April 25: W. H. Elson asks permission to quote.
2405. April 26: Sir George Douglas about the end of the War.
2406. May 6: Paul Jordan Smith sends praise of Hardy's poetry from California.

On 7 May 1919 Hardy wrote to Sir George Douglas that he had been doing nothing much—mainly destroying papers of the last thirty or forty years. One can judge of the wholesale nature of the destruction by noting the fact that the preceding 2406 letters (1970 of them *to* Hardy; 436 *from* him) represent a salvaging from 59 years (1860-1919), yet they make up a total of only 48% of the Max Gate Letters; the remaining 52% were all written in the last nine years of Hardy's life. What now follows has therefore not been subject to the culling which the preceding letters underwent.

2407. May 12: S. L. Bensusan sends a copy of the *Canadian Bookman* and asks permission to call at Max Gate to get Hardy's views.
2408. May 14: Amy Lowell about her polyphonic prose.
2409. May 15: Hardy to Dr. James Fitzmaurice-Kelly: expresses delight with the idea of marking the occasion of Edmund Gosse's seventieth

birthday by a testimonial. Rough draft, in pencil, unsigned (Hardy sent one guinea to the fund.)
2410. May 15: Arthur S. McDowall about Hardy's poem in the *Athenaeum*.
2411. May 16: W. Kean Seymour asks permission to quote.
2412. May 21: Edmund Gosse asks who drew the design for the original cover of *The Trumpet-Major* in 1880. (Hardy himself did.)
2413. May 21: Frederick Pickles asks permission to quote.
2414. May 23: Sir James Crichton Browne sends a memoir of a grandson of his who fell in the War.
2415. May 24: John Dublin thanks Hardy for a book of his poems.
2416. May 27: Brigadier-General John H. Morgan about the Peace Conference in Paris.
2417. May 31: The Secretary General of the Bibliothèque de la Guerre requests a bibliography of Hardy's war writings.
2418. June 2: Walter de la Mare sends birthday greetings.
2419. June 2: H. M. Hyndman sends birthday greetings.
2420. (c. June 2): Robert Lynd about his good intentions when he writes about Hardy's works.
2421. June 3: Frederic Harrison sends birthday greetings.
2422. June 5: Hardy to Florence Henniker; thanks for her good wishes on his 79th birthday; hopes she will come for a visit to Max Gate. Published in *Later Years*, pp. 191-192.
2423. June 5: H. Milford about granting permission to G. Zendequi to translate two of Hardy's poems into Spanish.
2424. June 6: Mrs. Dorothy Allhusen sends birthday greetings.
2425. June 12: Edgar Lee Masters, from Chicago, about the influence Hardy's poetry, especially his *Satires of Circumstance*, had on Masters' *Spoon River*; admires Hardy's work and his spirit profoundly.
2426. June 12: The League of Intellectual Solidarity for the Triumph of International Truth invites Hardy's participation.
2427. June 15: Hardy to The League of Intellectual Solidarity: rough draft in pencil; is not able to take active part.
2428. June 23: Lascelles Abercrombie thanks Hardy for a letter.
2429. June 28: Graham Peel asks permission to publish his musical setting for "The Oxen" under the title "Christmas Eve."
2430. (c. June 30): Hardy to Peel: rough draft of reply to Letter 2429; gives permission to publish if the title "The Oxen" is retained; however, "A Legend of Christmas Eve" could be used as a subtitle.
2431. July 4: Seymour again requests permission to quote.
2432. July 8: William Strang about his portrait of Hardy.
2433. July 13: Sydney C. Cockerell about corrections for a new edition of Hardy's works.
2434. July 19: The League of Intellectual Solidarity sends a detailed statement of its principles and aims.
2435. July 20: Hardy to H. J. Massingham: rough draft of reply to a solicitation of Hardy's support of a public protest about The Plumage Trade; specifies five modifications in Massingham's text before he could sign it.
2436. July 21: Massingham says Hardy's suggestions may be too late for use in a circular letter.

CHRONOLOGICAL LIST 123

2437. July 29: Robert Nichols about a young American artist, Rockwell Kent.
2438. August 5: J. M. Bullock thanks Mrs. Hardy for permission to print "The Darkling Thrush."
2439. August 8: Nichols thanks Hardy for his letter.
2440. August 12: W. F. Malden about The Wessex Saddle-back Pig Society.
2441. August 18: Mrs. Ethel F. Cowley thanks Hardy for information about Stinsford House, the vicarage.
2442. August 19: Sir George Douglas sends a copy of the *Hibbert Journal* containing his article on Goethe.
2443. August 22: E. K. Broadus about "the inanities of the laureateship."
2444. August 23: Hardy to Malden: rough draft in pencil, signed "T. H."; accepts honorary membership in The Wessex Saddle-back Pig Society.
2445. August 23: Rutland Boughton invites Hardy to attend the Glastonbury Music Festival.
2446. August 25: Malden again about the Pig Society.
2447. August 26: John C. Squire thanks Hardy for his willingness to contribute to the *London Mercury*.
2448. August 7: Jacqueline T. Trotter asks permission to include the "Song of the Soldiers" and "Jezreel" in an anthology to be sold for the benefit of the Soldiers & Sailors Help Society. (Hardy gave permission.)
2449. (n. d.): A. Edward Newton, from Philadelphia, invites Hardy to purchase a Walt Whitman medal for five dollars.
2450. September 1: Squire thanks Hardy for a poem ("Going and Staying") for the *London Mercury* (published in the November issue, p. 7).
2451. September 5: Ida Ragghiantiljero, an Italian widow, regrets Hardy is so little known in her country.
2452. September 12: Rockwell Kent (see Letter 2437) about his first discovery years ago of *Jude*.
2453. September 12: A. R. Powys about Symondsbury Church near Bridport.
2454. September 19: J. M. McCarthy about the Saddleback Pig Society.
2455. September 20: Hardy to the Secretary General of the Bibliothèque de la Guerre: copy of typed letter in reply to Letter 2417; lists as many of his war writings as he can remember; also a copy, in pencil, of the list sent to Paris: 17 poems, all in *Moments of Vision*.
2456. September 25: Gosse thanks Hardy for nearly 45 years of friendship.
2457. October 9: Cockerell about books on Napoleon.
2458. October 14: Maurice Baring says it was kind of Hardy to write about the 43 Poets' Tribute.
2459. October 15: Robert Bridges was pleased to contribute to the book on Hardy's 79th birthday; appreciates Hardy's writing his thanks to him.
2460. October 16: Chew inquires about J. W. Cunliffe's published (but erroneous) statement that *The Poor Man and the Lady* was recast and then published as *Desperate Remedies*.

2461. October 16: John Masefield says it was a pleasure to all of them [43 authors] to contribute to the book in Hardy's honor.
2462. October 17: A. E. Housman says Hardy was kind to let Housman know he liked his poem.
2463. October 17: Justice Sir Charles Darling invites Hardy to lunch.
2464. October 17: Sir Arthur Quiller-Couch sends a tribute.
2465. October 20: Maurice D. Colbourne says the Oxford University Dramatic Society (OUDS) proposes a production of *The Dynasts*.
2466. October 21: Maurice Hewlett about his journeys to and from Maiden Castle.
2467. October 22: George Blake sends a copy of *John O'London's Weekly*.
2468. October 23: Maurice D. Colbourne thanks Hardy for permission to give *The Dynasts* at Oxford.
2469. October 23: William Strang about his portrait of Hardy.
2470. October 23: Sylvia Townsend Warner asks permission to try to publish musical settings for three of Hardy's poems.
2471. October 24: Vernon Rendall wonders whether George Eliot got from Hardy the literary use of 'Wessex' as a territorial designation. Rendall has found 'Wessex' three times in *Daniel Deronda* (1876), whereas Hardy used the word in 1874.
2472. October 26: A. C. D. Lush congratulates Hardy on attaining the age of 79, and expresses pleasure in Hardy's books.
2473. October 29: E. Blake solicits Hardy's "recipe for success."
2474. October 30: J. J. Foster about his book on *Dorset Worthies*.
2475. October 30: Archie Whitfield asks about Hardy's earlier life.
2476. November 1: Florence Henniker pleased with tribute to Hardy from 43 poets; hopes the collection will be published in a little volume for his friends.
2477. November 2: Charles E. Gifford congratulates Hardy on his receipt of the testimonial from 43 fellow poets.
2478. November 6: Justice Sir Charles Darling thanks Hardy for a copy of Barnes's Poems.
2479. November 6: Strang about his portrait of Hardy.
2480. November 7: Hardy to Florence Henniker: both have been having colds; he refers to a manuscript that surprised him. (Poems by her?)
2481. November 11: Hardy to M. D. Colbourne: rough draft of letter about the details for the OUDS performance of *The Dynasts*.
2482. November 11: Hardy to Charles Morgan: rough draft in pencil; details for the OUDS performance of *The Dynasts*.
2483. November 17: Newman Flower solicits a poem for publication early next year.
2484. November 17: Lord Sandhurst sends an appeal in behalf of St. Bartholomew's Hospital.
2485. November 18: Hardy to Lord Sandhurst: rough draft of reply to Letter 2484; he must not at present write a special appeal.
2486. November 19: Thornycroft on various subjects.
2487. November 23: Florence Henniker about the Poets' Tribute from 43 fellow authors.
2488. November 23: Lord Sandhurst acknowledges Hardy's note.
2489. November 25: Gordon Bottomley thanks Hardy for his acknowledgment of B.'s contribution to the Poet's Tribute.

2490. (c. November 30): Hardy to Warner: rough draft in pencil; grants the permission requested in Letter 2470.
2491. November 30: Cockerell liked Hardy's poem in the *Mercury*.
2492. December 4: A. E. Drinkwater considers it a compliment to have been asked to produce *The Dynasts* for the OUDS.
2493. December 4. Elizabeth Robins asks for an autographed book "to help a hospital."
2494. December 5: Blanche A. Crackanthorpe expresses interest in the production of *The Dynasts* by the OUDS.
2495. December 5: Warner is grateful for the permission granted to her request in Letter 2470.
2496. December 6: Hardy to A. E. Drinkwater: rough draft of letter about the OUDS production of *The Dynasts*.
2497. December 8: Maurice D. Colbourne about the OUDS production of *The Dynasts*.
2498. December 9: Child met Cockerell in Cambridge.
2499. December 9: Sir C. P. Ibert thanks Hardy for a letter.
2500. December 9: Morgan invites Hardy to come to Oxford on 10 February 1920 to see *The Dynasts* performed by OUDS.
2501. December 9: William Lyon Phelps invites Hardy to come to Yale University and deliver two lectures under the Francis Bergin Memorial foundation.
2502. December 14: Morgan tells Hardy about OUDS arrangements for the *Dynasts* production.
2503. December 15: Hardy to W. H. Norris: rough draft of reply to Letter 2381; Gordon Gifford is a relative of Hardy and is in the offices of the London County Council.
2504. December 20: P. H. Pittwood appreciation.
2505. December 21: Mrs. Allhusen sends holiday greetings.
2506. December 21: Charles F. C. Wood is reading *The Mayor of Casterbridge* for the third time.
2507. December 24: Arnold Bennett thanks Hardy for his Christmas card and poem.
2508. December 24: J. Meade Falkner appreciation of Hardy's verse.
2509. December 24: Evelyn Gifford thanks Hardy for a triolet.
2510. December 26: Hardy to Phelps: rough draft of reply to Letter 2501: feels honored but cannot accept.
2511. December 27: Sir George Douglas sends New Year's greetings.
2512. December 27: Anita (Mrs. Ambrose) Dudley solicits a poem on the Royal Artillery.
2513. December 28: E. Graham sends an Old Dorset anecdote.
2514. December 28: J. Ellis McTaggart sends best wishes for the New Year.
2515. December 29: Lord Northcliffe thanks Hardy for his Christmas greetings.
2516. December 30: Hardy to Mrs. Dudley: rough draft of reply to Letter 2512; sends regrets, pleading exhaustion.
2517. December 30: Pollock sends a doggerel comment on the last volume of Hardy's poems, an amusing conversation overheard at the Mermaid.
2518. December 31: Hardy to McTaggart: rough draft in pencil; acknowledges best wishes in Letter 2514.

2519. December 31: Christopher Childs asks for help with regard to the Assistant Secretaryship of the Royal Society.
2520. December (?): Wilfrid Gibson sends a copy of the volume in which the poem Gibson had written for the Poets' Tribute first appeared.
2521. (n. d.): Raymond Abbott again from Ventnor on the Isle of Wight.
2522. (n. d.): Dorothy (Mrs. Cecil) Hanbury invites Hardy to dinner at Kingston Maurward House.
2523. (n. d.): Siegfried Sassoon tells Mrs. Hardy he will come on Wednesday and would like to take her and Mr. Hardy for a drive.
2524. (n. d.): H. Wilson solicits help in putting on a pageant for the benefit of disabled soldiers.
2525. (n. d.): Hardy to Wilson: rough draft of reply to Letter 2524: is unable to help.

1920

2526. January 5: J. Middleton Murry thanks Hardy for his Christmas card.
2527. January 7: August Brunius asks permission to adapt "The Distracted Preacher" for cinema production by a Swedish company of actors. Copy of the original letter, made when Hardy forwarded the original to Macmillan.
2528. January 7: Edmund Gosse invites Hardy to Weymouth and have lunch at the Gloucester Hotel, where there is a memorial tablet for which Hardy provided the wording.
2529. January 9: Harold Child is to see *The Dynasts* at Oxford next month.
2530. January 13: Justice Sir Charles Darling invites Hardy to dinner.
2531. January 14: Catherine (Mrs. Henry) Holiday is moved by Hardy's *Collected Poems*.
2532. January 17: Cecil Hanbury sends thanks for a book.
2533. January 18: Edmund Gosse about his earliest experiences at Weymouth in 1853.
2534. January 19: Charles Morgan about Hardy's presence at the OUDS performance of *The Dynasts* on 10 February.
2535. January 20: E. H. Moule about his brother Horace's pleasant visit with Hardy.
2536. January 21: George Sampson thanks Hardy for permission to quote *The Dynasts*.
2537. January 25: Hardy to Morgan: rough draft of reply to Letter 2534 about Hardy going to Oxford.
2538. January 25: Dowager Lady Ilchester is grateful for Hardy's note of condolence on the death of her daughter.
2539. January 26: Henry A. Lappin, from Buffalo, New York, praises Hardy's work.
2540. February 3: Lady Ilchester sends a copy of her husband's new book.
2541. February 12: A. B. Ramsay, President of Magdalene College, Cambridge, invites Hardy to the Pepys Dinner on 23 February.

2542. February 22: Murry solicits another poem for the *Athenaeum*.
2543. February 28: Hardy to Florence Henniker: had a very pleasant time at Oxford.
2544. February 28: Gordon Bottomley asks if he may call.
2545. March 1: Helen (Mrs. Harley) Granville-Barker sends greetings from Rome.
2546. March 2: Lord Ilchester pleased about Hardy's approval of his book.
2547. March 10: W. F. Malden about The Wessex Saddle-back Pig Society.
2548. March 10: Belle Willard (Mrs. Kermit) Roosevelt asks Hardy to autograph her copies of *Tess* and *Jude*.
2549. March 12: H. S. Milford asks permission to quote.
2550. March 23: John I. Fraser solicits support in a proposal to acquire Wentworth Place as a Keats Memorial House.
2551. March 25: Hardy to Fraser: rough draft of reply to Letter 2550: is willing to join the National Committee.
2552. April 1: Sir George Douglas hopes to call at Max Gate next week.
2553. April 9: Murry thanks Hardy for a letter.
2554. April 13: F. B. Fisher sends postage for a packet he had sent Hardy.
2555. April 13: John Tweed sends photograph of a statue of Sir John Moore.
2556. April 14: Rockwell Kent is sending a book by himself.
2557. April 15: Israel Cohen asks support of a proposal to establish a Jewish National Home in Palestine.
2558. (c. April 16): Hardy to Cohen: rough draft of reply to Letter 2557.
2559. April 18: Maurice Macmillan pleased Hardy is coming to his son's wedding.
2560. April 20: Humphry Ward sends thanks for Hardy's kind letter. [Mrs. Ward had just died.]
2561. April 21: Lady St. Helier hopes Mrs. Hardy will come to stay with her.
2562. April 22: F. B. Fisher about Colonel Holder's death and burial.
2563. April 22: C. A. Speyer asks permission to publish "When I set out for Lyonnesse" with his musical setting.
2564. April 23: John Gould Fletcher asks permission to dedicate to Hardy a poem to appear shortly in the *Yale Review*.
2565. April 26: Fletcher thanks Hardy for the permission granted.
2566. April 26: H. M. Massingham solicits support of Russian Intellectuals.
2567. April 27: Hardy to Macmillan: rough draft of letter forwarding the request in Letter 2527; Hardy says two of the Wessex novels have already been translated into Swedish.
2568. April 27: Speyer thanks Hardy for the permission requested in Letter 2563.
2569. May 2: Douglas about Hardy's poem in the *Athenaeum*.
2570. May 7: J. Ollendorff asks about film rights in *Tess*.
2571. (c. May 8): Hardy to Ollendorff: rough draft in pencil; the film rights have already been disposed of.
2572. May 12: Charles Whibley expresses gratitude for a letter.
2573. May 17: Leonard Rees solicits a contribution for the *Sunday Times*.

2574. (c. May 18): Hardy to Rees: rough draft of reply to Letter 2573; he is not able to find a suitable contribution.
2575. May 18: Maurice Hewlett sorry he is unable to be one of the deputation to greet Hardy on his 80th Birthday.
2576. May 21: John Galsworthy pleased at the prospect of seeing Hardy at Max Gate.
2577. June 1: Paul Jordan Smith asks permission to call.

On 2 June 1920 Hardy attained the age of 80. He received Birthday Greetings from 66 men and women, some of whom wrote just before or just after June 2 (on the date indicated in parentheses):

2578. Lascelles Abercrombie
2579. John E. Acland
2580. Dorothy Allhusen (31 May)
2581. Sherwood Anderson
2582. William Archer
2583. May Balfour (14 June)
2584. Arthur C. Benson
2585. Van Wyck Brooks
2586. James Branch Cabell
2587. Edward Clodd (31 May)
2588. Blanche Crackanthorpe
2589. Lord Curzon
2590. G. Lowes Dickinson
2591. John H. Dickinson
2592. Sir George Douglas (31 May)
2593. Theodore Dreiser
2594. Lord Fitzmaurice
2595. Newman Flower
2596. Winifred Fortescue (1 June)
2597. Bernard Frey
2598. Robert Frost
2599. H. M. King George V.
2600. Bertha George
2601. Lloyd George
2602. Charles E. Gifford
2603. Evelyn Gifford
2604. Margaret Gifford
2605. Edmund Gosse
2606. Harley Granville-Barker
2607. Robert Graves
2608. Cecil Hanbury
2609. E. C. Harcourt
2610. Frederic Harrison (31 May)
2611. Florence Henniker
2612. Joseph Hergesheimer
2613. J. G. Hicks
2614. H. M. Hyndman
2615. Lord and Lady Ilchester
2616. Dowager Lady Ilchester (31 May)
2617. Vachel Lindsay
2618. Frances Lockett
2619. Amy Lowell
2620. Arthur McDowall (1 June)
2621. Maurice Macmillan
2622. John Masefield
2623. S. G. Matthews
2624. Henry L. Mencken
2625. John H. Morgan (3 June)
2626. Lord Northcliffe
2627. T. P. O'Connor
2628. James Oppenheimer
2629. Sir Frederick Pollock
2630. Bishop Ridgeway
2631. Edwin Arlington Robinson
2632. Madeleine Rolland
2633. Romain Rolland
2634. Algernon Rose
2635. William Rothenstein
2636. Firmin Roz
2637. Lady St. Helier
2638. Charles A. Speyer
2639. Sara Teasdale
2640. Louis Untermeyer
2641. Carl Van Doren
2642. Humphry Ward
2643. Charles Whibley

2644. June 2: Edith Bateson about Hardy's poem "Often when Warring."
2645. June 4: Hardy to Florence Henniker: delighted to hear she is coming to Weymouth; Barrie is coming the next day.
2646. June 4: H. W. Massingham refers to page 310 in *The Nation*.
2647. June 9: A. C. Benson thanks Hardy for his letter.
2648. June 9: Alfred Gordon sends two books of his poetry.
2649. June 10: Foster again about *Dorset Worthies*.

2650. June 11: H. F. C. Marshall invites Hardy to dinner and asks for the honor of nominating him as a Steward of the Royal Literary Fund.
2651. June 12: Hardy to John G. Hicks: typed transcript (supplied by Howard Bliss?) of reply to an inquiry of 2 June 1920 (which Hardy did not retain), about his associations with St. Juliot, Cornwall, and its being the scene of *A Pair of Blue Eyes*.
2652. June (20?): E. Thommen sends praise and thanks from a Swiss reader at Basel.
2653. June 28: Hardy to General John H. Morgan: transcript (supplied by Howard Bliss?); thanks Morgan for his birthday greetings and refers to the OUDS performance of *The Dynasts*.
2654. June 29: Brenda Murray Draper offers a small volume of poems "because of *The Dynasts*."
2655. July 4: E. V. Lucas asks permission for Charles Henry Millyer to call.
2656. July 6: Raymond Abbott news from Ventnor.
2657. July 6: Florence Henniker hopes to arrive at the Museum in Dorchester at 2 P.M.
2658. July 7: Hardy to Florence Henniker: the Museum will be a good place to meet on Thursday.
2659. July 13: Algernon Rose about the Authors' Club.
2660. July 15: Hardy to Gordon: rough draft of reply to Letter 2648.
2661. July 16: Bliss asks if the manuscript of "The Night of Trafalgar" which he now owns is the original MS.
2662. July 16: Belle Roosevelt repeats her request of 10 March 1920.
2663. July 17: Hardy to Bliss: rough draft of reply to Letter 2661; the *original* is part of the MS. of *The Dynasts* in the British Museum.
2664. July 23: Smith repeats his request of 1 June 1920.
2665. July 27: Charles M. Doughty thanks Hardy for the loan of his doctor's academic robe to use at Cambridge University.
2666. July (?): Hardy to Algernon Rose: rough draft, in the hand of Florence Hardy, of reply to an inquiry about Paul Jordan Smith as a desirable member of the Authors' Club.
2667. August 5: Hardy to Florence Henniker: is sending a copy of *Two on a Tower* to complete her set of the novels but regrets her preference for the novels.
2668. August 10: B. Fossett Lock is grateful for sympathy from Hardy (in the loss of his wife?).
2669. August 12: W. M. Colles about a Press Service, and asks for a message to the American people.
2670. August 20: G. Herbert Thring is sending "the illuminated address."
2671. August 22: Stair A. Gillon appreciative letter.
2672. August 23: Hardy to Thring: a copy, in ink, of his letter thanking Thring for the Address from the Society of Authors on his 80th birthday.
2673. August 24: Ridgely Torrence asks for some of Hardy's poetry for publication in *The New Republic*.
2674. August 25: Hardy to Colles: rough draft of a reply to Letter 2669; has nothing new to say.
2675. August 28: Clyde A. Beals asks for an interview and an opportunity to take a picture of Hardy.
2676. (August ?): Mary Law appreciation from Ohio.

2677. September 1: Edmund Blunden sends a volume of his verse.
2678. September 4: Gordon Bottomley sends a copy of his book.
2679. September 13: Margaret F. Gifford about the death of Evelyn Gifford of Oxford.
2680. September 13: R. L. Pocock about the Guard House at Seatown.
2681. September 19: Edgar A. Mitchell about Hardy's descriptions of Wessex.
2682. September 30: Lady Ilchester solicits the proceeds of one performance of the dramatization of *The Return of the Native* for the benefit of the County Hospital.
2683. September (?): Mrs. Roosevelt sends two guineas to pay for the autographs she requested on 10 March 1920 (request repeated on 16 July). [Hardy signed her books on 30 September 1920 and returned them to Oyster Bay, New York.]
2684. October 4: Harold Child asks if he can see Hardy on an errand for the London *Times*.
2685. October 5: G. O. Lloyd appreciation from Warwick.
2686. October 14: Edith Orr, from Maine, appreciation of Hardy's work.
2687. October 15: Child says Hardy's poem reached him and will appear in *The Times* on 11 November.
2688. October 15: Gordon Robbins sends a proof of his poem "And there was a great calm," which is to appear in a special Armistice Day section of *The Times*, 11 November, on the occasion of the burial of the Unknown Soldier in Westminster Abbey.
2689. October 17: Elizabeth A. (Mrs. William) Sharp asks permission for a young friend to call at Max Gate.
2690. October 24: Florence Henniker on reading *Two On A Tower*.
2691. October 28: Cockerell ocean letter, en route to America.
2692. October 31: Hardy to Florence Henniker: thanks for her letter about *Two On A Tower*.
2693. November 9: Cockerell about the MS. of *A Group of Noble Dames* in the Library of Congress in Washington, D. C.
2694. November 13: Ezra Pound sends the November issue of *The Dial* and hopes Hardy's work may appear in it in America.
2695. November 13: W. Beach Thomas asks permission to call.
2696. November 18: Maria Sargent appreciation from Massachusetts.
2697. November 21: Florence Henniker about a poem published in *The Times* on Armistice Day.
2698. November 22: Vere Collins proposes to come to Dorchester to see Hardy.
2699. November 27: Mrs. Allhusen asks Hardy to join her committee.
2700. November 28: Hardy to Pound: rough draft of reply to Letter 2694; has searched but has not found a poem for *The Dial*.
2701. November 30: Mrs. Allhusen thanks Hardy for his letter.
2702. December 2: William Rothenstein is sending a book.
2703. December 6: Ada Foster (Mrs. Henry M.) Alden solicits a contribution to a memorial volume after editor H. M. Alden's death.
2704. December 6: Charles E. Gifford about committing "The Oxen" to memory.
2705. December 15: H. W. Stewart thanks Hardy for autographing a copy of his *Collected Poems*.
2706. December 17: Ford Madox Ford solicits a contribution to the *Manchester Guardian* about the bloodshed in Ireland.

2707. December 17: Alfred Noyes sends two typed pages of comment on Hardy's philosophy. See *Later Years*, p. 215.
2708. December 19: Hardy to Ford: rough draft of reply to Letter 2706; refuses to join in the protest.
2709. December 20: F. M. Rankin asks for support of a movement to reinstate the Slade Professorship of Fine Art at Oxford University.
2710. December 20: James M. Tuohy solicits (for the *New York World*) a statement of Hardy's position on Disarmament.
2711. December 21: Alfred Noyes thanks Hardy for elucidation of his philosophy. See *Later Years*, pp. 215-218.
2712. December 22: Hardy to Florence Henniker: thanks for her present; Mrs. Hardy's sister is coming to Max Gate for Christmas.
2713. December 23: Hardy to Noyes: copy of his letter about "the Scheme of Things," in reply to Noyes's letter of 21 December. Published in *Later Years*, p. 218.
2714. December 23: Hardy to Tuohy: rough draft of reply to inquiry of 20 December; approves of international disarmament "on the lines indicated."
2715. December 24: Eden Phillpotts about "When to drop the curtain."
2716. December 27: John W. Cunliffe asks permission to quote.
2717. December 27: Henry Hardy (not Hardy's brother) about the Hardy pedigree.
2718. December 29: Dorothy Allhusen sends best wishes for 1921.
2719. December 31: Foster again about *Dorset Worthies*.
2720. December (?): A. H. Giles about early "mumming" experiences.
2721. (n. d.): William Reptors sends a copy of *The Fourth Age*.
2722. (n. d.): Hamilton Fyfe solicits support of a petition for a Civil List pension for Frederic Villiers.
2723. (n. d.): Helen Thomas about her husband's poetry.
2724. (n. d.): Lady Ilchester about her son's tutor's calling at Max Gate to talk with Hardy.

1921

2725. January 1: John Galsworthy sends New Year's greetings.
2726. January 4: Margaret Boehm appreciation from Baltimore, Maryland.
2727. January 4: Lady St. Helier tells Hardy it was sweet of him to remember her.
2728. January 5: Luther Munday, a candidate for election to the Athenaeum Club, solicits support.
2729. January 6: John D. Wade, from Georgia, asks Hardy's opinion of the American writer A. B. Longstreet.
2730. January 7: Will T. Howe, from Cincinnati, Ohio, about Theodore Spicer-Simson's desire to make a bronze relief of Hardy.
2731. January 8: H. J. Strong asks where he can get the music composed by Gustav Holst for Hardy's poem "The Homecoming."
2732. January 9: Hardy to Ada F. Alden: rough draft of reply to her solicitation of 6 December 1920: sends her a letter of her late husband; if he finds more he will send them.

2733. (c. January 10): Hardy to Strong: rough draft of reply to Letter 2731; "The Homecoming" music published in London in 1913 by Stainer & Bell.
2734. January 12: Albert A. Cock about the establishment of an independent University of Wessex.
2735. January 12: James S. Wilson solicits a contribution to a Virginia volume.
2736. January 13: Samuel A. Nock sends a poetic tribute from Haverford College in America.
2737. January 14: Hardy to Cock: rough draft of reply to Letter 2734, which Hardy read with much interest.
2738. January 14: Mrs. Gertrude Probert appreciation.
2739. January 16: Luther Munday thanks Hardy for his support at the Athenaeum Club.
2740. (c. January 17): Hardy to Howe: rough draft of reply to Letter 2730; he is willing.
2741. January 18: Ian MacAlister invites Hardy to attend the dinner and meeting of the Royal Institute of British Architects.
2742. January 19: Cock again about a University of Wessex.
2743. January 20: Hardy to MacAlister: rough draft of reply to Letter 2741; regrets.
2744. January 20: G. Lowes Dickinson pleased at receiving Hardy's letter about his book.
2745. January 24: John B. Harford asks permission to quote two letters Hardy wrote to Bishop H. C. G. Moule of Durham.
2746. January 25: Thomas Loveday about the proposed University of Wessex.
2747. January 27: John Burns sends a New York publication.
2748. January 27: John W. Cunliffe thanks Hardy for granting the permission requested in Letter 2716.
2749. January 28: Arthur Symons has seen Gertrude Bugler as Eustacia in a performance in London of *The Return of the Native* as dramatized by T. H. Tilley. (The play was performed in Dorchester on 17-18 November 1920, and in London on 27 January 1921.)
2750. February 3: J. J. Foster about Hardy's portraits.
2751. February 4: Edmund Gosse about a portrait of Hardy.
2752. February 6: Mrs. Ada Foster Alden thanks Hardy for his reply to her appeal of 6 December 1920.
2753. February 8: Gosse thanks Hardy for his prompt and full reply.
2754. February 9: Edward Clodd about a Biographical Dictionary of Rationalists.
2755. February 9: Vere Collins to Cecil Hanbury about the Hardy birthplace at Higher Bockhampton.
2756. February 11: Hanbury about Hardy's birthplace.
2757. February 11: H. W. Massingham solicits a poem for *The Nation*.
2758. February 11: Ernest M. Wilkenham about Hardy's portrait in the National Portrait Gallery.
2759. February 14: Brigadier-General John H. Morgan about the disarmament of Germany.
2760. February 16: Hanbury to Collins about the Hardy birthplace at Higher Bockhampton.

2761. February 22: Collins asks if Hardy would care to write an Introduction to one of Shakespeare's plays for a new series to be published by Oxford University Press.
2762. March 4: H. F. C. Marshall acknowledges receipt of a cheque.
2763. March 8: John C. Squire thanks Hardy for a poem.
2764. March 12: Florence Henniker about de Selincourt's lecture on Keats.
2765. March 13: Mlle I. Lichnerorvicz asks permission to translate *The Woodlanders* into French.
2766. March 15: Irene K. Hyman asks explanation of reference to "the Swaffham tinker" in *The Return of the Native*.
2767. March (16): Hardy to Hyman: rough draft of reply to Letter 2766; story of "the Swaffham tinker" may be found in reference books, it is too long to repeat in a letter. The tradition has been printed many times.
2768. March 17: Howe again about a bronze portrait of Hardy to be made by Spicer-Simson.
2769. March 17: Arthur R. Reade asks for help in obtaining a Municipal Theatre for West Ham.
2770. March 17: Ridgely Torrence repeats request of 24 August 1920 for something for *The New Republic* to publish.
2771. March 19: Sidney Morgan submits a cinema scenario of *The Mayor of Casterbridge* for Hardy's suggestions.
2772. March 22: Hardy to Morgan: rough draft of reply to Letter 2771; he will "see to the dialect," and the general arrangement seems to be good.
2773. March 28: Cock further reports on plans for a University of Wessex.
2774. March 29: Mlle I. Lichnerorvicz repeats request of 13 March.
2775. March 30: Hardy to Torrence: rough draft in pencil; will turn his attention to some verses for his pages.
2776. April 1: C. H. B. Quennell about saving a specimen of old English farm waggons for a museum.
2777. April 2: Sidney Morgan is grateful for Hardy's corrections in the cinema scenario of *The Mayor of Casterbridge*.
2778. April 5: Hardy to General John H. Morgan: about Morgan's Berlin business and his visit to Vienna.
2779. April 7: Hardy to Quennell: rough draft in pencil; praises for his interest in old farm waggons.
2780. April 11: Robert Watson from Vernon, British Columbia.
2781. April 12: Quennell again about old Dorset waggons.
2782. (c. April 13): The Anglo-French Poetry Society invites Hardy to become an honorary member.
2783. April 14: Hardy to Florence Henniker: glad she liked his Keats poem.
2784. April 14: Edward Hudson about the graceful shape of the old waggons.
2785. (c. April 15): Hardy to Hudson: rough draft of reply to Letter 2784; fears the old type of country waggon has nearly disappeared.
2786. April 15: Florence Henniker pleased to have had a visit from Florence Hardy.

134 MAX GATE CORRESPONDENCE

2787. April 18: St. John Ervine proposes that a group of critics, dramatists, novelists, and poets honor Hardy on his next birthday by presenting a first edition of one of Keats's books to him.
2788. April 19: James B. Ritchie asks permission to dramatize and produce *The Three Strangers* at Kelvinside Academy. Hardy endorsed this letter: "Permission given."
2789. April 21: Hardy to Ervine: rough draft of reply to Letter 2787; the deputation will be welcome in June but he suggests a more modest gift, such as Winkle's *Cathedrals of England*.
2790. April 28: Charles A. Speyer about setting to music "My love's gone a-fighting."
2791. May 5: A. Methuen thanks Hardy for permission to quote.
2792. May 6: Harold Macmillan about a misprint in *The Dynasts*, "despise" instead of "despite."
2793. May 7: Hardy to Macmillan: rough draft of reply to Letter 2792; thanks for calling attention to the misprint in *The Dynasts*.
2794. May 13: T. Fisher Unwin asks for a photograph of Hardy to be reproduced in forthcoming volume entitled *Portraits of the Nineties*.
2795. (c. May 14): Hardy to Unwin: rough draft in pencil; sends a photograph taken about 1895.
2796. May 14: Lady Cynthia Asquith sends thanks for a visit.
2797. May 15: W. H. Davies solicits something for *The Forum*.
2798. May 16: Mrs. Dorothy Bosanquet about the death of her father, Bishop Moule.
2799. May 16: John C. Squire about the Hawthornden Prize.
2800. May 19: Ervine sends details about the arrangements for the June presentation of an "Address" to Hardy and gives a list of the signatures.
2801. May 20: James Barrie asks Hardy to cancel the visit he was to pay him, because of the death at Oxford, through drowning, of his son, Michael.
2802. May 21: Lady Asquith thanks Hardy for his letter to Barrie.
2803. May 21: H. M. Margoliouth about a branch of the English Association at Southampton.
2804. May 21: John C. Squire thanks for Hardy's very kind letter.
2805. May 23: Mrs. Dorothy Bosanquet thanks for Hardy's letter.
2806. May 25: Hamilton Fyfe thanks Hardy for his part in obtaining a Civil List pension for Frederic Villiers.
2807. May 25: Ezra Pound accepts Hardy's poem, "The Two Houses," for *The Dial*; it will be in the August number.
2808. May 26: Florence Henniker invites Hardy to come with his wife for a visit of several days.
2809. May 28: Robert Nichols news from Japan.
2810. May 29: Hardy to the Anglo-French Poetry Society: rough draft of reply to Letter 2782; pleased to accept the distinction.
2811. May 31: Margoliouth again about a branch of the English Association.
2812. (n. d.): B. Gurevich about an Italian translation of *Life's Little Ironies*.
2813. June 1: Yone Noguchi sends a book from Japan.

On 2 June 1921 Hardy attained the age of 81. He received Birthday

Greetings from a dozen men and women, some of whom wrote on days other than 2 June (as indicated by the dates in parentheses):

2814. Sydney C. Cockerell
2815. Maurice Colburne (3 June)
2816. Stephen Collins (3 June)
2817. Lord Curzon (3 June)
2818. Sir George Douglas (31 May)
2819. John Galsworthy
2820. Florence Henniker
2821. C. Rex Niven (22 June)
2822. Thomas A. Pearcy (1 June)
2823. Madeleine Rolland (5 June)
2824. Lord & Lady Shaftesbury (4 June)
2825. Charles Whibley (3 June)

2826. June 2: Ervine letter to accompany the Keats book to be presented to Hardy.
2827. June 2: C. R. Stride invites Hardy to visit Sturminster Newton on 9 June; Cecil Hanbury will arrange for transportation.
2828. June 3: Hardy to Ervine: rough draft of reply to Letter 2800.
2829. June 3: Newman Flower sends proofs of a poem which Cassells are to publish next autumn in their *Winter Annual.*
2830. June 3: John Pollock about views of *The Dynasts.*
2831. June 5: J. L. Hamilton requests permission to paint Hardy's portrait.
2832. June 5: E. A. Reynolds-Ball appreciation from Italy.
2833. June 6: Fyfe invites Hardy to comment on Tolstoy's proposed "League of Thinkers."
2834. June 6: A. P. Hatton solicits something for the first number of *The British Legion.*
2835. (n. d.): Hardy to Hatton: rough draft in pencil; gives permission to publish either of the War Poems, all of which are in *Collected Poems.*
2836. (June 8): Hardy to Stride: rough draft of reply to Letter 2827; hopes to come with Mrs. Hardy.
2837. June 8: Scofield Thayer acknowledges receipt of Hardy's poem "The Two Houses" to appear in the August number of *The Dial.*
2838. June 9: Madame Mary Duclaux (whom Hardy had known 30 years earlier as Mme Darmesteter) friendly letter.
2839. June 12: Theodore Spicer-Simson about his bronze medallion of Hardy.
2840. June 13: Muriel Stuart acknowledges Hardy's answer.
2841. June (13): W. H. Wagstaff has been elected a Vice-President of the Royal Society of Literature.
2842. June 14: Hardy to Wagstaff: rough draft of reply to Letter 2841; fears he will be unable to render any service to the Society.
2843. June 14: John Galsworthy regrets not seeing Hardy in London.
2844. June 20: Sir Henry Newbolt asks permission to quote Hardy in an anthology.
2845. June 23: Hardy to Newbolt: rough draft in pencil; gives permission to quote.
2846. June 25: J. W. Hamilton solicits support of a Magna Charta Day.
2847. July 2: Hardy to Florence Henniker: about the Burdon Hotel at Weymouth and a film version of *The Mayor of Casterbridge.*
2848. July 4: Nowell Smith solicits support about proposed alterations in the Lady Chapel of Sherborne Abbey.
2849. (c. July 5): Hardy to Smith: rough draft of reply to Letter 2848; will join Smith in signing a letter about it.

2850. July 5: Walter de la Mare about how he treasures the days at Dorchester.
2851. July 5: Florence Henniker on Walter de la Mare, etc.
2852. July 5: J. Middleton Murry about Hardy's poems, "Veteris Vestigia Flammae."
2853. July 12: N. R. Hariharaiyer, from Madras, about permission to prepare a volume of Hardy's poems for use in India. (Three previous letters on this subject are no longer present in the Max Gate files: 1. the first request Hardy received; 2. his reply dated 9 March 1921; 3. Hariharaiyer's reply of 25 April 1921.)
2854. July 15: Ernest Rhys about "The Superstitious Man." Asks if it can be called the best of Hardy's short stories.
2855. July 20: Ruth (Mrs. Henry) Head asks permission to compile a Hardy anthology for publication by Chatto & Windus.
2856. July 21: Hardy to Mrs. Head: rough draft of reply to Letter 2855; has no objection.
2857. July 21: Spicer-Simson about the medallion of Hardy.
2858. (c. July 22): Hardy to Spicer-Simson: rough draft of reply to Letter 2857.
2859. July 22: F. S. Flint glad to know his book interested Hardy.
2860. July 23: Mrs. Head thanks Hardy for his permission for the preparation of an anthology of his writings.
2861. July 24: John Masefield asks if he may call at Max Gate.
2862. July 28: A. Methusen note about a change in his anthology.
2863. July 31: John Hindsmith about the Omar Khayyam Club.
2864. August 4: Hardy to N. R. Hariharaiyer: rough draft; denies permission to publish a volume of his poems in India.
2865. August 5: Dorothy (Mrs. Cecil) Hanbury asks Hardy to stand godfather to her daughter Caroline. (Hardy consented.)
2866. August 5: Spicer-Simson again about his medallion of Hardy.
2867. August 7: Hardy to Mrs. Head: rough draft of reply to her letter of 23 July 1921; a long list of suggestions for her anthology.
2868. August 7: Hardy to Rhys: rough draft of reply to inquiry about "The Superstitious Man."
2869. August 8: Henry W. Sim appreciation from Valparaiso, Chile.
2870. August 10: Arthur Bryant asks permission to call.
2871. August 10: Hamilton repeats his request of 25 June 1921.
2872. August 15: Siegfried Sassoon, touring in Italy, has just come from Verona.
2873. August 16: Mrs. Head tells Hardy his letter of 7 August threw her back on her own judgment and has had a salutary effect on her.
2874. August 18: Mrs. Hanbury thanks Hardy for being willing to stand godfather to her daughter Caroline.
2875. August 21: Edgar A. Mitchell sends a copy of *In An Eastern Rose Garden.*
2876. (c. August 24): Douglas Fawcett, from Wenger, Switzerland, about *The Dynasts,* and sends a copy of his book, *Divine Imagining.*
2877. August 24: Abigail Brown Tompkins sends a water-color painting.
2878. August 27: Hardy to Hamilton: rough draft of reply to Letter 2871; thinks the scheme has a hopeful look.
2879. August 28: John Pollock is glad Hardy found his work worth notice.

2880. August 29: Hardy to Douglas Fawcett: rough draft of letter acknowledging receipt of a copy of *Divine Imagining*.
2881. (c. August 30): Fawcett discusses philosophical matters suggested by his reading of *The Dynasts*.
2882. August 31: Mrs. Hanbury thanks Hardy for a present, the MS. of a poem "To C. F. H." written for the occasion of the christening of Caroline Fox Hanbury. See *Later Years*, p. 224.
2883. September 1: A. Ivor Parry asks permission to quote.
2884. September 6: Otto Karl Müller asks permission to translate "A Tragedy of Two Ambitions" into German.
2885. September 8: Ervine note enclosing "the Tribute" which came to him from the binders today.
2886. (c. September 9): Hardy to Ervine: rough draft in pencil; acknowledgment of the Poets' Tribute; he feels more than he can express.
2887. September 10: Walter William Ouless asks if Hardy would sit for a portrait.
2888. (c. September 12): Hardy to Ouless: rough draft of reply agreeing to sit for a portrait.
2889. September 13: Samuel C. Chew asks permission to call at Max Gate.
2890. (c. September 15): Hardy to Chew: rough draft of reply to request for permission to call; will welcome Professor and Mrs. Chew, but wants nothing personal to be published after their visit.
2891. September 16: Nils Kittelsen asks for an interview, with a view to a report to be published in Stockholm.
2892. September 16: Hardy to Kittelsen: rough draft of reply; is not able to grant an interview.
2893. September 17: The Rev. Thomas J. Hardy sends a *Dorsetshire Garland*.
2894. September 19: E. Austin Hinton about a thesis on Hardy's poetry.
2895. September 22: Roger Ingpen invites Hardy to write a sonnet on Shelley for publication in a centennial edition of "Epipsychidion."
2896. September 24: Hardy to the Rev. Thomas J. Hardy: rough draft of reply to Letter 2893; the *Dorsetshire Garland* is new to him.
2897. September 24: Hardy to Ingpen: rough draft of reply to Letter 2895; may use either of Hardy's already published poems about Shelley.
2898. September 25: Harold Child has been requested to write more about Hardy's work.
2899. September 26: John Pollock about a little play of his.
2900. September 27: Parry repeats his request of 1 September.
2901. September 28: Ingpen thanks Hardy for the permission given in Letter 2897.
2902. September 29: Hardy to Parry: rough draft of reply to Letter 2900; asks who he is.
2903. September 29: William Nichols has finished the woodcut for Hardy's *Poems*.
2904. September 30: Parry says he will not trouble Hardy further.
2905. October 3: Siegfried Sassoon from Rome.
2906. October 5: Harold Spender invites Hardy to sign an "Address" to be presented to Frederic Harrison on his 90th birthday.
2907. October 5: Tuohy requests a comment on Disarmament.

2908. October 6: G. S. Churchill asks whether "The Burghers" (one of the *Wessex Poems*) is founded on fact.
2909. October 6: Hardy to Churchill: rough draft of reply to Letter 2908; Colliton House [in Dorchester] was in his mind as the scene of the enactment, but does not recall particulars.
2910. October 6: Hardy to Harold Spender: reply to Letter 2906; has signed the address with pleasure.
2911. October 9: Hardy to Mrs. Cecil Popham: remembers her half-sister, Mrs. Henry Reeve, very well.
2912. October 10: Ouless about Hardy's sitting for a portrait.
2913. October 11: Leonard Rees thanks Hardy for a kindness.
2914. October 17: Alfred Grey about Hardy's signing 14 vellum copies of his *Poems* for the Medici Society.
2915. October 18: Sir Hugh Clifford pleased to have heard from Hardy.
2916. October 18: Hardy to Tuohy: rough draft of reply to Letter 2907.
2917. October 19: A. E. Bevan asks permission to reprint. (Hardy gave permission to take any five pages of *The Trumpet-Major*.)
2918. October 20: Sir Henry Newbolt thanks Hardy for his contribution to Newbolt's Anthology.
2919. October 22: Tess M. Hope appreciation.
2920. October 25: Clifford J. Druse asks permission for a Christmas performance of a dramatization of *The Three Strangers*.
2921. October 25: Florence Henniker on Galsworthy's style and his detestation of the respectable.
2922. (c. October 26): Hardy to Druse: rough draft of reply to Letter 2920; no objection if the performance is limited to Christmas.
2923. October 26: Leslie Wylde thanks Hardy for a drive.
2924. October 27: Newman Flower sends a copy of Cassell's *Winter Annual* containing Hardy's poem "The Country Wedding."
2925. October 29: Claude G. Montefiore about the proposed University of Wessex.
2926. October 31: Hardy to Montefiore: rough draft in pencil; he agrees.
2927. November 1: Chew thanks Mrs. Hardy for her hospitality when he and Mrs. Chew called at Max Gate.
2928. November 1: Algernon Ward asks support of his candidacy for election as a Fellow of the Royal Society of Literature.
2929. November 2: Montefiore again about the proposed University of Wessex.
2930. November 2: Parry, despite having written Letter 2904, now writes peevishly if he may have the favor of a reply.
2931. November 2: Edward Shanks solicits a poem for the *London Mercury*.
2932. November 8: Sir George Douglas sends premature congratulations to Hardy "on winning the Nobel Prize."
2933. November 9: Shanks thanks Hardy for a poem for the *London Mercury*.
2934. November 14: Ernest J. White invites Hardy to attend a Special Meeting on 23 November when the Freedom of the City of Bath is to be bestowed on Frederic Harrison on his 90th birthday.
2935. November 15: Oscar Browning about Napoleon.
2936. November 18: John Buchan sends a 2-vol. *History of the War*.

2937. November 21: Esther Hallam Meynell about the great impression made by *The Dynasts* and the *Poems*.
2938. November 24: Browning about Napoleon and *The Dynasts*.
2939. November 27: Albert Sterling appreciation from Cincinnati, Ohio.
2940. November 30: Torrence says the publishers of *The New Republic* are happy to receive Hardy's poem ("The Haunting Fingers").
2941. December 5: Walter de la Mare thanks for two books Hardy had lent him.
2942. December 8: Torrence sends $100 in payment for the poem acknowledged in Letter 2940.
2943. December 8: Siegfried Sassoon admires Hardy's lines in the *Saturday Review*.
2944. December 11: Florence Henniker asks "Who is Haley?"
2945. December 13: Sir Arthur Spurgeon asks permission to print a letter of Hardy's.
2946. December 14: Hardy to Spurgeon: rough draft of reply to Letter 2945; gives permission but calls attention to two errors in the copy of his letter.
2947. December 19: Hardy to Florence Henniker: on the young architect who was the original of Stephen Smith in *A Pair of Blue Eyes;* on Walter de la Mare's recent poems, etc.
2948. December 19: Algernon Ward thanks Hardy for his kind action and says he has been elected a Fellow of the Royal Society of Literature.
2949. December 22: Vere Collins sends three guineas in payment for permission to include three poems in an anthology.
2950. December 22: Hamilton asks Hardy to suggest an Executive Vice-President.
2951. December 25: Mrs. Hanbury sends Christmas wishes.
2952. December 27: Gordon Gifford thanks Mrs. Hardy for a visit.
2953. (n. d.): August Brunius has sent his translation into Swedish of *The Return of the Native*.
2954. (n. d.): C. A. Dawson Scott about the P. E. N. Club.
2955. (n. d.): Scott again about the P. E. N. Club.
2956. (n. d.): W. H. Shewring appreciation from Bristol.

1922

2957. January 1: Edward Clodd about his reading.
2958. January 10: Cedric Chivers solicits something about Bath for the Bath Records Society.
2959. January 17: T. L. Davidson asks Mrs. Hardy for advice about putting on one of Hardy's dramatized novels.
2960. January 20: H. Nagaoka from Tokyo, about Japanese interest in the *Wessex Novels*.
2961. January 24: Joseph Anthony about a poem for the *Century Magazine* of New York.
2962. January 25: Hardy to Anthony: rough draft of reply to Letter 2961; hopes Anthony will get his contribution into the April number of the *Century*.

2963. January 29: Hardy to Chivers: rough draft of reply to Letter 2958; about presenting a replica of 'Aquae Sulis' in *Moments of Vision* as a Bath Record, if the Society promises it would not be sold.
2964. January 30: George Henry Payne asks for a contribution for *The Forum*.
2965. January 31: G. Lowes Dickinson thanks Hardy for his last book of poems.
2966. January 31: H. B. Elliott repeats his earlier request.
2967. January 31: Arnold W. Harwood solicits a preface for a book on architecture.
2968. February 1: Chivers sends a book of *Ancient Records* of Bath.
2969. February 2: Wade repeats request made in Letter 2729.
2970. February 6: Clotilda Marson about the *Collected Poems*.
2971. February 9: Frank Roscoe asks for support in protesting against the curtailment of national expenditure on education.
2972. February 10: Clifford Bax solicits a contribution to a new quarterly of Art and Letters.
2973. (c. February 11): Hardy to Bax: rough draft of reply to Letter 2972; regrets he can be of no service.
2974. February 13: Edmund Gosse friendly letter.
2975. (c. February 14): Hardy to Payne: rough draft of reply to Letter 2964; is unable to accommodate him.
2976. February 14: Bax is grateful for Hardy's reply to Letter 2972.
2977. February 14: H. B. Elliott again asks permission to quote.
2978. February 14: John C. Squire says The Riccardi edition [of Hardy's *Selected Poems*] is very fine.
2979. February 15: Sydney C. Cockerell about proofs and corrections in the forthcoming *Late Lyrics*.
2980. February 17: Cockerell about Mrs. Hardy's ill health.
2981. February 20: Hardy to Wade: rough draft of reply to Letter 2969; he has never read *Georgia Scenes*.
2982. February 21: Hardy to Sir Frederick Macmillan: carbon copy of typed letter; about proofs of *Late Lyrics*.
2983. February 22: Macmillan proposes 16 May as the date for publication of *Late Lyrics*.
2984. February 23: Hardy to Macmillan: rough draft; approves the May date for publishing *Late Lyrics*.
2985. February 24: H. Bonnaire about cinema rights in Hardy's novels.
2986. February 25: Cockerell about corrections in the proofs of *Late Lyrics*.
2987. February 25: Guy N. Pocock asks permission to quote from two novels.
2988. February 26: J. F. Symons-Jeune sends a pamphlet.
2989. February 26: H. W. Stewart thanks Hardy for autographing a copy of *The Dynasts*.
2990. February 27: Doris L. Causton appreciation.
2991. March 1: Hardy to Florence Henniker: he has been ill; Florence has had influenza; Emma's cousin, Charles Gifford, died last week; and "Wessex" (the dog) is ill.
2992. March 1: George T. Keating about a special binding to be put by Riviere & Son on a copy of *Selected Poems*.
2993. March 1: Riviere & Son to Keating about the special binding for Hardy's *Poems*.

2994. March 3: Sir Frederick Macmillan about selling poems to American magazines.
2995. March 6: Chivers thanks Hardy for the gift of a manuscript of part of his poem, "Aquae Sulis," referring to ancient Bath.
2996. March 7: Macmillan about cinema rights.
2997. March 8: N. R. Hariharaiyer sends a copy of his study of Hardy's *Return of the Native*.
2998. March 9: Mary Mackinnon appreciation from Australia.
2999. March 9: H. F. C. Marshall elected a Vice-President of the Royal Literary Fund.
3000. March 9: Sir Hama Thornycroft on various subjects.
3001. March 10: Hardy to Bonnaire: rough draft of reply to Letter 2985; unable to say which of his novels are still available for cinema production.
3002. March 10: Florence Henniker about various matters, including Sir James Barrie having been awarded the O. M., which she considers absurd.
3003. March 10: Macmillan about proofs of the May volume.
3004. March 12: Hardy to Marshall: rough draft in pencil; acknowledges receipt of Letter 2999.
3005. March 13: Andrew Bennett says the University of St. Andrews is going to confer the Honorary Degree of Doctor of Laws upon him.
3006. March 13: Cockerell about proofs and corrections in *Late Lyrics*.
3007. March 15: Hardy to Bennett: rough draft of reply to Letter 3005; thanks Bennett but says he cannot come to Scotland to receive the degree.
3008. March 16: W. M. Colles offers his services as literary agent, for the disposal of cinema rights in Hardy's novels.
3009. March 17: Hardy to Colles: rough draft of reply to Letter 3008; he is "not keen" on it.
3010. March 17: Bennett says the Senate of the University of St. Andrews will probably not insist on his presence to receive the honorary degree.
3011. March 17: Aylmer Maude about the need for a good translation of the works of Tolstoy into English.
3012. March 19: Hardy to Harley Granville-Barker; typed transcript; thanks for his new book.
3013. March 19: Hardy to Maude: rough draft of reply to Letter 3011; approves the idea.
3014. March 20: Colles again about marketing the film rights in the Wessex Novels.
3015. March 21: Juliet Lady Pollock admiration.
3016. March 23: Gilbert Murray testimonial about the ability of Charles King as a student at Oxford. (The testimonial reached Hardy later, with a letter from King dated 8 September 1924.)
3017. March 24: Cockerell again about corrections in the proofs of *Late Lyrics*.
3018. March 25: H. G. Mongruerly about Hardy's essay on Coloured Brick which won the Royal Institute of British Architects prize.
3019. (c. March 26): Hardy to Mongruerly: rough draft of reply to Letter 3018; the essay was lost.
3020. March 26: Cockerell returns the proofs of "Apology" which is to appear in *Late Lyrics*.

3021. March 27: Harold Child returns proofs.
3022. March 28: Markström appreciation from Upsala, Sweden.
3023. March 29: Petronella Nell sends a poem from Chiswick.
3024. March 30: W. M. Parker geographical letter.
3025. April 10: Ruby Poulsom appreciation.
3026. April 12: Rosaline Masson writes Hardy to contribute to a book to be entitled *I Can Remember Robert Louis Stevenson*.
3027. April 13: Robert Bridges thanks Hardy for his donation to the Society for Pure English.
3028. April 15: Theodore Spicer-Simson about his bronze medallion of Hardy.
3029. April 19: Willfrid F. Hodges about the Library at the Dorchester Grammar School.
3030. April 20: Frazier Hunt asks permission to call.
3031. April 25: Vere Collins says *Far from the Madding Crowd* has been prescribed for school examinations in Wales.
3032. April 26: Hardy to Hunt: rough draft of reply to Letter 3030; declines any kind of interview.
3033. April 28: T. Hidaka appreciation from a Japanese.
3034. May 2: John Buchan sends Volume III of his *History of the War*.
3035. May 3: Alfred Grey about Hardy signing a dozen vellum copies of *Selected Poems* published by the Riccardi Press.
3036. May 4: Bennett says the L.L.D. degree was conferred on him "in absentia" at St. Andrews on 3 May.
3037. May 5: Florence Henniker invites Hardy and his wife to visit in her new home in Highgate; comments on Barrie's plays.
3038. May 6: Hardy to Bennett: rough draft; acknowledges receipt of the L.L.D. diploma from St. Andrews.
3039. May 6: Armstrong Gibbs sends a musical setting for "When I set out for Lyonnesse."
3040. May 9: Hardy to Gibbs: rough draft in pencil; thanks for the music.
3041. May 9: Lola Fisher appreciation from Australia.
3042. May 9: Sir Frederick Macmillan about Hardy's autographing a first edition of *Desperate Remedies*.
3043. May 10: Newman Flower invites Hardy to dinner at the Savoy in London and offers to place a suite of rooms there at his disposal.
3044. May 12: Mrs. H. M. Hyndman solicits Hardy's support of a Memorial Committee.
3045. May 15: Flower regrets Hardy's recent illness prevents his attending the dinner at the Savoy.
3046. May 18: W. G. Bowman about establishing a new monthly magazine devoted to the Wessex Movement.
3047. May 18: John Purves solicits Hardy's recollections of R. L. Stevenson.
3048 May 19: Christos Djaferis appreciation from Turkey.
3049. May 21: Hardy to Dr. and Mrs. Head: rough draft; praises their anthology *Pages from the Works of Thomas Hardy* and offers some suggestions if a second impression of the book should be called for.
3050. May 23: Mrs. Allhusen thanks Hardy for a letter.
3051. May 23: Henry Head thanks Hardy for Letter 3049.
3052. May 23: Purves is grateful for Hardy's recollections of Stevenson.

3053. May 24: Octavia Gregory congratulates Hardy on *Late Lyrics;* especially likes the poem "To a Dumb Friend."
3054. May 25: Sir Frederick Macmillan writes about gift copies of *Late Lyrics and Earlier.*
3055. May 25: Rosaline Masson about plans for her book on Stevenson.
3056. May 26: Cockerell says *Late Lyrics* came today.
3057. May 26: Sir Frederick Macmillan about Mr. and Mrs. Henry Head's *Pages from the Works of Thomas Hardy.*
3058. May 26: E. L. (Mrs. James) Wright asks permission to use Hardy's poem "This is the weather the cuckoo likes" with music she has composed for it.
3059. May 27: Hardy to Bowman: rough draft of reply to Letter 3046; thinks the magazine could take up the matter of preservation of local names.
3060. May 27: Hardy to Rosaline Masson: rough draft of reply to Letter 3055; he intended his "page of recollections" for her, but it was sent by error to John Purves. (Refers to Robert Louis Stevenson.)
3061. May 27: David Sobol appreciation from New York City.
3062. May 28: Mrs. Jessie Adams asks permission to set several of Hardy's poems to music.
3063. May 28: Florence Henniker hopes to spend a week in Dorchester, 26 June to 1 July 1922, and would like to visit the country of *The Woodlanders.*
3064. May 29: Hardy to Florence Henniker (his last letter to her): is glad she is to be in Dorchester and he will show her the country of *The Woodlanders.*
3065. May 29: Charles A. Sackett appreciation from New York.
3066. May 30: Hardy to Macmillan: rough draft of reply to Letter 3057.
3067. May (?): Arthur Symons about Hardy's verses in *Late Lyrics.*
3068. June 1: Edward Clodd says Shorter has been to see him.

On 2 June 1922 Hardy attained the age of 82. He received birthday greetings from 34 men and women, some of whom wrote just before or just after 2 June (on the date indicated in the parentheses):

3069. R. Bickerstaffe
3070. A. H. Billington
3071. James & Edith Bradshaw
3072. John Buchan
3073. Katherine Burton
3074. James Cawson
3075. Harold Child
3076. Sydney Cockerell (1 June)
3077. Sir George Douglas (31 May)
3078. Edward & Emma Dugdale
3079. M. T. Evans
3080. Stanley Galpin
3081. Harry Goldman (30 April)
3082. Harley Granville-Barker
3083. C. N. Hardy
3084. Frederic Harrison (23 May)
3085. Florence Henniker
3086. Alida Lady Hoare
3087. Dorothea G. Hogg
3088. Audrey M. Little
3089. S. T. Lord
3090. J. H. Mills
3091. W. M. Parker
3092. Constance Pocock
3093. Jane Ratcliffe
3094. Walter H. Richter
3095. T. H. Rogers
3096. Siegfried Sassoon (1 June)
3097. Clement K. Shorter (1 June)
3098. J. S. Udal (1 June)
3099. Cecil Wedmore
3100. L. M. Whitby
3101. Winifred M. Williams
3102. Thomas J. Wise

3103. June 2: Bowman asks for an article for the new Wessex journal.

3104. June 2: John Hawke has read *Under the Greenwood Tree* many times; solicits help with a book on Wordsworth.
3105. (c. June 3): Hardy to Hawke: is unable to assist him.
3106. June 3: F. C. Owlett about the "Apology" in *Late Lyrics*.
3107. June 4: Mrs. M. M. Gordon sends her poem on *Tess*.
3108. June 5: Sir Clifford Allbutt personal letter.
3109. June 7: H. R. H. Princess Marie Louise about poems for the library in the Queen's Doll's House.
3110. June 8: Tom Bass appreciation from Manchester.
3111. June 8: C. W. Saleeby admires the new poems in *Late Lyrics* and is outraged at an article by Hewlett in *The Times*.
3112. June 10: Clive Holland asks Mrs. Hardy for permission to call at Max Gate with a view to writing on Hardy's Dorset.
3113. June 10: Harold Monro asks various questions about Hardy's poetry.
3114. June 10: Alfred Watkins about a booklet on Early Trackways.
3115. June 11: Hardy to Holland: rough draft in pencil; he has had to give up receiving writers about Dorset.
3116. June 11: Allbutt another personal letter.
3117. June 11: John Galsworthy thanks Hardy for *Late Lyrics*.
3118. June 14: Vere H. Collins has engaged himself to translate Mr. Hedgcock's book into English.
3119. June 15: Anthony Bertram appreciation.
3120. June 15: Edmund Blunden glad Hardy takes pleasure in his *Shepherd*.
3121. June 15: John Lane about adding a chapter on Hardy's poetry in a new edition of Lionel Johnson's *Art of Thomas Hardy*.
3122. June 15: A. J. Rhodes asks permission to reprint "The West-of-Wessex Girl" in the *Western Weekly News* of Plymouth.
3123. June 16: Hardy to Monro: rough draft of reply to Letter 3113; asks to be spared from replying to Monro's questions.
3124. June 16: R. Golding Bright asks about the film rights of *Tess*.
3125. June 16: Princess Marie Louise again about poems for the library in the Queen's Doll's House.
3126. June 16: W. Kean Seymour asks permission to quote.
3127. June 16: John C. Squire thanks Hardy for a reprint.
3128. June 17: Hardy to Bright: rough draft of reply to Letter 3124; the film rights have been sold.
3129. June 17: Hardy to Rhodes: rough draft of reply to Letter 3122; gives permission and suggests the poem "The Marble-streeted Town" also be used.
3130. June 17: Florence Henniker lists the poems she likes best in *Late Lyrics* and says the book is sadder in tone than he is.
3131. June 18: Hamlin Garland is again in England and wants to see Hardy while there.
3132. June 19: Mrs. G. A. Acland asks about "Acland" in *The Dynasts*.
3133. June 20: Captain Arnold Gathercole appreciation.
3134. June 20: A. D. Gristwood appreciation.
3135. June 21: Hardy to Mrs. Acland: rough draft of reply to Letter 3132; the Acland mentioned was not in the navy but was a brigadier-general in the army.
3136. June 21: Collins again about translating Hedgcock's French book on Hardy.

3137. June 22: Hardy to Collins: rough draft of reply to Letter 3136; disapproves of the plan to publish a translation of Hedgcock's book.
3138. June 22: Florence E. Hardy to Collins: typed copy of letter regarding his very objectionable proposal to translate Hedgcock's offensive book about Hardy into English.
3139. June 23: Nicholas Murray Butler invites Hardy to attend a Conference of British and American Professors at Columbia University in June 1923.
3140. (n. d.): Hardy to President Butler: rough draft of reply to Letter 3139; regrets he is unable to accept the invitation.
3141. June 23: Collins again about Hedgcock's French book on Hardy.
3142. June 24: Florence E. Hardy to Collins: another letter making it clear that Hedgcock's book is extremely objectionable in Hardy's eyes.
3143. June 26: Florence Henniker, from London; in an address at the Haymarket Theatre Sir Henry Newbolt recently stated that the four great writers who are the most sustaining and consoling are Shakespeare, Chaucer, Browning, and Hardy.
3144. June 26: George Newnes sends a book on science by J. Arthur Thomson.
3145. June 27: Collins again about the Hedgcock book.
3146. June 27: Robert Riviere & Son about the special binding for a copy of Hardy's *Selected Poems* for G. T. Keating, who wants Hardy to autograph the book.
3147. June 28: G. Julius Caesar asks some advice.
3148. June 28: Gertrude M. (Mrs. Waldo) Richards asks permission to quote.
3149. June 28: John Lane about the new edition of Lionel Johnson's book on Hardy.
3150. June 29: Hardy to Lane: typed copy to be signed "F. E. Hardy," replying to Letter 3149.
3151. June 30: Miss G. M. Faulding solicits a poem for a review.
3152. June 30: G. Herbert Thring asks if Hardy authorized a Czech translation of the *Romantic Adventures of a Milkmaid*.
3153. July 1: Hardy to Miss Faulding: rough draft of reply to Letter 3151; sends regrets.
3154. July 1: Garland repeats his desire to see Hardy while he is in England.
3155. July 2: Hardy to Thring: typed copy of answer to Letter 3152; does not remember authorizing a Czech translation of the *Romantic Adventures of a Milkmaid* and prefers to do nothing about the matter.
3156. July 2: Florence E. Hardy to Collins: typed copy of letter emphasizing Hardy's disapproval of Frank Hedgcock's book.
3157. July 2: Leo H. Wolf about a German translation of *Jude*.
3158. July 3: Hardy to Bowman: rough draft in pencil; is unable to contribute to his journal.
3159. July 3: Mira Duchess of Hamilton solicits help in protesting against present vivisectionist practices.
3160. July 3: Lane again about the projected edition of Lionel Johnson's *Art*.
3161. July 4: Garland thanks Mrs. Hardy for permission to call at Max Gate.

3162. July 4: Madame Henry appreciation.
3163. July 4: Thring about the drafting of a will.
3164. July 5: Hardy to the Duchess of Hamilton: copy of reply to her Letter 3159.
3165. July 5: Bowman again about the new magazine devoted to Wessex.
3166. July 5: Collins says he has written to Frank Hedgcock to withdraw his commitment to translate the French book, because Hardy does not wish an English translation published.
3167. July 7: Roger Ingpen sends a volume commemorating the centenary of Shelley's death.
3168. July 7: Walter Tittle asks permission to make a "dry-point" portrait of Hardy.
3169. (c. July 8): Hardy to Tittle: rough draft; is not able to sit to him.
3170. July 9: Florence E. Hardy to Collins: typed copy of a letter with further condemnation of Hedgcock's book.
3171. July 9: Hedgcock to Mrs. Hardy, explaining his position about the proposed translation by Collins.
3172. July 10: Hardy to George Newnes: rough draft; acknowledges the gift of a book on science.
3173. July 10: Lockwood Thompson appreciation from Cleveland, Ohio.
3174. July 11: Hardy to F. W. Slater (of Harper and Brothers): Copy of letter asking why their report of sales to the end of 1921 contains no returns for the Anniversary Edition in 21 volumes.
3175. July 12: Florence E. Hardy to Hedgcock: rough draft of letter, obviously inspired by Hardy, regretting Hedgcock's indulgence in personalities in his book.
3176. July 12: Vernon Hill about a first sitting for a portrait.
3177. July 12: Frederick Macmillan about the sale of *The Dynasts* and *Collected Poems* in America.
3178. July 12: Slater promises to investigate the failure of Harpers to report on sales of the Anniversary Edition.
3179. July 13: Bright inquires about the availability of *The Three Wayfarers* for production in New York.
3180. July 13: A. J. Rhodes thanks Hardy for permission to reprint his poems in the Plymouth *Western News*.
3181. July 15: Francis Macnamara about founding *The Wessex Review*.
3182. July 16: Mrs. Allhusen about the betrothal of her eldest daughter Madeleine.
3183. July 16: John C. Squire offers Hardy the presidency of The Architectural Club.
3184. July 17: Hardy to Squire: rough draft of reply to Letter 3183; has reservations about accepting.
3185. July 20: Hardy to Macnamara: rough draft of reply to Letter 3181; hopes the new *Review* will be a success.
3186. July 20: Walter de la Mare about publishers and permissions.
3187. July 20: Leonard Rees wants a poem for the *Sunday Times*.
3188. July 22: George Herbert Clarke asks permission to call.
3189. July 22: Wilfrid Gibson sends a copy of his new book.
3190. July 22: Margaret F. Gifford about Hardy's poem on the death of Evelyn Gifford.
3191. July 22: Ernest Greene appreciation.
3192. July 24: Hardy to Rees: rough draft of reply to Letter 3187; cannot find a poem to send to Rees.

CHRONOLOGICAL LIST

3193. July 26: Cyril W. Beaumont wants something by Hardy to publish.
3194. July 26: Alexander Kadison appreciation from New York.
3195. July 26: Mary Metzler appreciation from Luxembourg.
3196. July 27: Gibson is proud because his book has interested Hardy.
3197. July 31: Macnamara about the portrait of Hardy by Augustus John.
3198. August 1: The Duchess of Hamilton asks Hardy for a few lines to *The Times* about the Anti-Vivisection Society.
3199. August 1: Princess Marie Louise again about poems for the library in the Queen's Doll's House
3200. August 4: Raymond Abbott from Ventnor.
3201. August 4: Miss B. Cox asks Hardy's opinion of three MSS.
3202. August 4: Ouless tells Hardy his portrait was in the Royal Academy Exhibition.
3203. August 7: George J. Smyth about a California thesis about the influence of Euripides on the writings of Hardy.
3204. August 10: Sir Frederick Pollock on *Late Lyrics*.
3205. August 12: Ouless again about his portrait of Hardy.
3206. August 14: E. Lonsdale Deighton solicits an autograph line or two for sale to benefit British servicemen.
3207. August 15: George T. Keating says the specially-bound copy of *Selected Poems* has reached him and he is sending money to pay for the autograph Hardy had written in the book.
3208. August 16: W. Lock thanks Hardy for his sympathy upon the death of Lock's brother.
3209. August 17. Beatrice (Mrs. Leslie) Thomson sends thanks for Hardy's most recent book of poems.
3210. August 18: Moore & Minger, the firm of George T. Keating, send two guineas that were not enclosed in Letter 3207.
3211. August 19: Sir Frederick Pollock couples Turgeniev with Flaubert as artists.
3212. August 20: Edgar R. Brown asks permission to reprint "The Oxen."
3213. August 20: S. B. Siddall asks permission to print "The Homecoming" on a concert program.
3214. August 23: Hardy to Siddall: rough draft, in Hardy's hand; grants permission to print.
3215. August 26: J. B. Jones appreciation.
3216. August 29: Florence Henniker has not been well.
3217. September 2: Chew, from London, asks for suggestions for revisions in his book about Hardy.
3218. September 5: George Herbert Clarke sends thanks for a call at Max Gate.
3219. September 5: Ethel Millns asks if Hardy received a cheque in payment for permission to quote two poems.
3220. September 5: Mary (Mrs. Henry B. L.) Webb asks permission to dedicate her *Seven for a Secret* to Hardy.
3221. September 9: Dudley Field Malone offers his legal services in Paris or in New York.
3222. September 11: C. H. Hornby sends a shooting-seat.
3223. September 11: J. J. Walne about connecting Max Gate plumbing with the Dorchester Town Water Supply.

3224. September 12: Jim Tully, a California admirer, hopes Hardy has seen reviews of his autobiographical novel, *Emmett Lawler*.
3225. September 13: A. V. Houghton about the English Association.
3226. September 15: S. M. Ellis about his review of *Late Lyrics* in the *Fortnightly Review*.
3227. September 15: Houghton again about The English Association.
3228. September 15: Miss Daisy D. Solomon solicits a contribution for establishing an Olive Schreiner Memorial nursery in Cape Town.
3229. September 16: Miss Berenice C. Skidelsky asks permission to call.
3230. September 17: Florence Hardy to Chew: copy of a letter enclosing notes for the new edition of his book.
3231. September 18: Hardy to Miss Skidelsky: rough draft of reply to Letter 3229; is unable to give appointment.
3232. September 21: Stanley I. Galpin wants Hardy's opinion of Charles Dickens.
3233. September 22: Arthur S. Pearce asks advice on the rejection of poems by editors.
3234. September 22: Thring about the financial difficulties of the Society of Authors.
3235. September 23: Mrs. Allhusen asks advice about choosing hymns for Madeleine Allhusen's wedding service.
3236. September 25: Hardy to Galpin: rough draft of reply to Letter 3232; asks to be excused.
3237. September 27: Ian Hay Beith thanks Hardy for a gift.
3238. October 2: Mrs. Allhusen thanks Hardy for his help.
3239. October 2: Robert Graves thanks Hardy for his poem.
3240. October 2: Maurice Macmillan sends a book.
3241. October 4: Mrs. Jeanne S. Popham inquires about Hardy's letter to her sister about *The Trumpet-Major*.
3242. October 6: Hardy to Mrs. Popham: rough draft of reply to Letter 3241.
3243. October 7: Violet I. Balkwill to F. Kirkwood expressing ignorance, and curiosity, about the music mentioned in Hardy's novels.
3244. October 9: Butler Wood wants information about the music mentioned in Hardy's writings.
3245. October 10: Barbara Burkes appreciation from California.
3246. October 10: John C. Johnson asks about errors in books.
3247. October 12: Hardy to General John H. Morgan: typed transcript of letter about Napoleon's entrance into Berlin in *The Dynasts*. Hardy says that in composing *The Dynasts* the Battle of Leipzig bothered him more than Jena or Ulm. Published in *Later Years*, pp. 228-229.
3248. October 12: Lane about the Bibliography of First Editions to be included in the re-issue of L. Johnson's *Art*.
3249. October 12: David Platt appreciation.
3250. October 13: Collins about his position with regard to the now-cancelled plan to translate Hedgcock's book into English.
3251. October 13: Lady Agnes Grove about Edmund Gosse's article on Hardy's poems.
3252. October 13: Leonard Rees solicits a poem for the *Sunday Times*.
3253. October 13: Lady Agatha Russell about *Tess*.
3254. October 16: Johnson thanks Hardy for his reply to Letter 3246.

CHRONOLOGICAL LIST 149

3255. October 17: Chew to Mrs. Hardy in explanation of various revisions in his book on Hardy.
3256. October 17: T. M. Raff solicits a few lines for use at the Oswestry Grammar School.
3257. October 17: Filson Young solicits a poem for the *Saturday Review*.
3258. October 18: Rowland Grey (pen-name of Lillian Rowland-Brown) about her article on the women in Hardy's fiction, in the October *Fortnightly Review*.
3259. October 19: F. B. Bradley-Birt, from Calcutta, requests permission to quote.
3260. October 19: Cockerell about the draft of a memorial for Charles M. Doughty.
3261. October 19. Young thanks Hardy for his contribution to the *Saturday Review*.
3262. (c. October 20): Hardy to "Rowland Grey": copy of a letter commenting on her article "Certain Women of Thomas Hardy."
3263. October 21: Cockerell thanks Hardy for the Doughty Memorial.
3264. October 23: John Langdon Davies about making arrangements for an American filming of *Tess* in Dorset.
3265. October 23: Miss Rowland Grey again about the women in Hardy's fiction.
3266. October 23: General John H. Morgan about *The Dynasts*.
3267. October 24: Christian Barman wants an article for *Architecture*.
3268. October 24: J. A. Craig asks permission to quote.
3269. October 26: Davies again about making arrangements to film *Tess* in Dorset.
3270. October 27: Cockerell about seeking a pension for Charles M. Doughty.
3271. October 28: John Galsworthy thanks Hardy for reading his book.
3272. October 29: Hardy to Miss Weld: rough draft; asks help and permission for American photographing inside the [Bindon] Abbey enclosure for the film of *Tess*.
3273. October 30: Barman sends a supplement to his appeal in Letter 3267.
3274. October 30: Miss Rowland Grey again about her *Fortnightly* article on the women in Hardy's fiction.
3275. October 30: Sir Frederick Macmillan about corrections in *Collected Poems*.
3276. October 31: Charles Lapworth thanks Hardy for help in obtaining permission to take photographs at Bindon Abbey.
3277. October (?): Mrs. Allhusen asks help for the Irish loyalists.
3278. November 1: Hardy to the International Story Company of New York: copy of reply to their inquiry about motion-picture rights in *Tess* and *The Mayor*; film rights for *The Distracted Preacher* and *Romantic Adventures of a Milkmaid* are available. [Rights to *Tess* and *The Mayor* had been sold.]
3279. November 1: Barman sends a supplement to Letter 3267.
3280. November 2: Florence Henniker about the pleasant visit she has had from Mrs. Cockerell.
3281. November 2: H. A. Martin sends a proof of the program for the performance of *A Desperate Remedy*.
3282. November 3: Miss Rowland Grey further supplements her comments on her *Fortnightly* article about the women in Hardy's fiction.

3283. (c. November 5): Mrs. Allhusen thanks Hardy for his poems.
3284. November 5: Elizabeth Allhusen thanks Hardy for *The Woodlanders*.
3285. November 6: John E. Acland thanks Hardy for his list of Dorset "Worthies."
3286. November 6: Robert Bridges thanks Hardy for his message.
3287. November 7: Hardy to Slater (of Harpers): rough draft; about signing sheets for insertion into the so-called Anniversary Edition of Hardy's Works sold in America by Harper & Brothers.
3288. November 7: Slater reports New York sales of the Anniversary Edition have been very small.
3289. November 8: Lucy (Mrs. W. K.) Clifford asks Hardy to write a preface for a new edition of her novel, *Mrs. Keith's Crime*.
3290. November 9: Sir Frederick Macmillan inquires about an alleged misprint in *The Trumpet-Major*.
3291. November 10: E. M. Walker says Hardy has been elected to an Honorary Fellowship at Queen's College, Oxford.
3292. November 11: Hardy to Lucy Clifford: rough draft of reply to Letter 3289; has to confess he has never read her novel.
3293. November 11: Charles Morgan asks permission to call at Max Gate.
3294. November 12: Hardy to Macmillan: rough draft of reply to Letter 3290; it is *not* a misprint.
3295. November 13: A. C. Benson thanks Hardy for writing pleasantly about Benson's book.
3296. November 13: Sue M. (Mrs. C. P.) Farrell asks permission to quote Hardy in an anti-vivisection booklet.
3297. November 13: Ian MacAlister invites Hardy to serve on a committee for arranging a Commemoration of the Bicentenary of the death of Sir Christopher Wren.
3298. November 13: Ernest Rhys solicits an interview, in preparation for writing an article on Hardy's poetry.
3299. November 14: Hardy to Rhys: copy of reply to Letter 3298; not able to give interviews.
3300. November 14: Hardy to Pro-Provost Walker: rough draft of reply to Letter 3291; accepts the honor.
3301. November 14: May T. Dunn (daughter of William Barnes's second daughter, Mrs. Julia Dunn) asks for help in building a library in Ljubljana, Yugoslavia, for the promotion of the English language.
3302. November 14: Macmillan acknowledges receipt of Letter 3294.
3303. November 16: Thring asks about American piracy of *The Three Strangers*.
3304. November 16: Walker says Hardy's acceptance of the Honorary Fellowship at Queen's College pleases them.
3305. November 18: Lady Victoria Sackville asks Hardy to autograph some books.
3306. November 20: Hardy to Thring; rough draft of reply to Letter 3303; *The Three Strangers* is not copyright in America.
3307. November 20: Robert M. Smith submits an article (which has been accepted for publication by the *North American Review*) on the philosophical significance of Hardy's poetry.
3308. November 21: Commander W. W. Fisher invites Hardy and his wife to lunch on board H.M.S. *Queen Elizabeth*.

CHRONOLOGICAL LIST

3309. November 22: Hardy to Macmillan: rough draft; Hardy's trials with autograph hunters.
3310. November 22: General John H. Morgan congratulations on the Queen's College fellowship.
3311. November 23: Frederick Macmillan responds to letter about autograph hunters.
3312. November 23: George A. Macmillan asks about inserting a circular in *Collected Poems*.
3313. November 23: F. Dudley Taylor solicits a contribution to an album to be published by the Federation Interalliée des Anciens Combattants.
3314. November 24: Cockerell about returning books.
3315. November 25: Hardy to Lady Sackville: typed copy of reply to Letter 3305; he does not now sign his books without payment of a fee for the benefit of some charity.
3316. November 25: C. A. Dawson Scott about the P. E. N. Club.
3317. November 25: Edward Stevens about plans for printing some historical notes about the Gloucester Hotel at Weymouth.
3318. November 27: E. Godman Rumball, an American on Long Island, N. Y., sends thanks for Hardy's novels.
3319. November 28: Hardy to Stevens: rough draft of reply to Letter 3317; has read the historical notes by Mr. Pouncy and has nothing further to suggest.
3320. November 29: Hardy to E. L. Ling, then Mayor of Dorchester: rough draft; proposes improvements in the approach to Dorchester by the Wareham Road.
3321. November 29: Ian MacAlister invites Hardy to be "first Honorary Fellow" of the new Wessex Society of Architects.
3322. November 29: Mary Webb sends a copy of *Seven for a Secret* which she has dedicated to him.
3323. November 30: Princess Marie Louise about poems for the library in the Queen's Doll's House.
3324. (n. d.): Mrs. Allhusen after a call at Max Gate.
3325. (c. December 1): Hardy to Smith: rough draft of reply to Letter 3307; returns Smith's article with errors marked.
3326. December 1: George A. Cronshaw invites Hardy to attend the Christmas and New Year's Day "gaudies" at Queen's College, Oxford.
3327. December 1: Ling acknowledges Hardy's suggestion in Letter 3320.
3328. December 2: Hardy to MacAlister: rough draft; accepts invitation in Letter 3321.
3329. December 3: Lady Sackville about paying Hardy to autograph the books for sale to benefit a hospital.
3330. December 4: MacAllister thanks Hardy for Letter 3328.
3331. December 5: Rosaline Masson asks Hardy to sign the MS. of his contribution to her book *I Can Remember Robert Louis Stevenson*.
3332. December 5: Taylor thanks for Hardy's response to Letter 3313.
3333. December 6: Hardy to Cronshaw; rough draft of reply to invitation to attend holiday festivities at Queen's College.
3334. December 7: Hanbury thanks Hardy for his note.
3335. December 7: Slater about details connected with the American filming of *Tess*.

3336. December 11: H. A. Treble asks permission to reprint a chapter from *Under the Greenwood Tree*.
3337. December 14: Hardy to Sue M. Farrell: rough draft of reply to Letter 3296, granting permission.
3338. December 14: Smith regrets the tone of Hardy's reply to Letter 3307.
3339. December 14: Robert Whitehouse about film rights in *The Return of the Native*.
3340. (c. December 17): Hardy to Sir Frederick Macmillan: rough draft; discusses the use of a literary agent.
3341. December 18: Macmillan responds to Letter 3340.
3342. December 19: H. S. Milford sends a cheque for permission to quote.
3343. December 20: Hardy to MacAlister: rough draft of reply to Letter 3297; declines to serve on the Wren committee.
3344. December 20: Howard Corbett asks Hardy to autograph a copy of his "war poem" as published by *The Times*.
3345. December 21: Flower solicits an article on the beauty and wonders of Nature in the scheme of things.
3346. December 21: Florence Henniker sends the last of her extant letters, with New Year's wishes to Hardy and Florence.
3347. December 23: Madeleine Rolland Christmas greetings from Paris; still waiting for the proofs of a re-issue of her French translation of *Tess*.
3348. December 28: Alfred Pope about the Dorchester Grammar School.
3349. December 28: M. Sweetkind appreciation from America.
3350. December 29: Flower regrets Hardy cannot undertake the work solicited in Letter 3345.
3351. December 30: Hardy to A. G. Symonds: transcript; about the Dorchester Grammar School.
3352. December 30: W. Lock thanks for the loan of a book.
3353. December 30: Princess Marie Louise thanks for Hardy's letter.
3354. December 31: Mrs. Allhusen best wishes for 1923.
3355. December (?): Charles Cockerell sends sincere wishes, and a long poem.
3356. (n. d.): H. M. Forbes solicits a brief press interview.
3357. (n. d.): Mrs. Hanbury invites Hardy to tea.
3358. (n. d.): Mrs. Granville-Barker thanks Hardy for a present.
3359. (n. d.): Gustav Holst asks if he may call.
3360. (n. d.): Mrs. Hanbury again invites Hardy to tea.
3361. (n. d.): Forbes asks Hardy's opinion of John Masefield.
3362. (n. d.): Ulick de Mel, from Ceylon, asks for a contribution for the *St. Thomas Magazine*.
3363. (n. d.): Eugene O'Brien solicits a poem or a message for a Dundee student-anthology.
3364. (n. d.): Margaret Macnamara about the possibility of publishing the Evans or Tilley dramatizations of the Wessex Novels.
3365. (n. d.): Hardy to Macnamara: rough draft of reply to Letter 3364; publication is impossible.
3366. (n. d.): Thornycroft on a variety of subjects.
3367. (n. d.): The Reverend Laurence Tyler appreciation from America.
3368. (n. d.): Forbes telegraphs to ask Hardy's decision about the request in Letter 3361.

1923

3369. January 1: Harold Monro thanks Hardy for his letter and tells him about *The Chapbook*.
3370. January 3: Monro solicits a poem for the March issue of *The Chapbook*.
3371. January 3: Hester Ritchie asks for a letter of her mother, Lady Ritchie, which she could print.
3372. (c. January 4): Hardy to Monro: rough draft of reply to Letter 3370; hopes to send something soon.
3373. January 4: Gerald Duckworth sends payment for permission to include a poem in a Duckworth & Co. anthology.
3374. January 5: Sir Hama Thornycroft on various subjects.
3375. January 8: Thomas Moult asks permission to quote.
3376. January 9: Thornycroft supplement to his letter of the 5th.
3377. January 13: Behrens-Hagen appreciation from Norway.
3378. January 15: W. M. Colles asks if Hardy has any verse available which a literary agent might help him place.
3379. January 15: J. C. Squire will be glad to publish Hardy's poem "On the Portrait of a Woman about to be Hanged" (it appeared in the *London Mercury*, February 1923).
3380. January 16: Hardy to Colles: rough draft of reply to inquiry of the 15th; there are no more poems available at present.
3381. January 19: Hardy to an unnamed correspondent: rough draft in Hardy's hand; there are no dramatizations of Hardy's novels by himself [!].
3382. January 20: John Galsworthy friendly letter.
3383. January 20: Matthew Wordsworth about an amber-coloured butterfly found on Egdon Heath.
3384. January 29: Albert Berrisford appreciation from Kent.
3385. January 29: James Ismay asks for a contribution to a book dedicated to the men from Iwerne Minster who were in the war.
3386. January 30: Austin Harrison says it was kind of Hardy to write about Harrison's father and he values Hardy's sympathy.
3387. February 2: Ismay thanks for the consideration given his request of 29 January.
3388. February 2: Judge J. S. Udal pleased at Hardy's appreciation of his book.
3389. February 4: Ernest Rhys asks permission to include something by Hardy in Everyman's Library.
3390. February 4: Dennis Wilsden about the Hardy family pedigree.
3391. (c. February 5): Hardy to Sir Frederick Macmillan: rough draft; about answering Rhys's request in Letter 3389.
3392. February 5: Ismay thanks Hardy for sending a poem and some prose for insertion in a book dedicated to the men from Iwerne Minster.
3393. February 8: A. D. H. Allan asks Hardy to sit for a sketch-portrait for publication in the *Wessex Review*.
3394. February 8: S. Fisher solicits support of a move to obtain a pension for a daughter of a novelist known as "James Prior."
3395. February 8: Helen Gifford asks permission to translate "Hap" into French.

3396. February 9: John V. Lovitt (American Rhodes Scholar from Pennsylvania) invites Hardy to give a talk to the American Club at Oxford University.
3397. February 10: Hardy to Allan: rough draft of reply to Letter 3393; doubts he will be ready because he is ill with a chill.
3398. February 10: Hardy to Wilsden. rough draft of reply to Letter 3390; about the family pedigree.
3399. February 12: Hardy to E. J. Bodington: pointing out the errors in a lecture delivered by Bodington about the Wessex Novels and their author. Carbon copy of typed letter, signed "T. Hardy."
3400. February 12: R. L. Megroz inquires about Hardy's reminiscenses of schooldays.
3401. February 12: Squire about an Exhibition of modern English architecture which might interest Hardy.
3402. February 13: Hardy to Megroz: rough draft of reply to Letter 3400; is unable to answer his list of questions.
3403. February 13: Bodington thanks for Letter 3399.
3404. February 15: Hardy to Florence McNeill: rough draft; asks her to thank Kostos Palamas in Athens for the Greek poem on *Tess* sent to Hardy with a letter in French on 28 November 1918.
3405. February 21: Monro sends *Chapbook* proofs of Hardy's poem.
3406. February 24: A. V. Houghton about The English Association.
3407. February 24: Stephen Pickles appreciation.
3408. February 26: Frazier Hunt hopes he may be permitted to call at Max Gate sometime.
3409. February 26: Hilda M. Thorn asks permission to quote.
3410. February (?): Hardy to Bodington: rough draft of second letter about the errors in B's lecture about Hardy.
3411. February (?): Sir E. Ray Lankester sends a rare Christmas card for Hardy to see.
3412. February (?): Florence McNeill acknowledges Hardy's letter of the 15th.
3413. March 1: A. L. Kocher about books for young architects.
3414. March 1: Marion Nelson appreciation.
3415. March 1: G. W. Redway asks permission to quote from *The Dynasts*.
3416. March 1: W. G. Strickland asks Hardy to read a book of poems which he is sending and for which he will call later.
3417. (c. March 2): Hardy to Strickland: rough draft of reply to Letter 3516; finds it difficult to see visitors, and will return the book of poems.
3418. March 4: Lady Agnes Grove thanks for Hardy's kindness and patience in helping her.
3419. March 4: Henry Mitchell solicits a manuscript poem for the Christchurch Rectory in South Amboy, New Jersey.
3420. March 4: A. W. Reed sends a copy of *The Church Quarterly* containing a review of *Late Lyrics*.
3421. March 5: Hardy to Harley Granville-Barker: typed transcript of a letter welcoming him back from Rome.
3422. March 6: Harriet Monroe, from Chicago, about his corrections on the proofs of his poems in *The New Poetry*.
3423. March 6: Bryan O'Brien solicits a poem for *The Queen's College Miscellany* at Oxford. (Hardy sent "The Faithful Swallow.")

3424. March 7: A. Ivor Parry asks about quoting uncopyrighted material.
3425. March 8: Lady Agnes Grove personal letter.
3426. March 12: F. R. Yerbury invites Hardy to become an Honorary Member of The Architectural Association.
3427. March 13: Hardy to Yerbury: rough draft in pencil; he must forego the honor.
3428. March 14: Cecil Braithwaite asks Hardy to write a few lines for a book on fishing.
3429. March 16: Odin Gregory asks for Hardy's criticism of his work *Jesus*.
3430. March 19: Braithwaite thanks Hardy for his offer to help.
3431. March 20: Muirhead Bone asks for help in protesting against a proposal to charge admission to the British Museum.
3432. March 21: Sir Frederick Macmillan about a breach of copyright.
3433. March 23: Lady Victoria Sackville about paying Hardy to autograph some books for a sale to benefit a hospital.
3434. March 23: Verne Tewksbury appreciation from America.
3435. March 31: Granville-Barker asks for help in trying to obtain a Civil List Pension for William Dod.
3436. April 2: Norman Hapgood asks permission to call and solicits an article on religion.
3437. April 4: Alfred Pope about the Dorchester Grammar School.
3438. April 5: Hapgood is sorry Hardy cannot give the time for writing an article on religion.
3439. April 5: Sarah Meech Hardy Phillips about her uncle, a distant relative of Hardy.
3440. April 6: Vere Collins says a statement in *T. L. S.* that Hardy has "withdrawn from the arena" is not true.
3441. April 6: Geoffrey Whitworth asks support of a movement for obtaining a Civil List Pension for William Dod.
3442. April 9: James M. Fagan asks support of an appeal for a new Playhouse at Oxford.
3443. April 10: Alfred W. Anthony of New York City solicits an autograph letter.
3444. April 10: L. W. Hanna asks if Hardy plans to be in America next year.
3445. April 10: Sir James Marchant solicits an article on "Immortality."
3446. April 10: C. W. Napier appreciation.
3447. April 11: A. R. Powys asks Hardy to write an inscription for a new house which Lord Danby is building.
3448. April 12: Sydney C. Cockerell about folk songs and dances.
3449. April 12: H. Baillie Weaver solicits support of the work of the National Council for Animals' Welfare.
3450. April 13: Hardy to Sir James Marchant: rough draft of reply to Letter 3445; essays are out of his province.
3451. April 14: Hardy to Powys: rough draft of reply to Letter 3447; offers a choice of eight quotations from the Bible, Shakespeare, etc.
3452. April 14: Lady Ilchester about the death of Mrs. Henniker. (Obit. 4 April 1923.)
3453. April (14?): W. H. Ward invites Hardy to join the Wren Society.
3454. April 14: Charles Whitley promises to send proof of the poem Hardy is permitting Whitley to include in his Bath Anthology.

3455. April 15: Hardy to Ward: rough draft of reply to Letter 3453; regrets he must decline, due to increasing age.
3456. April 15: Madeleine Rolland, from Paris, says she and her brother are going to London and hope to call at Max Gate.
3457. April 16: Charles Morgan sends a copy of his novel.
3458. April 16: A. R. Powys thanks Hardy for the trouble he has taken with the inscription for Lord Danby's house.
3459. April 17: Galsworthy solicits a brief message for use at a meeting of the P. E. N. Club.
3460. April 17: R. Sheppard asks permission to quote.
3461. April 18: Cockerell about MSS. at the Bodleian Library.
3462. April 20: Hardy to Galsworthy, copy of reply to Letter 3459; feels he is too old to send any distinct message to the [P. E. N.] Club.
3463. April 20: A. E. (Mrs. Cecil) Chesterton solicits support of a petition on behalf of Walter Crotch.
3464. April 21: Marchant is sorry to receive Hardy's letter of 13 April.
3465. April 22: Braithwaite again thanks Hardy for his help.
3466. April 22: Llewelyn Powys about his book *Thirteen Worthies*.
3467. April 24: Hardy to Marchant: rough draft of reply to Letter 3464, again expressing regrets.
3468. April 24: Sheppard grateful for permission to quote a poem.
3469. April 29: John C. Johnson about the account of the Duchess of Richmond's ball in *The Dynasts*.
3470. April 30: I. W. Kitts acknowledges receipt of the autograph manuscripts of three poems on Plymouth by the Free Public Library of Plymouth.
3471. May 1: Roger Ferdinand, in French, from Paris, about his thesis at the University of Caen; asks permission to prepare a French scenario of *Tess;* or *The Trumpet-Major*, or *A Pair of Blue Eyes*.
3472. May 5: Kurt Busse writes about German translations.
3473. May 6: A. C. Benson invites Hardy to Cambridge.
3474. May 6: Galsworthy says he read a few words from Hardy's letter to him and they were received very well at the P.E.N. Club.
3475. May 8: Stafford Bourne asks permission to call.
3476. May 8: Harry Furniss is pleased Hardy will see him and give him time to make a sketch (next Saturday).
3477. May 8: Amy Lowell, from Boston, says *The Dynasts* is selling all the time; *The Dynasts* was her chief inspiration in doing her book *Can Grande's Castle*.
3478. May 8: Thring asks if Hardy would be interested in attending an international "Congress" of writers.
3479. May 9: Hardy to Thring: rough draft of reply to Letter 3478; is unable to participate.
3480. May 10: A. C. Benson thanks Hardy for his letter.
3481. May 10: Herbert W. Blundell solicits help in protesting against the Army's proposed "devastation of all the cliffs between Lulworth Cove and . . Mell Gap."
3482. May 10: Leonard Patten about Church Hope Cove, Portland.
3483. May 10: Madeleine Rolland tells Hardy how much she and her brother enjoyed their day at Dorchester and the hours spent with him.
3484. May 11: Frieda Pollard appreciation from America.
3485. May 14: John Williston appreciation.

3486. May 15: Austin H. Johnson solicits a poem for *The Cambridge Mercury*.
3487. May 16: Ward asks Hardy to reconsider his decision of 15 April.
3488. May 17: John Pollock writes for his father to thank Hardy for a very kind letter. Pollock is not out of the hospital yet.
3489. May 17: Virginia (Mrs. Leonard) Woolf solicits something of Hardy's for the *Nation and Athenaeum*.
3490. May 20: Hardy to Ward: rough draft of reply to Letter 3487; is compelled to adhere to his former decision.
3491. May 20: Hardy to Virginia Woolf: rough draft of reply to Letter 3489; refers to her father, Leslie Stephen, as one who influenced Hardy in many ways when he was a young man.
3492. May 21: Pittendrigh Macgillivray in appreciation of the *Collected Poems*.
3493. May 23: Sir Frederick Macmillan about film rights and German translations.
3494. May 23: Leonard Patten thanks Hardy for his suggestion about Church Hope Cove, Portland.
3495. May 24: Ernest Brennecke asks permission to call.
3496. May 27: Tom Clarke solicits a contribution to the Melbourne, Australia, *Herald*.
3497. May 29: Roger S. Loomis has sent a book of his, now asks permission to call at Max Gate.
3498. June (?): Brennecke is sending part of the manuscript of his book *Thomas Hardy's Universe*.
3499. June 1: E. Howes appreciation.

On 2 June 1923 Hardy attained the age of 83. Seventeen men and women remembered him and sent birthday greetings, either on 2 June or on the date indicated in parentheses:

3500. A. C. Benson (4 June)
3501. Lucy Clifford
3502. Vere Collins
3503. Sir George Douglas (1 June)
3504. Edward & Emma Dugdale
3505. St. John Ervine
3506. Stanley I. Galpin
3507. Lady Agnes Grove (1 June)
3508. Lady Ilchester (3 June)
3509. John H. Morgan (7 June)
3510. W. Hilton Nash
3511. W. M. Parker (3 June)
3512. Sir F. Pollock (4 June)
3513. Siegfried Sassoon
3514. Molly Stiff
3515. William Watkins
3516. Dr. Macleod Yearsley (1 June)

3517. June 2: S. Donald Cox asks Hardy to write a few lines about his favorite walk.
3518. June 2: Margaret Shewring asks the editor of *Chambers's Journal* if he plans to reprint Hardy's "How I Built Myself a House."
3519. June 7: Hardy to Dr. Yearsley: rough draft in pencil; about removing a gland from Mrs. Hardy's neck.
3520. June 7: John C. Johnson about an article on the Duchess of Richmond's ball on the eve of Waterloo.
3521. June 13: Mary S. Leitch, from Virginia, a sonnet addressed "To Thomas Hardy."
3522. June (?): Hardy to Leitch: rough draft, thanking her for the sonnet.
3523. June 13: George N. Northrop recalls a visit to Max Gate 18 years ago.

3524. June 14: Walter de la Mare, after a visit to Max Gate, exclaims about the joy it was.
3525. June 14: Dr. Macleod Yearsley advises Mrs. Hardy to let the gland in her neck alone.
3526. June 15: V. Joseph appreciation from Yugoslavia.
3527. June 18: Squire thanks Hardy for a letter and tells him Hewlett is dead.
3528. June 18: E. M. Walker invites Hardy to visit Queen's College at Oxford.
3529. June 20: Marion Buchanan appreciation.
3530. June 20: Rose Fyleman asks for a contribution to a projected monthly magazine for children.
3531. June 21: Walker is pleased at Hardy's acceptance of the invitation to visit Queen's College.
3532. June 24: Walker sends details about Hardy's visit to Queen's College.
3533. June 26: Cronshaw sends a copy of a *History of Queen's College*.
3534. July 2: Hardy to Granville-Barker: typescript copy of letter sent with a copy of *The Queen of Cornwall*, inviting comment on it.
3535. July 3: L. A. G. Strong asks permission to quote a poem.
3536. July 3: Thring about an inquiry sent to the Society of Authors.
3537. July 4: Hardy to Thring: rough draft of reply; is unable to give advice.
3538. July 4: Granville-Barker about *The Queen of Cornwall*.
3539. July 4: Paul S. Parsons asks permission to call.
3540. July 5: Hardy to Parsons: rough draft of reply to Letter 3539, referring Parsons to *Late Lyrics* and *Collected Poems* and to Hermann Lea's *The Wessex of Thomas Hardy*.
3541. July 6: Granville-Barker about the prospective production of *The Queen of Cornwall*.
3542. July 6: Elizabeth Hammell appreciation.
3543. July 6: Strong thanks Hardy for permission to quote.
3544. July 7: Ling asks help in revising an address.
3545. July 7: Lady Agatha Russell sends a book.
3546. July 8: Hardy to Sir George Douglas: transcript (made by May O'Rourke?); about Keats, *The Dynasts*, and other matters.
3547. July 9: Hardy to Granville-Barker: typed transcript; discusses details of staging for the projected production of *The Queen of Cornwall*.
3548. July 10: Marjorie Tilden thanks Hardy for a letter about her verses.
3549. July 12: J. F. Symons-Jeune hopes to call.
3550. July 16: Thring about a possible infringement of copyright.
3551. July 16: Jacqueline T. Trotter asks permission to quote.
3552. July 17: Hardy's sister Katharine ("Kate") about the visit of the Prince of Wales to Dorchester.
3553. July 17: Edgar A. Lane about the musical setting for *The Queen of Cornwall*.
3554. July 20: H. L. Burrows asks permission to quote.
3555. July 21: William Meade asks Hardy's opinion of enclosed verses.
3556. July 21: George C. Williamson, as a Trustee of the Keats House, Westworth Place, asks Hardy to write out the poem on Keats which he had contributed to the Keats Memorial volume.

CHRONOLOGICAL LIST

3557. July 23: P. N. Elven appreciation.
3558. July 24: Henry Hammond asks Hardy's critical opinion of a poem.
3559. July 28: J. Monte appreciation.
3560. (c. July 30): Franklin Dyall asks for help with a memorial on behalf of Charles Dalmon.
3561. July 30: Sydney Jeffery sends a copy of *The Warrington Examiner* from Lancashire containing a review of *Collected Poems*.
3562. July 31: Hardy to Hammond: rough draft of reply to Letter 3558; circumstances prevent his evpressing a critical opinion.
3563. August 1: Hardy to Dyall: rough draft of reply to Letter 3560; is not able to sign the petition.
3564. August 3: G. Currie Martin about the tour of Wessex he made, accompanied by Mrs. Gertrude Bugler of Beaminster.
3565. August 5: Mrs. Champ Clark flattery from Washington, D. C.
3566. August 7: Hamlin Garland may call on Hardy before he sails for America on the 17th.
3567. August 8: Garland will come to Max Gate on 10 August.
3568. August 8: Walter G. Kellogg solicits an autograph and a photograph.
3569. August 9: Daphne Bankes asks permission to call.
3570. August 11: May C. Hamilton sends her picture and praises *The Dynasts*.
3571. August 15: Hardy to Williamson: copy of reply to Letter 3556: is sending the manuscript of the poem on Keats.
3572. August 16: Mrs. Allhusen appeals for help in achieving the restoration of the spire of Stoke Poges Church.
3573. August 16: Williamson thanks Hardy for the poem on the Keats House.
3574. August 17: Irvin C. Poley about impeachments as "triumphs of justice" in *The Return of the Native*.
3575. August 19: Anna Lang sends appreciation from Cardiff, Wales.
3576. August 20: Clive Holland asks permission to call.
3577. August (21?): Hardy to Holland: rough draft of reply to Letter 3576; it would not be worth while to call for the purpose of getting an article.
3578. August 22: Mrs. Allhusen thanks Hardy for his letter.
3579. August 23: Henry Roe about Lieut. Frank George.
3580. August 24: William Toynbee sends a sonnet he has written to Hardy.
3581. (c. August 25): Hardy to Toynbee: rough draft of reply to Letter 3580.
3582. August 27: Hardy to Brennecke: rough draft of reply to Letter 3498 sent with his typescript of *Thomas Hardy's Universe;* although *Jude* is often cited as autobiographical, it is not.
3583. August 28: Charles A. Baker solicits help on behalf of Mrs. Charles Hardy of Puddletown, recently widowed.
3584. August 30: Loomis repeats his request of 29 May.
3585. (c. August 31): Hardy to Loomis: rough draft of reply to Letter 3584; Loomis may call on 12 or 13 September.
3586. September 5: Frank H. Knight appreciation.
3587. September 5: Dudley Field Malone sends some bottles of wine.
3588. September 8: Ian Hay Beith invites Hardy to the annual dinner of the Society of Authors.

3589. September 9: Mrs. Luce Wilks appreciation in French.
3590. September 11: Loomis will call on Thursday, 13 September.
3591. September 12: Fanny Butcher solicits Hardy's "Confessions" for the Chicago *Tribune*.
3592. September 16: John Coates asks how to pronounce "Lyonnesse."
3593. September 17: Lady St. Helier asks if she may call on 4 or 5 October.
3594. September 18: Hardy to Lady St. Helier: typed transcript of reply to Letter 3593; of course she may.
3595. September 21: Coates thanks Hardy for telling him how to pronounce "Lyonnesse."
3596. September 23: Clement K. Shorter about painters and other matters in *A Laodicean*.
3597. September 23: Shorter supplements his letter by further remarks on the back of a card.
3598. September 25: Flower solicits a poem for the Christmas Number of *Cassell's Magazine*.
3599. September 26: Geoffrey Lapage solicits help with regard to the Fiction Prize at Manchester University.
3600. September 27: F. deBurgh, a literary agent, solicits a short item.
3601. September 27: G. Currie Martin invites Hardy to become an Honorary Member of the Robert Louis Stevenson Club.
3602. September 27: Shorter remarks on Hardy's reply to Letter 3596: "What a stony-hearted monster you are becoming!"
3603. September 28: Hardy to Lapage: rough draft of reply to Letter 3599; beyond his physical powers to be any help.
3604. September 28: Hardy to Martin: rough draft of reply to Letter 3601; must decline due to his great age.
3605. September 28: Sheppard asks for a contribution to a *Call to National Righteousness*.
3606. September 29: Lady Alice Stuart of Wortley sends greetings from Tintagel in Cornwall.
3607. October 1: Bertram Fryer asks if Hardy would speak on a Broadcasting program.
3608. October 1: W. N. Shansfield to Edward Clodd about helping the Westminster Hospital.
3609. October 2: Lapage thanks Hardy for his reply of 28 September.
3610. October 2: Alexander Ross asks support of Lord Buckmaster as a candidate for the office of Lord Rector of Edinburgh University.
3611. October 2: W. N. Shansfield solicits help for the Westminster Hospital.
3612. October 3: Hedy Verena about a German translation of *Far from the Madding Crowd* or *Tess*.
3613. October 4: Hardy to Shansfield: rough draft of reply to Letter 3611; cannot help because he is too old.
3614. October 4: Tom Miners appreciation from Cornwall.
3615. October 6: Martin on the inaugural meeting of the Robert Louis Stevenson Club.
3616. October 12: Hugh Byas about a Japanese version of *Tess*.
3617. October 16: deBurgh repeats the solicitation of 27 September.
3618. October 17: Hardy to Byas: rough draft of reply; about *Tess* in Japanese.

CHRONOLOGICAL LIST 161

3619. October 17: Hardy to deBurgh: rough draft of reply to Letter 3617; regrets his inability to contribute.
3620. October 19: Percy G. Hardy wants an article for *The Westminsterian*.
3621. October 19: Leonard Rees solicits a special message for Armistice Day, for publication in the *Sunday Times*.
3622. October 20: Hardy to Rees: rough draft of reply; he is welcome to print in the *Sunday Times* any *one* of the poems on pages 507, 513, or 541 of *Collected Poems*.
3623. October 20: E. Lonsdale Deighton asks permission to reproduce in the *British Legion Autograph Album* the two lines from *Moments of Vision* which Hardy had written out in August 1922 for sale at a servicemen's benefit.
3624. October 20: J. W. Hamilton about a Song of Peace.
3625. October 21: Ford Madox Ford wants a contribution to the *Transatlantic Review*.
3626. October 22: Granville-Barker about the production of *The Dynasts*.
3627. October 22: Bernard Griffin asks permission to take photographs of Hardy in connection with the forthcoming production of *The Queen of Cornwall*.
3628. October 23: Hardy to Granville-Barker: typed transcript; about the sale of autograph letters and the craze for collecting.
3629. October 23: Hardy to Griffin: rough draft of reply to Letter 3627; has no objection to Griffin's request.
3630. October 24: Raymond Abbott last letter from Ventnor.
3631. October 24: S. H. Bathe asks permission to film *The Queen of Cornwall* production by the Hardy Players in Dorchester.
3632. October 24: George A. B. Dewar thanks Hardy for his letter.
3633. October 26: Marjorie G. Lachmund, from Yonkers, New York, asks Hardy, with his eyes shut, to draw a pig and send the drawing to her.
3634. October 29: Hardy to Granville-Barker: typed transcript of a letter about the production of *The Queen of Cornwall*.
3635. October 29: Hardy to Bathe: rough draft of reply to Letter 3631; is not yet able to give an answer.
3636. October 30: Bathe thanks Hardy for his reply.
3637. October 30: Benson sends good wishes.
3638. October 30: Granville-Barker again about *The Queen of Cornwall*.
3639. October 30: Florence E. Hardy to Ford Madox Ford: rough draft of a reply to be typed: "Mr. Hardy refuses . . . could do nothing."
3640. November 2: Andrew Halford appreciation from Leicester.
3641. November 6: Edward Clodd about religious ideas.
3642. November 8: Ford distressed to learn Hardy has been ill: solicits a poem from him later.
3643. November 9: Harold Child says *The Times* wants him to see the performance of *The Queen of Cornwall*.
3644. November 10: The Duchess of Hamilton invites Hardy to be one of the Vice-Presidents of the Anti-Vivisection Society.
3645. (c. November 10): Hardy to the Duchess of Hamilton: rough draft of reply to Letter 3644; avoids committing himself.
3646. November 11: Archibald Henderson asks permission to call.
3647. November 11: A. F. L. Webster about Dorset folk songs.

3648. (c. November 12): Hardy to Webster: rough draft of reply to Letter 3647; is unable to render much assistance.
3649. November 12: Child thanks Hardy for letter about *The Queen of Cornwall*.
3650. November 14: Ernest Rhys about Hardy's "She to Him" sonnet.
3651. November 14: C. A. Dawson Scott about the P.E.N. Club.
3652. November 15: Alfred Noyes sends a copy of an article he has written on *The Queen of Cornwall*.
3653. November 15: Hardy to Henderson: rough draft of reply to Letter 3646, denying permission to call.
3654. November 16: Henderson regrets illness forces Hardy to deny him permission to call.
3655. November 17: Cockerell thanks Hardy for a copy of his book.
3656. November 17: C. Rex Niven Christmas greetings from Nigeria.
3657. November 19: S. D. Green solicits a message for the students in the Trenton, New Jersey, High School.
3658. November 19: W. M. Parker on his visit to Max Gate in 1920.
3659. November 19: Harry Pouncy about his lectures on "The Wessex of Thomas Hardy."
3660. November 20: Augustus John says Cockerell has bought John's portrait of Hardy.
3661. November 21: Lord Ilchester thanks Hardy for a copy of his new work.
3662. November 22: A. B. Bater invites Hardy to give a lecture at Derby.
3663. November 22: Walter Tittle again appeals for permission to make a dry-point portrait of him.
3664. (c. November 23): Hardy to Tittle: rough draft of reply; does not wish to have any more sketches made of him.
3665. November 23: Granville-Barker about *The Queen of Cornwall*.
3666. November 24: Ian Hay Beith on the annual dinner of the Society of Authors.
3667. November 28: George Barnett solicits a bit of manuscript.
3668. November 28: S. Bernard Nutter about the Baptist minister in *A Laodicean*.
3669. November 28: Lady Alice Stuart of Wortley about a prospective visit to Dorchester.
3670. November 29: C. W. Williams about the performance of *The Queen of Cornwall* at Dorchester.
3671. November 30: Lady Ilchester praises *The Queen of Cornwall*.
3672. December 3: Brennecke asks permission to quote Hardy's letter about Schopenhauerian views.
3673. December 6: Cockerell about a Swinburne letter.
3674. December 10: Hardy to Clodd: typescript copy; refers to an American film of *Tess* in London. The typescript (supplied by Howard Bliss?) erroneously dates this letter in 1903; it is here assigned to 1923 on the strength of Hardy's reference to the American film of *Tess*; one was made in October 1922 (See Letters 3264, 3269, 3272, 3276); but Hardy's reference to a Dorchester performance of *The Woodlanders* suggests this letter may have been written in 1913 rather than in 1923.
3675. December 10: Cockerell again about the Swinburne letter.
3676. December 17: Karl Arns appreciation from Germany.

CHRONOLOGICAL LIST 163

3677. December 17: A. Dewitt appreciation.
3678. December 18: A. H. Edwards invites Hardy to become an Honorary Member of the Dorchester Rotary Club.
3679. December 20: Leonard Huxley sends a copy of the January 1924 *Cornhill* to show that Hardy's alliance with the magazine is treasured in the *Cornhill* memory.
3680. December 21: Hardy to Edwards: rough draft of reply to Letter 3678; is compelled to decline.
3681. December 22: Odell Shepard, from America, refers to a talk he had with Hardy in August 1922 about Bliss Carman; is sending a book about Carman's work.
3682. December 24: Sir George Douglas Christmas greetings.
3683. December 28: Edwards again about the Dorchester Rotary Club.
3684. December 28: William Watkins about the funeral of Sir Frederick Treves.
3685. December 31: Dewar asks for a poem for the *Nineteenth Century*.
3686. December 31: William Morris appreciation.
3687. (n. d.): Mrs. Hanbury asks about Mrs. Hardy's health.
3688. (n. d.): Masefield asks advice about publication.
3689. (n. d.): Lady St. Helier says Hardy is her "dearest Uncle Tom," a "devoted old Friend."
3690. (n. d.): Mrs. Hanbury invites Hardy to lunch.

1924

3691. January 1: Sir George Douglas tells Hardy a Glossary of his *Collected Poems* is needed.
3692. January 1: Charlotte Mew thanks for help in obtaining a Civil List Pension for her.
3693. January 1: Sir Hama Thornycroft New Year's Day letter.
3694. January 2: George A. B. Dewar asks for a contribution to the *Nineteenth Century*.
3695. (c. January 2): John Masefield thanks Hardy for his reply to Letter 3688.
3696. January 2: Stefan N. Mateusen, in Rumania, asks Hardy to send several of his masterpieces.
3697. January 4: Thomas Moult submits proofs of a poem Hardy had given him permission to reprint.
3698. January 5: Captain Fairholme asks for an ode for publication on the centenary of the Society for the Prevention of Cruelty to Animals.
3699. January 5: Newman Flower about Hardy's poem ["In the Evening"] to Sir Frederick Treves, of Dorchester, who had died at Vevey, Switzerland, on 7 December 1923.
3700. January 5: Anna, Lady Treves appreciation of Hardy's kindness in being present at her husband's funeral.
3701. January 6: John E. Acland about the manuscripts of the poems of William Barnes.
3702. January 6: Agnes Hyman appreciation.

3703. January 7: Ernest Brennecke has decided not to quote the expression of philosophical views, which he had asked permission to quote on 3 December 1923.
3704. January 10: J. T. Godwin of Dorchester consults Mrs. Hardy about the ceramic portrait of Hardy which Godwin has on sale.
3705. January 15: Cecil Braithwaite thanks Hardy for a letter about his book.
3706. January 15: Dewar thanks Hardy for his poem, "Xenophanes, the Monist of Colophon," for the *Nineteenth Century*.
3707. January 15: Roger S. Loomis thanks Hardy for permission to reprint his version of the St. George play.
3708. January 15: John H. Morgan about an article on Lord Morley.
3709. January 16: Wilfrid Gibson (detected in plagiarism by Hardy) says the apparent plagiarism was due to inadvertence.
3710. January 18: Hardy to Captain Fairholme: rough draft of reply to Letter 3698; will shortly have something for him.
3711. January 22: H. W. Garrod asks permission to add Hardy's name to a letter about Sir Walter Raleigh. (Hardy signed the letter on 25 January 1924 and returned it.)
3712. January 22: Mira, Duchess of Hamilton again solicits support of the anti-vivisection movement.
3713. January 22: W. Herbert about *Under the Greenwood Tree*.
3714. January 23: Captain Fairholme acknowledges Letter 3710, emphasizing that the ode is needed in time for the S.P.C.A. centenary.
3715. January 24: *Izvestia* solicits, through its London correspondent, Hardy's appreciation of Lenin.
3716. January 24: Morgan again about an article on Morley.
3717. January 26: T. H. Richie thanks Hardy for a gift.
3718. January 27: Hardy to Morgan: typed transcript; acknowledges receipt of Morgan's book on Germany.
3719. January 28: Harold W. V. Temperley about the wife-sale in *The Mayor of Casterbridge*.
3720. January (29?): Hardy to Temperley: rough draft of reply to Letter 3719; there were many wife-sales in the 1820s.
3721. January 29: Stanley I. Galpin about The Society of Dorset Men in London.
3722. January 30: Rutland Boughton, who was setting *The Queen of Cornwall* to music, accepts an invitation to Max Gate. (See his "Musical Association with Thomas Hardy" in *Musical News* for February 1928.)
3723. January 31: James Bone about two articles on Portland stone in *Country Life*.
3724. February 2: A. H. Edwards about the Dorchester Rotary Club.
3725. February 3: Elizabeth Allhusen thanks for a letter Hardy wrote her when she was ill.
3726. February 6: Lady Cynthia Asquith about a visit to Dorchester.
3727. February 6: Edward Stanhope Rodd invites Hardy to call at Launceston in Cornwall.
3728. February 7: Braithwaite again about his book.
3729. February 7: Elisabeth Marbury asks permission to arrange for an American production of *The Queen of Cornwall*.
3730. February 7: John S. Mayfield offers to pay for an inscribed copy of *Late Lyrics*.

3731. February 7: Isabel Smith asks Hardy to write a foreword to her novel.
3732. February 9: Hanbury about the sale of land on Egdon Heath.
3733. February 11: Braithwaite thanks Hardy for a letter.
3734. February 13: John Drinkwater about Barnes's *Poems*.
3735. February 15: Hardy to Drinkwater: rough draft of reply to Letter 3734; many of Barnes's poems have never been reprinted.
3736. February 15: F. T. Green about the Christmas Carol in *Under the Greenwood Tree*.
3737. February 16: Hardy to Green: rough draft of reply to Letter 3736; the Christmas Carol has not been sung in his part of England since 1840 or 1850.
3738. February 16: Drinkwater thanks Hardy for a letter.
3739. February 16: Lady Treves would like to use, in an inscription on Sir Frederick Treves's grave, some lines from Hardy's poem about him, published in *The Times*.
3740. February 18: Maud Liston from South Australia.
3741. February 18: C. A. Speyer about a musical setting he wishes to compose for Tristram's song in *The Queen of Cornwall*.
3742. February 20: Hardy to Speyer: rough draft of reply to Letter 3741; declines to supply the words requested by Speyer.
3743. February 21: S. D. Green, of Trenton, New Jersey, requests a reply to Letter 3657.
3744. February 22: Gerald Miller requests Hardy's signature on a letter soliciting funds for refugees in Greece.
3745. February 23: Hubert Bath asks permission to make a one-act operatic version of *The Three Strangers*.
3746. February 25: H. St. John E. Wrenford sends a copy of his song "Men of Devon."
3747. February 26: Lady Ilchester says her daughter Mary is engaged to Captain Herbert.
3748. February 27: The Countess of Lauderdale praises *Far from the Madding Crowd* and *The Return of the Native*, and says *Tess* long ago left a "wrong impression" on her.
3749. February 29: Gladys Fisher thanks Hardy for a letter about her enactment of the rôle of Queen in *The Queen of Cornwall*.
3750. February 29: Sir Frederick Pollock about the philosophy in Hardy's "Xenophanes" poem.
3751. March 1: Powys Evans asks Hardy to sit for a drawing to be published in the *London Mercury*.
3752. March (?): Hardy to Evans: rough draft of reply to Letter 3751; he will sit later in the year.
3753. March 3: Pollock continues discussion of the philosophy of "Xenophanes."
3754. March 4: John F. Childs about the Hardy family pedigree.
3755. March (7?): Hardy to Green: rough draft of reply to Letter 3743; advises the reading of his verse as containing a more condensed form of his views than can be gained from his prose.
3756. March 7: Evans thanks Hardy for his letter and hopes to make the drawing for the *London Mercury* later.
3757. March 10: Childs again about the Hardy pedigree.
3758. March 10: C. Rex Niven gossip from Nigeria.

3759. March 12: Henry B. Amos solicits Hardy's disapproval of "rabbit-coursing." (Hardy endorsed the letter in pencil.)
3760. March 16: Amos asks if Hardy would add stag-hunting.
3761. March 16: Frank Newnes about Drinkwater's *Outline of Literature*.
3762. March 18: Hardy to Amos: rough draft of reply; authorizes addition of "and captive stag-hunting" to his statement.
3763. March 18: Louis P. Lochner, from Berlin, Germany, praises *Tess*, which he read at the suggestion of Romain Rolland.
3764. March 19: Lord Ilchester sends a copy of his new book.
3765. March 23: Alfred W. Anthony of New York City wants a letter from Hardy.
3766. March 24: George A. Macmillan about the proofs of *The Queen of Cornwall* with Hardy's autograph corrections.
3767. March 26: Macmillan thanks Hardy for the gift of the autographed proofs of *The Queen of Cornwall*.
3768. March 31: Walter W. Blackie asks permission to quote from *Under the Greenwood Tree*.
3769. April 4: Thomas H. Ellis asks for (and gets) Hardy's autograph.
3770. April 4: Captain Fairholme tells Mrs. Hardy he has been unable to find a composer to provide the music for the ode, *Compassion*.
3771. April 4: Macmillan again about the proofs of *The Queen of Cornwall*.
3772. April 5: Hardy to Captain Fairholme: rough draft of reply to Letter 3770; Hardy will be pleased if he sends the words of *Compassion* to *The Times* for publication on 16 June 1924, the S.P.C.A. Centenary Day, and he may put "No Copyright" on the poem so that it may be widely copied.
3773. April 5: J. Middleton Murry thanks Hardy for his letter.
3774. April 8: Hardy to Kenneth R. Barnes: rough draft, in pencil, of a letter for F. E. H. to sign and send, asking Barnes why Hardy was not informed of a performance of *The Queen of Cornwall* by members of the Academy of Dramatic Art on 1 April 1924.
3775. April 8: C. Bohn Childs about Brennecke's book. *Thomas Hardy's Universe*.
3776. April 8: Everard J. Haynes invites Hardy to serve on a Committee for the International Congress on Architectural Education.
3777. April 8: Sir Henry Newbolt asks permission to quote.
3778. April 9: Hardy to Haynes: rough draft of reply to Letter 3776; is not able to undertake any function, but is willing to have his name used if desirable.
3779. April 9: Morgan sends an article on Lord Morley.
3780. April 10: Haynes pleased by Hardy's willingness to allow his name to be used as a Committeeman.
3781. April 11: R. R. B. Vakil, from Bombay, solicits Hardy's autograph.
3782. April 14: Newbolt thanks Hardy for permission to quote.
3783. April 15: A. Davies Adams explains how he came to compose music for *The Queen of Cornwall* without Hardy's knowledge or authorization.
3784. April 16: Camilla Selons thanks for visit to Max Gate.
3785. April 18: Margaret F. Gifford about her sorrow in the loss of her **daughter.**

CHRONOLOGICAL LIST

3786. April 18: Georgiana, Lady Macmillan made her acquaintance through *Under the Greenwood Tree* and has been a constant admirer since.
3787. April 21: Hardy to Morgan: typed transcript; about an article on Lord Morley.
3788. April 21: James Ismay asks Hardy to sign a photogravure of Augustus John's portrait of Hardy to be hung in the Village Club at Iwerne Minster.
3789. April 22: Green asks Hardy to autograph two volumes being sent to him from Trenton, New Jersey.
3790. April 26: Ismay thanks Hardy for signing the photogravure as requested in Letter 3788.
3791. April 27: Granville-Barker about Kean's appearance in Dorchester and about the old theatre there.
3792. April 28: Hardy to Granville-Barker: typed transcript; thanks for the particulars about Kean.
3793. April 28: George A. Cronshaw solicits a photograph of Hardy for hanging at Queen's College, Oxford.
3794. April 28: Winifred Stephens asks help in celebrating the fourth centenary of Pierre de Ronsard.
3795. April 29: C. Bohn Childs again about Brennecke's book, *Thomas Hardy's Universe.*
3796. April 30: John Shane sends a copy of his book of poems.
3797. April (?): Ian MacAlister invites Hardy to the Annual Dinner of the Royal Institute of British Architects.
3798. May 1: Vere Collins asks Hardy to autograph a copy of his poem on Shakespeare.
3799. May 3: Hardy to Adams: rough draft of reply to Letter 3783; can say nothing definite about publishing *The Queen of Cornwall* with music, since it may appear as an opera, with music by Rutland Boughton.
3800. May 9: Judge J. S. Udal about the Dorset Field Club.
3801. May 11: J. A. Pridham about a Garden Party at Puddletown.
3802. May 12: Hardy to Pridham: rough draft of reply to Letter 3801.
3803. May 12: Herbert Bates asks permission to quote five poems by Hardy and encloses an American stamp for Hardy's reply.
3804. May 14: E. V. Lucas asks Hardy to autograph his contribution to The Book of the Queen's Dolls' House Library.
3805. May 14: Pridham sends more information about the Garden Party at Puddletown.
3806. May 15: Laura O. (Mrs. Reginald T.) Gould asks about the stanzaic form used by Hardy in "When I set out for Lyonnesse."
3807. May 16: Hardy to Mrs. Gould: rough draft of reply to Letter 3806; the stanza is one of many varieties of Roundelay, Roundel, or Rondel.
3808. May 16: Lady Cynthia Asquith about *The Queen of Cornwall.*
3809. May 18: E. B. Poulton asks help in locating a passage in Hardy's work.
3810. May 19: T. M. Raff about Stephen Graham's *Life of Wilfrid Ewart.*
3811. May 20: Hardy to Poulton: copy of reply to Letter 3809; the story must be "The Superstitious Man's Story" in *Life's Little Ironies.*

3812. May 20: Hardy to Raff: rough draft of reply to Letter 3810; acknowledging receipt of book.
3813. May 21: T. Fisher Unwin about Brennecke's *Thomas Hardy's Universe*.
3814. May 22: Cockerell about the French.
3815. May 30: Ethel (Mrs. Sidney) Gutman, later Mrs. Ethel Lion, writes to Mr. Lewis Hind that she wants to get something [for the Bermondsey Book Shop] from Thomas Hardy.
3816. May 31: Edward Clodd chats about books.
3817. May 31: C. Lewis Hind says Mrs. Gutman (who with her husband opened the Bermondsey Book Shop) would like something from him for *The Bermondsey Book*.
3818. (c. June 1): Hardy to Hind: rough draft of reply to Letter 3817; is now of an age when he cannot promise anything.
3819. June 2: Annie Hemmekam asks permission to translate *Jude* into Dutch.

On 2 June 1924 Hardy attained the age of 84. Nineteen men and women remembered his birthday and sent greetings, on 2 June or on date indicated in parentheses:

3820. Cecil Braithwaite
3821. John H. Dickinson (4 June)
3822. St. John Ervine
3823. Newman Flower (1 June)
3824. Margaret Gifford
3825. Harley Granville-Barker
3826. Lady Agnes Grove
3827. Mrs. Cecil Hanbury (5 June)
3828. N. R. Hariharaiyer (12 May)
3829. Alda Hoar
3830. Lady Ilchester (31 May)
3831. J. W. Mackail (3 June)
3832. W. H. Perkins
3833. Alain Raffin
3834. Lady Agatha Russell (30 May)
3835. F. W. Slater (3 June)
3836. Muriel Stuart
3837. Charles Whibley
3838. F. Wortley

3839. June 2: J. Looker is about to publish (at Poole, Dorset) *A Guide to the Hardy Country*, for which he solicits a photograph and a list of Dorset names used in the novels.
3840. June 3: Hardy to Looker: rough draft of reply to Letter 3839; a list of names is available in Hermann Lea's book.
3841. June 3: G. Currie Martin queries Jack Squire's accuracy regarding *Under the Greenwood Tree*.
3842. June 5: Mary Fox-Strangways (daughter of Lady Ilchester) thanks Hardy for a copy of his poems.
3843. June 5: Bartos Zoltan about translating *Tess* and *Jude* into Hungarian.
3844. June 6: James T. Mackereth letter and three-page poem "To Thomas Hardy, O. M."
3845. June 9: Brennecke probes Hardy's philosophical views, especially with regard to Bergson.
3846. June 10: Speyer sends his musical setting for Tristram's song in *The Queen of Cornwall*.
3847. June 10: J. C. Squire about *The Dynasts*.
3848. June 11: Mrs. Lion solicits a poem.
3849. June 12: Christopher Whitfield asks how to get poetry published.
3850. June 13: Dr. Ernest N. Townley Clarke sends an article written by a friend of his about a visit to Egdon Heath.

CHRONOLOGICAL LIST

3851. June 13: C. A. Dawson Scott about the P.E.N. Club.
3852. June (14): Hardy to Scott: rough draft of reply to Letter 3851; for physical reasons, he is not able to take part.
3853. June 14: H. Irene Brown sends an American reader's response to the second chapter of *Far from the Madding Crowd*.
3854. June 15: Walter Oakeshott invites Hardy to a performance of Aeschylus by Balliol College players in Maumbury Ring at Dorchester.
3855. June 16: Arthur Bransden wants an autographed copy of one of Hardy's books.
3856. June 16: Max Judge asks Hardy to sign his name in an edition of fifty copies of his poem.
3857. June 17: Hardy to Oakeshott: rough draft of reply to Letter 3854; doubts being able to go to Maumbury Ring.
3858. June 17: Herman Livezey asks Hardy's opinion of Walt Whitman.
3859. June 18: Baron Georg Franckenstein, Austrian Minister in London wants Hardy to talk with Prince Rohan about a proposed International Review.
3860. June 18: Eden Phillpotts sends a book.
3861. June 19: Hardy to W. H. Perkins: rough draft, in pencil; recalls him as an undergraduate at Aberdeen. (Hardy used him as one of the argumentative sons of the Baptist minister in *A Laodicean*.)
3862. (c. April 19): Hardy to Prince Rohan: rough draft; will be unable to contribute to the proposed International Review because of his advanced age.
3863. June 19: Algernon Rose about The Authors' Club.
3864. June 21: Charles E. S. Chambers asks for a contribution to mark the Diamond Jubilee of Hardy's first appearance in *Chambers's Journal* in 1865.
3865. June 23: W. T. Shore asks for an interview with a view to writing an article for the American *Dearborn Independent*.
3866. June 24: Hardy to Shore: rough draft of reply to Letter 3865; is not able to comply.
3867. June 24: Cronshaw thanks Hardy for the etching of himself sent to Queen's College, Oxford.
3868. June 24: James Cross asks about the publisher, Kegan Paul.
3869. June 24: John H. Dickinson reports the St. Juliot Church is "now quite dry."
3870. June 24: Oakeshott asks if the players from Balliol College, Oxford, might give a performance of Aeschylus in the garden at Max Gate.
3871. June 25: Hardy to Cross: rough draft of reply to Letter 3868; he is not able to help.
3872. June 26: Hardy to Oakeshott: rough draft of reply to Letter 3870; wants to know the number of performers to give Aeschylus.
3873. June 26: John H. Morgan is grateful for permission to dedicate a book to Hardy.
3874. June 26: Sir Rennel Rodel asks support of a petition to admit Byron to Poets' Corner in Westminster Abbey.
3875. June 26: Edward Smith appreciation.
3876. June 27: Hardy to Rodel: rough draft of reply to Letter 3874; will give his name and support to the petition.

3877. June 27: Hardy to Chambers: rough draft of reply to Letter 3864; asks about the copyright in "How I Built Myself a House," which (before sending it in 1865 to the editor of *Chambers's Journal*) Hardy wrote to amuse some architect's pupils.
3878. June 28: Rodel thanks Hardy for his prompt reply.
3879. June 30: Dickinson thanks Hardy for a subscription for the church at St. Juliot.
3880. June (?): Hardy to Brennecke: rough draft of letter about his philosophical views; says he has never been influenced by Bergson.
3881. July 1: Chambers has found the 1865 receipt written out by his father and signed by Hardy, assigning copyright in "How I Built Myself a House" to *Chambers's Journal*.
3882. July 2: Pridham further information about the Garden Party at Puddletown.
3883. (c. July 3): Hardy to Pridham: rough draft of reply to Letter 3882.
3884. July 3: L. Ewart Skellern appreciation from Crewe, Cheshire.
3885. July 5: Hardy to Chambers: rough draft; encloses a poem, "A Bird-Scene at a Rural Dwelling," for publication in *Chambers's Journal* as solicited in Letter 3864.
3886. July 5: Cockerell about a Greek Dictionary.
3887. July 9: Wallace Brockway appreciation.
3888. July 9: John L. Hetheright from Birmingham.
3889. (c. July 10): Hardy to Hetheright: rough draft; acknowledges receipt of Letter 3888; is much obliged.
3890. July 10: Alfred Ludgate sends a copy of his first novel, *Mistress of Broad Marsh*.
3891. July 11: Chambers accepts Hardy's poem for publication in *Chambers's Journal*. (It appeared in January 1925 issue.)
3892. July 11: Poulton about a rare butterfly.
3893. July 11: Speyer asks why he has had no acknowledgment from Hardy of the musical setting sent him for Tristram's song in *The Queen of Cornwall*.
3894. July 11: Gertrude Trewern from Cornwall.
3895. July 12: M. M. Banaji asks Hardy's opinion of his book, *Sublime Though Blind*.
3896. July 12: B. E. Nicolls thanks Hardy for permission to read lines from *The Dynasts* in a B.B.C. broadcast.
3897. July 14: Hardy to Speyer: rough draft of reply to Letter 3893; cannot consent to publication of Tristram's song at present.
3898. July 14: F. G. Ellerton asks permission to quote.
3899. July 14: A. Herbert Evans forwards a letter from his son, Maurice Evans.
3900. July 14: Maurice H. Evans asks permission for an amateur Dramatic Society in London to enact *The Woodlanders*.
3901. July 15: Hardy to A. H. Evans: rough draft, denying permission to Evans' son Maurice.
3902. July 15: Odin Gregory sends MS. of his work *Cain* which he wishes to dedicate to Hardy.
3903. July 15: Ella G. Castleman Smith about a Garden Party at Ilsington.
3904. July 21: Serge Yourievitch asks to be allowed to model a bust of Hardy.

3905. July 22: Brennecke thanks Hardy for his comments on *Thomas Hardy's Universe*.
3906. July 22: Mrs. Ethel Gutman asks permission to publish Hardy's letter to Lewis Hind about the Bermondsey Book Shop.
3907. (c. July 23): Hardy to Mrs. Gutman: rough draft of reply to Letter 3906; has no objection to the letter being published.
3908. July 23: Cockerell about Yourievitch's proposal to do a bust of Hardy.
3909. July 25: Morgan solicits a testimonial for his book about Lord Morley.
3910. July 25: R. J. Wilkinson appreciation.
3911. July 27: Hardy to Yourievitch: rough draft of reply to Letter 3904; Hardy could not pay but would give a few sittings; also, he is not able to buy.
3912. July 28: Hardy to Morgan: typed transcript; declines suggestion that he write a testimonial for Morgan's book.
3913. (c. July 29): Hardy to Gregory: rough draft of reply to Letter 3902; reminds Gregory that Byron had written on the same subject.
3914. July 29: Morgan about the Nobel Prize Committee.
3915. July 30: Hardy to Ludgate: rough draft of reply to Letter 3890; he hopes to read Ludgate's novel.
3916. July 30: Chambers sends Hardy five guineas for his poem.
3917. August 1: Nelson Hardy sends a tribute from a ventriloquist.
3918. August 1: E. Millington-Drake, from the British Embassy in Brussels, asks Hardy to autograph a copy of *Late Lyrics*.
3919. August 2: Thornycroft again on art and books.
3920. August 5: Nicolls sends a copy of the program for the B.B.C. broadcast for 15 August, when lines from *The Dynasts* are to be read.
3921. August 6: Dorothy M. Macardle asks permission to submit a dramatized version in one act of "The Three Strangers."
3922. August 6: Thornycroft supplements his letter of 2 August.
3923. August 8: F. M. Marsden about the copy of *Late Lyrics* forwarded for Hardy's autograph (see Letter 3918).
3924. August 14: E. Millington-Drake thanks Hardy for autographing a copy of *Late Lyrics*.
3925. August 15: H. Watt about proofs of poems in magazines.
3926. August 16: L. S. Wood asks permission to quote.
3927. August 21: St. John Ervine definition of the meaning of Donaghodee, the name of a village in Belfast.
3928. August 21: Philip D. Sherman solicits an inscription in a copy of the first edition of *Tess*.
3929. August 23: H. Beadon requests permission to reprint *Compassion: An Ode*.
3930. (c. August 24): Hardy to Beadon: giving permission to reprint *Compassion*.
3931. August 24: Hardy to T. H. Tilley: rough draft; specifies five conditions on which Hardy is willing for the Dorchester players to perform his dramatization of *Tess*.
3932. August 24: Jamila Majid asks if the enclosed poems have any literary merit.
3933. August 29: Vere Collins detailed suggestions for two publishing projects.

3934. September 1: Powys Evans again asks Hardy to sit for a drawing planned for appearance in the *London Mercury*.
3935. September 3: Hardy to Evans: rough draft in which he declines "the opportunity" offered in Letter 3934.
3936. September 8: Charles King solicits a contribution to *The Torchbearer*.
3937. September 9: Hardy to King: rough draft of reply to Letter 3936; pleads inability.
3938. September 10: H. E. C. Brickell asks permission to call one of the teams at St. George's School, Portland, the Hardy House team.
3939. September 13: A. H. M. Sime asks permission to quote.
3940. September 17: Viscount Dillon requests Hardy sit for a photographer for producing a portrait for the National Portrait Gallery.
3941. September 18: Norman Gullick asks Hardy to write an introduction for a bibliography of Edmund Gosse.
3942. September 19: Hardy to Gullick: rough draft of reply to Letter 3941; feels it is more than he can do to write such an introduction.
3943. September 19: Ottoline Howell thanks Hardy for permission to call.
3944. September 20: Arthur C. Benson to "Dear Hardy."
3945. September 22: Cockerell about Mrs. Hardy's operation.
3946. September 22: Mrs. Granville-Barker invites Hardy to stay with her and Harley when Florence goes to the hospital for an operation.
3947. September 23: Drinkwater asks permission to dedicate his new book of poems to Hardy.
3948. September 24: Gustav Holst writes to the concert pianist Evelyn Stuart about his musical settings for Hardy's poems.
3949. September 25: Squire solicits something for the *London Mercury*. (Hardy sent "An East End Curate.")
3950. September 26: Gifford to Mrs. Florence Hardy about her operation; acknowledges a cheque sent on his sister's behalf.
3951. September 27: Cockerell on receiving Hardy's letter about Mrs. Hardy's health.
3952. September 29: C. Collier Abbott sends a "small tribute" to Hardy.
3953. September 29: Benson says Hardy was good to write to him.
3954. September 30: Cockerell has seen Mrs. Hardy at Fitzroy House.
3955. October 1: Cockerell on matters of health.
3956. October 1: Cockerell again about Mrs. Hardy's condition.
3957. October 1: James Sherren reports Mrs. Hardy's condition after her operation as "quite satisfactory."
3958. October 2: Cockerell again about Mrs. Hardy's condition.
3959. October 2: A. J. Gillam thanks Hardy for permitting the Dorchester Dramatic Society to produce his dramatization of *Tess*.
3960. October 2: Beecher Hogan appreciation from Yale College.
3961. October 3: Jacques Rivière solicits an article on Joseph Conrad for the *Nouvelle Revue Française*.
3962. October 4: Stair A. Gillon friendly letter.
3963. October 5: Hardy's sister Katharine about bringing Mrs. Hardy home from the hospital by car.
3964. October 5: Thornycroft writes the last of his splendid letters on art, books, etc.
3965. October 6: Cockerell about Mrs. Hardy's health.

3966. October 6: Dewar wants another poem for publication in the *Nineteenth Century*.
3967. October 8: Squire thanks Hardy for the poem "An East End Curate."
3968. October 10: J. B. Priestley sends a copy of his criticisms of contemporary writers.
3969. October 11. A. M. Parratt asks for the return to Australia of a photograph sent to Hardy in February.
3970. October 14: Lady Cynthia Asquith solicits a poem for publication in *The Flying Carpet*.
3971. October 15: Sasbrial appreciation from India.
3972. October 17: Lady Asquith thanks Hardy for "A Popular Personage at Home" (a poem about Hardy's dog "Wessex").
3973. October 20: Brennecke sends a copy of a New York edition of Middleton Murry's *Wrap Me Up in My Aubusson Carpet*.
3974. October 21: P. Anderson Graham sends a copy of the current issue of *Country Life* containing an article about Cerne Abbas.
3975. October 22: Hardy to Rivière: rough draft of reply to Letter 3961; regrets inability to write the article requested.
3976. October 23: Lady Asquith thanks Hardy for his letter.
3977. October 24: Delia Carroll appreciation.
3978. October 24: S. Hill asks Hardy to sign a copy of *Tess*.
3979. October 24: Walter E. Schott asks what London publisher might be interested in a book on the Sex Instinct.
3980. October 25: Dr. H. A. Lediard about the sleep-walking episode in *Tess*.
3981. October 25: Sam B. Sloan asks permission to quote from various Wessex Novels.
3982. October 25: Thomas J. Wise is glad to know a new volume of his *Catalogue* finds favor in Hardy's sight.
3983. October 26: Charles King thanks Hardy for taking an interest in him.
3984. (c. October 28): Masefield about *The Queen of Cornwall*.
3985. October 30: L. Everett replies to Hardy's complaint that his "wireless" set is not giving satisfaction.
3986. October 31: M. M. Banaji regrets Hardy is not able to express a critical judgment of B.'s book *Sublime*.
3987. November 1: Hanbury thanks Hardy for his congratulations on Hanbury's election.
3988. November 2: Hardy to Sybil Thorndike: rough draft of reply to some prior communication asking about the Dorchester performances of the *Tess* play on 26-29 November 1924.
3989. November (4?): Hardy to Sloan: rough draft of reply to Letter 3981; regrets that Professor Sloan's study of Hardy's work will be of only that part of it which he abandoned nearly thirty years ago.
3990. November 4: Margaret Drew asks permission to include *The Three Wayfarers* in the Play Lending Library of The Arts League.
3991. November 4: Mary Lady Wyndham asks for an autographed copy or two of *Tess* for a Bazaar Sale in aid of the Waifs and Strays.
3992. November 5: Sybil Thorndike says her husband, Lewis T. Casson, will be present to see the performance of *Tess* at Dorchester.
3993. November 7: Margaret Drew again about *The Three Strangers*.
3994. November 11: William Garwood appreciation.

3995. November 11: Sir Frederick Pollock congratulates Hardy on his honorary fellowship at Queen's College, Oxford.
3996. November 11: Sybil Thorndike reports the play (*Tess*) has arrived and she has started to read it.
3997. November 11: Yourievitch sends Hardy photographs of the bust he made of Hardy in August.
3998. November 12: Harold Child says the editor of *The Times* wishes him to write an account of *Tess*; he asks to see the dress rehearsal.
3999. November 12: P. Anderson Graham asks for a poem for publication in the Christmas number of *Country Life*.
4000. November 13: Hardy to Child: rough draft; about times for dress-rehearsals of *Tess*.
4001. November 14: Child will come to tea and will attend the dress rehearsal of *Tess*.
4002. November 17: Hardy to Parratt: rough draft of reply to Letter 3969; no trace of the letter or photograph can be found.
4003. November 17: Brennecke solicits consent to a biographical sketch.
4004. November 17: C. A. Lewis asks Hardy to speak a few words at the time of the B.B.C. broadcast of a *Tess* performance.
4005. November 17: Masefield asks permission to enact *The Queen of Cornwall*.
4006. November 18: Hardy to Dillon: rough draft of reply to Letter 3940; is physically unable to travel, but offers to supply a photograph of himself.
4007. November 19: Masefield thanks Hardy for permission to enact *The Queen of Cornwall*.
4008. November 19: Moult asks permission to quote.
4009. November 19: Graham pleased with Hardy's poem "Winter Night in Woodland" for publication in the Christmas number of *Country Life*.
4010. November 20: James Milner thanks for the suggestion made in Hardy's letter of 18 November to Dillon.
4011. November 20: Moult again asks permission to quote.
4012. November 22. Moult appeals to Mrs. Hardy for help in his attempt to pry permission out of Hardy.
4013. November 24: C. A. Lewis about Hardy's refusal to say a few words at the time of the B.B.C. broadcast of the *Tess* play.
4014. November 25: Philip Pearce solicits a funny verse in the Dorset dialect.
4015. November 25: Walter E. Schott asks for return of the copies of certain letters sent to Hardy soliciting his opinion.
4016. November 26: Hardy to Pearce: rough draft of reply to Letter 4014; he cannot produce such a verse.
4017. November 26: Hardy to Schott: rough draft of reply to Letter 4015; he has not yet read the letters.
4018. November 26: Child is grateful for permission to quote from the *Tess* play.
4019. November 26: Frederick Harrison, of the Haymarket Theatre in London, asks for a seat to see *Tess* performed in Dorchester.
4020. November 26: *Izvestia*, through its London correspondent, asks Hardy to express his opinion on the political situation created by the abandonment of the Anglo-Russian Treaties.
4021. November 26: Sybil Thorndike sends good wishes.

4022. November 27: Forbes-Robertson asks again about the acting rights of *Tess*.
4023. November 29: Hardy to Forbes-Robertson: rough draft of reply to Letter 4022; he does not at his age have any desire to see the *Tess* play acted in London, but years and years ago Forbes-Robertson and Mrs. Pat Campbell would have carried it off wonderfully. (See Letter 668.)
4024. November 29: Francis Needham about a pirated edition of *Compassion; An Ode*.
4025. November 29: B. F. Stevens & Brown ask Mrs. Florence Hardy about the MS. of *The Woodlanders* which they understand is for sale at one thousand pounds.
4026. November 29: W. O. Whinham thanks Hardy for permission for the Dorchester players to present *Tess* at Weymouth next month.
4027. November 30: Morgan about his "Morley book."
4028. December 1: Hardy to Morgan: typed transcript of letter about Morgan's Morley book.
4029. December 2: Harley Granville-Barker sends congratulations on *Tess* and reports Barrie sang its praises recently.
4030. December 3: Hardy to Granville-Barker: typed transcript; thanks for congratulations on the play, *Tess*.
4031. December 3: Schott again solicits Hardy's opinion on his book on the Sex Instinct.
4032. December 4: Child thanks Hardy for an autographed copy of *Tess*.
4033. (c. December 6): Masefield hopes to start rehearsing *The Queen of Cornwall* at Oxford soon.
4034. December 7: W. B. Beer appreciation.
4035. December (?): Masefield again about *The Queen of Cornwall*.
4036. December 8: Drinkwater thanks Hardy for a "present" (possibly a copy of *The Queen of Cornwall* in paper wrappers, which Hardy had had printed for private distribution).
4037. (c. December 9): Masefield thanks Hardy for a gift, possibly a copy of *The Queen of Cornwall* in paper wrappers.
4038. December 9: Child solicits a copy of the speech Hardy is to make at a dinner in Weymouth.
4039. December 10: Child thanks Hardy for help with a bibliography of Hardy's work.
4040. December 12: J. H. Fowler submits for inspection four short introductions he has written for an Indian edition of *Far from the Madding Crowd, The Return of the Native, The Trumpet-Major,* and *The Mayor of Casterbridge*.
4041. December 12: Yourievitch again about the bust for which Hardy had sat in August.
4042. December 13: Leonora W. Lockhart asks about Hardy's conception of The Immanent Will in *The Dynasts*.
4043. December 13: Harry Wheeler sends proofs of Hardy's portrait and asks for their return.
4044. December 15: Hardy to Wheeler: rough draft of reply to Letter 4043; approves the sale of three of the photographs and forbids the sale of two.
4045. December 15: B. E. Brenner asks permission for a dramatic performance of *Under the Greenwood Tree* for the benefit of a Congregational Church.

4046. December 15: E. F. Read solicits support of The Dorchester British Legion Military Band.
4047. December 15: E. N. Singleton informs Hardy there is a Thomas Hardy Study Club in Toronto, Canada.
4048. December 15: B. F. Stevens & Brown send Florence Hardy a cheque for £1000 for the MS. of *The Woodlanders*, which has been bought by Howard Bliss.
4049. (c. December 16): Hardy to Brenner: rough draft of reply to Letter 4045; grants permission to dramatize *Under the Greenwood Tree* and perform it.
4050. December 17: Hardy to Schott: has not been able to read his book through.
4051. December 18: Lady Asquith sends payment for the poem "A Popular Personage at Home" which Hardy had contributed to her book, *The Flying Carpet*.
4052. December 19: Frank Conlend asks for an article on "Literature" for *The Graphic*.
4053. December 19: Harper & Brothers inform Gunnar Gillhoff they are not in a position to negotiate about a German translation of *Tess*.
4054. December 20: Barrie about the possibility of Gertrude Bugler's appearing as "Tess" at the Haymarket Theatre in London.
4055. December 21: Harper & Brothers report to Hardy that Gillhoff had sought permission to make a German translation of *Tess*.
4056. December 23: F. T. Green about the Christmas carol in *Under the Greenwood Tree*.
4057. December 23: J. W. Mackail wishes he could have seen the recent [*Tess*] performance of the Dorchester Players.
4058. December 23: Schott again about his book on the Sex Instinct.
4059. December 24: Brenner thanks Hardy for granting permission for the dramatization of *Under the Greenwood Tree* and its performance by a Congregational Church group.
4060. December 26: Samuel Cohen invites Hardy to attend a debate at Cambridge University.
4061. December 26: W. S. Crockett suggests Hardy write a play about "Thomas the Rhymer."
4062. (c. December 27): Hardy to Cohen: rough draft of reply to Letter 4060; is not able to get to Cambridge.
4063. December 30: Benson appreciated Hardy's writing to him about his (Benson's) poems.
4064. December 31: Clodd plans to call at Max Gate.
4065. December 31: J. S. MacNutt asks Hardy to write a School Song for the Canford School at Wimborne.
4066. December (?): Hardy to the Mayor of Bournemouth: rough draft; about a possible performance of the *Tess* play at Bournemouth.
4067. (n. d.): Mrs. Hanbury thanks Hardy for his note after her husband had an operation.
4068. (n. d.): Masefield thanks Hardy for his letter.

1925

4069. January 1: William S. Dixon pleased about the re-publication of "How I Built Myself a House" in *Chambers's Journal*.

CHRONOLOGICAL LIST 177

4070. January 2: James Barrie about Yourievitch's bust of Hardy.
4071. January 3: Ernest Brennecke to C. K. Shorter about Hardy's disapproval of Brennecke's biography of Hardy.
4072. January 3: Charles W. Keppel asks about the origin of the name "Bathsheba" in *Far from the Madding Crowd*.
4073. January 6: Lady Cynthia Asquith wants another poem for publication.
4074. January 6: P. Anderson Graham sends payment for the poem "Winter Night in Woodland" published in the Christmas number of *Country Life*.
4075. January 6: Algernon Rose about the Authors' Club.
4076. January 7: Herbert Ashling thanks Hardy for his suggestion about a possible performance of his play in the Winter Gardens Pavilion at Bournemouth.
4077. January 7: Paul Bonnet solicits an autograph.
4078. January 7: George A. B. Dewar says Hardy's poem "The Absolute Explains" (to be published in the February *Nineteenth Century*) has moved him deeply.
4079. January 7: Lady St. Helier about E. Topham Forrest.
4080. January 7: Clement Shorter is glad Hardy will send him a poem for publication in *The Sphere*.
4081. January 8: N. R. Hariharaiyer repeats his request for permission to publish in India.
4082. January 9: E. A. Cross describes an American admirer's tour of "the Hardy country" and ends with a request for an autograph.
4083. January 13: Brennecke again to Shorter about his biography of Hardy. (Shorter forwarded the letter to Max Gate on 21 January.)
4084. January 15: Mlle Yvonne Salmon asks permission for a representative of the Alliance Française to call at Max Gate.
4085. January 17: Frederic F. Wheeler asks permission to call.
4086. January 19: Hardy to J. H. Fowler: rough draft; encloses some corrections of the Introductions Fowler had written for an Indian edition of four of the Wessex Novels.
4087. January 19: Hardy to MacNutt: rough draft of reply to Letter 4065; is unable to write a school song for him.
4088. January 19: Hardy to Yvonne Salmon: rough draft of reply to Letter 4084; Monsieur Lefevre may call.
4089. January 19: Howard Bliss sends thanks for a volume. (*The Woodlanders*?) See Letter 4048.
4090. January 21: Fowler thanks Hardy for the correction sent in Letter 4086.
4091. January 21: MacNutt thanks Hardy for Letter 4087.
4092. January 21: Shorter to Mrs. Hardy about Brennecke's objectionable *Life of Thomas Hardy*.
4093. January 22: Francis Day & Hunter, music publishers, inform Cockerell that "The Mocking Bird," a song Mrs. Emma Hardy used to sing (see Hardy's poem, "The Prophetess"), was composed by Edward Hoffman.
4094. January 23: Cockerell forwards the information in Letter 4093. (Hardy's poem, "The Prophetess," was published posthumously in *Winter Words*, 1928.)
4095. January 23: Charles Newland solicits Hardy's help.
4096. January 24: Wilbur Needham has found *Jude* very moving.

4097. January 24: D. C. Wren solicits Hardy's help.
4098. January 25: Richard A. Cordell sends thanks for having been permitted to call at Max Gate.
4099. January 27: Brennecke regrets Hardy's disapproval of B.'s biography of Hardy.
4100. January 28: Paul Kay solicits authorization of a dramatization of *The Hand of Ethelberta.*
4101. January 28: Ezra Pound to Hardy's "Secretary": offers to send Hardy the draft of his *Cantos*, but does not want to bother him with it.
4102. January 29: Henri Oppé asks for Hardy's autograph.
4103. January 29: W. M. Parker asks if Hardy ever received his booklet, *On The Track of the Wessex Novels.*
4104. January 29: Yvonne Salmon tells Mrs. Hardy she will accompany M. Lefevre when he comes to call on Hardy.
4105. January (30?): Hardy to Parker: rough draft; Parker's booklet did reach Hardy, and he thanks Parker.
4106. February 1: Hardy to Yvonne Salmon: rough draft of reply to Letter 4104.
4107. February 2: R. L. Pocock about the Dorset Antiquarian Field Club.
4108. February 4: Gertrude Bugler, after having been formally invited by Frederick Harrison (see Letter 4019) to play "Tess" at the Haymarket Theatre in London, tells Hardy she has written to Harrison that she cannot play 'Tess' after all. Her withdrawal was made at the request of Mrs. Florence Hardy, who made a trip to Beaminster to plead with Mrs. Bugler *not* to act in the play in London.
4109. February 4: J. C. Squire asks Hardy to judge a poetry competition.
4110. February (5?): Hardy to Paul Kay: rough draft; refuses to authorize the dramatization of *The Hand of Ethelberta.*
4111. February 5: Hardy to Squire: rough draft of reply to Letter 4109, is unable to judge a poetry competition.
4112. February 5: Cockerell about the spelling of a name in *The Dynasts.*
4113. February 5: J. W. Greenberg sends a copy of Brennecke's *Life and Art* from New York.
4114. February 5: The editor of *The Operative Builder* asks for a photograph of Hardy for use with an article on the Wessex Novels.
4115. February (6?): Hardy to the Editor of *The Operative Builder*: rough draft of reply to Letter 4114; encloses two portraits of Hardy and his autograph.
4116. February 9: Lady Agnes Grove about a prize that has been offered for the best essay on one of twelve books, *Tess* among them.
4117. February 10: Hardy to Granville-Barker: typed transcript; asks what would be involved in making arrangements for a London production of his *Tess* play.
4118. February 11: Sybil Thorndike hedges about accepting Hardy's *Tess* play for production.
4119. February 12: St. John Ervine comments on the *Tess* play.
4120. February 13: Granville-Barker responds to Hardy's letter of the 10th; says Winthrop Ames wants Hardy's play or nothing.
4121. February 13: M. Manent wants something for publication.
4122. February 14: A. G. Berrisford sends thanks.
4123. February 14: Lucile Burriss sends thanks.

4124. February 15: Christopher Childs asks if Hardy would propose his son for membership in the Athenaeum Club.
4125. February 16: S. McCrae sends thanks.
4126. February 18: Samuel A. Nock about the relative merits of Hardy's poetry and prose.
4127. February 19: Mrs. Cecil Hanbury thanks for Hardy's letter of sympathy after the death of her father.
4128. February 20: Alice Bossuet requests an option on making a French translation of *The Dynasts*.
4129. February 20: Charles I. Reid invites Hardy to make a lecture-tour in the United States in 1925-26.
4130. February 21: François Talva asks for Hardy's autograph.
4131. February 22: Ervine returns the MS. of Hardy's *Tess* play.
4132. February 24: Ernest B. Wood about a production of Rutland Boughton's musical setting for *The Queen of Cornwall*.
4133. February 25: T. G. Barber solicits support of a Byron Memorial Fund.
4134. February 26: Arthur S. McDowall to Mrs. Hardy about Hardy's poem in the *Nineteenth Century*. See Letter 4078.
4135. February (28?): Hardy to N. R. Hariharaiyer: rough draft; declines to authorize publication of any of Hardy's stories in India.
4136. March 3: Hardy to Nock: rough draft of reply to Letter 4126; Nock's opinion that Hardy's poetry is more important than his prose "is that of readers of the more advanced sort in England."
4137. March 3: Fr. Faehnert asks about German translations of *Tess* or *A Group of Noble Dames*.
4138. March 4: Henry J. Stone seeks support of the National Council for Animals' Welfare.
4139. March 6: Marie Flower asks about "the cliff without a name" in *A Pair of Blue Eyes*.
4140. March 6: Masefield explores the possibility of Hardy's visiting Oxford.
4141. March 6: L. H. C. Shuttleworth solicits an autograph MS. for the library of Cheltenham College.
4142. (c. March 7): Hardy to Marie Flower: rough draft of reply to Letter 4139; the Cliff is near Beeny.
4143. March 7: Wilkinson Sherren thanks Hardy for photographs of Yourievitch's bust.
4144. March 8: Mrs. Bugler thanks Hardy for sending *The Woodlanders* for her birthday.
4145. March 10: Hardy to W. Dawson & Sons: rough draft of reply to be signed ". . /Secretary"; Hardy has not written or authorized any biography of himself, and is not aware of any such book being published in England. (Brennecke's book was published in New York).
4146. March 10: Hardy to Schott: rough draft; he has not been able to form a critical estimate of S.'s book.
4147. March 10: Hardy to Shorter: rough draft, in Hardy's hand, (to be signed "F. E. H."); about a poem to be published in *The Sphere*. Shorter need not be concerned about American serial use of the poem. See Letter 4080.
4148. March 13: Albert Tustes, a French admirer, appreciation.
4149. March 14: Christopher Childs thanks Hardy for proposing his son for membership at the Athenaeum Club.

4150. March 14: Katherine C. Norwood sends thanks.
4151. March 14: *The Operative Builder* sends a copy of the March number containing an article about his literary work.
4152. March 16: E. Morton thanks Hardy for the gift of the MS. of "The Fallow Deer" to the library of Cheltenham College.
4153. March 17: Florence Burnand sends thanks.
4154. March 17: G. W. Forrest about Mrs. Anne Procter, who once told Forrest Hardy had named his heroine in *The Trumpet-Major* Anne after her.
4155. March 17: F. W. Slater about the prospective publication of Hardy's poem "Circus-Rider to Ringmaster" in *Harper's Magazine* for June 1925.
4156. March 18: Greenberg, New York publisher of Brennecke's *Life of Thomas Hardy*, sends a copy of the offensive book.
4157. March 19: Amy Lowell pleased by Hardy's letter (now in the Houghton Library, Harvard University) about her *Life of Keats*.
4158. March 19: L. H. C. Shuttleworth thanks Hardy for his gift to the library of Cheltenham College.
4159. March 23. Thomas Loveday asks if Hardy can be present at the University of Bristol on 9 June 1925 to receive the honorary degree of Litt.D.
4160. March 24: W. E. Lengel asks permission to call at Max Gate.
4161. March 25: Hardy to Loveday: rough draft of reply to Letter 4159; a physical difficulty will prevent his coming to Bristol to receive the degree offered him.
4162. March 31: C. Bohn Childs thanks Hardy for nominating him for membership in the Athenaeum Club.
4163. March 31: Henry Poulaille sends thanks.
4164. April 3: C. Bohn Childs about Brennecke's book *Life and Art in Thomas Hardy*.
4165. April 4: Miss "Rowland Grey" to her "Dear Master."
4166. April 7: Gerald Maxwell asks permission to call.
4167. April 9: Hardy to Maxwell: rough draft; is now compelled to decline interviews.
4168. April 10: The Duchess of Hamilton asks Hardy to write to the *Daily Mail* in her anti-vivisection campaign.
4169. April 12: Maxwell thanks Hardy for his letter.
4170. April 14: R. D. Blumenfield wants something for publication.
4171. April 14: Sir Daniel Godfrey invites Hardy to be present at Bournemouth when *The Queen of Cornwall* is performed on April 22, 23, or 25.
4172. April (15): Hardy to Godfrey: rough draft; he hopes to be present.
4173. April 17: C. Bohn Childs again about Brennecke's *Life and Art*.
4174. April 18: Hardy to Albert A. Cock: rough draft of reply to Cock's request for permission to call and discuss the establishment of a Hardy Chair at University College, Southampton.
4175. April 18: S. D. Green to May O'Rourke, Hardy's secretary, soliciting assistance in getting Hardy to autograph two books sent to him from Trenton, New Jersey.
4176. April 20: C. Bohn Childs third time about Brennecke's *Life and Art*.
4177. April 20: Forrest again about Mrs. Procter. See Letter 4154.

CHRONOLOGICAL LIST

4178. April 20: Bertram Fryer about a performance of *The Queen of Cornwall* by the Glastonbury Players.
4179. April 20: Godfrey again about Hardy's attending the Bournemouth presentation of his play.
4180. April 22: Frederick S. Mate, Mayor of Bournemouth, is pleased Hardy intends to attend the Bournemouth presentation of *The Queen of Cornwall* on Saturday, 25 April.
4181. April 23: Robert Birkmyre solicits something for publication in *Pauper's Pie*.
4182. April 24: Margaret Cox invites Hardy to be one of the Vice-Presidents of the English Folk Dance Society.
4183. April 24: E. L. Keen solicits something for publication.
4184. April 25: H. R. Shepherd solicits something for publication.
4185. April 25: Thring asks about an American piracy.
4186. April 26: Hardy to Mira, Duchess of Hamilton: rough draft of reply to Letter 4168; he cannot promise to write to the *Daily Mail*.
4187. April 26: Hardy to Thring: rough draft; asks him to send a copy of the American piracy.
4188. April 26: Arthur J. G. Russell writes about a Paper (or lecture) he had read on Hardy.
4189. April 26: M. E. E. Warren about the poem "Beeny Cliff."
4190. April 28: The Duchess of Hamilton again solicits support of her anti-vivisection efforts.
4191. May 1: Robert Carlton Brown solicits a contribution to the *British American*.
4192. May 2: D. L. Thornton asks for an autograph.
4193. May 4: British Broadcasting Co. thanks Hardy for permission to broadcast.
4194. May 4: Russell sends the "Paper" about which he wrote on 26 April.
4195. May 8: Max Salomon sends a copy of a German dissertation on Hardy's treatment of nature.
4196. May 9: Charles F. C. Wood solicits support of the Crosbie Wood Testimonial Fund.
4197. May (10?): Hardy to Wood: rough draft; he can express no opinion.
4198. May (11?): Hardy to Russell: rough draft; about the "Paper" Russell had sent on the 4th.
4199. May 11: Sam J. Banks asks permission to call at Max Gate.
4200. May 13: Harper & Brothers about an error in the check recently sent.
4201. May 14: Russell thanks Hardy for the return of his "Paper."
4202. May 15: Cock about establishing a Hardy Chair at University College, Southampton.
4203. May 16: J. M. Hogge invites Hardy to a Ramsay Macdonald Dinner.
4204. May 17: Lady Agnes Grove sends her essay on *Tess*, written when competing for the prize offered for the best essay on one of twelve books.
4205. May 18: Hardy to Cock: rough draft; does not oppose his proposal.
4206. May 19: Hardy to Hogge: rough draft of reply to Letter 4203; asks that his best wishes be conveyed to Macdonald, whose book Hardy has been reading.

4207. May 19: Cock about plans for a University of Wessex.
4208. May 20: Lady Asquith sends proof of his poem.
4209. May 20: A. G. Symonds about the Dorchester Grammar School.
4210. May 22: Stanley Kershaw sends thanks.
4211. May 23: Thomas Loveday asks if Hardy would receive a deputation from the University of Bristol to confer the honorary degree of Litt.D. on him.
4212. May 27: Hardy to Loveday: rough draft of reply to Letter 4211; accepts Loveday's proposal.
4213. May 28: F. Chudoba sends a copy of a monthly from Czechoslovakia in which C.'s article on Hardy's work is printed.
4214. May 28: Loveday is pleased Hardy will receive the honorary degree from the University of Bristol.
4215. May 29: F. Reunert gratitude from Pretoria, South Africa.

On 2 June 1925 Hardy attained the age of 85. Forty men and women sent him birthday greetings:

4216. Alfred W. Anthony (7 June)
4217. Lady Cynthia Asquith
4218. Arthur Barber
4219. Howard Bliss
4220. R. R. Bowker
4221. Sydney Cockerell (31 May)
4222. Arthur Compton-Rickett
4223. Mrs. Ethel Cowley
4224. Sir George Douglas
4225. Mrs. Emma Dugdale
4226. Robert Edgcumbe
4227. S. M. Ellis (31 May)
4228. St. John Ervine
4229. A. Farmery
4230. Newman Flower
4231. Stanley I. Galpin
4232. Margaret F. Gifford
4233. Edmund Gosse (1 June)
4234. Harley Granville-Barker
4235. Octavia Gregory
4236. Lady Agnes Grove (31 May)
4237. Mrs. Imigen Holst
4238. Stanley Kershaw
4239. Paul Lemperly
4240. Ramsey Macdonald
4241. Gilbert S. Macquoid
4242. Dudley Field Malone
4243. T. P. O'Connor
4244. Maud Oldaker
4245. Eden Phillpotts
4246. J. W. Pickstone
4247. Leonard Rees
4248. Harold W. Rodgers
4249. E. N. Singleton (9 May)
4250. J. R. C. Stephens
4251. May Stracey
4252. Edith C. Taylor
4253. Llewelyn Watkins
4254. Clara Watts-Dunton
4255. Charles Whibley

4256. June 2: Leonard Woolf thanks Hardy for his poem, "Coming up Oxford Street: Evening," for publication in *The Nation* (13 June 1925).
4257. June 3: Mrs. Dorothy Allhusen about her sorrow in a death in the family.
4258. June 3: John S. Mayfield sends a pencil sketch he had made of Hardy.
4259. June 4: Philo Calhoun, of Connecticut, asks to call with his wife.
4260. June 5: Stanley C. Nott appreciation.
4261. June 6: Mrs. Marion Christie Murray asks help in obtaining financial aid from the Royal Literary Fund.
4262. June 7: Hardy to Max Salomon: rough draft of reply to Letter 4195; Salomon seems not to have read Hardy's mature writings, only has early works.
4263. June 7: G. Lowes Dickinson introduces a Chinese friend who has translated some of Hardy's poems into Chinese.

4264.	June 7:	Stella E. Tyler asks Hardy's help.
4265.	June 8:	Grace Paterson wants Hardy's autograph.
4266.	June 8:	Apollo Valakiss writes appreciatively.
4267.	June 12:	Hardy to R. Golding Bright (drama agent): rough draft; has decided to withdraw the play of *Tess* from offer to managers.
4268.	June 12:	Robert Donald about the British Film industry.
4269.	June 14:	F. B. Bradley-Birt asks permission to quote.
4270.	June 15:	Bright returns MS. of Hardy's *Tess* play.
4271.	June 20:	W. Jaggard asks permission for an American friend's son to call.
4272.	June 22:	Wilfrid H. Hardy asks Hardy's help.
4273.	June 23:	Arthur C. Kennedy about the death of A. C. Benson.
4274.	June 23:	Loveday asks if 15 July would be convenient for Hardy to receive the deputation from the University of Bristol.
4275.	June 23:	Alfred B. Lamplugh about *A Pair of Blue Eyes*.
4276.	June 24:	Hardy to Loveday: rough draft; 25 July will be convenient.
4277.	July 2:	C. W. Saleeby calls attention to Hardy's remarks on a sentence in *The Dynasts* in an article in the current issue of the *Spectator*.
4278.	July 6:	Loveday glad Hardy will receive some of his friends when the University of Bristol confers on Hardy the honorary Litt.D. degree.
4279.	July 8:	Arthur Hanson expresses surprise and shock on seeing the American film version of *Tess*.
4280.	July 14:	Evelyn Sharp about the Folk Dances and Songs collected by her brother Cecil Sharp.
4281.	July 14:	Sydney Smith, of Edinburgh, asks if Hardy has letters from Donald Macleod, one time editor of *Good Words*, and if Hardy was called upon to alter the text of *The Trumpet-Major* to suit Macleod's standards.
4282.	July 15:	Hermione Baddeley congratulations on the success of the *Tess* play.
4283.	(c. July 16):	Hardy to Smith: rough draft of reply to Letter 4281.
4284.	July 20:	W. D. Coltart asks permission for a private performance of *The Queen of Cornwall*.
4285.	July 21:	William Blatchford appreciation.
4286.	July 21:	Harold Child says *Two on a Tower* plays an important part in Pryce's new book, *Romance and Jane Watson*.
4287.	July 21:	Vincent Waite sends thanks.
4288.	July 24:	Harold Child about the prospective production of *Tess* at the Barnes Theatre in London.
4289.	July 24:	Henry J. Timbres about *Tess*.
4290.	July 25:	Helen M. Beatty, from Pittsburgh, Pennsylvania, is sending a book relating to the philosophy of art; she recalls meeting Hardy almost twenty years ago.
4291.	July 29:	J. C. Squire thanks for two poems: "Cynic's Epitaph" and "Epitaph on a Pessimist"; they will be published together in the *London Mercury* for September 1925.
4292.	August 4:	Betty Thomas solicits an interview, with a view to playing Tess in the theater.
4293.	August 6:	Rutland Boughton about Gwen Ffrangcon-Davies as Tess.

4294. August 7: Cyril Hartmann asks permission to call at Max Gate.
4295. August 7: Shorter has sold Hardy's Christmas poem ["No Bell-Ringing: A Ballad of Durnover"] in America to the *Ladies Home Journal*.
4296. (c. August 10): Lucy (Mrs. W. K.) Clifford about Gwen Ffrangcon-Davies, the actress chosen to enact Tess.
4297. August 11: The Countess of Lauderdale apologizes for having confused his *Tess* with another book; has now read his novel and thinks highly of it.
4298. August 11: Alfred Zeitlin asks permission to arrange for an American production of *Tess*.
4299. August 12: E. H. Dring sends a reprint of a 1723 treatise on the Roman Amphitheatre at Dorchester.
4300. August 12: C. Burgas-Fernandez asks permission to put the *Tess* play onto the Spanish stage.
4301. August 12: Gwen Ffrangcon-Davies about her lines in *Tess*.
4302. (August 13): Hardy to Ffrangcon-Davies: rough draft; approves adding the few words she suggested.
4303. August 14: Hardy to Granville-Barker: typed transcript; about arrangements for producing the *Tess* play abroad.
4304. August 14: Ffrangcon-Davies thanks Hardy for his note and the script.
4305. August 15: Barrie advice about reserving American and Colonial rights in the *Tess* play.
4306. August 15: Henry Goddard Leach hopes to meet Hardy in October.
4307. August 16: Granville-Barker warns about parting with American rights in the *Tess* play.
4308. August 17: Thring warns about the need for a formal agreement for the production of a play.
4309. August 18: Robert Graves wants a poem for a new magazine coming out at Christmas.
4310. August 18: J. A. Hammerton asks permission to print outline studies of *Far from the Madding Crowd* and *Tess*.
4311. August 18: E. V. Lucas asks for permission for Reginald H. Roe (who knew Swinburne) to call at Max Gate.
4312. August 19: Hardy to Lucas: rough draft; gives Roe permission to call.
4313. August 19: Maria S. Gramazo appreciation.
4314. August 21: L. Edgar Young sends thanks.
4315. August 22: Hardy to Dring: rough draft; acknowledges Dring's letter, 4299 in this listing.
4316. August 22: Hardy to Granville-Barker: typed transcript; thanks for information about producing *Tess* abroad.
4317. August 24: Boughton about the production of *The Queen of Cornwall* at Glastonbury this year.
4318. August 25: Cockerell about corrections in the proofs of *Human Shows*.
4319. August 26: Roe sends thanks.
4320. August 26: Sheppard solicits a contribution for publication at Armistice time.
4321. August 29: Siegfried Sassoon about going to St. David's recently.
4322. (c. August 30): Hardy to Sheppard: rough draft of reply to Letter 4320.

4323. September 7: Harold Begbie asks for an interview.
4324. Sephember 8: Henry Arthur Jones tells what he felt and thought of the first performance of *Tess*.
4325. September 9: Hardy to Begbie: rough draft of letter declining to grant an interview.
4326. September 9: Mrs. Allhusen about *Tess* at the Barnes Theatre.
4327. September 9: Frederic d'Erlanger congratulations on the tokens of esteem and admiration Hardy is receiving.
4328. September 10: Burgas-Fernandez repeats his request for permission to present *Tess* on the Spanish stage.
4329. September 11: Cockerell returns some proofs of *Human Shows*.
4330. September 11: George McLean Harper sends a copy of the August 1925 *Scribner's Magazine* containing Harper's article on Hardy's poems.
4331. September 12: J. W. Kirby solicits an autographed letter to wish success to the vessel *Thomas Hardy*, a large steam-trawler built for deep-sea fishing off the coast of Iceland.
4332. September 13: Hardy to Jones: typed transcript; (supplied by Howard Bliss?) thanks for Jones's letter about *Tess* at the Barnes Theatre.
4333. September 14: Hardy to Kirby: rough draft; wishes the steam-trawler *Thomas Hardy* success.
4334. September 14: Cockerell about the proofs of *Human Shows*.
4335. September 14: A. H. Vincent inquires about film rights in the story Hardy has written for Messrs Cassell & Co.
4336. September 15: Ervine reports *Tess* is doing well at the Barnes Theatre.
4337. September 15: William K. Hill asks if *Far from the Madding Crowd* has ever been dramatized. If not, he would like to be allowed to submit a scenario.
4338. September 16: Samuel C. Chew, from Bryn Mawr, Pennsylvania, to Mrs. Hardy; refers to Brennecke's biography of Hardy and to Chew's criticism of it in a review.
4339. September 16: Jones consoles Hardy about the adverse remarks made by drama critics on the *Tess* play.
4340. September 17: Gordon Gifford to his "Dear Uncle" about *Tess* at the Barnes Theatre.
4341. September 20: Cockerell returns proofs of *Human Shows* with corrections.
4342. September 21: Richard D. Ware sends a poem from New Hampshire.
4343. September 23: James Smellie solicits help in phrasing a War Memorial.
4344. September 25: Hardy to Smellie: rough draft of reply to Letter 4343, enclosing four lines.
4345. September 26: G. W. Hinton offers an honorary membership in the Association of Alumni of the University of Bristol.
4346. September 26: H. Ketteringham about *The Mayor of Casterbridge*.
4347. September 27: Squire has seen *Tess* at the Barnes Theatre.
4348. September 28: Hardy to Hinton; rough draft; accepts honorary membership in the Association of Alumni of the University of Bristol.

4349. September 30: Boughton sends a subscription check for *The Queen of Cornwall* at the Glastonbury Music Festival.
4350. September 30: R. W. Gibbon asks about churning milk in *Tess*.
4351. September 30: Wilfred Grundy praises *The Dynasts* and says there are only three perfect writers in the handling of words: Horace, Kipling and Hardy.
4352. September 30: Murry returns proofs of *Human Shows*.
4353. October 1: Henry Broadbent about Hardy's epigram in the *London Mercury*.
4354. October 3: Broadbent anecdote about Robert Browning.
4355. October 4: Cockerell on the poems that are to appear in *Human Shows*.
4356. October 5: Stanley Lathbury sends photographs of the various members of the *Tess* company.
4357. October 5: Thring about Nathalia Crane and unauthorized publication in America.
4358. October 7: Serge Yourievitch says the bust for which Hardy sat in August 1924 was exhibited in the 1925 Royal Academy of Art exhibition in London.
4359. October 9: Barker Fairley sends some "lines" which had appeared about Hardy in the September *Canadian Forum*.
4360. October 14: Ffrangcon-Davies sends her photograph as Tess.
4361. October 15: D. Kennedy asks if Hardy would permit his name to be put forward for the Rectorship of St. Andrew's University.
4362. October 17: Hardy to Ffrangcon-Davies: rough draft; thanks the actress for her photograph.
4363. October 17: Hardy to Kennedy: rough draft of reply to Letter 4361; regrets he must decline.
4364. October 19: Gerald Barry solicits a contribution to the *Saturday Review*.
4365. October 19: Douglas Macmillan about the Folk Press.
4366. October (20): Hardy to Barry: rough draft of reply to Letter 4364; is not able to contribute.
4367. October 20: Hardy to Granville-Barker: typed transcript; about *Tess* at the Barnes Theatre.
4368. October 20: Moult asks permission to quote.
4369. October 20: Emil Roniger invites Hardy to join in acclaiming Romain Rolland on his 60th birthday.
4370. October 21: C. N. Heinchef sends proofs of "The Harvest Supper," to be published shortly by Cassell & Co.
4371. October 21: John T. Fripp about reading *Tess* at eighty.
4372. October 21: William K. Hill sends to Mrs. Hardy the scenario of *Far from the Madding Crowd*.
4373. October 22: Hardy to Roniger: rough draft of reply to Letter 4369; joins in homage to Romain Rolland.
4374. October 25: Bartos Zoltan asks permission to publish a Hungarian translation of *Tess*.
4375. October 27: Herbert Grimsditch sends a book he has just published about Hardy.
4376. October 27: A. S. Owen to W. Lock, Warden of Christ Church, Oxford, soliciting Lock's help in obtaining Hardy's permission to enact *The Three Strangers* at Keble College, Oxford.
4377. October 27: Lock about a dramatized form of *The Three Strangers*.

CHRONOLOGICAL LIST

4378. October 29: Douglas Macmillan asks support of the Folk Press.
4379. October 30: Hardy to Grimsditch: rough draft; thanks for the book sent with Letter 4375.
4380. October 30: Lock thanks Hardy for his reply and for the loan of his copy of *The Three Wayfarers*.
4381. October 30: Owen thanks Hardy for the loan of *The Three Wayfarers* and for permission to enact it at Keble College, Oxford.
4382. November 1: Mrs. M. Vaughan Clark sends thanks.
4383. November 1: Roger Ferdinand asks to adapt *Tess* for the stage in Paris.
4384. November 1: E. Graham sends a copy of a lecture given in Dorchester.
4385. November 2: Grimsditch thanks Hardy for his letter of 30 October 1925.
4386. November 2: Josiah C. Wedgwood asks Hardy to sign a protest.
4387. November 3: Hardy to Wedgwood: rough draft; he cannot comply.
4388. November 3: G. B. Besant asks permission to include one of Hardy's stories in *Standard Stories*.
4389. November 4: Douglas Macmillan thanks Hardy for suggestion about the Folk Press.
4390. November 9: Arthur David invites support of a plan to build a sanctuary for birds in Hyde Park to the memory of W. H. Hudson.
4391. November 10: Lady Alice Stuart of Wortley about *Tess* at the Barnes Theatre.
4392. November 10: Joan Young sends a book of hers and calls attention to a sonnet of hers printed in the *London Mercury*.
4393. November 11: Granville-Barker about a Spaniard who wishes to translate Hardy's plays.
4394. November 12: Hardy to Granville-Barker: typed transcript; about Hardy's and Granville-Barker's hopes for *The Madras House*.
4395. November 13: N. Dully is ready to produce a French dramatization of *Tess* at the Atelie Theatre in Paris if Hardy will permit Roger Ferdinand to dramatize the novel.
4396. November 14: Christine Beck about musical settings for Hardy's poems.
4397. November 16: Henry B. Amos solicits a message for use at a meeting of the League for the Prohibition of Cruel Sports.
4398. November 18: Stair A. Gillon sends a book.
4399. November 19: Hardy to Amos: rough draft of reply to Letter 4397; does not think much can be done.
4400. November 19: Thring asks about film rights in *The Mayor of Casterbridge*.
4401. November 23: Howard Bliss to Mrs. Hardy about *Human Shows*.
4402. November 24: John Lane solicits a poem for Queen Alexandra.
4403. November 24: Cockerell about *Human Shows*.
4404. November 24: Vere Collins asks permission to quote "The Going of the Battery."
4405. November 24: Mrs. Granville-Barker thanks Hardy for *Human Shows*.
4406. November 24: Hardy to Lane: rough draft of reply to Letter 4402; he is unable to comply.
4407. November 24: Barrie congratulations on the 100th performance of *Tess* in London.

4408. November 25: Granville-Barker congratulations on the 100th performance of *Tess*.
4409. November 26: Robert Bridges about *Human Shows*.
4410. November 27: Hardy to Thring: rough draft of reply to Letter 4400; film rights in *The Mayor* were purchased by a company some years ago.
4411. November 27: Lady Asquith wants another poem for publication.
4412. November 27: Collins praises *Human Shows*.
4413. December 1: James Bernard about broadcasts of the Trafalgar Scenes from *The Dynasts* which Hardy allowed Bernard to give last year.
4414. December 1: Frederick W. Heath offers ten guineas for the poem, "The Weary Walker," which appears in *The Bermondsey Book*.
4415. December 1: Eleanor Frances Young asks Hardy's permission for a Dramatics Class at Columbia University to present *The Three Strangers*, not Hardy's dramatization but one by Miss Young.
4416. December 2: A. R. Coster asks permission to take a photograph of the performance of *Tess* in the Max Gate drawing room when the cast from the Barnes Theatre comes to Dorchester.
4417. December 2: Mildred Gaskill asks for an autograph.
4418. December 2: Beryl Lewis sends a copy of an essay written by her son when he was at Marlborough College.
4419. December 2: Longman, Green & Co. asks permission to publish a passage in Rider Haggard's autobiography which refers to Hardy. (Hardy endorsed this letter: "No objection.")
4420. December 3: Hardy to Coster: rough draft of reply to Letter 4416; unable to let a photograph be taken of any performance.
4421. December 3: Owen returns Hardy's copy of *The Three Wayfarers*; says it will be given at Keble College next June.
4422. December 4: Hardy to Heath: rough draft; accepts offer made in Letter 4414.
4423. December 5: Henry A. Phillips asks permission to call.
4424. December 5: Rose L. Shefska solicits a manuscript.
4425. December 7: The Duchess of Hamilton invites Hardy to a meeting on anti-vivisection.
4426. December 7: J. A. Hammerton thanks Hardy for permission to print his "outline study" of *Tess*.
4427. December 7: Mrs. Thérèse Rich about *Tess*.
4428. December 8: Arthur J. Mayne thanks Hardy for the fine reception given the *Tess* cast from the Barnes Theatre when they came to enact the play at Max Gate.
4429. ("Wednesday"): Ffrangcon-Davies thanks Hardy for his kindness to the theater group.
4430. December 9: W. B. Beer sends thanks also.
4431. December 10: L. M. Lucas sends an etching of Tess's "old Manor House."
4432. December 10: Hardy to Lucas: rough draft; acknowledges gift of the etching.
4433. December 11: John Bargreen adds his thanks to the others'.
4434. December 11: Lucas glad Hardy likes the etching.
4435. December 14: St. John Adcock sends payment for permission to include some of Hardy's poems in an anthology.
4436. December 15: Daniel Critchley asks Hardy's help.

4437. December 15: Lady Millicent Hawes (formerly the Duchess of Sutherland) sends Christmas greetings.
4438. December 16: H. E. Piggott asks permission to quote "The Oxen."
4439. December 18: S. M. Ellis asks Hardy to write a foreword for his *Life* of G. P. R. James.
4440. December 19: Hardy to Granville-Barker: typed transcript; about G-B's play *The Madras House*.
4441. December 19: Henry Head thanks Hardy for a copy of *Human Shows*.
4442. December 19: John H. Morgan about the Treaty of Locarno.
4443. December 20: Cockerell about Blakiston's rudeness to Hardy.
4444. December 22: Mrs. Hanbury Christmas greetings; thanks Hardy for the book of poems he sent to her daughter Caroline.
4445. December 23: Hardy to H. F. C. Marshall: rough draft; about obtaining financial aid from the Royal Literary Fund for Miss Rosetta Spearing.
4446. December 23: Valentina Capocci, from Naples, Italy, asks permission to translate the *Tess* play into Italian.
4447. December 23: Granville-Barker thanks for Hardy's praise of *The Madras House*.
4448. December 23: Siegfried Sassoon about a journey to Salisbury, and sad thoughts of his uncle, Hamo Thornycroft, who had died.
4449. December 25: A. J. Armstrong, from Waco, Texas, solicits an autograph.
4450. December 25: John Birkley asks for the names of photographers from whom a good picture of Hardy can be obtained.
4451. December 25: Clemence Dane Christmas greetings; he has been reading *Human Shows* and sends thanks for it.
4452. (c. December 26): Hardy to Birkley: rough draft of reply to Letter 4450; names several photographers.
4453. December 26: E. Inglis-Arkell on a case of wife-selling like that in *The Mayor of Casterbridge*.
4454. December 27: Margaret F. Gifford thanks for a letter.
4455. December 27: Cecil Hanbury thanks for Hardy's concern about Mrs. Hanbury's operation.
4456. December 31: Hardy to A. G. Symonds: rough draft; about the Dorchester Grammar School.
4457. (n. d.): G. W. L. Day asks Hardy's help.
4458. (n. d.): G. D. Eliopoulo solicits an autograph.
4459. (n. d.): Gillon comments on Hardy's insight.
4460. (n. d.): George H. Leonard Christmas greetings from the University of Bristol.
4461. (n. d.): David C. Wilson asks for an autograph.

1926

4462. January 1: Everard G. Gilbert-Cooper letter of thanks.
4463. January 1: H. W. Lee invites Hardy to join the Hyndman Club.
4464. January 2: Hardy to Lee: rough draft; he cannot join a club of a political nature.

4465. January 6: Alfred Pope about the Dorchester Grammar School.
4466. January 12: Hardy to Morgan: typed transcript; comments on Morgan's article in the *English Review*.
4467. January 16: Y. Manuel-Lelis about publishing Hardy's poems in *La Revue Nouvelle*.
4468. January 16: Hester, Lady Pinney about Martha Brown, whose public execution for the murder of her husband Hardy had witnessed as a boy. See *Later Years*, p. 144.
4469. January 17: Ralph Chubb sends thanks.
4470. January 18: John H. Hutchinson about Hardy's "Epitaph on a Pessimist."
4471. January 18: The Duke of Portland asks advice about a Memorial to Queen Alexandra.
4472. (c. January 19): Hardy to Hutchinson: rough draft of reply to Letter 4470; refers Hutchinson to Mackail's *Select Epigrams*.
4473. January 19: Lina Baumann sends two essays which were given as a lecture to an English-speaking club at Zurich, Switzerland.
4474. January 19: Will Macmillan about English folk dances.
4475. January 22: Hardy to the Duke of Portland: rough draft of response to Letter 4471.
4476. January 22: Hardy to G. H. Thring: rough draft of letter forwarding an inquiry to the Council of The Society of Authors.
4477. January 23: Thring thanks Hardy for his letter.
4478. January 27: Macmillan again about English folk dances.
4479. January 29: Thring about the Czech translation of *The Return of the Native*.
4480. February 1: A. N. Richell solicits an autograph.
4481. February 2: Thring about a National Memorial to Queen Alexandra.
4482. February 3: J. Pomerantz asks permission to translate *Tess* into Yiddish.
4483. February 6: W. B. Maxwell asks Hardy's opinion of a proposal to send a delegation to France to represent the Society of Authors. (Hardy endorsed this letter: "approve sending.")
4484. February 10: Maxwell thanks Hardy for his letter.
4485. February 15: Alan W. Hazelton asks Hardy's help.
4486. February 17: John Kingsgate offers to sell a picture of the house at 16 Westbourne Park Villas where Hardy lived in the 1860s.
4487. February 22: Hardy to Kingsgate: rough draft; declines his offer.
4488. February 23: Hardy to the Rev. H. G. B Cowley: rough draft; about the bells at Stinsford Church.
4489. February 24: Rev. Cowley asks assistance for Stinsford Church.
4490. February 25: Rutland Boughton about an orchestral overture to *The Queen of Cornwall*.
4491. February 26: Charles H. Bates asks for support of a plan to memorialize William Blake.
4492. February 27: Hardy to the Rev. Cowley: rough draft; about Stinsford Church.
4493. February 28: Lotte Sternbach-Gärtner about translating Hardy's *Tess* play into German.
4494. February (?): Margaret Bradish solicits a message on "Animals in Captivity."

4495. February (?): Hardy to Margaret Bradish: rough draft; he has already taken a position on this matter.
4496. March 1: Hardy to Bates: rough draft of reply to Letter 4491; Bates's proposal has Hardy's approval.
4497. March 1: Eric Partridge asks permission to quote from *Under the Greenwood Tree.*
4498. March 2: J. L. Garvin wants a poem for publication in the *Observer* when that paper will be 135 years old; he would put it on the first page. (Hardy sent "The Aged Newspaper Soliloquizes.")
4499. March 3: Aylmer Maude proposes the formation of a Tolstoy Society.
4500. March 5: Ian MacAlister invites Hardy to serve on a committee for the British Architects' Conference.
4501. March 5: Hardy to MacAlister: rough draft; regrets he is unable to serve.
4502. March 5: Will Macmillan again about English folk dances.
4503. March 6: Garvin thanks Hardy for his poem "The Aged Newspaper Soliloquizes."
4504. March 17: Arnold Muntz about the Bergomask Players.
4505. March 18: Major O. W. White solicits a few lines for publication in the *Journal* of the Dorsetshire Regiment.
4506. March 18: T. R. Ybarra about Hardy's poem "The Aged Newspaper Soliloquizes."
4507. March 19: Hardy to Muntz: rough draft of reply to Letter 4504; is not able to accept Muntz's suggestion.
4508. March 20: White thanks Hardy for the few lines from *The Dynasts* enclosed in his letter.
4509. March 22: Thomas J. Wise about his *Catalogues* and comments on Wordsworth.
4510. March 23: A. E. Ovey wants something for publication.
4511. March 24: Wise, caught by Hardy in an error about Swinburne (eight years before the disclosures of Carter & Pollard), says Hardy's letter corrects an error he did not know to be an error; he enclosed a copy of the pamphlet preserving Swinburne's verses.
4512. March 24: Ybarra thanks Hardy for the loan of the MS. of "The Aged Newspaper Soliloquizes."
4513. March 25: Henry Arthur Jones about a National Theatre.
4514. March 31. J. S. Armour, from Patna, India, asks permission to quote "The Darkling Thrush."
4515. March 31: A. R. Powys to Oliver Dunn about the lodgings of Judge Jeffry at Dorchester. (Dunn forwarded this letter to Hardy on 17 April 1926.)
4516. April 3: Theodore Maynard sends a copy of the *Catholic World* for April 1926 containing an article he has written on Hardy's poetry.
4517. April 8: R. S. Malmud asks Hardy's help.
4518. April 9: Rev. Cowley again solicits help for Stinsford Church.
4519. April 10: F. W. Slater, of Harper & Brothers, asks if Hardy would permit his friend R. R. Bowker of New York to call.
4520. April 12: James F. Muirhead about a Swiss poet named Carl Spitteler.
4521. April 13: Hardy to Slater: rough draft; R. R. Bowker of New York may call.

4522. April 14: Marie C. Stopes solicits a letter from Hardy saying he thinks a play of hers, denied a license by the Government censor, should be licensed.
4523. April 14: Charles Wilson sends thanks.
4524. April 15: Thornton Butterworth asks if Hardy would waive a fee for permission to reprint.
4525. April 16: A. R. Powys asks Hardy to write about Judge Jeffry's lodgings in Dorchester.
4526. April (17?): Hardy to Maynard: rough draft of acknowledgment of Letter 4516; refers to Maynard's comments on harshness in Hardy's poetry. Hardy says this is deliberate, as a reaction from the Victorian poets.
4527. April 17: Oliver Dunn sends Hardy Letter 4515.
4528. April 18: Hardy to Powys: rough draft of reply to Letter 4525.
4529. April 18: E. Graham about literary prizes at the Dorchester Grammar School.
4530. April 19: Archibald Flower solicits help in raising funds for building a new Shakespeare Memorial Theatre at Stratford-on-Avon.
4531. April 19: James G. Leippert, from Kingston, New York, says he wishes to write a biography of Hardy, and requests answers to a group of questions.
4532. April 20: Mabel E. Mayo about a cat story.
4533. April 20: General Morgan about *The Dynasts*.
4534. April 22: George DuMaurier solicits an autograph to be sold for the benefit of The Actors' Orphanage.
4535. April 22: Philip Ridgeway asks Mrs. Hardy to send all the scripts she has of Hardy's plays, dramatized by himself or others. (A day later this request was repeated by telegram.)
4536. April 22: E. M. Walker sends personal thanks for the portrait sent by Hardy to Queen's College, Oxford.
4537. April 23: Hardy to Ridgeway: rough draft of reply to Letter 4535; Ridgeway might produce *The Queen of Cornwall* or *The Three Wayfarers*, but any novels dramatized by amateurs Hardy would not consent to have put on the regular stage.
4538. April 23: Benjamin DeCasseres sends a copy of his book, *Forty Immortals*, of which he considers Hardy to be one.
4539. (c. April 23): Madeline Mason-Manheim sends some of her writings; Arthur Symons told her she may write to Hardy.
4540. April 23: Arthur Symons asks if he can bring Madeline and her mother to call.
4541. April 24: Hardy to General Morgan: rough draft; acknowledges Morgan's letter about Napoleon and Waterloo.
4542. April 25: J. H. Edge asks Hardy's help.
4543. April 26: Hardy to Symons: rough draft of reply to Letter 4540; finds it difficult to see anybody at present.
4544. April 26: Roy McKay about the abridgment or simplification of Church creeds..
4545. April 27: Hardy to McKay: rough draft of reply to Letter 4544; is now too old to take up the questions McKay suggests.
4546. April 28: R. Williams thinks he has identified the work Hardy did in connection with the East Window of Littlebredy Church in about 1860.

4547. April 29: Eugene Field II, from Chicago, asks if any MS. of his father would be welcome by Hardy as a gift from Mrs. Field (his mother), and if Hardy would supply a MS. copy of "Men Who March Away" for the Field collection of MSS. (Hardy refused.)
4548. May 1: Walker sends official thanks of Queen's College, Oxford, for the portrait Hardy had sent.
4549. (c. May 3): Hardy to Leippert: rough draft of reply to Letter 4531; declines to answer the question put by Leippert.
4550. May 7: Dorothy H. Litchfield asks for Hardy's autograph.
4551. May 7: James Milne about the possibility of a film of something by Hardy.
4552. May (?): Squire explored the possibility of a Birthday Service as proposed by the B.B.C. for Hardy's 86th birthday.
4553. May (8?): Hardy to Milne: rough draft of reply to Letter 4551; it is too late for him to take up film-work.
4554. May 18: John Purves asks permission to reprint a poem.
4555. (c. May 19): Hardy to Purves: rough draft; denies the request made in Letter 4554.
4556. May 22: Martin Kennedy about *The Return of the Native*.
4557. (c. May 25): Harold J. Laski solicits a few words about H. M. Tomlinson, to assist him in getting some recognition and a little money.
4558. May 26: Hardy to Laski: rough draft of reply to Letter 4557; he has a high opinion of Tomlinson.
4559. May 27: Laski says it was most kind of him to send the note about Tomlinson.
4560. May 28: George S. Viereck would like to pay Hardy a brief visit in order to obtain information on his life, etc.
4566. May 30: D. S. Maccoll solicits support in opposing the proposal to erect a new bridge over the Thames near St. Paul's Cathedral.
4562. May 31: Hardy to Viereck: rough draft of reply to Letter 4560; regrets his inability to receive visitors.

On 2 June 1926 Hardy attains the age of 86. Nineteen men and women sent him Birthday Greetings and best wishes:

4563. Dorothy Allhusen (3 June)
4564. Anna J. P. Baxter
4565. Sydney Cockerell (1 June)
4566. Arthur Compton-Rickett
4567. Edward and Emma Dugdale
4568. St. John Ervine
4569. Annie Gifford
4570. Margaret Gifford
4571. Harley Granville-Barker (1 June)
4572. Annie Hardy
4573. Clive Holland
4574. Henry Leffert
4575. Paul Lemperly
4576. May O'Rourke
4577. Philip Ridgeway
4578. Algernon Rose
4579. Charles Whibley
4580. Sydney J. White
4581. Elizabeth Wigglesworth

4582. June 3: Hardy to Captain J. E. Acland, Curator of Dorset County Museum: rough draft; requests him to caution the museum porter against letting strangers draw from him any personal particulars about Hardy.
4583. June 3: J. B. Hobman apologizes for the inaccuracies in an article published by the *Westminster Gazette*.
4584. June 4: Hardy to Granville-Barker: typed transcript; thanks for his birthday greetings, and comments again on *The Madras House*.

4585. June 4: Acland replies to letter 4582.
4586. June 4: DuMaurier thanks Hardy for the autograph.
4587. June 4: Percy Smallman asks help in drafting a message from citizens of Weymouth to be sent to citizens of Weymouth, Massachusetts, U.S.A.
4588. June 5: W. G. Allen asks support of a protest against the proposed erection of a bridge across the Thames near St. Paul's Cathedral. See Letter 4561.
4589. June 7: Henry O. Lock, Dorchester solicitor, about the inaccuracies in an article about Hardy written by Thurston Hopkins.
4590. June 7: Hopkins apologizes for the inaccuracies in his article.
4591. June 7: C. H. Wolff thanks Hardy for his help in preparing a message to be sent to Weymouth, Mass.
4592. June 8: Donald Freeman, from New York, introduces Nickolas Muray, a celebrated New York photographer.
4593. June 8: Lock forwards a letter received from Thurston Hopkins; Lock says he is writing Hopkins as to the conditions on which Hardy will accept his apology.
4594. June 8: Lock to Hopkins, stating Hardy's terms as given in Letter 4595.
4595. June 8: Hardy to Lock: rough draft; states Hardy's conditions: 1. absolute withdrawal of his statements; 2. pays the legal expenses; 3. ceases to annoy in the future.
4596. June 8: Hardy to the editor of the *Dorset Echo*: rough draft of objections to the *Echo's* quoting the article in the *Westminster Gazette*, and pointing out the need to contradict the false charges in all issues of the *Echo*.
4597. June 9: Lock to Mrs. Hardy about Hopkins's offensive article on Hardy.
4598. June 9: Hopkins sends regrets and says he has written a public disavowal to the London *Evening News* and to the *Westminster Gazette*.
4599. June 9: Hopkins to Lock, a copy of his typed letter with his disavowal of the false statements published in the *Westminster Gazette*.
4600. June 9: Percy Smallman thanks Hardy for his message for the citizens of Weymouth, U.S.A.
4601. June 10: Lock forwards Hopkins's Letter 4599.
4602. June 11: Field is sending a book of Hardy's to be autographed.
4603. June 15: Alfred A. Wolmark reminds Hardy he had promised to sit for a pen-and-ink portrait.
4604. (c. June 16): Hardy to Wolmark: rough draft of reply to Letter 4603; will sit for the portrait any day after 4 July.
4605. June 18: Ernest Barker asks about Hardy's attendance at evening classes at King's College, London.
4606. June 18: James F. Muirhead about "the dram of eale" in *Hamlet* and the emendation proposed by Hardy in his letter to *The Times* (17 June 1926).
4607. June 19. Hardy to Barker: rough draft of reply to Letter 4605; Hardy attended the evening class in French in 1865-66.
4608. June 21: Nickolas Murray, a New York photographer, solicits a sitting.

4609.	June 21:	S. F. Peter about "the dram of eale" and the emendation proposed by Hardy in *The Times* (17 June 1926).
4610.	June 22:	W. Lock on the successful performance of *The Three Wayfarers* at Keble College, Oxford.
4611.	June (?):	John Masefield thanks Hardy for permission to call.
4612.	June 25:	Victor A. Gwatkin solicits a subscription for a memorial to Joseph Conrad to be erected in Canterbury.
4613.	June 25:	Masefield thanks Hardy for his welcome to Max Gate.
4614.	June 29:	Wolmark will come on 5 July to make the pen-and-ink portrait.
4615.	July 2:	S. D. Green again asks for Hardy's autograph in the two books sent from Trenton, New Jersey.
4616.	July 5:	Norman Bennet about birds in *Tess*.
4617.	July 6:	Edward Clodd about C. K. Shorter and his illness.
4618.	July 6:	A. R. Powys about the preservation of old cottages.
4619.	July 6:	Conrad Seiler asks permission to reprint *The Three Strangers*.
4620.	July 7:	F. Adams about Romany funeral customs.
4621.	July 7:	Edward Loud thanks Hardy for his gift to the Rotary Club of Weymouth, Massachusetts.
4622.	July 8.	Vere Collins asks help in answering questions put to him by a Vienna professor who is writing a book on English poetic meters.
4623.	July 8:	H. Dudley Swain asks about illustrated quarterlies.
4624.	July 9:	Hardy to Collins: rough draft of reply to Letter 4622; declines to answer the questions.
4625.	July 9:	Hardy to Swain: rough draft of reply to Letter 4623; does not know the answers.
4626.	July 10:	Swain again about illustrated quarterlies.
4627.	July 11:	Will Macmillan about folk dances and related matters.
4628.	July 12.	Hardy to Bennet: rough draft of reply to Letter 4616; he cannot remember.
4629.	July 12:	H. G. Harrison asks about matters in *The Dynasts*.
4630.	(c. July 13):	Hardy to Harrison: rough draft of reply to Letter 4629; refers Harrison to *Philippians* II, 2: "Fulfill ye my joy."
4631.	July 15:	Alyce L. Hoogs sends thanks.
4632.	July 15:	Boyle Lawrence solicits a comment, for publication in the *Morning Post*, on Rudyard Kipling's imperialistic tendencies.
4633.	July 16:	Louise Houde asks permission to quote.
4634.	July 17:	C. J. Arnell about a contest for producing the best epitaph to the memory of Tess of the D'Urbervilles.
4635.	July 20:	Marie C. Stopes about preserving the old cottage made famous as "Avice's Cottage" by Hardy's *The Well Beloved*.
4636.	July 25:	George Rylands asks permission to call.
4637.	August 7:	Harry K. Weymer asks permission to name a yacht *Thomas Hardy*.
4638.	August 9:	Philip Guedalla asks permission to call with his wife; says *The Dynasts* inspired him to write history.
4639.	August 11:	Dewitt MacKenzie asks permission to call.
4640.	August 13:	Rose Anne Goodman about King George the Third's "bathing van" at Weymouth.
4641.	August 18:	Charles W. Heathcote asks for Hardy's autograph.
4642.	August 20:	Charles Wilson solicits Hardy's help.

4643. August 24: Henry B. Amos solicits a message for the League for the Prohibition of Cruel Sports.
4644. August 25: E. H. Moule about "the many in Japan" who read and love Hardy's writings.
4645. August 26: Edward A. Cobby sends thanks.
4646. August 27: Macmillan again about English folk dances.
4647. August 28: Marie C. Stopes invites Hardy to attend a meeting of a committee in Portland, called by her to consider how best to preserve "Avice's Cottage" and other old cottages.
4648. August 28: Richard S. West about the Choruses in *The Dynasts*.
4649. August 29: Dorothy Allhusen about a call at Max Gate.
4650. August 29: T. E. Casson sends a poetic tribute.
4651. August 30: Ada Foster Alden thanks Hardy for a copy of his poems.
4652. September 1: Squire solicits "a few lines of commendation" of the *London Mercury*.
4653. September 2: Moule thanks Hardy for his letter.
4654. September 2: Charles E. Woods about "Unity" in *A Pair of Blue Eyes*.
4655. September 4: J. Marley asks for an autograph.
4656. September 5: William W. Wilson sends thanks.
4657. September 6: Hardy to Weymer: rough draft of reply to Letter 4637, granting permission.
4658. September 6: N. M. Cameron thanks Hardy for his recollections of Country Dances and for permission to print them in the English Folk Dance Society *News*.
4659. September 8: Augusta (Mrs. Henry) Everett solicits Hardy's autograph on a print from *Vanity Fair*.
4660. September 9: Hardy to Mrs. Everett: rough draft; declines to autograph the print from *Vanity Fair*.
4661. September 9: S. Miyashima thanks Hardy for permitting a young Japanese admirer to call.
4662. September 10: John Drinkwater to Mrs. Hardy about the matinee of his dramatization of *The Mayor of Casterbridge* to be given at Weymouth on 20 September.
4663. September 10: Ervine about dramatizing *Jude*.
4664. September 10: Edward Warren on reading *The Mayor of Casterbridge* for the third or fourth time.
4665. September 12: Robert Pearsall asks about the pupils of Sir Arthur Blomfield in the early 1860s.
4666. September 13: E. Haigh Thoxoe solicits Hardy's signature on a portrait.
4667. September 14: Ervine about Maumbury Ring, Maiden Castle, and other landmarks near Dorchester.
4668. September 15: Francis Claymore asks Hardy's help.
4669. September 15: Edward Warren thanks Hardy for a reply.
4670. September 16: Mrs. Hanbury note to accompany a box of grapes sent to Max Gate.
4671. September 17: Hardy to Pearsall: rough draft of reply to Letter 4665.
4672. September 18: Archibald Flower solicits support in efforts to raise money for building a new Shakespeare Memorial Theatre at Stratford-on-Avon.

4673. September 21: Lord Coleridge asks support of a movement to mitigate cruelty to animals.
4674. September 21: Thomas A. Pearcy congratulations on Drinkwater's dramatization of *The Mayor of Casterbridge*.
4675. September 21: Louise Prussing asks for autograph in a copy of *The Mayor of Casterbridge*.
4676. September 23: Dame Georgiana Bullen solicits support of a drive for the benefit of crippled children.
4677. September 23: Mabel (Mrs. Cook) Collins solicits a contribution in support of a movement for setting up a model abattoir where humanely slaughtered meat will be offered to the public.
4678. September 24: Florian Williams about the proofs of the letterpress attached to the music of *The Queen of Cornwall*.
4679. September 25: Alfred Hale sends a copy of his musical setting for Hardy's poem "Rose-Ann."
4680. September 28: Hardy to Hale: rough draft; acknowledges receipt of Hale's music and says it has the proper lilt.
4681. September 28: Acland thanks Hardy for the gift of a *New Testament* in shorthand for the Dorset County Museum.
4682. September 28: Rose I. M. Lucas offers to sell Hardy the plot for a story.
4683. (c. September 29): Hardy to Lucas: rough draft of reply to Letter 4682; he would never use any story but his own.
4684. September 29: Betty Ross solicits an interview.
4685. September 30: Hardy to Ross: rough draft of reply to Letter 4684; must refuse to meet interviewers.
4686. October 2: T. S. Denbow asks Hardy's help.
4687. October 4: Wilfred P. H. Warner solicits a message for the League for the Prohibition of Cruel Sports.
4688. October 4: Malcolm Watson asks for a contribution to a Shakespearean Souvenir Programme at Drury Lane.
4689. October 5: Acland says he has been able to date the shorthand *New Testament* A.D. 1690.
4690. October 7: W. Kent about the allusion to Milton in Hardy's poem "Lausanne."
4691. October 6: Hardy to Kent: rough draft of reply to Letter 4690; the passage will be found in "The Doctrine and Discipline of Divorce" in Milton's *Prose Works*.
4692. October 9: N. M. Cameron about Country Dances and her editorial note in the *English Folk Dance Society News*.
4693. October 9: Wilfrid F. Hodges about the Old Boys' Club at the Dorchester Grammar School.
4694. October 9: Marie C. Stopes on the committee meeting at Portland to consider preservation of "Avice's Cottage."
4695. October 11: Algernon Rose about The Authors' Club.
4696. October 12: Hardy to Watson: rough draft of reply to Letter 4688; encloses copy of a part of the Ms. he wrote in 1916.
4697. October 13: Watson sends thanks.
4698. October 14: Hardy to Warner: rough draft of reply to Letter 4687; he thinks not much can be done.
4699. October 14: O. H. Forsyth-Major ask Hardy about a report that he once met a young lady in Switzerland and presented her with some of his books.

4700. October (15): Hardy to Forsyth-Major: rough draft of reply to Letter 4699; the story is entirely fictitious.
4701. October 17: W. P. D. Stebbing sends a thirty-pound legacy left to him by Stebbing's father.
4702. October 18: Arthur Lamsley asks permission to call.
4703. October 19: Mrs. G. Millard sends thanks.
4704. October 20: Rutland Boughton gossipy letter.
4705. October 20: Thomas M. Cornell solicits Hardy's opinion about the possibility of dramatizing *The Mayor of Casterbridge*.
4706. October 20: Hodges again about the Old Boys' Club at the Dorchester Grammar School.
4707. October 23: J. J. Aston invites Hardy to lunch at the office of *The Times*.
4708. October 27: Cameron again about old Country Dances.
4709. October 30: Ernest F. Kevan asks why books like *Tess* are written.
4710. November 1: Cecil Hanbury proposes paying a visit to Hardy's birthplace at Higher Bockhampton.
4711. November 4: George Blake solicits Hardy's autograph.
4712. November 4: W. R. Wood asks about the meaning of "tacker-haired" in *The Romantic Adventures of A Milkmaid*.
4713. November 6: Hardy to Wood: rough draft of reply to Letter 4712; "Tacker-haired" meant in old Dorset wiry-black-haired; "tacker" being formerly the Dorset name for a shoemaker's thread, which is black and something like wire.
4714. November 9: J. C. Maxwell Garnett to Sir Arthur Carlton about a pageant on behalf of the League of Nations Union.
4715. November 13: A. T. Atherton solicits something for publication.
4716. November 16: J. D. Parsons about doubts concerning authorship of the plays attributed to Shakespeare.
4717. November 17: Hardy to Parsons: rough draft of reply to Letter 4716; the testimonies of Heminge, Condell, Jonson and many others set at rest all doubts on the matter.
4718. November 17: Sam Logan asks permission to use slides of Max Gate and Hardy when he gives a public lecture.
4719. November (18?): Hardy to Logan: rough draft of reply.
4720. November 19: Ernest Barker invites Hardy to the Annual Dinner of Old Members at King's College, London.
4721. (c. November 20): Ursula Greville says that when she sings "The Fallow Deer" she wishes he was in her audience.
4722. November 20: Sir Alfred J. Rice-Daley asks where Hardy resided in Kensington.
4723. November 22: Hardy to Rice-Daley: rough draft of reply to Letter 4722; (1) in 1894 and 1896 he and Mrs. Hardy lived at 16 Pelham Crescent—they had the whole house; (2) in 1898-1899 in Wynstay Gardens; (3) in 1887 in Campden Hill Road.
4724. November 22: Sir Frederick Pollock about Hamlet's "dram of eale" and Hardy's emendation of it in his letter to the London *Times*, 17 June 1926.
4725. November 23: Hardy to Barker: rough draft of reply to Letter 4720; unable to attend the dinner in London.
4726. November 23: Hardy to Ursula Greville: rough draft; thanks for her letter.

CHRONOLOGICAL LIST

4727. (c. November 25): Hardy to W. L. Courtney: rough draft of reply to a solicitation of a poem for the *Fortnightly Review* (Courtney wished to print Hardy's poem on Shakespeare). Hardy points out that this poem is not new; it came out in 1916; he can send a new poem if Courtney wishes.
4728. November 25: Dorothy Allhusen sends a book.
4729. November 26: Courtney accepts Hardy's offer of a new poem for publication in the *Fortnightly Review.*
4730. November 26: Alfred Powell asks Mrs. Hardy if it would be possible for Hardy to write an appeal in support of the movement by the Royal Society of Arts for the preservation of the Ancient Cottages of England.
4731. November 27: G. K. Menzies solicits an appeal for the Preservation of Old Cottages.
4732. November 27: May Morris asks support of the appeal.
4733. (c. November 28): Hardy to Menzies: rough draft of reply to Letter 4731; encloses all he feels able to say.
4734. November 29: Dorothy Allhusen from Basingstoke after the death of her daughter Elizabeth.
4735. November 29: Galsworthy sends greetings before sailing for South Africa.
4736. December 1: C. Guise Mitford asks permission to dedicate a novel to Hardy.
4737. December 2: Sir Arthur Carlton solicits a contribution from Hardy to a Pageant for the League of Nations Union.
4738. December 2: Miss M. Elizabeth Pearson asks Hardy to autograph a copy of *Tess* for sale to raise funds for a library for the Blind.
4739. December 3: Caradog Pritchard sends a tribute from a young Welshman.
4740. December 3: Cecil Wedmore solicits some verse on behalf of young prisoners.
4741. December 4: H. Cotton Minchin sends a copy of *The Mercury Book.* (Minchin's "Story of the MS. [of *Far from the Madding Crowd*]" appeared in the *Morning Post,* London, 28 January 1928, just after Hardy's death. See Letter 2272.)
4742. December 5: May Morris thanks Hardy for his support.
4743. December 6: Basil Dalton about "lost books" and solicits Hardy's "list" of great books which have been "still-born."
4744. December 7: Hardy to Dalton: rough draft of reply to Letter 4743; can think of only one at the moment—Charles C. Colton's *Lacon* (published about 1820) that might be included in Dalton's category, though it can scarcely be called a *great* book.
4745. December 7: Harry E. King about the publication of *The Three Wayfarers.*
4746. December 7: P. Macer-Wright requests something for publication.
4747. December 11: Samuel J. Banks sends thanks.
4748. December 13: H. Newman solicits an interview.
4749. December 14: Hardy to Minchin: rough draft of thanks for the copy of the *Mercury Book.*
4750. December 14: Hardy to Macer-Wright: rough draft of reply to Letter 4746; it is out of his power to provide something.
4751. December 14: Oenone Grove acknowledges Hardy's letter written after Lady Grove's death.

4752. December 14: Florian Williams sends a copy of a Special Edition (50 copies) of *The Queen of Cornwall* with Rutland Boughton's music.
4753. December 15: Hardy to Newman: rough draft of reply to Letter 4748; is not able to grant an interview.
4754. December 15: Hardy to Williams: rough draft of thanks for the copy of the Special Edition of *The Queen of Cornwall*.
4755. December 17: L. S. Amery solicits a poem for the use of the Empire Marketing Board.
4756. December 18: Rice-Daley again about Hardy's house (No. 20) in Wynstay Gardens.
4757. December 19: Hardy to Amery: rough draft of reply to Letter 4755; regrets inability to write the poem.
4758. December 20: Walter H. Parker asks for Hardy's autograph.
4759. December 22: H. M. Tomlinson will read "The Oxen" on Christmas Eve.
4760. December 23: Amery regrets Hardy's inability to supply the poem requested in Letter 4755.
4761. December 25: Edward Clodd illegible Christmas letter.
4762. December 27: Sylvia Dunn requests something for publication.
4763. (n. d.): Beatrix M. Cave appreciation of the permission granted to the Bournemouth Dramatic Club to perform *The Three Strangers*.
4764. (n. d.): Marshall Kirby sends a poetic tribute from California.
4765. (n. d.): Thomas X. Lewis sends thanks.
4766. (n. d.): Ezra Pound about his own poetry.

1927

4767. January 1: Alfred Powell asks Mrs. Hardy to thank Hardy for phrasing an appeal for the committee of the Royal Society of Arts.
4768. January 3: Leonard Woolf to Mrs. Hardy, presenting the request of the Princesse Marguerite di Bassiano for a short story by Hardy for her Parisian quarterly *Commerce*.
4769. January 4: Frederick Medway solicits a foreword for a work he has written on the Royal Navy.
4770. January 5: Ivor Nicholson solicits a few lines for publication in the *Pall Mall Magazine*.
4771. January 6: Hardy to Medway: rough draft of reply to Letter 4769; impossible for him to write the foreword Medway has requested.
4772. (c. January 6): Hardy to Nicholson: rough draft of reply to Letter 4770; cannot comply because of the state of his health.
4773. January 9: Medway regrets Hardy is unable to write a foreword for his book.
4774. January 12: John H. Dickinson sends a book on St. Juliot.
4775. January 12: Alban Dobson asks permission to quote one or two letters Hardy wrote to his father, Austin Dobson, in 1907-08.
4776. January 18: Professor J. Helder solicits a contribution to a book on Immortality.

4777. January 19: Sir John Owen asks permission to take two photographs of Hardy's head for use in a cinema series on "Ability."
4778. January 21: Cicely Hornby about T. E. Lawrence's book.
4779. January 21: Berkeley C. Williams about the death of Hardy's dog "Wessex."
4780. January 26: A. Watson Bain asks about the pronunciation of "Dynasts."
4781. January 26: John Galsworthy, from Cape Town, South Africa, sends condolence on the death of "Wessex."
4782. January 26: Merrill Moore sends thanks.
4783. January 27: Sylvia Beach solicits help in protesting against the pirating of Joyce's *Ulysses*.
4784. January 28: J. B. Fuller wants a short poem on Beethoven's centenary.
4785. February 1: Mira, Duchess of Hamilton invites Hardy to honor the International Anti-Vivisection Congress (which is to meet in London in July) by accepting election as Vice-President.
4786. February 8: E. W. Smerdon, one of the "Hardy Players" in Dorchester, about Hardy's line for him in *The Queen of Cornwall*.
4787. February 11: George Feith solicits Hardy's autograph.
4788. February 14: Samuel Burns about an autographed copy of *Tess*.
4789. February 16: Hardy to Burns: rough draft of reply to Burns's inquiry.
4790. February 18: Cyril Clemens appreciation and thanks.
4791. February 18: F. Wooding solicits an autographed copy of a book by Hardy for sale for the benefit of the Royal Infant Orphanage. (Hardy endorsed this letter: "Sent *Two On A Tower*. 2 Mar 1927.")
4792. February 20: Henry Cavendish, after reading *Tess*, asks what is meant by the story.
4793. February 21: Walter de la Mare tells Mrs. Hardy he was pleased to receive Hardy's poem.
4794. February 21: Newman Flower about his purchase of *Cassell's Magazine*.
4795. February 21: G. Hewitt solicits support of a Community Theatre Society and offers Hardy the vice-presidency.
4796. February (22): Hardy to Hewitt: rough draft of reply to Letter 4795; he is unable to accept the honor.
4796. February 22: Sir Mark Hunter about the proposed University of Wessex.
4798. February 22: A. G. Symonds about the Dorchester Grammar School.
4799. February 24: Hardy to Cavendish: rough draft of reply to Letter 4792; cannot tell him more than is expressed in the book.
4800. February 24: Hardy to Symonds: rough draft of reply to Letter 4798.
4801. February 24: Henry B. Amos solicits a message for the League for the Prohibition of Cruel Sports.
4802. February 25: Hardy to Amos: rough draft of reply to Letter 4801.
4803. February 25: Hardy to Hunter: rough draft of reply to Letter 4797; sincere wishes for the success of the proposed University of Wessex.
4804. February 26: Hunter again about plans for the University of Wessex.

4805. February 28: D. Macgillivray solicits Hardy's autograph in a copy of one of his books for the library of Dalhousie University in Halifax, Nova Scotia. (Hardy endorsed this letter: "Book posted to Halifax 2 March 1927.")
4806. March 3: Harold Child was proud and glad to see Hardy recently.
4807. March 4: Christopher Hudson about reviewing *Late Lyrics*.
4808. March 4: T. R. Warner solicits Hardy's autograph.
4809. March 7: Walter J. Berkowitz asks Hardy to autograph two books, one of them not by Hardy.
4810. March 7: Boyle Lawrence asks for a letter about Esperanto for publication in the London *Morning Post*.
4811. March 8: Newman Flower thanks Hardy for his congratulation and good wishes on Flower's purchase of *Cassell's Magazine*.
4812. March 9: N. Brown solicits an article on fair treatment for animals for publication in *The Spectator*.
4813. March 10: D. B. Browne asks what Hardy would charge to sign a thousand copies of his portrait.
4814. March 10: Thomas J. Gannon about the authenticity of a card bearing Hardy's autograph.
4815. March 11: Princesse Marguerite di Bassiano, having (apparently) received no response to her request (presented by Leonard Woolf, see Letter 4768), again solicits a short story for publication in her Parisian quarterly, *Commerce*. (Whether by oversight or by other cause of delay, no response was made to this request until after Hardy's death ten months later. Then Mrs. Hardy sent a poem entitled "Felling a Tree." It was published in the Winter 1928 issue of *Commerce*, Paris, pp. 6-9. When this poem was collected in *Winter Words* in 1928, the title was changed to "Throwing a Tree." An article about the Princesse in the *Atlantic Monthly*, February 1965, p. 81, identifies her as Marguerite Chapin Caetani.)
4816. March 12: Emily A. Paas appreciation.
4817. March 12: Symonds again about the Dorchester Grammar School.
4818. March 15: Helder again solicits a contribution to a book on Immortality.
4819. March 16: Hardy to Brown: rough draft of reply to Letter 4812; because of his age Hardy is now forced to leave such matters to younger men.
4820. March 16: C. Lacey acknowledges Hardy's gifts.
4821. March 17: Margot Asquith invites Hardy to endow a hospital bed.
4822. March 18: G. K. Menzies thanks Hardy for writing an appeal for the Royal Society of Arts.
4823. March 19: Charles Ganz solicits a few lines for publication on the Beethoven Centenary.
4824. March 19: W. Winslow Hall asks Hardy to permit his nomination for the presidency of the Bournemouth Literature and Art Association.
4825. March 20: W. D. Croft about the letter Hardy wrote previously on the subject of English folk dances.
4826. March 21: Hardy to Ganz: rough draft of reply to Letter 4823; sends regrets.
4827. March 21: Hardy to Hall: rough draft of reply to Letter 4824; he must decline.

4828. (c. March 22): Hardy to Croft: rough draft of reply to Letter 4825; grants permission to publish his letter in the *Journal of the English Folk Dance Society.*
4829. March 22: Weymer about the authenticity of an autograph letter signed "Thomas Hardy."
4830. (c. March 24): Hardy to Gannon: rough draft of reply to Letter 4814; the writing on the card is *not* the handwriting of Thomas Hardy.
4831. March 25: G. Herbert Thring thanks Hardy for his letter.
4832. March 26: Francis Dodd about Hardy's sitting for a portrait for publication in a new Macmillan book.
4833. March 28: William K. Hill to Mrs. Hardy: Alec Rea has consented to read Hill's scenario of *Far from the Madding Crowd.*
4834. March 28: Erich Weltzien from Berlin, thanks Hardy for a copy of *The Dynasts.*
4835. March 29: W. A. Pickard-Cambridge sends a book of Dorset Carols.
4836. March 31: Ezra Pound about "Propertius Soliloquizes" and others of his own poems.
4837. April 5: Hardy to Weymer: rough draft of reply to Letter 4829; the letter was not written by Hardy.
4838. April 5: Dodd hopes to be present next Wednesday to continue the portrait.
4839. April 5: Florence Greg sends an article she has written for possible publication in an American magazine.
4840. April 7: Esmé Bruce asks permission to photograph Hardy in his garden.
4841. April (8): Hardy to Bruce: rough draft of reply to Letter 4840; is unable to grant Bruce a sitting.
4842. April 13: Symonds again about the Dorchester Grammar School.
4843. April 16: Cecil Wedmore asks permission to dedicate his "Mendip novel" to Hardy.
4844. April 18: Hardy to Weltzien: rough draft of reply to Letter 4834; too much attention is given to sport in England.
4845. April 19: Walter A. Briscoe about the publication in book form of the dramatizations of *Tess* and *The Mayor of Casterbridge.*
4846. April 19: The Bishop of Liverpool solicits a paper for publication in a series of religious books on *Affirmations.*
4847. April (20): Hardy to Briscoe: rough draft of reply to Letter 4845; there is no possibility of the text of *Tess* as a play being published, and the same applies to *The Mayor of Casterbridge.* (The text of *Tess*, as a play, has, however, been subsequently published: see *"Tess" in the Theatre* by Marguerite Roberts, University of Toronto Press, 1950.)
4848. April 20: Sherwood Anderson thanks Hardy for a kind letter about a book Anderson had sent.
4849. April 21: M. S. Mok solicits Hardy's autograph in three books.
4850. April 22: Weltzien about *The Dynasts.*
4851. April 23: J. W. Robertson Scott sends a copy of the first number of *The Countryman.*
4852. May 3: H. Latimer solicits Hardy's autograph.
4853. May 5: Emily A. Paas sends thanks.

4854. May 9: Sylvestre Dorian solicits Hardy's autograph on a photograph.
4855. May 9: Edna Porter asks if Hardy has ever written a poem for Helen Keller; if so, she wishes to use it in an anthology.
4856. May 12: E. N. Singleton solicits Hardy's autograph on a photograph.
4857. May 13: G. Gilliat solicits Hardy's estimate of British literary progress in the hundred years during which *The Evening Standard* has been published.
4858. May 16: Charles H. Bates about a tablet to William Blake to be placed in the crypt of St. Paul's Cathedral.
4859. May 16: H. C. Manning about "the dram of eale" in *Hamlet*.
4860. May 17: Henry Goddard Leach about a prize offered by *The Forum* in New York for the best translation of a poem by Claudel (the French ambassador in Washington, D. C.), and invites Hardy to compete.
4861. May 19: Ian MacAlister invites Hardy to lend his name as a member of the Grand Committee for the British Architectural Conference.
4862. May 19: Ernest Noble asks permission to reprint "To Shakespeare after Three Hundred Years."
4863. May 19: Sotheby & Co. ask if Hardy would object to the sale by auction of a letter he wrote to Reginald Bosworth Smith.
4864. (n. d.): Hardy to Mrs. R. Bosworth Smith: sends *A Pair of Blue Eyes* which she may keep until she is done with it.
4865. May 20: Hardy to Sotheby & Co.: copy of reply to Letter 4863; he would rather it should have been destroyed.
4866. May 20: E. Channon solicits Hardy's autograph.
4867. May 21: Hardy to MacAlister: rough draft of reply to Letter 4861; prefers not to have his name used:
4868. May 21: Hardy to Noble: rough draft of reply to Letter 4862; gives the requested permission.
4869. May 21: James Mortimer has met a nephew of Hardy's.
4870. May 23: Hardy to Harley Granville-Barker: typed transcript; he liked *Waste*.
4871. May 24: Charles Wilson solicits Hardy's autograph in a book of his.
4872. May 25: J. M. Baroody, from Syria, asks the return of some MSS. sent to Hardy.
4873. May 26: Granville-Barker says it was good of Hardy to write about *Waste*.
4874. May 26: Stan Lee Kapustka asks advice about college courses at the University of Illinois.
4875. May 28: H. Lawrence about false allegations made by one James Mortimer. See Letter 4869.
4876. May 29: Hardy to Lawrence: rough draft of reply to Letter 4875; the man was an imposter.
4877. May 29: R. Edwards asks for a contribution to a school magazine.
4878. May 30: Caroline M. Hill asks permission to quote two poems.
4879. May 31: Symonds again about the Dorchester Grammar School.
4880. June 1: Georges Lasselin, from Paris, acknowledges receipt of a letter from Hardy; he is writing an article on "Men and Women in the Works of T. H."

4881. June 1: Upton Sinclair asks Hardy's opinion about the decency of *Oil*.

On 2 June Hardy attained the age of 87. Seventeen men and women sent him Birthday Greetings and best wishes:

4882. Edward Clodd
4883. Sydney Cockerell
4884. Arthur Compton-Rickett
4885. R. E. Crompton
4886. Sir George Douglas
4887. George Drayton
4888. John Drinkwater
4889. S. M. Ellis
4890. St. John Ervine
4891. Stanley Galpin
4892. Margaret Gifford
4893. Cyril A. Munro
4894. A. R. Powys
4895. Philip Ridgeway
4896. T. H. Tilley
4897. Philip Tomlinson
4898. Charles Whibley

4899. June 7: M. A. Mugge asks help in publishing matters.
4900. June 8: Richard Gillbard about the Dogs' Protection Bill.
4901. (c. June 9): Hardy to Gillbard: rough draft of reply to Letter 4900.
4902. June 14: E. A. Knapp-Fisher solicits support of an appeal for the Abbey.
4903. June 17: A. B. Ramsay sorry Hardy is unable to accept an invitation to Magdalene College, Cambridge.
4904. June 18: Knapp-Fisher acknowledges Hardy's letter of regret.
4905. June 19: Hardy to Crompton: rough draft; thanks for birthday greetings on 2 June.
4906. June 19: John S. Kenyon about the Dorset pronunciation of "r" in *Tess*.
4907. June 21: Sir Robert Edgcumbe is pleased at the thought of having Hardy lay the foundation-stone of the newly planned Dorchester Grammar School.
4908. June 22: J. Hawkesby-Mullins solicits an autograph.
4909. June 23: Hardy to Kenyon: rough draft of reply to Letter 4906; sorry about the gradual loss of "r" in Dorset speech so that it hardly exists now in the speech of well-bred people.
4910. June 24: Bates invites Hardy to the unveiling of a tablet to William Blake in the crypt of St. Paul's Cathedral.
4911. June 25: Hardy to Sinclair: rough draft of reply to Letter 4881; thanks for the copy of *Oil*.
4912. June 25: W. S. Spantoz appreciation.
4913. June 29: H. N. Hurst, from South Africa, suggests Hardy read *The Book of Truth*.
4914. June 29: Lasselin writes in French about a visit to Dorchester.
4915. June 30: Muriel Stuart sends a copy of her *Selected Poems* which she has dedicated to him.
4916. July 1: James Stanley Little about the Shelley Memorial Trust.
4917. July 4: Fred F. Footlet solicits a sitting in order to make a lithographic portrait.
4918. July 4: Thomas Wood about *Late Lyrics and Earlier*.
4919. July 5: Emmeline (Mrs. W. H.) Harrison regrets not being able to meet Hardy.
4920. July 5: Louise Moog, a Dutch girl, from The Hague, after reading *Tess*.

4921. July 7: Hardy to Footlet: rough draft of reply to Letter 4917; he is unable to give a sitting.
4922. July 9: Hardy to Douglas: typed transcript of reply to Sir George's birthday greetings.
4923. July 10: Eleanor C. Koenig, from Hartford, Connecticut, sends a copy of her book, *Herb Woman.*
4924. July 11: Douglas pleased to get a letter from Hardy.
4925. July 14: C. Bohn Childs about literary agencies.
4926. July 14: William M. Meredith thanks Hardy for a pleasant call at Max Gate.
4927. July 14: Verla West, from Los Angeles, California, about her high-school task of composing a sonnet; encloses a copy of her sonnet "To Thomas Hardy."
4928. July 18: Arnold Dawson asks for a brief interview.
4929. July 18: Frances G. Gibbs (Mrs. O. L. Keith, of Columbia, South Carolina) says she is interested to learn he is now writing poetry.
4930. July 20: Hardy to Dawson: rough draft; declines permission for an interview.
4931. July 22: J. A. Allen asks permission to reprint Hardy's speech at the opening of the New Dorchester Grammar School.
4932. July 23: Hardy to Allen: rough draft of reply to Letter 4931; does not wish it to be reprinted.
4933. (c. July 24): Hardy to Koenig: rough draft of reply to Letter 4923.
4934. July 24: Alfred Pope about the new Dorchester Grammar School.
4935. July 25: Frederic Whyte asks how Heinemann came to publish *Desperate Remedies* in 1892.
4936. (c. July 26): Hardy to Whyte: rough draft; does not know the answer to Whyte's question.
4937. July 27: Lewis Horrox asks Hardy to lend his name as a patron of University College in Exeter.
4938. July 28: Jacques-Emile Blanche in praise of Hardy's books.
4939. July 30: Wolmark about an exhibition of his art in London; it will include the portrait of Hardy made in July 1926.
4940. August 2: W. G. Lockett, from the British Consulate in Davos, Switzerland, solicits, for the benefit of charitable work in Davos, any book of Hardy's.
4941. August 3: Hardy to Horrox: rough draft of reply to Letter 4937; does not consent to lend his name as a patron.
4942. August 3: Squire solicits a comment on the Protection of Stonehenge from further deterioration. (Hardy's reply to this solicitation is now in the Colby College Library.)
4943. August 4: Hardy to Gibbs: rough draft of reply to Letter 4929; her interest in having discovered that he writes verse is gratifying to him—he has been writing it more than thirty years.
4944. August 4: Mrs. Cecil Hanbury sends a note with some fruit.
4945. August 4: Gustav Holst asks permission to dedicate a new orchestral composition entitled *Egdon Heath* to Hardy. (It was published in 1928 by Novello & Co.)
4946. August 7: C. Greenway solicits a photograph.
4947. August 8: Mrs. G. Cobban sends two of her poems and solicits his help in getting her work published.

CHRONOLOGICAL LIST

4948. August 10: Hardy to Mrs. Cobban: rough draft of reply to Letter 4947; he is not able to help her.
4949. August 15: Roger Ingpen says his sister, Mrs. Walter de la Mare, suggests he call on Hardy, and he asks if next Wednesday will be convenient.
4950. August 15: G. L. Springham asks where the parish of Springham in *The Trumpet-Major* is.
4951. August 16: Hardy to Springham: rough draft of reply to Letter 4950; Springham is an invented name.
4952. August 16: Emily Hallowell asks aid on behalf of Sacco and Vanzetti in America.
4953. August 21: Richard Lindebury sends thanks.
4954. August 25: Martin J. Youdelman solicits a statement about Zola.
4955. August 26: H. O. Lock about the wording on a plaque to be affixed to the house in South Street, Dorchester, in which William Barnes once conducted his school.
4956. August 28: James O'Rourke asks permission to call.
4957. August 29: Lady Elizabeth Lewis thanks Hardy for his sympathy.
4958. August 30: Miss Gwladys Harris pleasure in visiting the scene of *Desperate Remedies*.
4959. August 31: N. C. Raad solicits an Introduction for a book of poems.
4960. September 1: W. T. Shore asks help for The Boy Scouts Association.
4961. September 2: Hardy to Shore: rough draft; sends regrets.
4962. September 5: Leslie A. Boosey asks about the possibility of using a shorter title for "In Time of the Breaking of Nations."
4963. September 5: Margaretta L. (Mrs. Frank E.) Lemon asks permission to quote.
4964. September 5: Kuo Yu-shou asks permission to call.
4965. September 6: Hardy to Boosey: rough draft of reply to Letter 4962; suggests five other possible titles.
4966. September 9: Hardy to Raad: rough draft of reply to Raad's request: is sorry to decline.
4967. September 10: F. Stamper about an inferior performance of the *Tess* play at the Weymouth Pavilion.
4968. September 12: Henry Goddard Leach, through his assistant in the office of *The Forum* in New York, solicits an autographed photograph suitable for framing.
4969. September 13: Godfrey Elton sends Hardy some books borrowed from his college library at Oxford.
4970. September 14: John W. Symons about *A Pair of Blue Eyes*.
4971. September 16: Thoreau MacDonald sends thanks.
4972. September 18: Lillah, Lady Keeble, from Lulworth Castle, Wareham, asks if she and her husband may call. (She had met Mrs. Hardy when she was Lillah McCarthy, Mrs. Granville-Barker.)
4973. September 23: Miss Gwladys Harris thanks Hardy for the gift of his poems.
4974. September 24: Berton Braley asks permission to quote.
4975. September 27: L. Bradbury sends payment for permission to quote three poems.
4976. September 29: Danford Barney sends thanks.
4977. September 30: Vivian de Sola Pinto sends a copy of his book *Sir Charles Sedley*.

4978. October 1: Lady Keeble thanks Hardy for a book of his poems.
4979. October 3: William Maxwell has found the Mary Queen of Scots poem and the author.
4980. October 3: Carrol Romer solicits an article on George Meredith for the *Nineteenth Century*.
4981. October 4: Hardy to Romer: rough draft; agrees to write an article on George Meredith.
4982. October 4: A. Wilson solicits "a word of farewell to two pairs of nightingales" who are to be sent to New Zealand.
4983. October 5: Romer thanks Hardy for being willing to write the article on George Meredith.
4984. October 5: Sotheby & Co. ask permission to sell four of Hardy's letters.
4985. October 7: Maxwell sends some notes about the song "Annie Laurie."
4986. October 7: Herman Ould introduces Kuo Yu-shou from China.
4987. October 7: Kuo Yu-shou repeats his request for permission to call; wishes to translate Hardy's works into Chinese.
4988. October 13: Romer thanks Hardy for the MS. of his article on George Meredith.
4989. October 14: William M. Meredith thanks Hardy for his article about his father George Meredith, written for the *Nineteenth Century*.
4990. October 15: Acland about moving "the pavement," a recently discovered Roman floor, to the Dorset County Museum.
4991. October 16: Charles Whibley announces his approaching marriage to Sir Walter Raleigh's daughter Philippa.
4992. October 17: Henry O. Lock again about the dates to be used on the plaque to be affixed to the house where William Barnes conducted his school.
4993. October 17: Maxwell withdraws the wrong information given Hardy in Letter 4985.
4994. October 23: de Sola Pinto thanks Hardy for his letter and is glad Hardy found *Sedley* pleasant reading.
4995. October 28: Georgina Mase sends a copy of an anthology in which two of his poems were, with his permission, included.
4496. October 29: L. W. Payne, from Austin, Texas, solicits a personal word for a class at the University of Texas.
4997. October 31: Francis de Kiss solicits Hardy's recollections of Kossuth's stay in England.
4998. (c. October ?): Sheegee Yoshivara asks Macmillan & Company to forward to Hardy a poem from a Japanese admirer. (Sir Frederick Macmillan forwarded the poem on 31 October.)
4999. October 31: Macmillan forwards a letter from a Japanese admirer.
5000. November 1: de Sola Pinto thanks Hardy for signing a photograph for the library of University College in Southampton.
5001. November 1: Kenneth Vickus thanks Hardy for the signed photograph presented to the University College Library at Southampton.
5002. November 1: I. Wynne-Roberts asks for Hardy's opinion of an "Ode to Apollo" enclosed.
5003. November 2: Nancy Sheppard asks permission to make a "portrait-drawing" for publication in *The Bookman*.

CHRONOLOGICAL LIST

5004. November 3: Hardy to de Kiss: rough draft of reply to Letter 4997; Hardy never met Kossuth.
5005. November (3): Hardy to Sheppard: rough draft; he cannot sit for a portrait but he would lend a photograph for use in *The Bookman*.
5006. November 7: Wedmore acknowledges receipt of Hardy's letter about his Mendip novel.
5007. November 9: Elton thanks Hardy for the return of the books sent him in September from Oxford.
5008. November 9: Edmund Gosse about raising money for the benefit of John Middleton Murry.
5009. November 9: Gosse again on the same subject.
5010. November 10: Yutaro Ito sends a copy of a Japanese translation of *Jude* which Hardy had authorized in 1923.
5011. November 10: Charles H. Robinson about Paula's baptism in *A Laodicean*.
5012. November 12: Mrs. Sarah A. Tooley asks permission to call with a view to writing an article for American readers.
5013. November (13): Hardy to Mrs. Tooley: rough draft of reply to Letter 5012; he must forgo all interviews; suggests she write an article about *The Dynasts* from the books themselves.
5014. November 13: Lasselin says the *Revue Hebdomadaire* of Paris is going to dedicate one of its first numbers in 1928 to Hardy's work.
5015. November 14: Florence T. Bullen asks if she would be right in tracing the influence of de Maupassant in Hardy's short stories.
5016. November 14: Hardy to Bullen: rough draft; she appears to have a very slight knowledge of literary chronology, or she would be aware that many of Hardy's novels and stories preceded in date those of the French novelist.
5017. November 14: Lady Keeble is memorizing Hardy's poems in the book he gave her in September.
5018. November 14: Yvonne Salmon to Mrs. Hardy about her translation of Pitt's speech in *The Dynasts*.
5019. November 14: Vincent Starrett, from Chicago, asks about a four-page leaflet of notes on *The Dynasts*.
5020. November 17: Gosse about getting £250 from the Prime Minister for "J. M. M."
5021. November 18: J. T. Godwin asks about Hardy's family "Coat of Arms."
5022. (n. d.): Hardy to Mlle Salmon: rough draft of reply to Letter 5018; approves of her French translation of a passage in *The Dynasts*.
5023. November 18: Yvonne Salmon says she would not leave out anything.
5024. (c. November 19): Hardy to Godwin: rough draft of reply to Letter 5021; the Arms of the Hardys of Dorchester can be found in Hutchins' *History of Dorset* (II, 385, and IV, 433), but he himself has never used them.
5025. November 23: Hardy to Lasselin: rough draft; acknowledges Lasselin's help in making French translations of Hardy's work.
5026. November 23: George Grant sends official thanks for the signed photograph presented to the library of University College at Southampton.

5027. November 28: Poppie Tunstall sends a copy of her first novel.
5028. November 29: Mina Condrow asks Hardy's opinion of the influence exerted on dialects by the "refined accents" of B. B. C. announcers.
5029. November 30: Hardy to Granville-Barker; typed transcript; on G-B's *Prefaces to Shakespeare*. Hardy has always held *Lear* to be unactable.
5030. November (?): Hardy to Starrett: rough draft of reply to Letter 5019; he has never written any leaflet called *Notes on "The Dynasts"*; it was probably prepared by the London producer of the selection of scenes from the drama acted some years ago.
5031. December 2: Horace Morgan sends thanks.
5032. December 2: Doris Thorne asks help in obtaining some recognition for her father, Henry Arthur Jones, in his 77th year.
5033. December 6: Cronshaw invites Hardy to visit Queen's College, Oxford, on 1 January 1928 for the New Year's Day "gaudy."
5034. December 6: John M. Hightett asks advice about finding a publisher for his poems.
5035. (c. December 7): Hardy to Hightett: rough draft; he is not aware of any method of getting a publisher, except that of sending the manuscript to one who publishes.
5036. December 10: Hardy to Cronshaw: rough draft of reply to Letter 5033; regrets inability to visit Queen's College.
5037. December 10: Yvonne Salmon has completed the translation of *The Dynasts* into French.
5038. December 24: Gosse says Hardy's poem in today's *Times*, entitled "Christmas in the Elgin Room, British Museum," is a fine one.

1928

5039. January 1: Ezra Pound again about sending some of his "Cantos."

* * * * *

Hardy died on 11 January 1928. Thereafter only two letters survived the bonfire tended by Mrs. Hardy in the Max Gate garden.

5040. February 13, 1929: Howard Bliss to Mrs. Florence Hardy about receiving "Old Mrs. Chundle" today. (She had sold this story to the *Ladies' Home Journal* for publication in February 1929; it was also published in a 38-page book, New York, Crosby Gaige, 1929. These publications took place without the knowledge or consent of Sydney Cockerell. He vehemently rebuked her and she promised not to do such a thing again. But in 1934 she arranged for a private printing of *An Indiscretion in the Life of an Heiress* without consulting Cockerell. In March 1935 he wrote her that, apart from her solemn promise after the unfortunate incident of "Old Mrs. Chundle," it was her duty to consult him inasmuch as Hardy had appointed Cockerell one of his literary executors.)

5041. August 10, 1933: John Galsworthy thanks Mrs. Hardy for lending him some of the autograph letters he had written to Hardy in earlier years.

ALPHABETICAL INDEX OF HARDY'S CORRESPONDENTS

(Numerals refer to the LETTERS as they are numbered in the Chronological List. Hardy's own letters are indicated by a parenthetical "H" after the letter-numeral. In the case of those correspondents whose extant letters are quite numerous (more than fifty, for example), there has seemed little to be gained by listing them all here. To list each of the 150 letters to Mrs. Henniker would certainly serve no useful purpose. In such cases the numerals of the first and the last letters are given, and between the two numerals the *total* number of the letters to and from that correspondent is stated.)

Abbey, Edwin A.: 239
Abbott, C. Collier: 3952
Abbott, Edward: 127
Abbott, Raymond: 2215, 2240, 2358, 2521, 2656, 3200, 3630
Aberconway, Marya: 486
Abercrombie, Lascelles: 1599, 1908, 2428, 2578
Academy, The, editor of: 736(H)
Acland, Mrs. G. A.: 3132, 3135(H)
Acland, Capt. John E. (Curator, Dorset County Museum): 1229, 1511, 1586, 1749, 1751, 2579, 3285, 3701, 4582(H), 4585, 4681, 4689, 4990
Adams, A. Davies: 3783, 3799(H)
Adams, F.: 4620
Adams, Mrs. Jessie: 3062
Adams, W. Davenport: 240
Adcock, St. John: 4435
Adlam, Frank: 1096
Ainley, Henry: 1900
Alden, Ada Foster (Mrs. Henry M.): 2703, 2732(H), 2752, 4651
Alden, Henry M.: 155

Aldrich, Thomas Bailey: 197, 217, 221, 292
Alexander, Sir George: 519, 521, 718, 720
Allan, A. D. H.; 3393, 3397(H)
Allbutt, Sir T. Clifford: 837, 1423, 1654, 1801, 3108, 3116
Allen, Grant: 608, 666
Allen, J. A.: 4931, 4932(H)
Allen, W. G.: 4588
Allhusen, Dorothy (Mrs. Henry): 1210, (total: 30 letters), 4734
Allhusen, Elizabeth: 3284, 3725
Allingham, Helen Paterson (Mrs. William): 160
Alma-Tadema, Sir Laurence: 686
Alma-Tadema, Laura (Mrs. Laurence): 265, 375
Amery, L. S.: 4755, 4757(H), 4760
Ames, Percy W.: 1615, 1616(H), 1619, 1655, 2174, 2175(H)
Amos, Henry B.: 3759, 3760, 3762(H), 4397, 4399(H), 4643, 4801, 4802(H)
Anderson, M.: 1587

Anderson, Sherwood: 2581, 4848
Andrews, A. R.: 1524
Anglo-French Poetry Society. 2782, 2810(H)
Animal's Friend, editor of: 652(H)
Anthony, Alfred W.: 3443, 3765, 4216
Anthony, Joseph: 2961, 2962(H)
Archer, William: 2582
Armour, J. S.: 4514
Armstrong, A. J.: 4449
Armstrong, Walter: 1314
Arnell, C. J.: 4634
Arnold, Edward A.: 311, 395, 397
Arnold, W. R.: 1214, 1220(H), 1222
Arns, Karl: 3676
Aronstein, Phil: 1830
Ashling, Herbert: 4076
Asquith, Lady Cynthia: 2796, 2802, 3726, 3808, 3970, 3972, 3976, 4051, 4073, 4208, 4217, 4411
Asquith, Elizabeth: 1904, 1914
Asquith, the Rt. Hon. Herbert Henry: 1291, 1293, 1418, 1420, 1522, 1883
Asquith, Margot Lady: 1727, 1728, 1786, 1891, 4821
Aston, J. J.: 4707
Atherton, A. T.: 4715
Atkinson, Judge H. Tindal: 209, 254, 255, 266, 295
Austin, Alfred: 472
Authors' Club: 1656
Ayscough, John: 1378

Baber, Sydney M.: 1765
Baddeley, Hermione: 4282
Bagot, Richard: 2205, 2206
Bain, A. Watson: 4780
Bainton, George: 340
Baker, Charles A.: 3883
Baker, Charlotte Lozier: 2226
Balfour, Alice: 1637
Balfour, Lady Betty: 1163, 1164
Balfour, May: 2583
Balkwill, Violet I.: 3243
Ball, J. Evelyn: 867
Banaji, M. M.: 3895, 3986

Bancroft, Sir Squire: 544, 1282, 1657
Bankes, Daphne: 2218, 3569
Banks, Samuel J.: 4199, 4747
Barber, Arthur: 4218
Barber, T. G.: 4133
Barclay, Thomas: 1783
Bargren, John: 4433
Baring, Maurice: 2458
Barker, Ernest: 4605, 4609(H), 4720, 4725(H)
Barker, Harley G.: see Granville-Barker, Harley.
Barker, James D.: 2223, 2227(H), 2349, 2351(H)
Barker, Lillah (Mrs. Granville): see Keeble, Lillah Lady.
Barman, Christian: 3267, 3273, 3279
Barnes, Kenneth R.: 3774(H)
Barnes, L. L.: 314
Barnes, William M.: 361
Barnett, George: 3667
Barney, Danford: 4976
Baroody, J. M.: 4872
Barrie, Sir James M.: 379, (total: 31 letters), 4407
Barry, Gerald: 4364, 4366(H)
Bass, Tom: 3110
Bassiano, Princesse Marguerite di (Marguerite Chapin Caetani): 4815
Bastow, Henry R.: 2, 3, 4, 6, 10, 12, 13, 1196
Bater, A. B.: 3662
Bates, Charles H.: 4491, 4496(H), 4858, 4910
Bates, Herbert: 3803
Bateson, Edith: 2644
Bath, Hubert: 3745
Bathe, S. H.: 3631, 3635(H), 3636
Baumann, Lina: 4473
Bax, Clifford 2972, 2973(H), 2976
Baxter, Anna J. P.: 4564
Baxter, Lucy E.: 315, 317
Bazile, Georges: 1531, 2239
Beach, Sylvia: 4783
Beadon, H.: 3929, 3930(H)
Beals, Clyde A.: 2675
Beament, W. O.: 1794, 1795(H)
Beatty, Helen M.: 4290
Beaumont, Cyril W.: 3193
Beck, Christine: 4396

ALPHABETICAL INDEX

Beckett, Pat à: 1359, 1360
Beer, M.: 1192, 1193(H)
Beer, W. B.: 4034, 4430
Beerbohm, Max: 1141
Beesly, E. S.: 1629
Begbie, Harold: 4323, 4325(H)
Behrens-Hagen: 3377
Beith, Ian Hay: 3237, 3588, 3666
Bell, C. Moberly: 1277, 1424
Bell, F. Mackenzie: 1425
Bennet, Norman: 4616, 4628(H)
Bennett, Andrew: 3005, 3007(H), 3010, 3036, 3038(H)
Bennett, Arnold: 2334(H), 2335, 2507
Benson, Arthur Christopher: 932, (total: 28 letters), 4063
Benson, Sir Frank R.: 634, 635
Bensusan, S. L.: 2407
Berger, A.: 601
Bergerat, Emile: 1533, 1535(H)
Beringer, Esmé: 1925
Berkowitz, Walter J.: 4809
Bernard, James: 2219, 4413
Berrisford, Albert: 3384
Berrisford, A. G.: 4122
Bertram, Anthony: 3119
Besant, G. B.: 4388
Besant, Walter: 134, 147, 148, 174, 178, 193, 194, 242, 251, 253, 343, 382, 398, 401, 443, 494, 796
Bevan, A. E.: 2917
Bickerstaffe, R.: 3069
Billington, A. H.: 3070
Binghams, George: 119
Binyon, Laurence: 1269, 1288, 1328, 2245
Birkley, John: 4450, 4452(H)
Birkmyre, Robert: 4181
Birrell, Augustine: 648, 2359, 2362
Black, William: 111, 211, 230, 269, 270, 294
Blackie, Walter W.: 3768
Blackmore, Richard D.: 101, 104
Blackwood, John: 138
Blackwood, William: 344, 348, 350
Blake, George: 2467, 4711
Blake, E.: 2473
Blakeney, E. H.: 2074
Blanchamp, H.: 433(H)
Blanche, Jacques-Emile: 1091, 1093, 1097, 1128, 1130, 1132, 1135, 1151, 1228, 4938

Bland, F. M.: 1322
Blatchford, William. 4285
Blind, Mathilda: 503
Bliss, J. Howard: 2661, 2663(H), 4089, 4219, 4401, 5040
Blomfield, Arthur W.: 122, 327, 383
Blomfield, Charles J.: 825, 826(H)
Blumenfeld, R. D.: 4170
Blundell, Herbert W.: 3481
Blunden, Edmund: 2677, 3120
Bodington, E. J.: 3399(H), 3403, 3410(H)
Boehm, Margaret: 2726
Boggs, Thomas: 576
Bok, Edward W.: 250
Bolce, Harold: 2030, 2031(H)
Boncher, Léon: 113
Bone, James: 3723
Bone, Muirhead: 3431
Bonnaire, H.: 2985, 3001(H)
Bonnet, P.: 4077
Boosey, Leslie A.: 4962, 4965(H)
Borsa, Mario: 915, 916(H), 930
Bosanquet, Dorothy: 2798, 2805
Bossuet, Alice: 4128
Bottomley, Gordon: 2489, 2544, 2678
Boughton, Rutland: 2445, 3722, 4293, 4317, 4349, 4490, 4704
Boulton, Sir Harold: 1184, 1526
Bourne, Stafford: 3475
Bowker, R. R.: 4220
Bowman, W. G.: 3046, 3059(H), 3103, 3158(H), 3165
Bradbury, L.: 4975
Bradish, Margaret: 4494, 4495(H)
Bradley, A. C.: 1487, 1723
Bradley, Henry: 450
Bradley, W. T.: 1734
Bradley-Birt, F. B.: 3259, 4269
Bradshaw, James & Edith: 3071
Bradzky, Leon: 1787
Braley, Berton: 4974
Braithwaite, Cecil: 3428, 3430, 3465, 3705, 3728, 3733, 3820
Bransden, Arthur: 3855
Brennecke, Ernest: 3495, 3498, 3582(H), 3672, 3703, 3845, 3880(H), 3905, 3973, 4003, 4071, 4083, 4099
Brenner, B. E.: 4045, 4049(H), 4059
Brereton, Clouderley: 1846

Brickell, H. E. C.: 3938
Bridges, Robert: 2459, 3027, 3286, 4409
Bright, R. Golding: 3124, 3128(H), 3179, 4267(H), 4270
Briscoe, Walter A.: 4845, 4847(H)
British Broadcasting Co.: 4193
Broadbent, Henry: 4353, 4354
Broadley, A. M.: 1223, 1363(H)
Broadus, E. K.: 2443
Brockway, Wallace: 3887
Bromley, W.: 980
Bronner, Milton: 2402
Brooks, Edward D.: 2080, 2116
Brooks, Van Wyck: 2585
Brougham, ed.: 1952
Brown, Edgar R.: 3212
Brown, H.: 1171
Brown, H. Irene: 3853
Brown, N.: 4812, 4819(H)
Brown, Robert Carlton: 4191
Brown, William Adams: 1379
Browne, D. B.: 4813
Browne, Sir James Crichton: 532, 1498, 2414
Browning, Oscar: 2935, 2938
Browning, Robert: 363
Bruce, Esmé: 4840, 4841(H)
Brunius, August: 2527, 2953
Bryant, Arthur: 2870
Bryce, James Lord: 1845
Buchan, John: 2207, 2936, 3034, 3072
Buchanan, Marion: 3529
Buchanan, Robert: 517
Buckle, G. E.: 741, 1283
Bugler, Gertrude (Mrs. Ernest): 4108, 4144
Bulkeley, H. C.: 2144, 2246
Bulkeley, H. F.: 2344
Bullen, Florence T.: 5015, 5016(H)
Bullen, Dame Georgiana: 4676
Bullock, J. M.: 2438
Burgas-Fernandez, C.: 4300, 4328
Burkes, Barbara: 3245
Burnand, Florence: 4153
Burns, John: 2747
Burns, Samuel: 4788, 4789(H)
Burriss, Lucile: 4123
Burrows, H. L.: 3554
Burrows, John: 1496
Burton, Katherine: 3073
Bury, J. B.: 1545

Busse, Kurt: 3472
Butcher, Fanny: 3591
Butcher, S. H.: 1051, 1058
Butler, J. Montagu: 1721
Butler, Nicholas Murray: 3139, 3140(H)
Butterworth, Thornton: 4524
Buxton, Charles Roden: 1170, 1225
Byas, Hugh: 3616, 3618(H)

Cabell, James Branch: 2586
Caesar, G. Julius: 3147
Caetani, Marguerite Chapin: see Bassiano, Princesse
Caine, Hall: 365, 1843, 1872, 1877, 2265, 2292, 2293, 2295(H), 2296, 2298, 2299
Calhoun, Philo C.: 4259
Cameron, N. M.: 4658, 4692, 4708
Campbell, Beatrice Stella (Mrs. Patrick): 630, 631, 633, 642, 665, 667, 669, 697, 704, 705(H), 725, 726, 730, 740, 868
Capocci, Valentina: 1920, 4446
Carlton, Sir Arthur: 4737
Carnarvon, Lord: 192
Carnarvon, Lady: 276
Carr, J. Comyns: 181, 208, 214, 215, 216, 220
Carré, Jean-Marie: 1486
Carroll, Delia: 3977
Cartwright, Charles: 1234, 1237(H)
Cassell & Co.: 4370
Casson, T. E.: 4650
Caulfeild, Edward B.: 984, 988
Causton, Doris L.: 2990
Cave, Beatrix M.: 4763
Cavendish, Henry: 4792, 4799(H)
Cawson, James: 3074
Cecil, Gertrude L. E. G.: 1983
Cervesato, Arnaldo: 879, 887(H)
Chambers, Charles E. S.: 3864, 3877(H), 3881, 3885(H), 3891, 3916
Channon, E.: 4866
Chapman, Frederick: 16, 17, 18
Chatto and Windus: 128, 131
Chesterton, A. E. (Mrs. Cecil): 3463

ALPHABETICAL INDEX 215

Chew, Samuel C.: 2261, 2271(H), 2284, 2287(H), 2460, 2889, 2890(H), 2927, 3217, 3230(H), 3255, 4338
Child, Harold: 1272, 1289, (total: 28 letters), 4288, 4806
Childs, Borlase: 420
Childs, C. Bohn: 3775, 3795, 4162, 4164, 4173, 4176, 4925
Childs, Christopher: 416, 419, 2519, 4124, 4149
Childs, John F.: 2197, 2200, 2203, 2204, 2234, 3754, 3757
Chivers, Cedric: 2958, 2963(H), 2968, 2995
Choate, Joseph H.: 1032, 1037
Chubb, Ralph: 4469
Chudoba, F.: 4213
Churchill, G. S.; 2908, 2909(H)
Churchill, Lord Randolph: 587
Churchill, Violet: 1701
Clark, Genevieve Bennett (Mrs. Champ): 1414, 1502, 2089, 2319, 3565
Clark, Mrs. M. Vaughan: 4382
Clarke, Ernest N. Townley: 3850
Clarke, George Herbert: 2211, 2328, 2342, 3188, 3218
Clarke, Tom: 3496
Claymore, Francis: 4668
Clayton, Arthur E.: 2125, 2129(H)
Clemens, Cyril: 4790
Clibborn, William: 677
Clifford, Sir Hugh: 972, 2915
Clifford, Lucy (Mrs. W. K.): 1426, 3289, 3292(H), 3501, 4296
Clodd, Edward: 473(H), 480(H), 593, 594(H), 650(H), 775(H), 794(H), 918(H), 948(H), 1119-(H), 1122, 1155, 1188(H), 1238-(H), 1367, 1483(H), 1853(H), 1902(H), 1913, 2587, 2754, 2957, 3068, 3641, 3674(H), 3816, 4064, 4617, 4761, 4882
Clothier, G. L.: 1044
Coates, John: 3592, 3595
Cobban, Mrs. G.: 4947, 4948(H)
Cobby, Edward A.: 4645
Cochrane, Arthur: 1219
Cock, Albert A.: 2734, 2737(H), 2742, 2773, 4174(H), 4202, 4205-(H), 4207
Cockerell, Charles: 3355

Cockerell, Sir Sydney C.: 1566, (total: 69 letters), 4883
Cohen, Israel: 2557, 2558(H)
Cohen, Samuel: 4060, 4062(H)
Colbourne, Maurice D.: 2465, 2468, 2481(H), 2497, 2815
Coleridge, Stephen, Lord: 1754, 1755, 1803, 2243, 4673
Colles, W. M.: 2669, 2674(H), 3008, 3009(H), 3014, 3378, 3380(H)
Collier, John: 141, 146
Collins, Mabel (Mrs. Cook): 4677
Collins, Stephen: 1427, 2816
Collins, Vere: 2698, 2755, 2761, 2949, 3031, 3118, 3136, 3137(H), 3138(H), 3141, 3142(H), 3145, 3166, 3170(H), 3250, 3440, 3502, 3798, 3933, 4404, 4412, 4622, 4624(H)
Coltart, W. D.: 4284
Colvin, Sir Sidney: 1724, 1736, 1737, 1840, 1841, 1849, 1957
Comber, Robert S.: 2086, 2260
Compton-Rickett, Arthur: 1635, 1636(H), 2070, 4222, 4566, 4884
Condrow, Mina: 5028
Conlend, Frank W.: 4052
Conyers, Louisa: 2166
Coombs, E. H.: 755, 756(H)
Cooper, J. Paul: 2397, 2398(H)
Corbett, Howard: 3344
Cordell, Richard A.: 4098
Cornell, Thomas M.: 4705
Cornford, F. M.: 1508
Cornford, Frances (Mrs. F. M.): 1380
Cornford, Leslie Cope: 1012, 1036(H)
Cornhill Magazine: 1125
Cornish, Blanche Warre: 2288
Coster, A. R.: 4416, 4420(H)
Cotten, Lyman A.: 1506
Cotton, Vere E.: 1926
Courtney, W. L.: 1180, 1212, 2001, 4727(H), 4729
Cousin, D. R.: 2384
Cowley, Mrs. Ethel F.: 2441, 4223
Cowley, H. G. B.: 1707, 2387, 4488(H), 4489, 4492(H), 4518
Cox, Miss B.: 3201
Cox, Margaret: 4182
Cox, S. Donald: 3517

216 MAX GATE CORRESPONDENCE

Crackanthorpe, Blanche A. (Mrs. Montagu): 695, 1043, 1400, 1493, 1659, 1928, 2041, 2152, 2494, 2588
Crackanthorpe, Montagu: 1428, 1494
Craig, Gordon: 1586
Craig, J. A.: 3268
Craigie, Pearl Mary (Mrs. Reginald W.; pen-name: John Oliver Hobbes): 626, 654, 679, 732, 765, 792
Creczowska, Mary G.: 1829
Crewe, Lord: 489, 506, 507, 512, 828, 1371, 1888
Crickmay, G. R.: 19, 33
Critchley, Daniel: 4436
Crockett, W. S.: 4061
Croft, W. D.: 4825, 4828(H)
Crompton, R. E.: 4885, 4905(H)
Cronshaw, George A.: 3326, 3333(H), 3533, 3793, 3867, 5033, 5036(H)
Crookes, Sir William: 1482
Cross, E. A.: 4082
Cross, James: 3868, 3871(H)
Cunliffe, John W.: 2716, 2748
Curle, James: 1696
Curzon, George, Lord: 501, 586, 588, 839, 1253, 1254, 1259, 1402, 1538, 1709, 1834, 2076, 2589, 2817

Dalton, Basil: 4743, 4744(H)
Daly, J. B.: 236
Dane, Clemence: 4451
Daniels, Bradford K.: 404
Darling, Justice Sir Charles: 364, 2463, 2478, 2530
Darmesteter, Mme Mary: see Duclaux, Madame Mary
Darnkhanavola: 1539
Darwin, Sir Francis: 1381, 1644, 2266
David, Arthur: 4390
Davidsohn, Doris: 1176
Davidson, T. L.: 2959
Davies, John Langdon: 3264, 3269
Davies, W. H.: 1947, 2797
Davray, Henri D.: 862
Dawes, R. N.: 2158
Dawson, Arnold: 4928, 4930(H)

Dawson, Colonel Douglas: 1472
Dawson & Sons, W.: 4145(H)
Day, G. W. L.: 4457
Day & Hunter, Francis: 4093
Deane, A. C.: 2309, 2310(H)
Debenham, Ernest R.: 2324
deBurgh, F.: 3600, 3617, 3619(H)
de Bury, Mme Blaze: 761
De Casseres, Benjamin: 941, 4538
Deighton, E. Lonsdale: 3206, 3623
deKiss, Francis: 4997, 5004(H)
de la Fontaine, Alfred: 946
de la Mare, Walter: 2345, 2418, 2850, 2941, 3186, 3524, 4793
Deland, Mrs. Margaret: 498
de la Pasture, Betty: 1429
deMel, Ulick: 3362
Denbow, T. S.: 4686
d'Erlanger, Baron Frederic: 939, 1116, 1126, 1127, 1297, 1331, 1335, 1338, 1405, 1647, 1660, 4327
Derosne, Bernard: 187, 188(H), 189, 191, 249, 263, 370, 396
DeTabley, Lord: 584, 597, 628
Dewar, George A. B.: 1052, 1194, 1349, 1693, 1738, 1760, 1907, 2033, 3632, 3685, 3694, 3706, 3966, 4078
Dewitt, A.: 3677
Dickinson, G. Lowes: 2590, 2744, 2965, 4263
Dickinson, John H.: 1703, 1718, 1937, 2110, 2591, 3821, 3869, 3879, 4774
Dicksen, Frank: 161
Dilke, Ethel Clifford: 1905
Dillon, Viscount: 3940, 4006(H)
Dixon, William S.: 4069
Djaferis, Christos: 3048
Dobson, Alban: 4775
Dobson, Austin: 1202, 1260, 1430
Dodd, Francis: 4832, 4838
Donald, Robert: 1249, 1252(H), 4268
Donaldson, S. A.: 1711, 1741, 1763, 1769, 1796
Dorchester Town Clerk: 935(H)
Dorian, Sylvestre: 4854
Dorset County Chronicle, Editor of: 938(H)
Dorset Echo, Editor of: 4596(H)
Doughty, Charles M.: 2665
Douglas, Sir George B.: 89, 527, (total: 33 letters), 4924

Douglas, James: 1651, 1652(H)
Doyle, A. Conan: 1432
Draper, Brenda Murray: 2654
Drayton, George: 4887
Dreiser, Theodore: 2593
Drew, Margaret: 3990, 3993
Dring, E. H.: 4299, 4315(H)
Drinkwater, A. E.: 1885, 1886(H), 2492, 2496(H)
Drinkwater, John: 1369, 1372, 1377, 1969, 2286, 3734, 3735(H), 3738, 3947, 4036, 4662, 4888
Drummond, Dolores: 212
Druse, Clifford Jr.: 2920, 2922(H)
Dublin, John: 2415
Duckworth, Gerald: 3373
Duclaux, Mme Mary: 504, 2838
Dudley, Anita (Mrs. Ambrose): 2512, 2516(H)
Duffin, H. C.: 1408
Dugdale, Edward and Emma: 3078, 3504, 4225, 4567
Dully, N.: 4395
Du Maurier, George: 87, 162, 165, 166, 168, 169, 172, 176, 4534, 4586
Dumur, Louis: 993, 1000(H)
Duneka, F. A. (of Harpers): 1756(H), 1860, 1864(H)
Dunn, J. Nicol: 863, 901, 1018, 1019(H)
Dunn, May T.: 3301
Dunn, Oliver: 4527
Dunn, Sylvia: 4762
Dyall, Franklin: 3560, 3563(H)

East, Alfred: 1401, 1433, 1534, 1547
Edgcumbe, Sir Robert Pearce: 378, 1434, 2314, 4226, 4907
Edge, J. H.: 4542
Edwards, A. H.: 3678, 3680(H), 3683, 3724
Edwards, R.: 4877
Egerton, George: 655
Eldridge, Joseph: 499, 500(H)
Elgar, Sir Edward: 1739, 1742
Eliopoulo, G. D.: 4458
Ellerton, F. G.: 3898
Elliott, H. B.: 2154, 2157, 2966, 2977
Elliott, Hubert J.: 1304

Ellis, Havelock: 243, 244, 409, 410(H)
Ellis, S. M.: 3226, 4227, 4439, 4889
Ellis, Thomas H.: 3769
Elson, W. H.: 2404
Elton, Godfrey: 4969, 5007
Elven, P. N.: 3557
Ervine, St. John: 2787, 2789(H), 2800, 2826, 2828(H), 2885, 2886(H), 3505, 3822, 3927, 4119, 4131, 4228, 4336, 4568, 4663, 4667, 4890
Evans, A. Herbert: 1537, 1540(H), 3899, 3901(H)
Evans, Maurice: 3900
Evans, M. T.: 3079
Evans, Powys: 3751, 3752(H), 3756, 3934, 3935(H)
Everett, Augusta Stewart (Mrs. Henry): 4659, 4660(H)
Everett, Cyril R.: 884
Everett, L.: 3985

Faehnert, Fr.: 4137
Fagan, James M.: 3442
Fairholme, Captain: 3698, 3710(H), 3714, 3770, 3772(H)
Fairley, Barker: 4359
Fairweather, Mrs. Winnie: 1939
Falkner, J. Meade: 1094, 1161, 1592, 2508
Farmery, A.: 4229
Farrell, Sue M. (Mrs. C. P.): 3296, 3337(H)
Faulding, Miss G. M.: 3151, 3153(H)
Fawcett, Douglas: 2876, 2880(H), 2881
Fawcett, Millicent: 485, 490
Fawcett, Mrs. M. G.: 1178, 1181(H), 1182
Feith, George: 4787
Fenn, George Manville: 170, 171, 345
Ferard, Arthur G.: 1175
Ferdinand, Roger: 3471, 4383
Fernandez-Burgas, C.: see Burgas-Fernandez, C.
Ffooks, E. A.: 1792, 2187

Ffrangcon-Davies, Gwen: 4301, 4302(H), 4304, 4360, 4362(H), 4429
Field, Eugene II: 4547, 4602
Findlay, Charles F.: 96
Fisher, F. B.: 2554, 2562
Fisher, Gladys: 3749
Fisher, Lola: 3041
Fisher, S.: 3394
Fisher, Commander W. W.: 1417, 1435, 1788, 1790, 1930, 3308
Fiske, Mrs. Minnie Maddern: 723, 779
Fitzmaurice, Lord: 2594
Fitzmaurice-Kelly, Dr. James: 2409(H)
Fletcher, John Gould: 2564, 2565
Flint, F. S.: 2859
Flood, W. H. Grattan: 1835, 1836(H)
Flower, Archibald: 4530, 4672
Flower, Marie: 4139, 4142(H)
Flower, Newman: 1389, 2483, 2595, 2829, 2924, 3043, 3045, 3345, 3350, 3598, 3699, 3823, 4230, 4794, 4811
Footlet, Fred F.: 4917, 4921(H)
Forbes, H. M.: 3356, 3361, 3368
Forbes-Robertson, Sir Johnston: 618, 629, 649, 658, 662, 664, 668, 676, 780, 4022, 4023(H)
Ford, Ford Madox: 2706, 2708(H), 3625, 3639(H), 3642
Forman, W. Courthope: 2353
Forrest, E. Topham: 1185
Forrest, G. W.: 4154, 4177
Forsyth-Major, O. H.: 4699, 4700(H)
Fortescue, John W.: 1477, 1576, 1578
Fortescue, Winifred (Mrs. John W.): 2596
Fortnightly Review: 438
Foster, J. J.: 320, 2192, 2474, 2649, 2719, 2950
Foster, J. V.: 452, 453
Fosyth, Neil: 1334
Fowler, J. H.: 4040, 4086(H), 4090
Fox-Strangways, Mary: 2302, 3842
Frampton, George: 1436, 1662
Franckenstein, Baron George: 3859
Frankland, J. W.: 1106
Franklyn, Annie S.: 135

Fraser, John I.: 2550, 2551(H)
Frazer, Sir James G.: 1072, 1076
Freeman, Donald: 4592
Frey, Bernard: 2597
Fripp, John T.: 4371
Frith, W. P.: 167
Frohman, Daniel: 680
Frost, Robert: 2598
Fryer, Bertram: 3607, 4178
Fuller, J. B.: 4784
Furley, J. S.: 1933, 1936
Furniss, Harry: 3476
Fyfe, Hamilton: 1550(H), 2722, 2806, 2833
Fyfe, J. H.: 88
Fyleman, Rose: 3530

G_____, W. E.: 459
Galpin, Stanley: 3080, 3232, 3236(H), 3506, 3721, 4231, 4891
Galsworthy, John: 1339, 1551, (total: 25 letters), 4781, 5041
Gannon, Thomas J.: 4814, 4830(H)
Ganz, Charles: 4823, 4826(H)
Gardiner, Alfred G.: 1244, 1255
Gardiner, H. Balfour: 1002, 1295, 1296(H), 1298, 1307
Gardner, Nelson: 1490
Garland, Hamlin: 802, 3131, 3154, 3161, 3566, 3567
Garnett, Edward: 1055
Garnett, J. C. Maxwell: 4714
Garnett, Richard: 888, 889, 897, 902, 929
Garrod, H. W.: 3711
Garvin, J. L.: 1078, 1098, 2105, 4498, 4503
Garwood, Helen: 1312
Garwood, William: 3994
Gaskell, Lady Catherine Milnes: 362, 400, 556, 563
Gaskill, Mildred: 4417
Gathercole, Arnold: 3133
Geach, Joseph: 1704, 1706, 1716
George the Fifth, His Majesty King: 2599
George, Bertha: 2600
George, Ernest: 1388
George, Frank William: 1714, 1772, 1955, 1993, 1994

ALPHABETICAL INDEX

George, Lloyd: 2601
Gibbon, R. W.: 4350
Gibbs, C. Armstrong: 3039, 3040(H)
Gibbs, Frances G. (Mrs. O. L. Keith): 4929, 4943(H)
Gibson, Wilfrid: 2520, 3189, 3196, 3709
Gifford, Annie: 4569
Gifford, Charles E.: 1437, 1499, 1663, 1729, 1731, 2477, 2602, 2704
Gifford, E. Hamilton: 75, 77
Gifford, Evelyn: 2148, 2509, 2603
Gifford, Gordon: 2952, 3950, 4340
Gifford, Helen: 3395
Gifford, Kate: 1805, 1892
Gifford, Leonie: 1648
Gifford, Lilian: 1784, 2060
Gifford, Mrs. Margaret F.: 2604, 2679, 3190, 3785, 3824, 4232, 4454, 4570, 4892
Gilbert-Cooper, Everard G.: 4462
Gilder, Jeannette L.: 698, 699(H), 700
Giles, A. H.: 2720
Gillam, A. J.: 3959
Gillbard, Richard: 4900, 4901(H)
Gilliat, G.: 4857
Gillon, Stair A.: 1991, (total: 15 letters), 4459
Gissing, George: 386, 644, 816, 987
Glasier, J. Bruce: 2170
Gleaves, Captain Albert: 1504
Godfrey, Sir Daniel: 4171, 4172(H), 4179
Godwin, J. T.: 3704, 5021, 5024(H)
Goldman, Harry: 3081
Gollancz, Israel: 1086, 1088(H), 1844, 2012, 2014(H), 2048, 2051, 2188
Golland, Florence: 1664, 1733
Goode, W. A. M.: 1906
Goodman, Rose Anne: 4640
Gordon, Alfred: 2648, 2660(H)
Gordon, Mrs. M. M.: 3107
Gorst, Herbert C.: 1643
Goschen, Max: 1697
Gosse, Sir Edmund: 180, 246, (total: 64 letters), 5020, 5038
Gosse, Ellen (Mrs. Edmund): 1665
Gould, Laura O. (Mrs. Reginald T.): 3806, 3807(H)

Gow, James: 1631
Gower, G. Levenson: 2032
Gowing, Richard: 97, 98
Graham, E.: 2513, 4384, 4529
Graham, P. Anderson: 3974, 3999, 4009, 4074
Graham, R. B. Cunningham: 1077, 1316, 2235
Gramazo, Maria S.: 4313
Grant, George: 5026
Granville-Barker, Harley: 1862, 1863(H), (total: 44 letters), 4873, 5029
Granville-Barker, Helen (Mrs. Harley): 2545, 3358, 3946, 4405
Granville-Barker, Lillah, (Mrs. Harley): see Keeble, Lady Lillah
Graves, Robert: 2364, 2368, 2400, 2607, 3239, 4309
Green, F. T.: 3736, 3737(H), 4056
Green, Roma: 1759
Green, S. D.: 3657, 3743, 3755(H), 3789, 4175, 4615
Greenberg, J. W.: 4113, 4156
Greene, Ernest: 3191
Greenhill, A. G.: 770
Greenway, Rev. C.: 4946
Greenwood, F.: 213, 235
Greg, Florence: 4839
Gregory, Lady Augusta: 1329, 1345
Gregory, Octavia: 3053, 4235
Gregory, Odin: 3429, 3902, 3913(H)
Grein, Jack T.: 390
Greville, Ursula: 4721, 4726(H)
Grey, Alfred: 2914, 3035
Grey, Miss Rowland: 3258, 3262(H), 3265, 3274, 3282, 4165
Grierson, H. J. C.: 1071, 2123
Grieves, James P.: 2000
Griffin, Bernard: 3627, 3629(H)
Grimsditch, Herbert B.: 4375, 4379(H), 4385
Gristwood, A. D.: 3134
Grogan, Lady Ellinor: 1909
Grosart, A. B.: 356, 357(H)
Grove, Lady Agnes: 1439, 1807, 3251, 3418, 3425, 3507, 3826, 4116, 4204, 4236
Grove, Oenone: 4751
Grundy, Wilfred. 4351
Guedalla, Philip: 4638
Gullick, Norman: 3941, 3942(H)

Guppy, Henry: 1593
Gurevich, B.: 2812
Gutman, Ethel (Mrs. Sidney): 3815, 3906, 3907(H)
Gwatkin, Victor A.: 4612

Hadden, J. Cuthbert: 1507
Haggard, H. Rider: 924, 926(H), 928, 1440, 1590, 1747
Hale, Alfred: 4679, 4680(H)
Hale, William Bayard: 1373
Hales, John W.: 508, 509(H), 511
Halford, Andrew: 3640
Hall, W. Winslow: 4824, 4827(H)
Hallowell, Emily: 4952
Hamilton, J. L.: 2831
Hamilton, J. W.: 2846, 2871, 2878(H), 2950, 3624
Hamilton, Mira Duchess of: 3159, 3164(H), 3198, 3644, 3645(H), 3712, 4168, 4186(H), 4190, 4425, 4785
Hamilton, May Cleland: 3570
Hammell, Elizabeth: 3542
Hammerton, J. A.: 4310, 4426
Hammond, Henry: 3558, 3562(H)
Hanbury, Cecil: 2532, 2608, 2756, 2760, 3334, 3732, 3987, 4455, 4710
Hanbury, Dorothy (Mrs. Cecil): 2002, (total: 19 letters), 4670, 4944
Hand, Thomas W.: 1617
Hankey, Mr.: 1821(H)
Hanna, L. W.: 3444
Hannan, Charles: 999(H), 1022(H), 1023
Hannay, Cathcart: 1995
Hansen, A.: 107
Hanson, Arthur: 4279
Hapgood, Norman: 3436, 3438
Harcourt, E. C.: 2609
Hardy, Annie: 4572
Hardy, C. N.: 3083
Hardy, Emma (Mrs. Thomas): 272(H), (total: 74 letters), 1549(H). These 74 letters have all been published in *"Dearest Emmie"* (London, Macmillan, 1963).

Hardy, Florence (Mrs. Thomas): 3138, 3142, 3156, 3170, 3175(H?), 3230(H?), 3582(H), 3639
Hardy, Henry (not the novelist's brother): 2717
Hardy, Katharine (sister): 2552, 3963
Hardy, Nelson: 3917
Hardy, Percy G.: 3620
Hardy, Rev. Thomas J.: 2893, 2896(H)
Hardy, Wilfrid: 4272
Hare, John: 696, 701, 702, 703
Harford, John B.: 2745
Hariharaiyer, N. R.: 2853, 2864(H), 2997, 3828, 4081, 4135(H)
Harper & Brothers: 156(H), 159, 163(H), 204, 234, 349, 673(H), 675(H), 681, 687, 728, 1934, 4053, 4055, 4200
Harper, George McLean: 4330
Harris, Miss Gwladys: 4958, 4973
Harris, Rendel: 2291, 2294(H), 2297
Harrison, Austin: 1374, 1441, 1559, 3386
Harrison, Emmeline (Mrs. W. H.): 4919
Harrison, Frederic: 278, (total: 43 letters), 2610, 3084
Harrison, Frederick: 682, 4019
Harrison, H. G.: 4629, 4630(H)
Harrison, L. G.: 2274, 2275(H)
Harsley, Fred: 1340, 1341(H)
Hart, Sir Robert: 1442
Hartmann, Cyril: 4294
Harwood, Arnold W.: 2967
Hatton, A. P.: 2834, 2835(H)
Hawes, Lady Millicent (formerly the Duchess of Sutherland): 978, 979, 1092, 4437
Hawke, John: 3104, 3105(H)
Hawkesby-Mullins, J.: 4908
Hawkins, Anthony Hope: 925, 927, 1443
Haynes, Everard J.: 3776, 3778(H), 3780
Hazelton, Alan W.: 4485
Head, Henry: 3049(H), 3051, 4441
Head, Ruth (Mrs. Henry): 2855, 2856(H), 2860, 2867(H), 2873

ALPHABETICAL INDEX

Heath, Frederick W.: 4414, 4422(H)
Heathcote, Charles W.: 4641
Hedgcock, Frank A.: 1204, 1221, 1476, 3171, 3175(H)
Heidbrink, F. H.: 870
Heinchef, C. N.: 4370
Helden, J.: 4776, 4818
Helm, W. H.: 1311
Hemmekam, Annie: 3819
Henderson, Archibald: 3646, 3653(H), 3654
Henniker, Arthur: 814(H), 1134(H)
Henniker, Florence (Mrs. Arthur): 541(H), 1399, 1444, (total: 188 letters, 150 *to* her, 38 *by* her), 3280, 2346
Henry, Mme: 3162
Henschel, G.: 613
Herbert, A.: 334, 354
Herbert, Lady Winifred: 275, 296
Herbert, W.: 3713
Hergesheimer, Joseph: 2612
Herkomer, Sir Hubert von: 1243, 1383, 1419, 1445
Herkomer, "Maggie" Lady: 1827
Herriot, G.: 284, 287, 609, 610(H), 611(H), 612
Hertz, Rabbi J. H.: 2337
Hetheright, John L.: 3888, 3889(H)
Hewitt, G.: 4795, 4796(H)
Hewlett, Maurice: 885, 1318, 1321, 1323(H), 1324, 1325(H), 1326, 1327(H), 1330, 1407, 1446, 1667, 2466, 2575
Hicks, John George: 2613, 2651(H)
Hidaka, T.: 3033
Higbee, Mrs. Frank D.: 861(H)
Hightett, John M.: 5034, 5035(H)
Hill, Caroline M.: 4878
Hill, S.: 3978
Hill, Vernon: 3176
Hill, William K.: 4337, 4372, 4833
Hind, Arthur M.: 351
Hind, C. Lewis: 734, 1107, 1113, 3817, 3818(H)
Hindsmith, John: 2863
Hinton, E. Austin: 2894
Hinton, G. W.: 4345, 4348(H)
Hion, Yrjo: 1226

Hoar, Alda: 3829
Hoare, Alida Lady: 1799, 3086
Hobbes, John Oliver: *see* Craigie, Mrs. Pearl
Hobman, J. B.: 4583
Hodges, Wilfrid F.: 3029, 4693, 4706
Hogan, C. Beecher: 3960
Hogg, Dorothea G.: 3087
Hogg, James: 225(H), 226, 227(H)
Hogge, J. M.: 4203, 4206(H)
Holder, Rev. Caddell: 42
Holiday, Catherine (Mrs. Henry): 2531
Holland, Clive: 872, 1089, 1102(H), 3112, 3115(H), 3576, 3577(H), 4573
Holman-Hunt, Edith: 1921
Holst, Gustav: 1491, 1523, 1564, 1575, 3359, 3948, 4945
Holst, Imogen: 4237
Holt, Henry: 52, 57, 65, 67, 72, 78(H), 103(H), 129
Holzmann, M.: 307, 316
Hoogs, Alyce L.: 4631
Hope, Tess M.: 2919
Hopkins, Arthur: 125, 126
Hopkins, Robert Thurston: 4590, 4598, 4599
Hornby, C. H. S-I.: 3222
Hornby, Cicely: 4778
Horrox, Lewis: 4937, 4941(H)
Houde, Louise: 4633
Houghton, A. V.: 3225, 3227, 3406
Houghton, Lord: *see* Crewe, Marquis of
Housman, A. E.: 833, 849, 852, 1668, 1774, 1897, 2462
Housman, Laurence: 974, 975(H), 982, 983(H)
Howard, Richard N.: 853
Howe, Will T.: 2730, 2740(H), 2768
Howells, Ottoline: 3943
Howells, William Dean: 491, 798, 844, 1422, 1610
Howes, E.: 3499
Hudson, Christopher: 4807
Hudson, Edward: 2784, 2785(H)
Hudson, Sir Robert: 1447
Hueffer, Ford Madox: *see* Ford, Ford Madox
Hueffer, Francis: 124

Hughes, Charles: 976
Humanitarian League: 1195(H), 1387(H)
Hunt, Frazier: 3030, 3032(H), 3408
Hunt, Violet: 1038, 1039(H), 1263
Hunter, Sir Mark: 4797, 4803(H), 4804
Hurst, H. N.: 4913
Hutchinson, John H.: 4470, 4472(H)
Hutton, Edward: 1048
Hutton, John: 49, 53, 54, 56, 82, 183, 281
Hutton, Richard H.: 223
Huxley, Leonard: 3679
Hyman, Agnes: 3702
Hyman, Irene K.: 2766, 2767(H)
Hyndman, H. M.: 2313, 2419, 2614
Hyndman, Mrs. H. M. ("Rosalind Travers"): 1898, 3044

Ibert, Sir C. P.: 1884, 2499
Ilchester, Lord: 2546, 2615, 3661, 3764
Ilchester, Helen Lady: 1589, (total: 22 letters), 3747, 3830
Ilchester, Dowager Lady Mary: 1818, 1819, 1824, 1842, 1940, 1961, 1975, 2022, 2538, 2616
Inge, Dean W. R.: 2238
Inglis-Arkell, E.: 4453
Ingpen, Roger: 2895, 2897(H), 2901, 3167, 4949
International Story Company: 3278(H)
Irving, H. B.: 747, 749, 769
Irving, Sir Henry: 442, 537
Isbister, William: 99, 142(H)
Ismay, James: 3385, 3387, 3392, 3788, 3790
Ito, Yutaro: 5010
Izvestia, London correspondent of: 3715, 4020

Jacks, L. P.: 1287, 1479
Jackson, Henry: 1007, 1207, 1208
Jaggard, W.: 4271

James, Henry: 388, 1986, 1988, 1990
James, M. R.: 2338
Jarvis, Charles W.: 390, 391(H), 394, 435, 444
Jeffery, Sydney: 3561
Jennings, L. J.: 90
Jeune, Mary: *see* Lady St. Helier
John, Augustus: 3660
Johnson, Anna (Mrs. David): 2354
Johnson, Austin H.: 3486
Johnson, John C.: 3246, 3254, 3469, 3520
Johnson, Lionel: 790
Johnson, William Savage: 891
Johnston, Bertha: 1317
Jones, Henry Arthur: 565(H), 589, 595(H), 684(H), 719(H), 1137, 1138(H), 1357(H), 1411(H), 4324, 4332(H), 4339, 4513
Jones, J. B.: 3215
Joseph, V.: 3526
Judge, Max: 3856
Jullien, Jean: 2113, 2115(H)
Jüngling, Paul: 182

Kadison, Alexander: 3194
Kapustka, Stan Lee: 4874
Kay, Paul: 4100, 4110(H)
Keating, George T.: 2355, 2992, 3207, 3210
Keeble, Lillah Lady (here listed are all the letters from her, whether signed Lillah McCarthy, Mrs. H. G. Barker, Mrs. H. Granville-Barker, or as Lady Keeble): 1410, 1412(H), 1634, 4972, 4978, 5017
Keen, Edward L.: 4183
Kellner, Leon: 678
Kellogg, Walter Guest: 3568
Kennedy, Arthur C.: 4273
Kennedy, D.: 4361, 4363(H)
Kennedy, Martin: 4556
Kent, Charles W.: 1301, 1306(H)
Kent, Rockwell: 2452, 2556
Kent, W.: 4690, 4691(H)
Kenyon, F. G.: 1577
Kenyon, John S.: 4906, 4909(H)
Keppel, Charles W.: 4072

ALPHABETICAL INDEX

Kershaw, Stanley: 4210, 4238
Ketteringham, H.: 4346
Kevan, Ernest F.: 4709
King, Charles: 3936, 3937(H), 3983
King, Harry E.: 4745
Kingsgate, John: 4486, 4487(H)
Kingsley, Mary St. Leger (pen-name "Lucas Malet"): 474, 478, 481, 483, 524
Kipling, Rudyard: 750, 751, 752, 753, 757, 760
Kirby, J. W.: 4331, 4333(H)
Kirby, Marshall: 4764
Kittelsen, Nils: 2891, 2892(H)
Kitts, I. W.: 3470
Knapp-Fisher, E. A.: 4902, 4904
Knight, Frank H.: 3586
Knollys, Lord: 1421
Knowles, James: 1029
Kocher, A. L.: 3413
Koenig, Eleanor C.: 4923, 4933(H)

Lacey, C.: 4820
Lachmund, Marjorie G.: 3633
Lamboth, Paul: 1981, 1982
Lamplugh, Alfred B.: 4275
Lamsley, Arthur: 4702
Landesberger, D. R.: 1868
Lane, Edgar A.: 3553
Lane, John: 447, 1740, 1785, 3121, 3149, 3150(H), 3160, 3248, 4402, 4406(H)
Lang, Andrew: 402, 403, 492, 493
Lang, Anna: 3575
Lang, John Marshall: 1073, 1075, 1216
Lange, W.: 105
Lankester, Sir E. Ray: 2004, 3411
Lanoire, Maurice: 1351
Lapage, Geoffrey: 3599, 3603(H), 3609
Lappin, Henry A.: 2539
Lapworth, Charles: 3276
Larbaud, Valery: 1290, 1497
Laski, Harold J.: 4557, 4558(H), 4559
Lasselin, Georges: 4880, 4914, 5014, 5025(H)
Lathbury, Stanley: 4356

Latimer, Rev. H.: 4852
Lauderdale, Countess of: 3748, 4297
Laurie, Alan: 2085
Law, Mary: 2676
Lawrence, Boyle: 4632, 4810
Lawrence, H.: 4875, 4876(H)
Leach, Henry Goddard: 4306, 4860, 4968
League of Intellectual Solidarity: 2426, 2427(H), 2434
Leathes, Stanley: 2156
Lediard, H. A.: 3980
Lee, H. W.: 4463, 4464(H)
Lee, Sir Sidney: 1083, 1121, 1177, 1348, 1448
Leffert, Henry: 4574
Legge, Col. Henry C.: 1481
Leighton, Sir Frederick: 330
Leippert, James G.: 4531, 4549(H)
Leitch, Mary S.: 3521, 3522(H)
Lemon, Margaretta L. (Mrs. Frank E.): 4963
Lemperly, Paul: 4239, 4575
Lengel, W. E.: 4160
Leonard, George H.: 4460
Levine, Isaac: 1525, 1528(H), 1541, 1553, 1560
Lewis, Arnold H.: 2393
Lewis, Beryl: 4418
Lewis, C. A.: 4004, 4013
Lewis, C. Sothern: 605
Lewis, Lady Elizabeth: 1543, 1548, 1595, 1669, 1810, 4957
Lewis, Thomas X.: 4765
Lichnerorvicz, Mlle I.: 2765, 2774
Lindebury, Richard: 4953
Lindsay, Vachel: 2617
Ling, E. L.: 1492, 3320(H), 3327, 3544
Linton, Mrs. E. Lynn: 376, 387, 619, 621, 637
Lion, Mrs. Ethel: 3848, 3906
Liston, Maud: 3740
Litchfield, Dorothy H.: 4550
Little, Audrey M.: 3088
Little, James Stanley: 1831, 4916
Litwinski, Dr. L.: 2182, 2183(H)
Liverpool, Bishop of: 4846
Livezey, Herman: 3858
Lloyd, Bertram: 2237
Lloyd, G. O: 2685
Lochner, Louis P.: 3763

Lock, B. Fossett: 271, 273, 1246, 2084, 2668
Lock, Henry Osmond: 4589, 4593, 4594, 4595(H), 4597, 4601, 4955, 4992
Lock, John H.: 337
Lock, W.: 2069, 3208, 3352, 4377, 4380, 4610
Locke, W. J.: 758, 759(H)
Locker, F.: 151
Locker, W. Arthur: 286, 407
Lockett, Frances: 2618
Lockett, W. G.: 4940
Lockhart, Leonora W.: 4042
Lodge, Sir Oliver: 2021
Logan, Sam: 4718, 4719(H)
Londonderry, Marchioness of: 1778, 1941, 2053
Longman, C. J.: 341
Longmans, Green & Co.: 4419
Looker, J.: 3839, 3840(H)
Loomis, Roger S.: 3497, 3584, 3585(H), 3590, 3707
Lord, S. T.: 3089
Loud, Edward I.: 4621
Loveday, Thomas: 2746, 4159, 4161(H), 4211, 4212(H), 4214, 4274, 4276(H), 4278
Lovitt, John V.: 3396
Lowell, Amy: 1874, 1929, 2356, 2408, 2619, 3477, 4157
Lowell, James Russell: 173
Lowell, William: 164
Lowndes, F. S. A.: 1449
Lucas, E. V.: 2269, 2272(H), 2655, 3804, 4311, 4312(H)
Lucas, L. M.: 4431, 4432(H), 4434
Lucas, Rose I. M.: 4682, 4683(H)
Lucas, Symour: 1450
Lucy, Sir Henry: 694
Ludgate, Alfred: 3890, 3915(H)
Lund, Reginald: 876
Lush, A. C. D.: 2472
Lushington, Susan: 1670
Lushington, Vernon: 1451
Lynd, Robert: 1854, 2420
Lyon, Henry C.: 2391
Lyttleton, Edith (Mrs. Alfred): 1594
Lytton, Lord: 336, 405, 451, 454

MacAlister, Ian: 1258, 2741, 2743(H), 3297, 3321, 3328(H), 3330, 3343(H), 3797, 4500, 4501(H), 4861, 4867(H)
Macardle, Dorothy M.: 3921
McCarthy, Desmond: 1148, 1292
McCarthy, J. M.: 2454
McCarthy, Justin: 335, 582
McCarthy, Lillah: see Lady Keeble
MacCartie, Miss Mary: 1079
McClure, Edmund: 313
McClure, John: 2185
Maccoll, D. S.: 4561
MacColl, N.: 308, 309, 310
McCrae, S.: 4125
MacDonald, Ramsay: 4240
MacDonald, Thoreau: 4971
McDowall, Arthur S.: 2410, 2620, 4134
McFadden, A. G.: 237
Macgillivray, D: 4805
Macgillivray, Piltendrigh: 3492
Machlachlen, Angus: 1505, 1510, 1609
McIlvaine, Clarence W.: 458, 919, 920(H), 921(H), 1611
MacIlvaine, H. C.: 1978, 2020(H)
MacKay, Eneas: 2102, 2103(H)
McKay, Roy: 4544, 4545(H)
Mackail, J. W.: 2101, 2108, 2162, 3831, 4057
MacKenzie, Dewitt: 4639
Mackereth, James T.: 3844
Mackinnon, Mary: 2998
Macleod, Donald: 139, 140
Macmillan, Alexander: 15, 20, 34, 274, 291, 297, 299, 300, 323, 328, 359
Macmillan, Douglas: 4365, 4378, 4389
Macmillan, Sir Frederick: 931(H), 937, (total: 34 letters), 3493, 4999
Macmillan, George, A.: 136, 1016, 1017(H), 1145, 1248, 1672, 1812, 2096, 3312, 3766, 3767, 3771
Macmillan, Georgiana Lady: 3786
Macmillan, Harold: 2792, 2793(H)
Macmillan, Helen (Mrs. Maurice): 1673, 1813
Macmillan, M. K.: 30, 31
Macmillan, Maurice: 1980, 2304, 2559, 2621, 3240

Macmillan, Will: 4474, 4478, 4502, 4627, 4646
Macmillan & Company: 1354(H)
Macnamara, Francis: 3181, 3185(H), 3197
Macnamara, Margaret: 3364, 3365(H)
McNeill, Florence: 3404(H), 3412
MacNutt, J. S.: 4065, 4087(H), 4091
Macquoid, Gilbert S.: 4241
Macquoid, Katharine S.: 79
McTaggart, J. Ellis: 1453, 1708, 1828, 2514, 2618(H)
Macer-Wright, P.: 4746, 4750(H)
Machen, Arthur: 2281, 2282(H)
Madan, F: 1579
Maddison, F.: 1699, 1700(H)
Maguire, Julia (Mrs. Rockfort): 1454
Maitland, F. W.: 1080, 1081, 1084, 1090, 1136, 1140, 1149, 1150, 1152, 1154, 1156, 1158, 1179
Maitland, R. E. F.: 1767
Majid, Jamila: 3932
Malden, W. F.: 2440, 2444(H), 2446, 2547
Malet, Lucas: see Mary St. Leger Kingsley
Malmud, R. S.: 4517
Malone, Dudley Field: 3221, 3587, 4242
Manent, M.: 4121
Manning, H. C.: 4859
Manuel-Lelis, Y..: 4467
Maquarie, Arthur: 2189, 2190(H)
Marbury, Elisabeth: 3729
Marchant, Sir James: 3445, 3450(H), 3464, 3467(H)
Margoliouth, H. M.: 2803, 2811
Margueritte, Eve (Madame Paul): 1350
Marie Louise, Her Royal Highness Princess: 3109, 3125, 3199, 3323, 3353
Marks, Mrs. Lionel: see Peabody, Josephine Preston
Markström, ———: 3022
Marley, J.: 4655
Marsden, F. M.: 3923
Marsh, E.: 2347
Marshall, Grace E. (Mrs. T. H.): 2231

Marshall, H. F. C.: 2650, 2762, 2999, 3004(H), 4445(H)
Marson, Clotilde: 2970
Marston, R. B.: 233
Martens, Maarten: 947, 1489
Martin, G. Currie: 3564, 3601, 3604(H), 3615, 3841
Martin, H. A.: 3281
Martin, Julia Augusta: 8, 41, 84, 326, 381
Mase, Georgina: 4995
Masefield, John: 1584, 1887, 1895, 2461, 2622, 2861, 3688, 3695, 3984, 4005, 4007, 4033, 4035, 4037, 4068, 4140, 4611, 4613
Maskeleyne, Inez S.: 1343
Mason-Manheim, Madeline: 4539
Massingham, H. J.: 2435(H), 2436
Massingham, H. W.: 2280, 2283, 2566, 2646, 2757
Masson, Rosaline: 3026, 3055, 3060(H), 3331
Masterman, Charles F. A.: 1866, 1867
Masters, Edgar Lee: 2425
Mate, Frederick S.: 4066(H), 4180
Mateusen, Stefan N.: 3696
Math, Manuel: 1024
Matthews, S. G.: 2623
Maude, Aylmer: 3011, 3013(H) 4499
Maxwell, Gerald: 4166, 4167(H), 4169
Maxwell, Perriton: 1600, 1601(H)
Maxwell, W. B.: 4483, 4484
Maxwell, William: 4979, 4985, 4993
Mayfield, John S.: 3730, 4258
Maynard, Theodore: 4516, 4526(H)
Mayne, Arthur J.: 4428
Mayo, Mabel E.: 4532
Mayor of London: 2320(H)
Meader, William: 3555
Medway, Frederick: 4769, 4771(H), 4773
Megroz, R. L.: 3400, 3402(H)
Mencken, H. L.: 2624
Menzies, G. K.: 4731, 4733(H), 4822
Meredith, George: 302, 804, 1087, 1313
Meredith, William M.: 1342, 4926, 4989

Metcalf, L. G.: 338, 342(H), 355
Methuen, A.: 2791, 2862
Metzler, Mary: 3195
Mew, Charlotte: 3692
Meynell, Esther Hallam: 2937
Meynell, Wilfrid: 238, 1346, 1722
Middleton, H. B.: 2062
Midleton, Madeleine Lady: 2172
Milford, H. S.: 2191, 2216, 2423, 2549, 3342
Millard, Mrs. G.: 4703
Miller, Gerald: 3744
Millington-Drake, E.: 3918, 3924
Millns, Ethel: 3219
Mills, J. H.: 3090
Milman, Lena: 555(H), 561(H), 568(H), 575(H), 579(H), 1270
Milne, James: 2378, 4551, 4553(H)
Milner, James: 4010
Minchin, H. Cotton: 4741, 4749(H)
Miners, Tom: 3614
Minoura, K.: 1200, 1205(H)
Minto, W.: 102
Mitchell, Edgar A.: 2681, 2875
Mitchell, Henry: 3419
Mitchell, P. G.: 1315
Mitford, C. Guise: 4736
Miyashima, S.: 4661
Mok, M. S.: 4849
Mongruerly, H. G.: 3018, 3019(H)
Monro, Harold: 3113, 3123(H), 3369, 3370, 3372(H), 3405
Monroe, Harriet: 2045, 2046(H), 2047(H), 2120, 3422
Monte, J. 3559
Montefiore, Claude G.: 2925, 2926(H), 2929
Moog, Louise: 4920
Moore, George: 774
Moore, Merrill: 4782
Morgan, Arthur E.: 2194, 2198, 2199(H)
Morgan, Charles: 2482(H), 2500, 2502, 2534, 2537(H), 3293, 3457
Morgan, Horace: 5031
Morgan, John H.: 2098, 2146(H), 2221(H), 2252, 2416, 2625, 2653(H), 2759, 2778(H), 3247(H), 3266, 3310, 3509, 3708, 3716, 3718(H), 3779, 3787(H), 3873, 3909, 3912(H), 3914, 4027, 4028(H), 4442, 4466(H), 4533, 4541(H)

Morgan, Sidney: 2771, 2772(H), 2777
Morley, John: 32, 247, 268, 288(H), 289, 518, 554, 910, 1630
Morris, May: 1710, 4732, 4742
Morris, Mowbray: 306, 399
Morris, William: 464
Morris, William (not *the*): 3686
Morrison, W.: 533
Mortimer, James: 4869
Morton, E.: 4152
Moule, A. C.: 2300
Moule, Arthur E.: 981, 998
Moule, Charles W.: 50, 949, 2315
Moule, E. H.: 2535, 4644, 4653
Moule, George E.: 1565
Moule, Handley C. G.: 1782
Moule, Henry J.: 195, 196, 198, 219, 256, 318, 346, 347, 510, 602, 607, 714, 767, 857, 858, 904, 962, 963, 964, 965, 966
Moule, Horace M.: 1, 5, 7, 9, 11, 14, 22, 36, 51
Moult, Thomas: 3375, 3697, 4008, 4011, 4012, 4368
Mount Batten, Colonel: 1455
Muchall, Mary: 257, 260, 261
Mugge, Mase A.: 4899
Muirhead, James F.: 4520, 4606
Müller, Otto Karl: 2884
Mullins, E. Roscoe: 332
Munday, Luther: 2728, 2739
Munro, Cyril A.: 4893
Muntz, Arnold: 4504, 4507(H)
Muray, Nickolas: 4608
Murray, Gilbert: 1370, 3016
Murray, Sir James: 1074, 1115, 1495, 1536, 1552, 1768, 1771
Murray, Mrs. Marion Christie: 4261
Murry, John Middleton: 2386, 2389(H), 2390, 2394, 2526, 2542, 2553, 2852, 3773, 4352

Nagoaka, H.: 1757, 2960
Nairne, Canon A.: 2352
Napier, C. W.: 3446
Nash, W. Hilton: 3510
Needham, Francis: 4024
Needham, Wilbur: 4096
Nell, Petronella: 3023

ALPHABETICAL INDEX

Nelson, Marion: 3414
Nethersole, Olga: 604, 641, 729, 743
Nevill, Lady Dorothy: 445, 449, 475, 505, 515, 534, 581, 812, 819, 822, 873, 1056, 1456 1512
Nevinson, Henry W.: 973, 1027, 1129, 1169, 1347
New, Edmund H.: 834, 856, 905
Newbolt, Sir Henry: 936, 1014, 1028, 1060, 1061, 1120, 1308, 1409, 1597, 1623, 1625, 2230, 2844, 2845(H), 2918, 3777, 3782
Newland, Charles: 4095
Newman, H.: 4748, 4753(H)
Newnes, Frank: 3761
Newnes, George: 3144, 3172(H)
Newton, A. Edward: 2312, 2449
Nichols, Robert: 2029, 2437, 2439, 2809
Nichols, William: 2903
Nicholson, Ivor: 4770, 4772(H)
Nicoll, W. Robertson: 448, 456, 457, 460, 461(H), 536
Nicolls, B. E.: 3896, 3920
Nimmo, James V.: 689, 690(H)
Niven, C. Rex: 2821, 3656, 3758
Noble, Ernest: 4862, 4868(H)
Nock, Samuel A.: 2736, 4126, 4136(H)
Nodal, J. H.: 112
Noel, Roden: 482(H), 502
Noguchi, Yone: 1557, 2813
Norris, W. H.: 2381, 2503(H)
North, E. Jean: 1362
Northcliffe, Lord: 1457, 2327, 2515, 2626
Northrop, George N.: 3523
Norwood, Katherine C.: 4150
Nott, Stanley C.: 4260
Novello & Co.: 2163, 2165(H), 2168(H)
Noyes, Alfred: 1500, 2707, 2711, 2713(H), 3652
Nutter, S. Bernard: 3668

Oakshott, Walter: 3854, 3857(H), 3870, 3872(H)
O'Brien, Bryan: 3423
O'Brien, Eugene: 3363

O'Connor, T. P.: 469, 614, 801, 943, 2627, 4243
O'Dell, G. E.: 1715
Ogden, C. K.: 2126, 2133, 2184, 2186(H)
Ogle, John W.: 352
Oldaker, Maud: 4244
Oliphant, Mrs. M. O. W.: 224
Oliver, John: 1527
Ollendorff, J.: 2570, 2571(H)
Operative Builder, The, editor of: 4114, 4115(H), 4151
Oppé, Henri: 4102
Oppenheimer, James: 2628
O'Rourke, James: 4956
O'Rourke, May: 4576
Orr, Alexandra Leighton (Mrs. Sutherland): 145, 206
Orr, Edith: 2686
Osgood, James Ripley: 426
Ould, Herman: 4986
Ouless, Walter William: 2887, 2888(H), 2912, 3202, 3205
Overy, Thomas: 114
Ovey, A. E.: 4510
Owen, A. S.: 4376, 4381, 4421
Owen, Sir John A.: 4777
Owlett, F. C.: 3106

Paas, Emily A.: 4816, 4853
Palamas, Kostos: 2350
Palmer, Cecil: 2339, 2340(H)
Parker, Walter H.: 4758
Parker, W. M.: 3024, 3091, 3511, 3658, 4103, 4105(H)
Parkes, Kineton: 2365
Parratt, A. M.: 3969, 4002(H)
Parrott, Walter: 1640
Parry, A. Ivor: 2883, 2900, 2902(H), 2904, 2930, 3424
Parsons, Alfred: 412, 434, 1458, 1674, 1705
Parsons, J. D.: 4716, 4717(H)
Parsons, Paul S.: 3539, 3540(H)
Partridge, Eric: 4497
Pasco, E.: 1031
Paterson, Grace: 4265
Paterson, Helen: *see* Mrs. William Allingham
Patmore, Coventry: 312

Patmore, H. G. (Mrs. Coventry): 793
Paton, W. R.: 787
Patten, Leonard: 3482, 3494
Paul, C. Kegan: 117, 143, 144, 184, 185, 228, 298, 465
Paul, M. E.: 2195
Payne, George Henry: 2964, 2975(H)
Payne, James: 321, 322, 331
Payne, L. W.: 4996
Peabody, Josephine Preston: 1416, 1602, 2114
Pearce, Arthur S.: 3233
Pearce, Philip: 4014, 4016(H)
Pearcy, Thomas A.: 2822, 4674
Pearsall, Robert: 4665, 4671(H)
Pearson, Miss M. Elizabeth: 4738
Peel, Graham: 2429, 2430(H)
Peet, William H.: 248
Pembroke, Earl of: 476, 477, 488
Pendleton, Charlotte: 847, 848(H)
Pennell, Joseph: 1062
Perkins, Rev. T.: 1162
Perkins, W. H.: 3832, 3861(H)
Peter, S. F.: 4609
Peters, G. E.: 977
Petrie, W. M. Flinders: 1987, 2039
Phelps, William Lyon: 2501, 2510(H)
Philips, Austin: 2092
Philips, George Morris: 2369
Phillips, Henry A.: 4423
Phillips, Sarah Meech: 3439
Phillips, Stephen: 869
Phillpotts, Eden: 1034, 1035, 2715, 3860, 4245
Pickard-Cambridge, W. A.: 4835
Pickles, Frederick: 2413
Pickles, Stephen: 3407
Pickstone, J. W.: 4246
Piggott, H. E.: 4438
Pike, Laurence: 820
Pinero, Sir Arthur W.: 1068
Pinney, Lady Hester: 4468
Pinto, Vivian de Sola: 4977, 4994, 5000
Pittwood, P. H.: 2504
Platt, David: 3249
Pocock, Constance: 3092
Pocock, Guy N.: 2379, 2987
Pocock, R. L.: 2680, 4107
Poley, Irvin C.: 3574

Pollard, Frieda: 3484
Pollock, Sir Frederick: 520, 845, (total: 22 letters), 4724
Pollock, John: 1063, 2830, 2879, 2899, 3488
Pollock, Juliet Lady: 3015
Pomerantz, J.: 4482
Ponsonby, Sir Henry F.: 177
Pont, Albert: 1025
Poole, D. Lewis: 1473
Pope, Alfred: 3348, 3437, 4465, 4934
Popham, Mrs. Jeanne S.: 1791(H), 2911(H), 3241, 3242(H)
Porter, Edna: 4855
Porter, Robert P.: 2013, 2015(H)
Porthays, Vicomte J. de: 912, 914(H)
Portland, Duke of: 4471, 4475(H)
Portman, Lord: 1745
Poulaille, Henry: 4163
Poulsom, Ruby: 3025
Poulton, E. B.: 3809, 3811(H), 3892
Pouncy, Harry: 3659
Pouncy, Walter: 2257, 2258(H)
Pound, Ezra: 2694, 2700(H), 2807, 4101, 4766, 4836, 5039
Powell, Alfred: 4730, 4767
Powys, A. R.: 2382, 2383(H), 2453, 3447, 3451(H), 3458, 4515, 4525, 4528(H), 4618, 4894
Powys, John Cowper: 1963, 1976, 2318
Powys, Llewelyn: 3466
Pretor, Alfred: 1003, 1004
Pridham, J. A.: 3801, 3802(H), 3805, 3882, 3883(H)
Priestley, J. B.: 3968
Pritchard, Caradog: 4739
Probert, Mrs. Gertrude: 2738
Procter, Mrs. Anne Benson: 73, 76, 100, 115, 116, 153, 154, 158, 199, 231, 241, 258, 262, 264, 267
Prussing, Louise: 4675
Purves, John: 3047, 3052, 4554, 4555(H)
Putnam, Herbert: 1588

Queensbury, Marchioness of: 871

ALPHABETICAL INDEX

Quennell, C. H. B.: 2776, 2779(H), 2781
Quiller-Couch, Sir A.: 952, 1160, 1641, 2124, 2321, 2385, 2464
Quilter, Harry: 367, 368, 369, 373

Raad, N. C.: 4959, 4966(H)
Raff, T. M.: 3256, 3810, 3812(H)
Raffin, Alain: 3833
Ragghiantiljero, Ida: 2451
Raleigh, Sir Walter A.: 1189, 1191, 1230, 1231, 1261
Ralston, W. R. A.: 201, 203(H)
Ramsay, A. B.: 2541, 4903
Rankin, F. M.: 2709
Ratcliffe, James: 3093
Raulbach, Herman: 692
Rawnsley, H. D.: 900
Read, E. F.: 4046
Reade, Arthur R.: 2769
Reayner, J. L.: 2072, 2073(H)
Redway, G. W.: 3415
Reed, A. W.: 3420
Rees, Leonard: 2573, 2574(H), 2913, 3187, 3192(H), 3252, 3621, 3622(H), 4247
Reeve, Christine (Mrs. Henry): 293, 301(H)
Reid, Charles I.: 4129
Reid, Stuart J.: 513
Reid, T. Wemyss: 432
Rendall, Vernon: 2471
Reptors, William: 2721
Reunert, F: 4215
Reynolds-Ball, E. A.: 2832
Rhodes, A. J.: 3122, 3129(H), 3180
Rhys, Ernest: 2854, 2868(H), 3298, 3299(H), 3389, 3650
Rice, Wallace: 1065
Rice-Daley, Sir Alfred J.: 4722, 4723(H), 4756
Rich, Mrs. Therèse: 4427
Richards, John Morgan: 1186
Richards, Gertrude M. (Mrs. Waldo): 3148
Richardson, H. Stephens: 1139(H), 2177, 2179(H)
Richardson, Nelson W.: 1247
Richell, A. N.: 4480
Richie, T. H.: 3717

Richmond, Bruce L.: 1556, 1932, 2167, 2316
Richmond, John: 1546
Richter, Walter H.: 3094
Ridgeway, Bishop of Salisbury: 2630
Ridgeway, Philip: 4535, 4537(H), 4577, 4895
Ritchie, Lady (Thackeray's daughter): 1530, 2138, 2142
Ritchie, Hester: 3371
Ritchie, James B.: 2788
Rivière, Jacques: 3961, 3975(H)
Rivière & Son, Robert: 2993, 3146
Robbins, Gordon: 2688
Roberts, W. J.: 2224, 2225(H), 2229
Robertson, David A.: 2247, 2268(H)
Robins, Elizabeth: 683, 685, 1040, 1041, 2493
Robinson, Charles H.: 5011
Robinson, Charles J.: 415
Robinson, Edwin Arlington: 2631
Robinson, J. R.: 333
Robinson, Mabel: 1695, 1814
Rodd, Edward Stanhope: 3727
Rodel, Sir Rennel: 3874, 3876(H), 3878
Rodgers, Harold W.: 4248
Roe, Henry: 3579
Roe, Reginald H.: 4319
Rogers, T. H.: 3095
Rohan, Prince: 3862(H)
Rolland, Madeleine: 688, 693, 717, 803, 805, 1099, 1166, 1215, 1279, 1376, 1513, 1694, 2632, 2823, 3347, 3456, 3483
Rolland, Romain: 2633
Romer, Carrol: 4980, 4981(H), 4983, 4988
Roniger, Emil: 4369, 4373(H)
Roosevelt, Belle Willard (Mrs. Kermit): 2548, 2662, 2683
Roscoe, Frank: 2971
Rose, Algernon: 1384, 2634, 2659, 2666(H), 3863, 4075, 4578, 4695
Rose, James: 1174
Roseberry, Lord: 906, 1012
Ross, Alexander: 3610
Ross, Betty: 4684, 4685(H)
Rothenstein, Sir William: 722, 843, 955, 1064, 1108, 1109(H), 1606,

1627, 1959, 1960, 2044, 2049, 2052, 2635, 2702
Rouht, Arthur: 245
Rowland-Brown, Lillian: see Grey, Rowland
Royce, John: 956, 957(H)
Roz, Firmin: 1159, 2636
Rumball, E. Godman: 3318
Rumbold, Charles E. A. L.: 137, 1646, 1997
Russell, Lady Agatha: 179, 3253, 3545, 3834
Russell, Arthur J. G.: 2075, 4188, 4194, 4198(H), 4201
Rylands, George: 4636

Sackett, Charles A.: 3065
Sackville, Lady Victoria: 3305, 3315(H), 3329, 3433
St. Helier, Lady (previously Mrs. C. Stanley, Mrs. Francis Jeune, and Mary Lady Jeune): 542, 580, (total: 28 letters), 3689, 4079
Saintsbury, George: 615, 616
Saleeby, Dr. C. W.: 1910, 1916, 1917, 1927(H), 1944, 2095, 3111, 4277
Salmon, Mlle Yvonne: 4084, 4088(H), 4104, 4106(H), 5018, 5022(H), 5023, 5037
Salomon, Max: 4195, 4262(H)
Salt, Henry S.: 886, 890(H), 892
Sampson, George: 2536
Sandhurst, Lord: 2484, 2485(H), 2488
Sargent, John S.: 1598
Sargent, Maria: 2696
Sarum, John: 358, 360
Sasbrial: 3971
Sassoon, Aline Lady: 1015
Sassoon, Siegfried: 2043, 2055, 2178, 2202, 2333, 2348, 2403, 2523, 2872, 2905, 2943, 3096, 3513, 4321, 4448
Saunders, T. Bailey: 1461
Saxelby, F. O.: 1501, 1514(H), 1515, 1516, 1520, 1521(H), 1562(H)
Schott, Walter E.: 3979, 4015, 4017(H), 4031, 4050(H), 4058, 4146(H)

Schuster, Sir Claud: 1856, 1857, 1858(H), 1861, 2035, 2037
Schwartz, P.: 1676
Scott, C. A. Dawson: 2954, 2955, 3316, 3651, 3851, 3852(H)
Scott, J. W. Robertson: 4851
Searle, W. Townley: 1752, 1753(H)
Seccombe, Thomas: 840, 841, 1206, 1462
Secretary General, Bibliothèque de la Guerre: 2417, 2455(H)
Seiler, Conrad: 4619
Selons, Camilla: 3784
Serjeant, William: 1677
Seymour, Horace: 252
Seymour, W. Kean: 2411, 2431, 3126
Shaftesbury, Constance Countess of: 2078, 2081, 2082
Shaftesbury, Lord and Lady: 2824
Shane, John: 3796
Shanks, Edward: 2931, 2933
Shansfield, W. N.: 3608, 3611, 3613(H)
Shapcote, Dorothy: 2009
Sharp, Elizabeth A. (Mrs. William): 2689
Sharp, Evelyn: 2140, 2141(H), 4280
Sharp, William: 1005
Shefska, Rose L.: 4424
Shepard, Odell: 3681
Shepherd, H. R.: 4184
Sheppard, Nancy: 5003, 5005(H)
Sheppard, Rev. R.: 3460, 3468, 3605, 4320, 4322(H)
Sheridan, Mary (Mrs. Algernon): 1678, 1777, 1977, 2010
Sherman, Philip D.: 3928
Sherren, James: 3957
Sherren, Wilkinson: 1850, 4143
Shewring, Margaret: 3518
Shewring, W. H.: 2956
Shinohara, K.: 1702
Shipley, Maynard: 958, 959(H)
Shore, W. T.: 3865, 3866(H), 4960, 4961(H)
Shorter, Clement K.: 446, 516, 733, 739, 1463, 2090, 2091(H), 3097, 3596, 3597, 3602, 4080, 4092, 4147(H), 4295
Shudscanoff: 1825, 1999
Shuttleworth, L. H. C.: 4141, 4158

ALPHABETICAL INDEX

Siddall, Dr. S. B.: 3213, 3214(H)
Sim, Henry W.: 2869
Sime, A. H. M.: 3939
Sinclair, May: 1273, 1278, 1333, 1337, 1518
Sinclair, Upton: 4881, 4911(H)
Singleton, E. N.: 4047, 4249, 4856
Skellern, L. Ewart: 3884
Skidelsky, Miss Berenice C.: 3229, 3231(H)
Slater, F. W. (of Harpers): 2107, 2109(H), 3174(H), 3178, 3287(H), 3288, 3335, 3835, 4155, 4519, 4521(H)
Slater, John: 1157
Sloan, Sam B.: 3981, 3989(H)
Smallman, Percy: 4587, 4600
Smellie, James: 4343, 4344(H)
Smerdon, E. W.: 4786
Smith, Edward: 3875
Smith, Ella G. Castleman: 3903
Smith, Emily Genevieve: 55
Smith, Evangeline F.: 1464
Smith, George: 83, 85, 91, 130, 157
Smith, H. W.: 1232, 1233(H)
Smith, Hippisley: 764, 766
Smith, Isabel M.: 2259, 2262, 3731
Smith, J. Alexander: 530, 531(H)
Smith, Logan Pearsall: 1761, 1762(H)
Smith, Nowell: 2848, 2849(H)
Smith, Paul Jordan: 2363, 2406, 2577, 2664
Smith, R. Bosworth: 1111, 1187
Smith, Mrs. R. Bosworth: 4864
Smith, Reginald J.: 202, 1146, 1209
Smith, Robert M.: 3307, 3325(H), 3338
Smith, S. H. Spencer: 467
Smith, Rev. Sydney: 4281, 4283(H)
Smith, T. Roger: 39
Smith, Elder & Co.: 62, 63, 64, 92, 106
Smyth, George J.: 3203
Sobol, David: 3061
Solomon, Miss Daisy D.: 3228
Sotheby & Co.: 4863, 4865(H), 4984
Spantoz, W. S.: 4912
Spassky, Vera: 514, 522, 523, 529, 560
Spender, Harold: 2906, 2910(H)
Spender, J. A.: 823

Speyer, Charles A.: 2357, 2361(H), 2366, 2563, 2568, 2638, 2790, 3741, 3742(H), 3846, 3893, 3897(H)
Spicer-Simson, Theodore: 2839, 2857, 2858(H), 2866, 3028
Spottiswoode, W. Hugh: 1021
Springham, G. L.: 4950, 4951(H)
Spurgeon, Sir Arthur: 875, 893, 2945, 2946(H)
Squire, Sir John C.: 2447, (total: 22 letters), 4652, 4942
Stainsby, Henry: 1730(H), 1732
Stamper, F.: 4967
Starrett, Vincent: 5019, 5030(H)
Stead, W. T.: 659, 660(H), 784, 785(H)
Stebbing, W.: 1558, 1713, 2233
Stebbing, W. P. D.: 4701
Stephen, Leslie: 43, 44, (total: 27 letters), 374, 783
Stephens, J. R. C.: 4250
Stephens, Winifred: 3794
Sterling, Albert: 2939
Sternbach-Gärtner, Lotte: 4493
Steuart, J. A.: 421
Stevens, Edward: 3317, 3319(H)
Stevens, Henry: 200, 218, 222
Stevens & Brown, B. F.: 1642, 1797, 1798(H), 4025, 4048
Stevenson, Robert Louis: 282, 303, 304
Stewart, H. W.: 2705, 2989
Stiff, Molly: 3514
Stirling, Arthur: 653
Stone, Henry: 2305
Stone, Henry J.: 4138
Stone, W. M.: 2307, 2311
Stopes, Marie C.: 4522, 4635, 4647, 4694
Stracey, May: 4251
Strang, William: 497, 1465, 1478, 1480, 1488, 1816, 2432, 2469, 2479
Strange, H. D.: 2370, 2371(H)
Strickland, W. G.: 3416, 3417(H)
Stride, C. R.: 2827, 2836(H)
Strong, H. J.: 2731, 2733(H)
Strong, L. A. G.: 3535, 3543
Stuart of Wortley, Lady Alice: 2127, 2222, 2341, 3606, 3669, 4391
Stuart, Muriel: 2057, 2058(H), 2840, 3836, 4915
Sturgeon, Mary C.: 1353
Suart, Evelyn: 1352

Sully, James: 799, 1042, 1653, 1683
Sutherland, Millicent Duchess of: see Hawes, Lady Millicent
Sutro, Alfred: 830, 1889
Sutro, Esther (Mrs. Alfred): 1881, 1882(H)
Swain, H. Dudley: 4623, 4625(H), 4626
Sweetkind, M.: 3349
Swinburne, A. C.: 329, 647, 735, 781, 1010
Symonds, A. G.: 1309, 1688(H), 1689, 1690(H), 1698, 2228(H), 4209, 4798, 4800(H), 4817, 4842, 4879
Symonds, John Addington: 380, 468, 471
Symons, Arthur: 859, 1046, 1123, 1167, 1240, 2159, 2317, 2749, 3067, 3351(H), 4456(H), 4540, 4543(H)
Symons, A.: 1649, 1650(H)
Symons, John W.: 4970
Symons-Jeune, J. F.: 1878, 1972, 2077, 2289, 2988, 3549

Tadema, Laurence Alma: see Alma-Tadema, Sir Laurence
Talva, François: 4130
Tauchnitz, Freiherr von: 108, 110, 120, 121, 123, 132, 150, 229, 525
Taylor, Edith C.: 4252
Taylor, F. Dudley: 3313, 3332
Teasdale, Sara: 2639
Teck, Prince Alexander George of: 1529
Tedder, Henry R.: 1466
Temperley, Harold W. V.: 3719, 3720(H)
Tennyson, Hallam: 152
Terriss, William: 744, 745
Terry, Ellen: 603, 656
Tewksbury, Verne: 3434
Thayer, Scofield: 2837
Theodore, Frank: 1931
Thomas, Betty: 4292
Thomas, Edward: 1165, 1946, 1949, 1951
Thomas, Helen (Mrs. W. B.): 2723
Thomas, John: 210
Thomas, W. Beach: 2695

Thomas, William M.: 389
Thommen, E.: 2652
Thompson, Sir Henry: 418
Thompson, Lockwood: 3173
Thomson, Beatrice (Mrs. Leslie): 3209
Thomson, Winifred: 598, 600, 625, 627, 754(H), 824(H), 2270, 2290
Thorn, Donaldson R.: 1070
Thorn, Hilda M.: 3409
Thorndike, Sybil (Mrs. Lewis T. Casson): 3988(H), 3992, 3996, 4021, 4118
Thorne, Doris (Arthur Jones): 5032
Thornton, D. L.: 4192
Thornycroft, Sir Hamo: 1919, 1935, (total: 23 letters), 3922, 3964
Thoxoe, E. Haigh: 4666
Thring, G. Herbert: 922(H), 923, (total: 40 letters), 4481, 4831
Thyen, G.: 186(H), 190(H)
Tilden, Marjorie: 3548
Tilley, T. H.: 3931(H), 4896
Tillotson & Son: 324
Timbres, Henry J.: 4289
Tinsley, William: 21, 23, 24, 25, 26, 27, 28, 29(H), 35(H), 37(H), 38, 40(H), 45(H), 46(H), 86(H)
Tittle, Walter: 3168, 3169(H), 3663, 3664(H)
Tolbort, Caroline J.: 319
Tomabeclus, H.: 2264
Tomlinson, H. M.: 4759
Tomlinson, Phillip: 4897
Tompkins, Abigail Brown: 2877
Tomson, Rosamund (Mrs. Arthur): 384, 385, 417, 423, 462, 463(H)
Tooley, Mrs. Sarah A.: 5012, 5013(H)
Torrence, Ridgely: 2673, 2770, 2775(H), 2940, 2942
Toynbee, William: 3580, 3581(H)
Traill, H. D.: 807
Travers, Rosalind: see Mrs. H. M. Hyndman
Treble, H. A.: 3336
Trevelyan, G. M.: 1320
Treves, Anne E., Lady: 3700, 3739
Treves, Sir Frederick: 838, 1066, 1067, 1299, 1468, 1519, 1679, 1817
Trewern, Gertrude: 3894
Trotter, Jacqueline T.: 2448, 3551

ALPHABETICAL INDEX

Tullidge, H. E.: 149
Tully, Jim: 3224
Tunstall, Poppie: 5027
Tuohy, James M.: 2710, 2714(H), 2907, 2916(H)
Turner, K. Amy: 2023
Turner, Thackeray: 424, 430, 1131
Tussaud, John: 1469
Tustes, Albert: 4148
Tweed, John: 2555
Tyler, Harry W.: 2068
Tyler, Rev. Laurence: 3367
Tyler, Stella E.: 4264
Tyndall, Walter: 1085

Udal, Judge J. S.: 285, 1485, 3098, 3388, 3800
Unknown correspondent: 1114(H)
Untermeyer, Louis: 2640
Unwin, T. Fisher: 2794, 2795(H), 3813
Unwin, W. C.: 207
Urlan, Kurt: 1764

Vakil, R. R. B.: 3781
Valakiss, Apollo: 4266
Valaskaki, S.: 1563
Vanbrugh, Irene: 1143
Van Doren, Carl: 2641
Venables, E. Malcolm: 2326
Verena, Hedy: 3612
Verity, Heron B.: 408
Vickus, Kenneth: 5001
Viereck, George S.: 4560, 4562(H)
Vincent, A. H.: 4335
Vizetelly, Ernest A.: 441

Wade, John D: 2729, 2969, 2981(H)
Wagstaff, W. H.: 2841, 2842(H)
Waite, Vincent: 4287
Walker, E. M.: 3291, 3300(H), 3304, 3528, 3531, 3532, 4536, 4548
Wallis, Whitworth: 1582, 1607
Walne, J. J.: 3223

Ward, A. Helen: 1302, 1303(H)
Ward, A. W.: 1717
Ward, Algernon: 2928, 2948
Ward, Humphry: 2117, 2122, 2147, 2395, 2560, 2642
Ward, Mary A. (Mrs. Humphry): 487, 864, 907
Ward, W. H.: 3453, 3455(H), 3487, 3490(H)
Ware, Richard D. 4342
Warner, P. H. Lee: 2150
Warner, Sylvia Townsend: 2470, 2490(H), 2495
Warner, T. R.: 4808
Warner, Wilfred P. H.: 4687, 4698(H)
Warren, Edward: 4664, 4669
Warren, M. E. E.: 4189
Warren, Sir T. Herbert: 1355, 1358, 1361
Waters, F. H.: 2017, 2018(H)
Watkins, Alfred: 3114
Watkins, Llewelyn: 4253
Watkins, William: 1250, 1284, 1286, 1680, 3515, 3684
Watson, Malcolm: 4688, 4696(H), 4697
Watson, Sir William: 455, 632, 1245, 1681, 1945, 2217
Watson, Grant: 1966
Watson, Robert: 2780
Watt, H.: 3925
Watts-Dunton, Theodore: 791, 795, 908, 911, 1470, 1628, 1682
Watts-Dunton, Clara (Mrs. T.): 606, 2374, 4254
Waugh, Arthur: 933
Weaver, H. Baillie: 3449
Webb, Mary (Mrs. Henry B. L.): 3220, 3322
Weber, A.: 909
Webster, A. F. L.: 3647, 3648(H)
Wedgwood, Josiah C.: 4386, 4387(H)
Wedmore, Cecil: 3099, 4740, 4843, 5006
Wedmore, Frederick: 470, 538
Weld, Miss: 3272(H)
Wells, H. G.: 2139, 2376
Wells, Thomas B.: 1390, 1392(H)
Weltzien, Erich: 4834, 4844(H), 4850

Wendheim, Marie von: 479, 596
West, Richard S.: 4648
West, Verla: 4927
Weymer, Harry K.: 4637, 4657(H), 4829, 4837(H)
Wharton, Mrs. Edith: 1989, 1992, 2050
Wheeler, Frederic F.: 4085
Wheeler, Harry: 4043, 4044(H)
Wheeler, W. Reginald: 2151
Whetham, C. Dampier: 2277, 2279
Whetham, Catherine D.: 2399
Whibley, Charles: 942, 1471, 1687, 1912, 1943, 2306, 2572, 2643, 2825, 3837, 4255, 4579, 4898, 4991
Whinham, W. O.: 4026
Whitby, L. M.: 3100
White, Ernest J.: 2934
White, O. W.: 4505, 4508
White, Sydney J.: 4580
White, Thomas: 986
Whitehouse, Robert: 3339
Whitfield, Archie: 2475
Whitfield, Christopher: 3849
Whitley, Charles: 3454
Whitworth, Geoffrey: 3441
Whymper, Edward: 1386
Whyte, Frederic: 4935, 4936(H)
Widger, Howard D.: 2323
Wigglesworth, Elizabeth: 4581
Wilkenham, Ernest M.: 2758
Wilkinson, Marguerite: 2375
Wilkinson, R. J.: 3910
Wilks, Mrs. Luce: 3589
Williams, Anna: 535
Williams, Berkeley C.: 4779
Williams, C. W.: 3670
Williams, Florian: 4678, 4752, 4754(H)
Williams, R.: 4546
Williams, R. Vaughan: 1054, 1294, 1375
Williams, W. H.: 1365, 1366(H)
Williams, Winifred M.: 3101
Williamson, George C.: 3556, 3571(H), 3573
Williston, John: 3485
Wilmhurst, George: 283(H)
Wilsden, Dennis: 3390, 3398(H)
Wilson, A.: 4982
Wilson, Charles: 4523, 4642, 4871
Wilson, David C.: 4461
Wilson, H.: 2524, 2525(H)

Wilson, Sir James: 1984
Wilson, James S.: 2735
Wilson, William W.: 4656
Wimborne, Lady C.: 2131, 2132(H), 2135
Wimborne, S.: 2273, 2276(H)
Windle, Sir Bertram C. A.: 707, 708, 917
Winslow, Henry: 2330, 2336
Wise, Thomas J.: 3102, 3982, 4509, 4511
Withers, Percy: 1979
Wolf, Leo H.: 3157
Wolff, C. H.: 4591
Wolmark, Alfred A.: 4603, 4604(H), 4614, 4939
Wolseley, Lord: 835
Wood, Butler: 3244
Wood, Charles F. C.: 2506, 4196, 4197(H)
Wood, Ernest B.: 4132
Wood, Sir Evelyn: 1948, 2003
Wood, L. S.: 3926
Wood, Thomas: 4918
Wood, W. R.: 4712, 4713(H)
Wooding, F.: 4791
Woods, Charles E.: 4654
Woolf, Leonard: 4256, 4768
Woolf, Virginia (Mrs. Leonard): 1922, 3489, 3491(H)
Woolner, Thomas: 205
Wordsworth, Matthew: 3383
Wortley, F.: 3838
Wren, D. C.: 4097
Wrenford, H. St. John E.: 3746
Wright, C. Hagberg: 1241, 1251
Wright, E. L. (Mrs. James): 3058
Wright, Edward: 1197, 1198(H), 1199
Wylde, Leslie: 2923
Wyndham, Mary Lady: 3991
Wynne-Roberts, I.: 5002

Ybarra, T. R.: 4506, 4512
Yearsley, Macleod: 3516, 3519(H), 3525
Yeats, William Butler: 1624
Yerbury, F. R.: 1869, 1870(H), 3426, 3427(H)

York, William H.: 259, 280
Yoshivara, Sheegee: 4998
Youdelman, Martin J.: 4954
Young, Eleanor Frances: 4415
Young, Filson: 3257, 3261
Young, James Carleton: 850
Young, Joan: 4392
Young, L. Edgar: 4314
Young, Robert: 710

Yourievitch, Serge: 3904, 3911(H), 3997, 4041, 4358
Yu-shou, Kuo: 4964, 4987

Zangwill, Israel: 1045, 1344
Zeitlin, Alfred: 4298
Zivny, L. J.: 1310
Zoltan, Bartos: 3843, 4374

INDEX OF REFERENCES TO HARDY'S WORKS

(Numerals refer, not to pages in this book, but to the LETTERS as numbered in the Chronological List.)

Abbey Mason, The, 1611
Absolute Explains, The, 4078
Aged Newspaper Soliloquizes, The, 4498, 4503, 4506, 4512
And there was a great calm, 2687, 2688
Aquae Sulis, 2963, 2995
At Lanivet, 2267
At the Word "Farewell", 2267
Autumn in the Park, 1759

Bird-Scene at a Rural Dwelling, A, 3885, 3891
Budmouth Dears, 2393
Burghers, The, 2908, 2909

Changed Man, A, 1756, 1773, 1778
Christmas Ghost-Story, A, 823
Church Romance, A, 1167
Circus-Rider to Ringmaster, 4155
Compassion, 3770, 3772, 3929, 3930, 4024
Country Wedding, The, 2924
Cry of the Homeless, 1988, 1990
Cynic's Epitaph, 4291

Dead Drummer, The, 818
Desperate Remedies, 20, 21, 24, 26, 27, 28, 29, 35, 49, 79, 370, 410, 567, 2460, 4935, 4936
Distracted Young Preacher, The, 844, 3278
Duke's Reappearance, The, 712

Dynasts, The, 710, 989, 1001, 1008, 1009, 1010, 1011, 1026, 1047, 1051, 1063, 1100, 1110, 1118, 1124, 1198, 1203, 1224, 1236, 1238, 1239, 1240, 1242, 1256, 1313, 1519, 1577, 1637, 1862, 1863, 3469, 4042

East End Curate, An, 3949, 3967
Enter a Dragoon, 844
Epitaph on a Pessimist, 4291, 4470
Fallow Deer, The, 4152, 4721
Far from the Madding Crowd, 58, 59, 60, 61, 62, 66, 67, 68, 69, 70, 73, 74, 78, 79, 83, 84, 85, 105, 106, 107, 113, 131, 151, 181, 214, 248, 352, 464, 608, 634, 761, 895, 1034, 1091, 1153, 2018, 2259, 2269, 2272
Fellow Townsmen, 1057
Few Crusted Characters, A, 412
Fire at Tranter Sweatley's, The, 103
For Conscience' Sake, 433

God's Funeral, 1643
Going and Staying, 2450
Group of Noble Dames, A, 407, 411, 436, 451, 454, 456, 459, 463, 1226, 1588, 2693

Hand of Ethelberta, The, 87, 90, 91, 92, 93, 94, 95, 2213, 2214, 4100, 4110
Haunting Fingers, The, 2940

INDEX OF REFERENCES

How I Built Myself a House, 3518, 3864, 3877, 3881, 4069
Human Shows, 4318, 4329, 4341, 4403, 4405, 4409, 4412

Imaginative Woman, An, 1587
In a Wood, 1054
In the Evening, 3699
Indiscretion in the Life of an Heiress, An, 129
Interlopers at the Knap, 265

Jezreel, 2340, 2343, 2448
Jingle on the Times, A, 1914
Jude the Obscure, 640, 647, 648, 650, 651, 652, 653, 654, 655, 656, 657, 662, 663, 666, 674, 677, 762, 864, 947, 1091, 2235, 4096

Laodicean, A, 159, 163, 166, 172, 184, 204, 206, 228, 551, 552, 3596, 3861
Late Lyrics, 2982, 2983, 2984, 2986, 3006, 3017, 3054, 3067, 3106, 3204, 4918
Lausanne, 4690, 4691
Life's Little Ironies, 583, 585, 587, 589, 678, 1226, 2812, 3811
Life's Opportunity, 979

Market Girl, The, 983
Maumbury Ring, 1277, 1282, 1283
Mayor of Casterbridge, The, 286, 295, 300, 303, 337, 479, 596, 977, 1166, 1234, 1414, 1586, 3719
Moments of Vision, 2238, 2241, 2242, 2244, 2318, 2367, 3623

New Year's Eve, 1180, 1183
Night of Trafalgar, The, 1061
No Bell-Ringing, 4080, 4295

Old Mrs. Chundle, 5040
On the Portrait of a Woman about to be Hanged, 3379
On the Western Circuit, 601
Oxen, The, 2150, 2429, 2430, 2704, 3212, 4759

Pair of Blue Eyes, A, 37, 38, 40, 45, 46, 53, 54, 56, 57, 65, 106, 117, 793, 898, 2651, 2947, 4139, 4142, 4275, 4654, 4864

Poems of 1912-13, 1848
Poems of the Past and the Present, 906, 907, 910, 911, 1579
Poor Man and the Lady, The, 15, 16, 17, 18, 1145, 2460
Popular Personage at Home, A, 3972
Profitable Reading of Fiction, The, 338
Prophetess, The, 4093, 4094

Queen of Cornwall, The, 3538, 3541, 3547, 3553, 3627, 3634, 3638, 3643, 3649, 3652, 3665, 3766, 3767, 4005

Return of the Native, The, 118, 125, 126, 130, 131, 135, 137, 143, 380, 464, 603, 870, 1646, 2231, 2353, 2766
Romantic Adventures of a Milkmaid, The, 1611, 3152, 3278, 4712, 4713

Satires of Circumstance, 1887, 1888, 1893, 1897, 1912, 1922, 1929, 2318, 2425
Singer Asleep, A, 2374
Song of the Soldiers, 1859, 1860, 2163, 2165, 2223, 2349, 2448
Song of the Soldiers' Wives, 863, 901
Spectre of the Real, The, 571, 573, 605
Spring Call, The, 1125
Sunday Morning Tragedy, A, 1212
Superseded, The, 876
Superstitious Man, The, 2868, 3811

Tess of the D'Urbervilles, 324, 397, 399, 427, 437, 438, 439, 458, 465, 466, 467, 469, 470, 472, 473, 474, 475, 476, 477, 478, 492, 493, 514, 520, 522, 525, 526, 529, 530, 531, 532, 533, 535, 560, 603, 604, 613, 629, 630, 668, 669, 673, 697, 705, 717, 721, 733, 779, 1770, 2327, 3980, 3998, 4001, 4004, 4023, 4302
Three Strangers, The, 504, 539, 540, 1057, 2788, 2920, 4376, 4377, 4619
Three Wayfarers, The, 539, 542, 543, 695, 701, 860, 1589, 1798, 3179, 4380, 4381, 4421, 4537, 4610
Time's Laughingstocks, 1364, 1367, 1368, 1370, 1371, 1374, 1512, 1592, 1947

To Meet, or Otherwise, 1793
To Shakespeare, 2051, 4696
Tragedy of Two Ambitions, A, 375, 376, 377, 379, 601, 1593, 2884
Tramp-Woman's Tragedy, A, 990, 1044, 1113
Trumpet-Major, The, 133, 136, 139, 140, 142, 148, 149, 177, 178, 179, 180, 182, 183, 187, 188, 191, 249, 293, 301, 563, 564, 1013, 1077, 1572, 1791, 2412
Two Houses, The, 2807, 2837
Two on a Tower, 221, 228, 233, 236, 245, 292, 1115, 2667, 2690, 4286, 4791

Under the Greenwood Tree, 30, 31, 32, 34, 35, 41, 43, 52, 54, 55, 86, 508, 714 871, 1597, 1787, 3104, 3736, 3737, 3786

Waiting Supper, The, 349
Well-Beloved, The, 731, 732, 734, 736, 737, 741, 742, 748, 845, 1049
Wessex Folk, 1744
Wessex Poems, 772, 773, 781, 783, 786, 788, 790, 791, 794, 1552, 1582, 1607
Wessex Tales, 354, 359, 362, 363, 364, 366
When I Set Out for Lyonnesse, 2357, 2361, 2366, 2563, 2568, 3806, 3807
Why Did I Sketch, 2267
William Barnes, 202, 308, 314, 840
Winter Night in Woodland, 4009
Withered Arm, The, 223, 341, 344, 348, 350
Woodlanders, The, 291, 297, 298, 299, 306, 323, 324, 325, 328, 330, 339, 345, 351, 389, 390, 391, 394, 567, 1545, 2226, 3900, 4144

Xenophanes, the Monist of Colophon, 3706, 3750, 3753

Year's Awakening, The, 1826